Educational Psychology

Visit the *Educational Psychology*, first edition, companion website at
www.pearsoned.co.uk/markswoolfson to find valuable student learning
material including:

- Relevant research articles on key topics discussed across the book
- Web links to specific sites of interest including journal references to
  facilitate in-depth independent research

Educational Psychology

The impact of psychological research on education

Lisa Marks Woolfson

Prentice Hall
is an imprint of

Harlow, England • London • New York • Boston • San Francisco • Toronto
Sydney • Tokyo • Singapore • Hong Kong • Seoul • Taipei • New Delhi
Cape Town • Madrid • Mexico City • Amsterdam • Munich • Paris • Milan

For Esther and Seth

Pearson Education Limited
Edinburgh Gate
Harlow
Essex CM20 2JE
England

and Associated Companies throughout the world

Visit us on the World Wide Web at:
www.pearsoned.co.uk

First published 2011

© Pearson Education Limited 2011

ISBN: 978-0-273-72919-8

British Library Cataloguing-in-Publication Data
A catalogue record for this book is available from the British Library

Library of Congress Cataloging-in-Publication Data
A catalog record for this book is available from the Library of Congress

10 9 8 7 6 5 4 3 2 1
15 14 13 12 11

Typeset in 10/13.5 pt Palatino by 73
Printed by Ashford Colour Press Ltd., Gosport

Brief contents

Contents

Supporting resources

Visit **www.pearsoned.co.uk/markswoolfson** to find valuable online resources.

Companion website for students

- Relevant research articles on key topics discussed across the book
- Web links to specific sites of interest including journal references to facilitate in-depth independent research

Also: The companion website provides the following features:

- Search tool to help locate specific items of content
- E-mail results and profile tools to send results of quizzes to instructors
- Online help and support to assist with website usage and troubleshooting

For more information please contact your local Pearson Education sales representative or visit **www.pearsoned.co.uk/markswoolfson**

Guided tour

Learning outcomes

By the end of this chapter you should be able to:

● Understand how to critically evaluate papers

● Appreciate the features of a well-designed study to identify strengths and weaknesses in journal papers

● Understand the different parameters for evaluating quantitative and qualitative studies

● Understand how to evaluate the extent to which a suggested educational intervention may be considered effective.

Learning outcomes list the topics covered in the chapter and what you should have learnt by the end.

KEY CONCEPTS

Checklist for critical analysis for quantitative studies

1 **Conceptualisation and theoretical framework**

● Is the research problem made explicit and is there a clear rationale for the study?

● Is the research problem underpinned by psychological theory?

● How well have the major theoretical concepts been explained and defined?

● How well does the literature review locate this study within previous studies in this area?

● Are research questions or hypotheses clearly stated and testable, with relationships between variables proposed?

2 **Design**

● What is the research design, e.g. randomised controlled trial, quasi-experimental, single case experimental design, observation, etc.?

● Consider how well possible extraneous confounding variables are controlled, how threats to internal validity are dealt with and discussed, and how design could be improved.

Key concepts boxes highlight an important issue or point to think about.

EXAMPLES Teacher perceptions of troublesome behaviour

1 Lawrence and Steed (1986) surveyed UK head teachers in 85 primary schools and monitored incidents in 77. The behaviours they saw as concerning were: not listening, aggression towards other pupils, poor concentration, disobedience and defiance of the teacher. The researchers randomly selected a day for teachers to record disruptive behaviours. Aggression, disobedience, poor concentration, clowning and defiance were reported as the most frequently occurring. The head teachers in this survey viewed their older pupils, i.e. the 9–11-year-olds, as presenting most of the behavioural problems.

2 Wheldall and Merrett (1988) carried out a similar survey with 32 primary schools and 198 teachers, also in the UK. Their study was with classroom teachers rather than head teachers. They reported 'talking out of turn' and 'hindering other children' as the most troublesome, the most commonly occurring, and indeed they were also identified as the most troublesome behaviours of the most troublesome students.

3 Jones, Charlton and Wilkin's (1995) study included primary school teachers, and also middle school teachers. Fifty-four teachers based on the island of St Helena

Examples of studies and applications relating to a topic are included throughout.

QUISSET *Now go beyond the text . . . look it up yourself!*

Explore your library's electronic databases to investigate 'prevalence/incidence'.

- What explanations have been offered in the literature for differing rates across different countries?
- How might differences in current rates be explained?
- Identify a question of your own to consider here.

Questions to **I**nform **S**tudent **S**tudy and **E**ngagement with the **T**opic (**QUISSET**s) provide questions to think about and refer you to online resources to help you answer them.

 Group activity (for 2–6 people)

Join up with some friends to discuss.

Having read the chapter and worked through the QUISSETS, you now have some understanding of the arguments about the occurrence of autism. So here's the question for you to consider as a group . . .

'Has the rate of autism increased over the years?' Support your arguments with evidence.

Divide the group in half. Half the group (one person/pair/group of three) is to research and present the argument that autism has indeed increased and provide evidence from studies to support this. The other half (person/pair/group of three) is to present the arguments that there are other explanations for any apparent increase and that there are no changes in the numbers of children with autism.

Hint: Make sure you have studied original journal papers to see how studies were carried out, how autism was defined, what age groups were studied, and what tools were used for diagnosis. Are there differences in these between studies? Your QUISSET research should help here. What are the unresolved issues here?

Group activities are suggestions of things you can do in a class or group to explore the topic further.

IN FOCUS

The Clackmannanshire studies

In the UK the work of Johnstone and Watson was influential in persuading educators of the benefits of synthetic phonics. These studies were considered in the Rose Report that advocated synthetic phonics.

Johnstone and Watson carried out a series of studies comparing analytic and synthetic phonics in Clackmannanshire in Scotland. They focused on 300 children in their first year of schooling and their progress was regularly followed up and reported on the Scottish government website (Johnstone and Watson, 2003, 2005; Watson and Johnstone, 1998) and in a peer-reviewed journal (Johnstone and Watson, 2004). The study comprised three groups, synthetic phonics, a typical analytic phonics group which was the standard teaching method in Scottish schools at study start, and a third analytic phonics + phonological awareness group. Children in the study received 16 weeks of 20 minutes' training each day. Watson and Johnstone (1998) initially reported that the synthetic phonics group was reading seven months ahead of the other two groups and ahead of their chronological age, and were spelling eight to nine months ahead. This group also read irregular words better and could read previously unseen words by analogy. By the end of their primary schooling, with 95 boys and 84 girls still in the sample they reported that the group, now in Primary 7, were now reading three years six months ahead of their chronological age and spelling one year nine months ahead.

In focus boxes take a more detailed look at a key study in a particular topic area.

sample they reported that the group, now in Primary 7, were now reading three years six months ahead of their chronological age and spelling one year nine months ahead.

 Debate

Join up with some friends to discuss.

Read the reports by Johnstone and Watson on the Clackmannanshire studies. Consider the arguments presented by Wyse and Goswami (2008). Argue the case for and against the superiority of synthetic phonics.

Suggested **debates** help you to use your knowledge and understanding to talk about current issues in educational psychology.

---

onwards to more complex cognitive levels may be viewed as an example of a personal change model of development.

 Revision activity

Revise Piagetian stages of intellectual development from your earlier studies of psychology. Consider them within the concept of a personal change model.

Can you think of any other developmental models that use the idea of stages to explain not engaging in the relevant tasks better but also, and more importantly, differently?

Revision activities help you look back over what you've learnt.

---

constructive way forward. Further research is still needed to demonstrate the efficacy of current assessment and intervention approaches.

Further study

Go to the website www.pearsoned.co.uk/markswoolfson for the following starter articles:

Elliott, J. (1999). Practitioner review: school refusal: issues of conceptualisation, assessment and treatment. *Journal of Child Psychology and Psychiatry, 40*(7), 1001–12.

Kearney, C. (2008a). School absenteeism and school refusal behaviour in youth: a contemporary review. *Clinical Psychology Review, 28*, 451–71.

Further study boxes at the end of each chapter point you towards further reading and interesting articles.

Visit the companion website accompanying this book at **www.pearsoned.co.uk/markswoolfson**.

Explore topics in more depth by viewing the journal articles available and links to relevant further reading.

Acknowledgements

For research assistance, thanks are due to Rhona Jackson Taylor for her thorough work on several of the book's chapters. Thanks also to Gillian Eadie.

For thoughtful reading of specific chapter drafts, my thanks to Thusha Rajendran, Simon Hunter and Marc Obonsawin.

For well-judged editorial advice and support, thanks to Janey Webb and also to Christina Venditti who managed the book's production, both at Pearson Education.

Finally, my thanks to Richard, Tessa, Eve, Fergal and, of course, lovely Esther and Seth.

Publisher's acknowledgements

Our thanks to the following reviewers for their valuable time and feedback:

Dave Putwain, Edge Hill University
Susan Atkinson, Leeds Metropolitan University
Sarah Crafter, The University of Northampton
Mei Mason-Li, Southampton Solent University
Carrie Winstanley, Roehampton University
Simon Gibbs, Newcastle University
Kieron Sheehy, The Open University

We are grateful to the following for permission to reproduce copyright material:

Figures
Figure on page 62 from 'Reading the mind in the eyes' test revised version: A study with normal adults and adults with Asperger syndrome or high-functioning autism, *Journal of Child Psychology and Psychiatry*, 42(2), figure 1&2, p. 242 (Baron-Cohen, S., Wheelwright, S., Hill, J., Raste, J., & Plumb, I. 2001), reproduced by permission of John Wiley & Sons Inc.; Figure on page 67 from Defining and quantifying the social phenotype in autism, *American Journal of Psychiatry*, 159:6, figure 1, p. 898 (Klin, A., Jones, W., Schultz, R., Volkmar, F., & Cohen, D. (2002)), reprinted with permission from the American Journal of Psychiatry (copyright 2002), American Psychiatric Association; Figure on page 68 from Two-year-olds with autism orient to non-social contingencies rather than biological motion, *Nature* 459, figure 1a, pp. 257–261 (Klin, A., Lin, D., Gorrindo, P., Ramsay, G., & Jones, W. 2009), reproduced by permission from Macmillan Publishers Ltd; Figure on page 72 from An islet of ability in autistic children: A research note, *Journal of Child Psychology and Psychiatry*, 24(4), figure 1, p. 615 (Shah, A. & Frith, U. 1983), reproduced by permission of John Wiley & Sons Inc.; Figure on page 70 from Association between two distinct executive tasks in schizophrenia: a functional transcranial Doppler sonography study, *BMC Psychiatry* 6:25, figure 2, p. 5 (Feldmann, D., Schuepbach, D., von Rickenbach, B., Theodoridou, A., & Hell, D. 2006), originally published by BioMed Central; Figure 7.1 adapted from *Phonological skills and learning to read,*

Hillsdale, NJ: Lawrence Erlbaum Associates (Goswami, U., & Bryant, P. 1990) figure 1, p. 219; Figure 7.4 adapted from DRC: A dual route cascaded model of visual word recognition and reading aloud, *Psychological Review*, 108, figure 1, pp. 204–256 (Coltheart, M., Rastle, K., Perry, C., Langdon, R., & Ziegler, J. 2001), published by the American Psychological Association (APA), adapted with permission; Figure on page 144 from Definitions of bullying: A comparison of terms used, and age and gender differences, in a fourteen-country international comparison, *Child Development*, 73(4), figure 1, p. 1123 (Smith, P. K., Cowie, H., Olafsson, R.F., Liefooghe, A. P.D. Almeida, A., Araki, H., del Barrio, C., Costabile, A., Dekleva, B., Houndoumadi, A., Kim, K., Olajsson, R.P., Ortega, R., Pain, J., Pateraki, L., Schafer, M., Singer, M., Smorti, A., Toda, Y., Tomasson, H., & Wenxin, Z. 2002), reproduced by permission of John Wiley & Sons Inc.; Figure 9.1 adapted from Attitudes and behaviour of children towards peers with disabilities, *International Journal of Disability, Development and Education*, 46(1), figure 3, pp. 35–50 (Roberts, C., & Smith, P. 1999), reprinted by permission of the publisher (Taylor & Francis Group, http://www.informaworld.com); Figure 10.2 from A unified theory of development: a dialectic integration of nature and nurture, *Child Development*, 81(1), figure 5, p. 10 (Sameroff, A. 2010), reproduced by permission of John Wiley & Sons Inc.; Figure 10.3 adapted from Transactional regulation: The developmental ecology of early intervention (Sameroff, A. & Fiese, B.) in *Handbook of Early Childhood Intervention* 2nd Ed.; Figure 7.3 (J. Shonkoff & S. Meisels (Eds.) 2000), reproduced by permission of Cambridge University Press; Figure 11.2 from Family wellbeing and disabled children: A psychosocial model of disability-related child behaviour problems, *British Journal of Health Psychology*, 9(1), pp. 1–13 (Woolfson, L. 2004); Figure on page 269 from *The connections between language and reading disabilities*, Mahwah NJ: Lawrence Erlbaum (Turkeltaub, P., Weisberg, J., Flowers, D., Basu, D., & Eden, G. 2005) figure 1, pp. 103–130, H. Catts & A Kamhi (Eds.)

Tables

Table 8.1 from Bullying and symptoms among school-aged children: International comparative cross sectional study in 28 countries, *European Journal of Public Health*, 15(2), pp. 128–132 (Due, P., Holstein, B., Lynch, J., Diderichsen, F., Gabhain, S., Scheidt, P., Currie, C., & The Health Behaviour in School-Aged Children Bullying Working Group 2005), by permission of Oxford University Press and the authors.

In some instances we have been unable to trace the owners of copyright material, and we would appreciate any information that would enable us to do so.

Part 1

INTRODUCTION

The study of the application and impact of psychology in education is a highly popular option within undergraduate psychology degrees. You might have chosen this area because you are considering a career in education, perhaps planning on postgraduate training as an educational psychologist or as a teacher. Perhaps you have a personal interest in this area because you yourself have dyslexia or a disability, or you have a sibling who has special educational needs or a significant educational difficulty. Perhaps you have chosen to study this topic simply because you want to engage with applied psychology, real-life applications of psychological theories and concepts.

This book is designed as a sourcebook to help you pursue your interest in the study of educational psychology. Part 1 of the book comprises three introductory chapters to set the context for the topics to be discussed in Parts 2, 3 and 4. Chapter 1 explains how the book is organised and how you can actively study the topics, using this as a sourcebook to guide your critical reading of original academic papers in peer-reviewed journals. Chapter 2 considers what makes academic educational psychology a distinct discipline. It addresses and attempts to resolve current dilemmas of identity within the field. The third chapter in this introductory section deals with how to read journal papers critically. This is a key skill for psychology students and one that is central to the book. You should expect to use this skill throughout your study of this book whenever you are reading the original journal papers suggested in each chapter.

- Chapter 1 How to use this book
- Chapter 2 What is educational psychology?
- Chapter 3 How to read journal papers critically

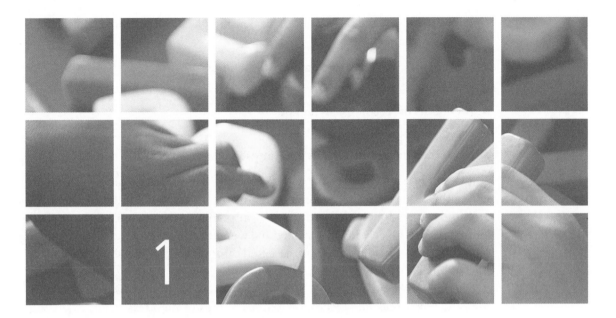

How to use this book

This book is designed for advanced students of psychology, in particular undergraduate students in their final or penultimate year. This means that your lecturers do not want you to rely on a textbook for your studies. They see this as 'spoon-feeding'. Instead they want you to read widely around the topics by researching primary references in peer-reviewed academic journals. That means you need to read the original authors' papers and not only rely on secondary reports, other authors' interpretation of what was said or found in a research study.

This textbook is designed to help you do this. It aims to help you understand key concepts and issues by explaining these before guiding you through critical reading of relevant primary journal articles. Its central focus is on helping you to develop as an independent, active learner, identifying your own issues and concerns, rather than being dependent only on what has been told to you by your tutors or that you have read in your textbook. Critical analysis rather than description is your objective here.

The book will introduce and explain key ideas and key themes. While your first task is to understand these, in final-year undergraduate psychology courses, this is not sufficient in itself. The book is designed to help develop your own awareness of the controversies, complexities, debates and what issues are still currently unresolved. The aim is to help you learn how to critically evaluate conflicting arguments and evidence and ultimately to develop your own considered view.

Think of each chapter as if it were a background lecture on the topic. Each chapter will provide:

- A list of the chapter's learning outcomes
- Key concepts and underlying psychological theories
- An outline of recent research in the area
- Discussion of methodological issues
- Discussion of current debates and unresolved issues.

At the end of each chapter you will be directed to web links which will provide you with key starter journal references. In the boxes throughout the chapters you will find directed activities and discussion points to focus your study of these journal papers. Once you have tackled the web-linked papers you will be ready to undertake wider reading yourself, accessed through your university library using the reading list of references.

Chapters provide additional explanatory boxes to add to your understanding of key concepts and issues, or with examples of the ideas being discussed. Chapters also provide activities to help you think critically about the issues that are being raised. These activities may be carried out individually but you might find it more useful to discuss them with friends in pairs or small groups as that will allow you to hear other viewpoints. It is more challenging to have to express your ideas aloud to see how well your arguments stand up to someone who wants to argue in a different direction. In any case, talking ideas through with friends is generally more enjoyable. Thinking critically about research need not be a solitary activity.

A distinctive feature of this book is the presence of **QUISSET**s in each chapter. These are **Questions to Inform Student Study and Engagement with the Topic**. QUISSETs are designed to encourage you to look beyond this book in order to engage with the available literature in greater depth. Each QUISSET will focus your attention on a question or issue by asking you to make use of the electronic databases and study sources to which you have access to weigh up the arguments on a particular issue.

The book is organised in four parts. Parts 2, 3 and 4 are organised using the ecological systems divisions of classroom level, whole-school level and beyond the school. Within each of these levels I have selected topics of interest whose primary research focus is at that level. This book does not claim to cover every topic in the application of psychology to education. It couldn't. What it aims to do is select a representative and topical range of areas.

2

What is educational psychology?

As a student of psychology, you will not be surprised to learn that the answer to the apparently simply question 'What is educational psychology?' is complex. There has been a dilemma of identity in educational psychology throughout the twentieth and into the twenty-first century, concerned with identifying how the two disciplines of education and psychology combine. This short chapter indicates some of the current debates and identifies how educational psychology is conceptualised in this book.

Looking back at a changing relationship between psychology and education

The focus of educational psychology as a discipline has changed over the twentieth century with the shifting nature of the relationship between psychology and education. This started as a uni-directional relationship, where psychology developed theories, for example of learning, and education simply applied them to the classroom (Mayer, 1992). In reviewing the content of papers over the twentieth century in one key journal, *Journal of Educational Psychology*, Ball (1984) noted a trend away from practical problems for teachers delivering a curriculum to a more academic, experimental, testing-out of theories. Theories and measurement tools that had been developed in laboratory settings were applied to real-life classrooms. Thus research in the 1920s was predominantly concerned with measurement of intelligence and measurement of motivation, and the 1930s' focus on learning was typically on measurable aspects of learning such as handwriting (O'Donnell and Levin, 2001). Similarly, from the 1960s through to 2000, studies of learning tended to address small measurable parts of learning processes rather than the larger educational outcomes that teachers wanted to know more about (O'Donnell and Levin, 2001). The result was a perception that academic educational psychology was too reductionist and did not engage sufficiently with the complexities of children's behaviour in the classroom (Levin and O'Donnell, 1999); that it had in effect 'disconnected' itself from the reality of the daily classroom (Grinder, 1989).

Educational psychology: is it for teachers, for academics, or for practitioner educational psychologists?

Alongside divisions in educational psychology as signified by publication in academic journals, a lack of consistency of subject matter within educational psychology textbooks was noted (Blair, 1949; Tyler, 1956), reflecting what Grinder (1989) referred to as 'fractionation' in the discipline. The audience for such texts varied considerably in their needs and in what information they needed to abstract from such books. Teachers wanted educational psychology books and papers to provide practical guidance to classroom problems they would be faced with in their work. The educational psychology of theorists and researchers, however, needed to reflect the development and testing-out of theories that explain the psychological processes underlying learning, quite a different focus of interest from the more direct, proximal one of teachers in the here-and-now of the classroom. Added to this mix was the relatively new profession of educational psychologist practitioners who also studied educational psychology but whose role in dealing with problems of education was quite different from that of the 'frontline' role of teachers and for whom an educational psychology text needed to serve quite a different purpose. Clearly such diversity of audience and diversity of need resulted in a confusingly wide range of subject matter in textbooks.

This dilemma about whether educational psychology should be about practical problems or theoretical problems seems to have rather dominated the field. This is not only an issue about content but is also about methodology. It has been suggested that many in education who are critical of the empirical, evidence-based approach favoured by academic psychologists prefer instead to view personal voice, opinion and anecdote as sources of knowledge (Good and Levin, 2001). The view taken in this book is that qualitative narrative data are indeed important sources of evidence when analysed rigorously, but that a single person's description of their own experience in the classroom is best used to illustrate a point that has emerged from theory that has been tested out, and should not be treated as received wisdom in itself. It is central here to recognise the different status of a theory that might be implicit within a person's account of their experience but has not been further tested out, compared to a theory that is formulated explicitly and then systematically tested with findings carefully interpreted and critically examined, in terms of their relative contribution to knowledge. The book's focus is on the latter. Its methodology is unapologetically psychological in that regard.

Integrating psychology and education for the twenty-first century

In any case, some have suggested that divisions between education and psychology are both artificial and unnecessary (e.g. Lunt and Majors, 2000), and that the two disciplines may be more usefully viewed as interacting and interconnecting (Norwich, 2000). This book certainly takes the view that such polarisation is unhelpful and instead aims to show that education and psychology can work beautifully together, by education providing real-life problems for psychology to study as advocated by Mayer (2001) and Norwich (2000).

We can see how such divisions might have arisen. The beginnings of educational psychology are usually credited to Edward Thorndike with his 1903 text *Educational Psychology*. Thorndike carried out experiments and viewed education from this scientific perspective in contrast to John Dewey whose ideas about education were also highly influential but whose concern was with the philosophy of education, with political and social aspects of education. Already, even then, divisions in focus had emerged, with educational psychology theorists subsequently aligning themselves with either a more 'psychological' (Thorndike) or 'educational' (Dewey) approach to their research and thinking about educational psychology (O'Donnell and Levin, 2001).

This book adopts a broad view of educational psychology, viewing it as the investigation of how psychological principles are applied to the development and education of children, both those who are typically developing and those with difficulties in learning, as mediated by teachers, parents and carers within the contexts of both the school and the home environment.

In his review of educational psychology research over the previous 25 years, McInerney (2005) pointed out that modern educational psychology now covers many more research areas than it once did, which reflects new areas of interest such as neuroscience and the emergence of new problems, but also that some of the old problems such as improving literacy are still around. In this book I have attempted to reflect current concerns. The book does not recognise a division between practical and theoretical problems of educational psychology but instead attempts to integrate these by starting from practical problems and examining the impact of psychological theory, principles and perspectives on these educational problems. The selection of practical problems was influenced by the kinds of problems that would concern teachers and would involve advice and intervention from the local educational psychology service. It proposes a coherent view of educational psychology as a distinct academic discipline that integrates theoretical underpinnings from developmental, health, social and clinical psychology in order to apply them to problems of education. Nolen (2009) pointed out some might then argue that such an overlap means educational psychology is not a distinct discipline, but this book's argument is that the distinctiveness of the discipline relates to the nature of the real-life problems to which we apply these theories – all related to educational phenomena. This book takes the view throughout that educational practice can only usefully advance if it is based on evidence-based approaches that have been shown to work by the careful interpretation of well-designed research studies.

References

Ball, S. (1984). Educational psychology as an academic chameleon: An editorial assessment after 75 years. *Journal of Educational Psychology, 76*(6), 993–9.

Blair, G. (1949). The content of educational psychology. *Journal of Educational Psychology, 40*(5), 267–74.

Good, T. and Levin, J. (2001). Educational psychology yesterday, today and tomorrow: Debate and direction in an evolving field. *Educational Psychologist, 36*(2), 69–72.

Grinder, R. (1989). Educational psychology: The master science. In M. Whittrock and F. Farley (eds), *The future of educational psychology: The challenges and opportunities.* Hilllsdale, NJ: Lawrence Erlbaum (pp. 3–18).

Levin, J. and O'Donnell, A. (1999). What to do about educational research's credibility gaps? *Issues in Education: Contributions from Educational Psychology, 5,* 177–229.

Lunt, I. and Majors, K. (2000). The professionalisation of educational psychology. *Educational Psychology in Practice, 15,* 237–45.

Mayer, R. (1992). Cognition and instruction: On their historic meeting within educational psychology. *Journal of Educational Psychology, 84,* 405–12.

Mayer, R. (2001). What good is educational psychology? The case of cognition and instruction. *Educational Psychologist, 36*(2), 83–8.

McInerney, D. (2005). Educational psychology – theory, research, and teaching: A 25-year retrospective. *Educational Psychology, 25,* 585–99.

Nolen, A. (2009). The content of educational psychology: An analysis of top ranked journals from 2003 through 2007. *Educational Psychology Review, 21,* 279–89.

Norwich, B. (2000). *Education and psychology in interaction: working with uncertainty in interconnected fields.* London: Routledge.

O'Donnell, A. and Levin, J. (2001). Educational psychology's healthy growing pains. *Educational Psychologist, 36*(2), 73–82.

Tyler, F. (1956). Educational psychology. *Annual Review of Psychology, 7,* 283–304.

How to read journal papers critically

Now that Chapter 2 has helped us to understand what our subject matter, educational psychology, is, we will move on in this chapter to build up our skills in analysing papers critically so that we can better judge the strength of case they argue. As we are very clear that educational psychology is the application of psychological theories, models and methodologies to investigate problems, questions and issues in educational and home settings, when we read a journal paper we will certainly then want to critically examine the paper's exposition of each of these in turn to evaluate how convinced we are of the strength of the author's findings and the conclusions that s/he draws from them.

Educational psychology has an ongoing interest in journal papers reporting the outcomes of educational, cognitive or psychosocial intervention approaches to improve behavioural, emotional or educational problems that have presented in the classroom. For researchers in educational psychology, this interest might primarily be directed at whether improvements were reported in the paper and whether the study's design allows us to be confident that these improvements are a result of the intervention and not explained by confounding variables that were not controlled for. More importantly, researchers want to know this finding is generalisable, whether this same intervention approach could usefully be applied to other classrooms where teachers report similar problems. The education practitioner is also interested in generalisability but more particularly with respect to his/her own classroom: 'Does the study show that this intervention approach will work in my classroom as well as it seems to have worked in the study reported in the paper?' In order to provide some tools for addressing these important questions of intervention effectiveness, the chapter will focus in particular on issues of study design as these have very important implications for the strength of study findings, how much information can be reliably drawn from different designs, and where caution in interpretation should be exercised.

Learning outcomes

By the end of this chapter you should be able to:

- Understand how to critically evaluate papers
- Appreciate the features of a well-designed study to identify strengths and weaknesses in journal papers
- Understand the different parameters for evaluating quantitative and qualitative studies
- Understand how to evaluate the extent to which a suggested educational intervention may be considered effective.

The development of critical thinking is seen as a key graduate skill. In the box below I have provided a checklist to guide your critical review of studies that you read. After reading a paper using such a checklist, ultimately what you want to decide, bearing all the following points in mind, is 'What does this study contribute to the issues?'

KEY CONCEPTS

Checklist for critical analysis for quantitative studies

1 **Conceptualisation and theoretical framework**
   - Is the research problem made explicit and is there a clear rationale for the study?
   - Is the research problem underpinned by psychological theory?
   - How well have the major theoretical concepts been explained and defined?
   - How well does the literature review locate this study within previous studies in this area?
   - Are research questions or hypotheses clearly stated and testable, with relationships between variables proposed?

2 **Design**
   - What is the research design, e.g. randomised controlled trial, quasi-experimental, single case experimental design, observation, etc.?
   - Consider how well possible extraneous confounding variables are controlled, how threats to internal validity are dealt with and discussed, and how design could be improved.
   - Are variables operationalised, and are cut-off points for categories justified?

- Are measures chosen of demonstrated reliability and validity?
- Can you generalise findings to a broader population from the sample?

3 Results and discussion
- Are statistical analyses appropriate?
- How are extraneous variables controlled for in the analysis?
- Are interpretation of results and conclusions drawn in keeping with the results presented – no over-claiming. Are there other ways of interpreting the findings?
- What are the limitations of the study and how do they affect interpretation of the findings or limit possible conclusions?

(Adapted from Rudestam and Newton, 2007)

The above checklist first of all suggests that you consider theoretical issues to examine the psychological theory that underpins the study and decide whether the background literature review sufficiently argues a case that these research questions need to be asked, or that the intervention evaluated in this study is likely to be successful. This is another way of saying that the study should have a strong rationale to justify its being carried out, and all its underlying concepts should be explained clearly. The literature review then should lead to explicitly stated research questions and an explanation of research design that reads almost like a recipe in that its description is sufficiently detailed to allow the reader (if s/he wanted to) to carry out exactly the same study in the same way. In the next section we will consider in some detail issues of design and how these can limit the conclusions that might be drawn from the study.

Evidence-based practice

In the world of applied psychology in which educational psychology is firmly located, there has been a major focus in recent years on helping practitioners identify from research study evidence those practices that have been shown to be most effective not only for intervention, but also for the purpose of assessment, decision-making and evaluation of services (Hoagwood and Johnson, 2003). While psychologists have been concerned with integrating scientific evidence into their practice for the last sixty years (Levant, 2005), they are of course not the only professional group to demonstrate an interest in evidence-based practice (EBP). Medicine has been a leader in developing guidelines on EBPs with other paramedical professions, for example physiotherapy and occupational therapy, following suit (Kratochwill, 2007). Indeed, Slavin (2008a) suggested that education professionals today are at much the same pre-scientific point that medical practitioners were 100 years ago. The development of EBP in medicine has meant that

Source: Photofrenetic/Alamy

A task force was appointed to determine effective intervention

rather than doctors relying only on their own knowledge, experience, preferences, word-of-mouth or intuition when they make clinical decisions about patient treatment, they can now utilise best practice guidelines on, for example, how to treat asthma. These are guidelines that are based on rigorous analysis of the most up-to-date research evidence. In 2005, the American Psychological Association (APA) appointed a Task Force to consider how to determine whether evidence pointed to an intervention being effective or not.

The Task Force defined EBP in psychology as 'the integration of the best available research with clinical expertise, in the context of patient characteristics, culture and preferences'. This definition of EBP is similar to that used previously in medicine.

This is the transition that the evidence-based reform movement wants us to make in education, too, so that practitioners in classrooms choose to implement programmes that have been demonstrated to be effective, rather than making decisions based on word-of-mouth or custom as is too often the case in education (Slavin, 2008a, 2008b).

How to evaluate study designs

In starting the process of critically examining different study designs, let us begin with a hierchical distinction made by The British Psychological Society who distinguished what they referred to as 'research' from 'audit' (BPS, 2005). 'Audit' is a valuable study design with the purpose of surveying the outcomes of a routine clinical treatment for individuals or groups, or for gathering data on the process or experience of individuals' participation in intervention. Audit findings, however, are largely of interest only to the local team of practitioners where the data were collected with a view to improving their service provision.

In contrast, the BPS viewed 'research' as concerned with

> generating new knowledge that will have general application, as for example in determining whether a new treatment is superior to an existing one or evaluating whether a particular theory provides an adequate explanation for a clinical phenomenon.
>
> (BPS, 1995, p. 8).

The APA provided a more detailed hierarchy of research evidence also for psychologists working in health settings, with respect to how well each study design can contribute to conclusions about whether an intervention actually causes behavioural change (APA Presidential Task Force, 2006; Levant, 2005). A hierarchical approach to using the best available evidence for guiding healthcare practice has also been adopted in the UK by the National Institute for Clinical Excellence (NICE) and by the Cochrane Collaboration. While these hierarchies have been developed for those working in healthcare rather than educational contexts, researchers carrying out psychological studies in the field of education have found them useful, and they are certainly referred to in many of the papers referenced throughout this textbook. Similar guidelines though have now been developed for those carrying out research in educational contexts (who may or may not also be psychologists), for example, 'What Works Clearinghouse' (WWC) guidelines from the US Department of Education, Institute of Educational Science. As well as offering research guidelines, the WWC operates as a source of evidence-based studies to provide education practitioners with accessible information about what works in educational settings. In the UK, the Best Evidence Encyclopaedia at the University of York similarly reviews research on programmes that have been carried out in schools, as does the Evidence for Policy and Practice Information and Coordinating Centre at the Institute of Education of the University of London, both with the purpose of making accessible to practitioners reliable information about what practices are known to work.

As we have defined educational psychology in Chapter 2 as 'the investigation of how psychological principles are applied to the development and education of children', we will introduce here common guidelines for EBP synthesised from the disciplines of both psychology and education in order for you to use them as a guide to inform your critical reading of the quality of evidence presented in research papers as you work through the topics and debates in this book.

Examples of different research designs are presented in Figure 3.1 below in descending order. These are likely to correspond with the different kinds of studies and evidence that you will probably come across when reading in a particular topic area in educational psychology.

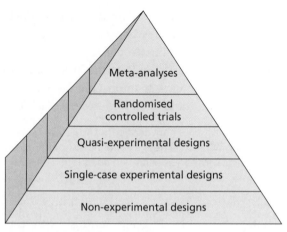

Figure 3.1 **Hierarchy of evidence**

Randomised controlled trials (RCTs)

Within most hierarchical systems, meta-analyses and randomised controlled trials are considered as providing the most robust evidence that an intervention works. A meta-analysis is a review where there is a synthesis of the results of many different studies. This will be discussed in Chapter 4.

RCTs are where participants are randomly allocated to an intervention group that receives the programme that is being examined in the study, or to a comparison group which doesn't receive the programme. The aim is to reduce any possible bias that may exist between groups if pre-existing groups were used (see quasi-experimental groups below). When reading a report of an RCT in a journal paper you should also consider if there has been significant attrition from groups between pre- and post-intervention measurements and whether this loss of participants could now result in a biased, rather than the intended randomly allocated, sample. If, for example, in a programme designed to help parents manage their children's behaviour better, there is a drop-out of intervention-group parents, it could disproportionately be those parents whose children present the most challenging behaviour because they find it very difficult to comply with the programme demands. Although then because of random allocation, the two groups were equivalent when assessment data was gathered before the intervention (pre-test), at the time of post-intervention evaluations (post-test), bias may now have been introduced through attrition with an intervention group comprised of those children whose behaviour is least challenging, while the comparison group has retained the full range of severity of behaviour problems.

Quasi-experimental designs

Quasi-experimental designs are considered as a weaker design but are common in education where intervention is often at the level of a class, and children usually are not randomly allocated to classes. Quasi is Latin for 'as if', so this is almost an experimental design. You might also see it also referred to as a non-randomised pre-post design. A quasi-experimental design uses pre-existing groups, e.g. a class where a teacher is already using a particular intervention or has volunteered to do so, compared with a class who is not experiencing this intervention. Because of the non-random allocation to conditions, the two class groups may not be equivalent, so this design may be strengthened by the study author demonstrating that there is equivalence on relevant variables and that the groups did not differ significantly from each other at study start even though there was not random allocation.

Even so, we still do not know to what extent the groups might differ on important extraneous variables that the study did not measure, therefore we must be cautious about inferring from a non-randomised design like this that the intervention was successful in causing the outcome. There may be other explanations that owe more to possible biases between the two groups, e.g. maybe the intervention group comprised a more able group than that of the comparison, so they were more responsive to the programme. Or perhaps the intervention group had a highly experienced and effective teacher and the improvements were due to the effectiveness of the teacher rather than the effectiveness of the programme. These extraneous variables in quasi-experimental designs are considered as threats to the internal validity of the study. We need to examine the paper critically to see what attempts were made to identify and control for them as this will strengthen the extent to which we can conclude that the study has indeed shown the intervention programme to be successful, rather than some other factor having caused the positive outcome.

The nature of applied psychological and educational research typically requires work to be carried out in a 'field' setting where it can be difficult to control not only allocation to groups but also a range of other factors that affect the internal validity of the study. It is important when reading a research report critically that you keep a close eye then on a variety of possible threats to the internal validity of the study's conclusions (see Key Concepts Box).

KEY CONCEPTS

Threats to internal validity of a study

This issue of internal validity (Campbell and Stanley, 1966; Cook and Campbell, 1979) is an important one in examining designs that applied psychology researchers use in school settings. Researchers hope to establish causal connections between an intervention and behavioural change, or between a manipulation of a particular variable and an outcome. While these relationships may indeed exist, they cannot necessarily be inferred from a quasi-experimental or one-group pre-test-post-test designs because of threats to that study's internal validity in that particular context. In short these are threats to the study's ability to be able to draw the conclusions it might want to draw about causality.

Threats to internal validity identified by Cook and Campbell (1979) include:

History. Let us consider a situation where Class A receives an intervention and at post-test shows improvements in the measured behavioural outcome variable. Can we conclude the intervention caused this improvement? Perhaps it did, but events other than the intervention may have taken place between pre- and post-test that caused the change, and the study design does not control for these. An enthusiastic new teacher had just taken over Class A. Was the change due to the intervention or due to the enthusiasm and skills of the new teacher, regardless of what intervention was being administered? Thus history threatens the internal validity of concluding that the intervention caused the outcome.

Maturation. This is an important issue in any research with children who are developing and maturing anyway without any intervention. Could Class A just growing older have caused the effect, without any intervention? Both maturation and history are significant threats to the internal validity of one-group pre-test-post-test designs.

Statistical regression. An example of this would be where participants are allocated to an intervention on the basis of their low pre-intervention scores. This often happens in education where children who are poorer in some area are selected to receive an intervention that targets that area. However, if there is unreliability in the test measures used, then regression to the mean is likely to occur, where extreme low scorers at pre-test will score higher at post-intervention testing. This can look as though the intervention was successful but the effect may instead be due to regression to the mean.

Selection. This is a problem in quasi-experimental designs where there may be some difference between the groups. For example, the children in Class A may be brighter than the children in Class B. The children's ability, rather than the intervention, could explain the differences observed between intervention and comparison groups. In addition, selection might also interact with another threat to internal validity. For example, it might interact with history where Class A have the enthusiastic new teacher and Class B, the comparison group, have a rather bored teacher. Thus not only are the groups different from each other (selection) but different events happened to them between pre- and post-testing (history).

Mortality. This threat relates to drop-out from the study (attrition) and causes concerns as to whether groups that were matched at pre-test are now still similar if there has been differential drop-out from the groups.

Random allocation to groups rules out threats to internal validity as on average each group will be similar in terms of history, selection and maturation. Neither will regression to the mean be a problem as extreme pre-test scores will be randomly allocated across the groups (Cooke and Campbell, 1979). Threats to internal validity, however, are not ruled out by the design itself in quasi-experimental designs, so when reading a study with a quasi-experimental design, the extent to which each possible threat to validity has been addressed should be considered critically as it will impact on the strength of the conclusions that may be drawn.

The APA's (2002) policy statement established efficacy, i.e. 'systematic and scientific evaluation', as the first criterion for determining whether or not an intervention works. The second criterion related to the clinical utility of the intervention, its usefulness in the real-world setting where it would be delivered. Efficacy studies are designed to address threats to internal validity. External validity on the other hand is more about the generalisability of the study and is better addressed by effectiveness research (see Key Concepts Box).

KEY CONCEPTS

What is the difference between effectiveness and efficacy studies?

The terms 'effectiveness' and 'efficacy' should not be used interchangeably. Much of educational psychology research comprises *effectiveness* studies which evaluate interventions in their real-world, everyday settings. These often use pre-existing groups comparing participants who are already allocated to classes, teachers and intervention programmes in their school setting. This is known as a quasi-experimental design. Effectiveness research, however, is strong in ecological validity.

Efficacy research on the other hand will involve random allocation into the conditions to be compared and will be carried out under more carefully controlled conditions. This usually means that individual participants are randomly allocated to conditions, or for studies in schools often random allocation to conditions is carried out at the level of the school or the class, rather than at the level of the individual child. Furthermore in efficacy research, participants are selected for, and excluded from, the study according to specific criteria. The influence of bias and other possible confounding variables is thus addressed by the study design. Efficacy research then provides a measure of the effect of the intervention under ideal conditions and allows us to establish causal relationships between interventions and outcomes.

Whether a causal relationship still holds when the intervention is delivered in the real-world classroom setting, however, is the business of effectiveness research. It may be, for example, that a programme has demonstrated its efficacy in a study using RCT or indeed in a series of studies, but that it is difficult for teachers to implement it regularly or with fidelity to the required programme elements when they have other curricular, behavioural and administrative matters to attend to in their classrooms on a day-to-day basis. Thus the programme 'works' in that it can deliver the required outcomes, but is impractical and difficult to implement in a real-world setting, and so cannot be used effectively in the classroom context.

Remember though not to conclude that a treatment that has not yet been subject to controlled trials with demonstrated efficacy does not work. It is simply that an evidence base to support it is not currently available. It may be in the future. Or it may not . . .

Single-case experimental designs

Next down in the hierarchy of evidence in Figure 3.1, below the quasi-experimental design is the single-case experimental design. The single-case here may be an individual child or an individual class. In this design a baseline measure is taken before the intervention is introduced, and then the same variable is measured at the end of the intervention period, which should show improvement if the intervention worked. There is no control or comparison group. The single-case provides its own control in this design for comparison. Following cessation of the intervention another measure is then taken which is expected to show a return to the baseline measure, and that it was the intervention that was causing the improvement. You may see this referred to in the literature as A-B-A design, where A is the baseline measurement phase, B is the measurement post-intervention, and the second A refers to the return to no intervention. This is usually repeated a number of times (multiple baseline) in an attempt to demonstrate causality, that manipulation of the intervention variable causes a change in the outcome measure, that is reversed when the intervention is no longer in place and which is observed when the intervention is repeated. A minimum of four phases (ABAB), replication, and randomisation can help reduce threats to internal validity in this design (Kratochwill, Hitchcock, Horner, Levin, Odom, Rindskopf, *et al.*, 2010; Kratochwill and Levin, in press).

Non-experimental design

The previous designs which we have discussed are all experimental designs which make attempts to minimise bias by controlling for possible confounding variables, with varying degrees of stringency, to try to demonstrate that the intervention caused the outcome. Compare the above, which all have inbuilt comparisons, to the one-group pre-test-post-test design where there is only an intervention group and no comparison group. You may often read reports of studies with this design where an intervention was administered to one class or group and measurements were carried out pre- and post-intervention to record change. As there is no comparison group in this design, then there is no attempt to control for threats to internal validity. Events other than the intervention may have caused any changes that were recorded and so claims for the efficacy of the intervention cannot be viewed as convincing (see Key Concepts Box on Threats to Internal Validity of a Study).

This one-group pre-test-post-test above is an example of a descriptive study in which quantitative measures are used to record and describe changes observed. An audit or survey of the experiences of participants who took part in an intervention programme would also be considered a non-experimental design for the same reasons. Other examples of non-experimental data are anecdotal reports, personal opinion and expert opinion. In the absence of more robust findings, expert opinion can sometimes be the best option available. Qualitative data are often gathered in the form of participant experiences of the intervention process. What these varied non-experimental study designs have in common is that they provide valuable descriptions of intervention experiences but we cannot infer causality from their findings with confidence.

Qualitative data

Qualitative data in educational psychology studies are typically data in the form of words from interviews, from observation or from document examination. These data are viewed as providing rich description contributing to an in-depth understanding of the meaning of the experience for that person. Quantitative data on the other hand are data in the form of numbers.

To carry out good qualitative research data should be submitted to rigorous and transparent analysis. Just as there is a hierarchy of evidence for quantitative research design and analysis, we may consider there to be a parallel hierarchy for qualitative data. Daly, Willis, Small, Green, Welch, Kealy *et al.* (2007) suggested that anecdotal descriptions of single-case studies would be at the lower end of this hierarchy, followed by descriptive studies that provide selected quotes but provide only a very limited analysis of the data. Next up in this proposed hierarchy are studies of a specific sample where there is thorough conceptual thematic analysis of all the data that were gathered. The limitations on this study design are in terms of its generalisability because of the lack of diversity of the sample. At the top of Daly *et al.*'s qualitative hierarchy are studies with diverse samples where there has also been a conceptually based thematic analysis, and which therefore allow the findings to be generalised beyond the sample under study. Guidelines are evolving for ensuring quality (e.g. Lincoln and Guba,1985; Miles and Huberman, 1994). Miles and Huberman (1994), for example, provide a list of criteria for evaluating qualitative research that parallel objectivity, reliability and validity criteria used in evaluating quantitative studies.

- **Confirmability** – are the study's methods sufficiently well detailed so that this study can be replicated by others? Would the findings be the same, or were there researcher biases that contributed to the reported findings? The concept of confirmability shares similarities with the idea of objectivity in quantitative research.

- **Dependability** – the issue here is the reliability of results, i.e. whether due care and attention have been taken in the process of designing and carrying out the study. For example, are there clear research questions and a design that is coherent with these? Were checks made on the coding for bias? Is there some degree of convergence across data collected by different participant groups where such convergence would be anticipated?

- **Credibility** – this is akin to internal validity of quantitative studies. Miles and Huberman (1994) viewed this as the key question for the study: are the findings truthful? Different ways of considering this relate to how well the understandings that comprise the findings from the qualitative data are meaningful and make sense to the range of stakeholders that are interested in these findings. Are results supported by triangulation of findings collected by different methods and from different participant groups? To what extent was evidence that did not support these findings considered and to what extent were alternative interpretations and explanations examined?

- **Transferability** – this is about the generalisability of the study. Transferability in qualitative research is similar to the idea of external validity in quantitative research. Do the findings on the perspectives of this group of teachers in this school have a wider relevance to other teachers and other schools, or are the findings only of local interest? In order to allow the reader to make this judgment the study should be sufficiently detailed in its description of the sample and in its representation of data collected, so that the reader can determine whether the characteristics and experiences of the teachers in the study school can be compared to teachers in other schools.

- While it has been argued in this chapter that well-designed quantitative research makes the strongest contribution to answering questions of causality in relation to the efficacy of the intervention, qualitative studies have a significant contribution to make to studies of programme effectiveness, providing participant perspectives on their experiences of the programme in real-life educational settings, as opposed to carefully managed and controlled programmes of efficacy research.

It is also important in qualitative studies for the author to have made very clear what their own theoretical perspective is, so that their own values, their role and interest in the study topic are made explicit (e.g. Elliott, Fischer and Rennie, 1999). If you read a study reporting widespread parent support for a commercial parenting programme, the findings would resonate differently with you if you knew the study author was the same person who had developed the programme and would benefit financially from its take-up, compared to your interpretation of the findings if you understood the author to be an independent researcher with no particular perspective on the programme's utility.

Mixed methods research

Qualitative and quantitative studies can work together in different ways. This is referred to as mixed methods research in which these two methods may be used together. They can be used in a range of ways. For example, different and **complementary** questions may be explored by qualitative and quantitative methods, e.g. where qualitative interviews on teachers' experience of the process of implementing the intervention complement data on programme outcomes from experimental studies; or they may be used for **triangulation** purposes where qualitative data may be used to support and confirm findings from quantitative studies; or one method may be used to **expand** findings obtained by the other method, e.g. parent questionnaires show improved child behavioural outcomes so parents may then be interviewed to explore parental perceptions of these behavioural changes in more detail (Greene, Caracelli and Graham, 1989).

This chapter has presented the case for a hierarchy that values objective, evidence-based findings over more subjective, descriptive, opinion-based findings in determining whether interventions work or not. We have seen that this view has been adopted in medicine, in psychological research, and is now also recommended in education research. However, this set of research values, which Issitt and Kyriacou (2009) characterised as an 'RCT privileged version of evidence-based discourse', is not without its critics. One can question whether indeed any research can be considered as completely objective. It can be argued that even apparently objective, positivist, quantitative studies are carried out by researchers whose views, values and interests have influenced the filtering procedure that is necessary to decide which studies will be covered in the literature review and which not, and what research questions are to be examined. Scott (2007), for example, has argued that rather than relying only on empirical evidence, i.e. scientific realism, a *critical realist* approach to research evaluation is needed, which allows us to recognise that there are good reasons for preferring one theory over another. Critical realism advocates that in order to understand the social world of education we need to include, but also go beyond, the empirical domain, to include the study of values and to take account of the complexity of the social context in which educational interventions take place (e.g. Kelly and Woolfson, 2008; Nash, 2005). This calls for a rather more eclectic version of evidence-based discourse that recognises the relative contribution of a range of quantitative and qualitative methodologies rather than valuing only RCT evidence (Issitt and Kyriacou, 2009).

Evidence in education research

We have argued in this chapter that evidence from each of the designs described can contribute something to our understanding of intervention efficacy. It is, however, RCTs that are viewed by APA, WWC and NICE as the most stringent means of doing this because they are viewed as strongest at removing threats to the internal validity of the study, i.e. the possibility that any changes measured may be due to a variable other than the intervention itself. The importance of rigorous experimental design for influencing educational policy decisions in the UK is only recently being recognised (e.g. Slavin, 2008a). Furthermore, in education the most appropriate design may be the cluster RCT, where random allocation is at the level of the school or the class (Tymms, Merrell and Coe, 2008). This is important for educational research as in practice educational interventions are implemented at the whole-school, whole-class or whole-group level, so the cluster RCT may have greater ecological validity. However, Tymms *et al.* pointed out that cluster RCTs have significant implications for sample size with larger samples being required compared to the method of randomly allocating individuals to conditions. Requiring a larger sample makes the cluster RCT a more costly and less frequently used method in the UK educational context (Biggs, 2008; Slavin, 2008c).

In any case while the RCT is *necessary* for establishing causality, a successful RCT is not *sufficient* for ensuring that what worked in a carefully managed experimental study will be successfully rolled out in classrooms as part of the usual day-to-day routine (e.g. Chambers, 2008; Newman, 2008). It has been argued in this chapter that both efficacy and effectiveness studies have a role to play in establishing the value of a particular intervention for teachers in schools. Efficacy studies using RCTs can determine the causal link between intervention and behavioural outcome, and effectiveness studies using quasi-experimental, single-case and qualitative studies of the process of change can then examine the practicality of their situated use in the particular classroom.

Many of the studies discussed in this book relate to this topic of intervention effectiveness, while others focus more on developing our theoretical understanding of aspects of children's development and learning within a school setting. Nonetheless the substantial body of guidance that has grown through the EBP movement provides us with an excellent starting point for understanding the relative strengths and weaknesses of different designs, the robustness of the evidence they provide, and which research questions these designs are best equipped to answer.

This may all begin to sound a bit familiar to you if you are currently in the process of designing a research study yourself. Yes indeed, the same elements that your supervisor is querying in your study are exactly those that you will examine when you read other people's published studies. This time instead of being on the receiving end of your supervisor's (helpful and encouraging) criticism, you are now the critic of someone else's work. Critical analysis and designing and carrying out a piece of research are two sides of the same coin.

From working with both undergraduates and postgraduates I know that students are well able to think critically. They often say though that they are uncomfortable or unsure about doing this. Many students have shared with me the nagging doubt that they feel it is not really appropriate for them to express critical opinions about the published work of more senior academics. This is the same body of work that they have used to build up their knowledge and understanding of the discipline of psychology. Can it not be trusted? Some feel that if work has been published then surely it must be 'correct', and that it would be 'cheeky' for them to comment negatively. While this speaks volumes for the respect for their 'elders' that students and young people in general are often accused of as lacking, such a polite view hinders critical thinking.

Students in the final years of their undergraduate courses and those on postgraduate programmes need to adjust to a gear change where they are dealing much more with work in progress, ongoing research programmes and theory building. In the earlier years of your psychology course the focus is more on learning about well-established paradigms within the discipline. Moving to your final undergraduate year and beyond, though, the game moves on. Rather than textbooks you find yourself working much more with original journal articles. Aligned with this thinking, this book sees itself as a sourcebook to guide you to examine relevant journals, rather than suggesting that what you need to study educational psychology at an advanced level can be found all in one book.

So, even though papers have been published, there may still be flaws and weaknesses that limit the importance of the findings. If you have to decide whether an intervention 'works' sufficiently to recommend to a school or a local authority that they should invest time and resources in its implementation, then you need to be able to consider the strengths and weaknesses of studies critically. My purpose here is to give you the confidence to read research papers critically and to be prepared to find flaws that could impact on your interpretation of the findings. Any such critique should, however, always use polite and respectful language. Your critique refers to the study's design or the paper's interpretation of the findings or conclusion, not to the authors personally.

References

American Psychological Association (2002). Criteria for evaluation treatment guidelines. *American Psychologist, 57*, 1052–9.

American Psychological Association Presidential Task Force on Evidence-Based Practice (2006). Evidence-based practice in psychology classroom behaviour problems. *American Psychologist, 61*(4), 271–85.

Biggs, D. (2008). Synthesising causal inferences. *Educational Researcher, 37*(1), 15–22.

British Psychological Society (2005). *Good practice guidelines for the conduct of psychological research within the National Health Service: A guide for managers, LREC members, and psychological researchers.* Leicester: The British Psychological Society.

Campbell, D. and Stanley, J. (1966). *Experimental and quasi-experimental designs for research.* Chicago: Rand McNally.

Chambers, B. (2008). Open Dialogue peer review: A response to Tymms, Merrell and Coe. *The Psychology of Education Review, 32*(2), 9–10.

Cook, T. and Campbell, D. (1979). *Quasi-experimentation: Design analysis issues for field settings.* Boston: Houghton Mifflin.

Daly, J., Willis, R., Small, J., Green, N., Welch, M., Kealy, E., *et al.* (2007). A hierarchy of evidence for assessing qualitative health research. *Journal of Clinical Epidemiology, 60*(1), 43–9.

Elliott, R., Fischer, C., and Rennie, D. (1999). Evolving guidelines for publication of qualitative research studies in psychology and related fields. *British Journal of Clinical Psychology, 38*, 215–29.

Greene, J., Caracelli, V., and Graham, W. (1989). Toward a conceptual framework for mixed-method evaluation design. *Educational Evaluation and Policy Analysis, 11*(3), 255–74.

Hoagwood, K. and Johnson, J. (2003). School psychology: A public health framework: 1 From evidence-based practice to evidence-based policies. *Journal of School Psychology , 41*, 3–21.

Issitt, J. and Kyriacou, C. (2009). Epistemological problems in establishing an evidence base for classroom practice. *The Psychology of Education Review, 33*(1), 47–51.

Kelly, B. and Woolfson, L. (2008). Developing a system of complementary frameworks. In B. Kelly, L. Woolfson, and J. Boyle eds. *Frameworks for practice in educational psychology* (pp. 237–50). London: Jessica Kingsley Publishers

Kratochwill, T. (2007). Preparing psychologists for evidence-based school practice: Lessons learned and challenges ahead. *American Psychologist, 62*(8), 829–43.

Kratochwill, T., Hitchcock, J., Horner, R., Levin, J., Odom, S., Rindskopf, D., and Shadish, W. (2010). Single-case designs technical documentation. Retrieved on September 13 2010 from What Works Clearinghouse website: http://ies.ed.gov/ncee/wwc/pdf/wwc_scd.pdf

Kratochwill, T. and Levin, J. (In press). Enhancing the scientific credibility of single-case intervention research: Randomization to the rescue. *Psychological Methods*.

Levant, R. (2005). *Report of the 2005 Presidential Task Force on evidence-based practice*. Washington, DC: American Psychological Association.

Lincoln, Y. and Guba, E. (1985). *Naturalistic inquiry*. Beverly Hills, CA: Sage.

Miles, M. and Huberman, A. (1994). *Qualitative data analysis: An expanded sourcebook*, 2nd edn. Thousand Oaks, CA: Sage.

Nash, R. (2005). Explanation and quantification in educational research: The arguments of critical and scientific realism. *British Educational Research Journal, 31*(2), 185–204.

Newman, M. (2008). Open Dialogue peer review: A response to Tymms, Merrell and Coe. *The Psychology of Education Review, 32*(2), 14–16.

Rudestam, K. and Newton, R. (2007). *Surviving your dissertation: A comprehensive guide to content and process* 3rd edition. London: Sage.

Scott, D. (2007). Critical realism and statistical methods – A response to Nash. *British Educational Research Journal, 33*(2), 141–54.

Slavin, R. (2008a). *Evidence-based policies for education in the United Kingdom*. 28th Vernon-Wall Lecture. Leicester: The British Psychological Society.

Slavin, R. (2008b). Evidence-based reform in education: What will it take? *European Educational Research Journal, 7*(1), 124–8.

Slavin, R. (2008c). Perspectives on evidence-based research in education. *Educational Researcher, 37*(1), 5–14.

Tymms. P., Merrell, C., and Coe, R. (2008). Education policies and randomised controlled trials. *The Psychology of Education Review, 32*(2), 3–7.

US Department of Education Institute of Educational Sciences (2008). *What Works Clearinghouse procedures and standards handbook*. US Department of Education. Accessed 12 September 2009. Available from world wide web at http://ies.ed.gov/ncee/wwc/help/idocviewer/Doc.aspx?docId=19&tocId=1

PSYCHOLOGY RESEARCH AT CLASSROOM LEVEL

I have structured the parts of this book to align them with different ecological levels of analysis. This approach builds on Bronfenbrenner's (1979) social ecological model which identifies a series of microsystems nested within each other which influence each other. Bronfenbrenner gave the analogy of a set of Russian dolls with each doll nested inside a larger doll. I made use of this conceptualisation in a model I developed for informing the work of practitioner educational psychologists (Woolfson, 2008). I think it provides an equally useful structure for this book too.

Here's how it works. Think of the classroom as one of the microsystems that the child inhabits and in which s/he interacts. This microsystem will influence the child's learning, development and behaviour. In turn, however, the classroom is nested within the wider context of the school, which itself is nested within the wider community. The wider community is nested within a broader society. Each of these influence, and is influenced by, the other. We will structure our examination of developmental and educational problems then within the contexts of these three ecological levels, the classroom, the school and the wider community with respect to the target level for the primary focus of research and intervention for a topic.

It is important that you understand the importance of this structure in helping to ensure that you do not think of the difficulties children experience as due only to problems within the child. Practitioner educational psychologists have moved away from this 'within-child deficit' model where a child's educational or behavioural difficulties are viewed solely as characteristics of the child and now work to conceptualise developmental problems at a more systemic level. Often other children in the class will experience similar problems to some degree. Examination of topics at the ecological levels of the class and the school allows us to consider the relationship between child problems and the environment within which the problem characteristics present, and the interactions between the two. The child cannot exist outside these systems, so in order to study children to propose appropriate interventions, we must study them within a context. Much of the work of the practitioner educational psychologist now targets the environmental context, to work with teachers and parents, rather than with the child individually. Our structure here reflects that philosophy.

Part 2 then deals with three topics at the level of the classroom.

- Chapter 4 Managing behaviour
- Chapter 5 Autism
- Chapter 6 School refusal

References

Bronfenbrenner, U. (1979). *The ecology of human development*. Cambridge, MA: Harvard University Press.

Woolfson, L. (2008). The Woolfson *et al*. Integrated Framework: an executive framework for service-wide delivery. In B. Kelly, L. Woolfson, and J. Boyle (eds) *Frameworks for practice in educational psychology*. London: Jessica Kingsley Publishers (pp. 121–36).

Managing behaviour

How to manage children's behaviour in the classroom is a key area for teachers: new teachers starting out in their career in the classrooms worry particularly about maintaining control in the classroom. Learning and management of behaviour go hand-in-hand. Effective learning cannot take place in classroom settings where behaviour is beyond the teacher's control, where the rules of what is acceptable are unclear or inconsistently upheld and where the teacher is unsure if individuals will cooperate with carrying out instructions and requests made to the class. Such an environment can feel unsafe and threatening to children and is not conducive to learning. Disruptive behaviour has been shown to predict poorer academic performance (e.g. Wentzel, 1993). Parents are concerned for their children's education and even their safety when they have concerns about the behaviour of other children in the class. Teacher received wisdom advises student teachers to get the class to behave first, then teach them. But what are the behaviour problems that commonly present in the classroom and, looking beyond folk wisdom, what does research suggest as effective ways to manage these problems?

Learning outcomes

By the end of this chapter you should be able to:

- Understand the nature and extent of behaviour problems that present in classrooms
- Evaluate the effectiveness of different intervention approaches
- Understand what meta-analysis is
- Appreciate the methodological difficulties in effectiveness research.

Within education we tend to refer to classroom behaviours that are problematic as 'social, emotional and behaviour difficulties' (SEBD). Health and child psychiatric workers refer rather to 'child and adolescent mental health' but the problems that are implied by each of these terminologies are essentially the same area (Wolfendale, 1996). The British Psychological Society had a working party looking at this in the mid-1990s with reports taken from different concerned professional discipline groups. The definition used by the working party was:

> Child and adolescent mental health problems are those in which displays of emotions, behaviours or social relationships are sufficiently marked or prolonged to cause suffering or risk to development in the child, and/or distress or disturbance in the family, school or community.   Wolfendale, 1996

While medical/psychiatric/health professionals use internationally accepted classification systems such as the Diagnostic and Statistical Manual of Mental Disorders (DSM-IV) published by the American Psychological Association (APA) and the International Classification of Diseases (ICD-10) published by the World Health Organization, in education professionals have tended not to employ diagnostic categories but instead are characteristically more concerned with functionality rather than diagnosis. However, some of the research that we will examine in this chapter and throughout the book has roots in clinical child psychology and psychiatry, for example the research on children with attentional deficit hyperactivity disorder. Research from this more medical/health background typically uses DSM or ICD diagnostic categories to define study samples and its findings are of importance to education professionals even though the perspective may be different.

In education we view it as important to evaluate the systemic factors that illuminate how and why problematic behaviour presents in the classroom context. We are interested in how to intervene and manage behaviour using classroom-level psychosocial intervention approaches. This emphasis on classroom contextual factors is the case both for general low-level classroom problem behaviours such as chatting instead of working, that all children engage in to a greater or lesser extent, as well as for more chronic diagnosed disorders. We do therefore have concerns that diagnostic labels can imply rather that the problem is located within the child, pathologising the child and suggesting that intervention need only be directed to the child, and that the classroom environment in which the problem presented need not also be examined or changed. Be aware of these issues as you read the different studies. We'll look at both kinds of research in this chapter.

What behaviours need managing in the classroom?

It has been estimated that around 10% of British children of school age have psychiatric disorders that result in social, emotional or behavioural difficulties (Meltzer, Gatward, Goodman and Ford, 2000). This covers a range of problems not all of which present as problematic behaviour that requires management in the classroom. A distinction is often made between externalising, outwardly directed behaviours such as disruptive classroom behaviour or aggression towards peers or adults, and internalising behaviour problems directed inwards, such as anxiety and depression. Our focus in this chapter will be only on externalising, disruptive behaviours as these are the ones that present as troublesome in the classroom. As well as day-to-day, low-level, disruptive behaviours such as talking in class or not getting on with work, this will include behaviours diagnosed as attention deficit hyperactivity disorder (ADHD), and to a lesser extent oppositional defiance disorder (ODD) and conduct disorder (CD) which often coexist with ADHD (Hinshaw and Park, 1999; King *et al.*, 2005), which can mean that teachers may have to manage children who present with ADHD alongside oppositional behaviours.

Attention deficit hyperactivity disorder (ADHD)

ADHD refers to impairments in attention, hyperactivity and impulsivity that affect social and academic areas of a child's life (Polanczyk, De Lima, Horta, Biederman and Rohde, 2007) and are evident in at least two settings, typically school and home. It is now the most common childhood behavioural disorder (Rowland, Lesesne and Abramowitz, 2002). World-wide prevalence was recently reported as 5.3% for children and adolescents (Polanczyk and Rohde, 2007); and 3–9% in the UK (NICE, 2008). No differences were found in prevalence between the US and UK/Europe (Polanczyk *et al.*, 2007). DSM-IV (APA, 1994) identified three ADHD subtypes: a combined type where both inattention and impulsivity symptoms are present (ADHD-C); a primarily inattentive type (ADHD-I/ADHD-PIT) where the child presents mainly inattention behaviours; and a primarily hyperactive impulsive type (ADHD-H-I). There has, however, been some controversy about these subtypes with some authors (e.g. Hinshaw, 2001; Pelham, 2001) arguing that it is not always possible or useful to distinguish subtypes.

QUISSET*	*Now go beyond the text ... look it up yourself!*	

Explore your library's electronic databases to investigate 'ADHD'.

- What explanations have been offered in the literature for differing rates of ADHD across different countries?

* What's a QUISSET? Questions to Inform Student Study and Engagement with the Topic (see Chapter 1)

Oppositional defiance disorder (ODD)/Conduct disorder (CD)

Oppositional behaviour is defiant, disobedient, provocative, argumentative, hostile behaviour that occurs more frequently and is more excessive in comparison to the occasional disobedient episodes that all children engage in at times. For a child's behaviour to be diagnosed as ODD, this behaviour needs to cause impairment in social or academic functioning (APA, 1994). Behaviour for CD diagnosis is regarded as more severe than that for ODD. It may involve actual physical aggression towards people and/or animals, destructive behaviour such as fire-setting, and behaviours such as house-breaking, car theft. Again the pattern of behaviour needs to be repeated and persistent.

There are two CD subtypes:

- child-onset (symptoms appear by age ten years)
- adolescent-onset (symptoms emerge after age ten).

Those diagnosed with child-onset CD tend to be male, experience difficulties in peer social interactions, are likely to have had a diagnosis of ODD when they were younger, and are more likely to present with disruptive behaviour problems that will persist (APA, 1994). Prevalence rates for CD and ODD are difficult to measure because studies differ in the methodologies and criteria they use (Lahey, Miller, Gordon and Riley, 1999). A figure of 9.5% was suggested for the US (Nock, Kazdin, Hiripi and Kessler, 2006).

Troublesome classroom behaviours

Behaviours leading to exclusion

In addition there are other lower-level behaviours that are troublesome in the classroom but which need not be part of a diagnosed condition. If we look at exclusion data as a marker of the kinds of behaviours that schools find unacceptable this gives us a good indication of the nature of problems experienced as problematic in classrooms. In England, for example, there were 8680 permanent exclusions from primary, secondary and special schools during 2006–7, i.e. 0.12% of the number of school children (Department for Children, Schools and Families, 2008). Boys' exclusions represent 80% of this, a rate which has been stable for the past five years. There were also 425 600 exclusions for fixed periods. That is to say, schools perceived behaviour sufficiently problematic to require these children to be removed from school for a period of time, permitting them to return when that period was finished. Within these figures, 39% of pupils were excluded more than once. Again boys predominate, with 75% of the fixed period exclusions. Scottish figures which combine temporary and permanent exclusions reported 39 717 exclusions of 20 600 different pupils in 2007/8. Only 3873 of these were identified as having social, emotional or behavioural difficulties, so there is clearly a much larger undiagnosed group of children who also present significant management problems in classrooms. As in English schools, boys accounted for 79% of exclusions in the Scottish data (Scottish Government, 2009).

What were the reasons for these exclusions? In Scotland, 33% were due to 'general or persistent disobedience', 26% were 'verbal abuse of members of staff' and 17% were 'insolent or offensive behaviour' (Scottish Government, 2009). A similar picture emerged in England with 'persistent disruptive behaviour' the most common reason (Department for Children, Schools and Families, 2008). Excluding a child represents the most serious action the school can take, and therefore what schools perceive as the most serious behavioural infringements. However, there are also lower-level behaviours that require management by teachers. Now let us turn from government data to research studies to find out more about these.

Disruptive classroom behaviours

Let us first clarify what we mean by disruptive behaviour. Merrett and Wheldall's (1984) definition is still good for this purpose today. It views behaviour as disruptive when it interferes with the pupil's own learning, or the learning of classroom peers, or with the teacher's ability to carry out his/her work properly. Several studies have examined the kinds of behaviours that teachers experience as disruptive (see Examples Box). You can see that a consistent picture emerges from these data. Aggression, poor concentration, stopping other children getting on with their work, talking out of turn, non-compliance tend to be the behaviours that teachers perceive as frequent and problematic.

EXAMPLES Teacher perceptions of troublesome behaviour

1 Lawrence and Steed (1986) surveyed UK head teachers in 85 primary schools and monitored incidents in 77. The behaviours they saw as concerning were: not listening, aggression towards other pupils, poor concentration, disobedience and defiance of the teacher. The researchers randomly selected a day for teachers to record disruptive behaviours. Aggression, disobedience, poor concentration, clowning and defiance were reported as the most frequently occurring. The head teachers in this survey viewed their older pupils, i.e. the 9–11-year-olds, as presenting most of the behavioural problems.

2 Wheldall and Merrett (1988) carried out a similar survey with 32 primary schools and 198 teachers, also in the UK. Their study was with classroom teachers rather than head teachers. They reported 'talking out of turn' and 'hindering other children' as the most troublesome, the most commonly occurring, and indeed they were also identified as the most troublesome behaviours of the most troublesome students.

3 Jones, Charlton and Wilkin's (1995) study included primary school teachers, and also middle school teachers. Fifty-four teachers based on the island of St Helena took part. Results were very similar to Wheldall and Merrett's (1988), with 'talking out of turn', 'facing away from work' and 'disturbing others' reported as the most commonly occurring and the most troublesome misbehaviours.

4 Houghton, Wheldall and Merrett (1988) collected data from 251 teachers in six UK secondary schools in the West Midlands. The most common problem behaviours were again reported to be 'talking out of turn' and 'hindering other children'. The third most common reported in their study was 'slowness'.

5 Beaman, Wheldall and Kemp (2007) reviewed more recent studies from the period 1994-2005 that were carried out in Australia, US, Malta, Hong Kong and Greece, in both primary and secondary schools. 'Talking out of turn' was again both the behaviour teachers most frequently reported and that they also perceived as the most disruptive. This finding seemed to be consistent across countries and regardless of the age of class taught.

You may want to argue that the above studies should be read with caution as all rely on teacher self-report, which may be neither a reliable nor a valid measure of their actual classroom experiences. For example, an Australian working group found that teachers reported that there had been a significant increase over the years in the numbers of pupils presenting with problem behaviours in the classroom. However, when this perception was validated against teacher estimates of proportions of pupils with behaviour difficulties over the years, the estimates of the problems were actually the same and there was no change (Jacobs, 2005). Turnuklu and Galton (2001) carried out one of the few studies that did not rely on questionnaire methodology. Instead they employed structured observation, along with semi-structured interviews. Even with a different methodology, they still found that students talking noisily when they should not have been doing so, and moving about the classroom inappropriately, were the most common misbehaviours, comprising 75% of all disruptive behaviours.

Prevalence

Depending on child age and local factors in identification of troublesome behaviours, there are variations in the numbers of pupils presenting with problematic behaviours reported in studies (Beaman *et al.*, 2007). For example, in Hong Kong, a figure of 15% of pupils with troublesome behaviour was reported for both primary and secondary schools (Leung and Ho, 2001; Ho and Leung, 2002), although it is more usual for studies to show a rise of troublesome pupils in the class as children get older (e.g. Arbuckle and Little, 2004; Beaman *et al.*, 2007; Oswald, 1995). Beaman and Wheldall (1997) suggested that, on balance, teachers might expect to have from two to nine students with some level of problematic behaviour in a class of 30.

Time spent managing disruptive behaviours

Behaviours that seem to be most troublesome to teachers in the classroom tend to be low-level, trivial, but nonetheless persistent (Beaman and Wheldall, 1997; Beaman *et al.*, 2007; Houghton, Wheldall and Merrett, 1988; Little, 2005). While externalising behaviours (e.g. aggression, impulsivity, non-compliance, rule-breaking) are more serious and more difficult to manage in a classroom, they are relatively rare, estimated at around 3–5% (Jacob, 2005; Jenson, Olympia, Farley and Clark, 2004; Kazdin, 1995). However, when you also factor into the daily classroom situation these lower-level disruptive behaviours discussed above, you can see that teachers have to spend a considerable amount of their time managing behaviour, a recognised prerequisite for effective teaching and learning to take place in the classroom (Brophy, 1985). Half of all teachers said that they had to spend more time on managing behaviour than they thought they should (Beaman and Wheldall, 1997), and Little (2005) reported 68% of teachers saying they spent too much time on this. However, these views very clearly depend on subjective teacher judgments as to how much time they should be spending on managing behaviour. If, as a teacher, you think a significant part of your work is behaviour management then you would give a different response to this question compared to a teacher who thinks little time should be spent on this, that children should come to school already knowing how to behave, and that the teacher's job is to teach. This would be the case even when both of you are actually spending exactly the same amount of time on sorting out management issues. The first teacher would feel s/he is spending the right amount of time and the second teacher would feel it's too much time and they should be getting on with educating children, their real work. Indeed in two Chinese studies, Ding, Li, Li and Kulm (2008) reported only 34% of teachers who felt they spent too much time on discipline in the classroom, and Shen, Zhang, Zhang, Caldarella, Richardson and Shatzer (2009) reported 45%. These figures were low in comparison to the Western studies reported above, which the authors explained was likely to be due to cultural differences between Chinese and Western teachers. It is interesting to note that while these studies both reported talking out of turn to be a significant problem, unlike the Western studies it was only the second most significant problem with non-attention perceived as the main problem for Chinese teachers.

 ## Debate

Join up with some friends to discuss.

Behavioural problems in the classroom are those child behaviours that are experienced as problematic by the teacher. Consider to what extent problematic classroom behaviour might be a function of:

- the individual child
- teacher perceptions
- teacher management and organisation
- the demands of the learning task
- classroom conventions around sitting still and working quietly
- context – social, cultural, environmental.

Behavioural interventions

Having established the kinds of behaviours that teachers are concerned about, let us look at research evidence for the effectiveness of behavioural strategies for managing these disruptive behaviours. It should be noted that teacher experience may be a factor here, with newer teachers reporting they have to spend more time on behaviour problems and that they are less able to find ways to deal with them (Shen, Zhang, Zhang, Caldarella, Richardson and Shatzer, 2009).

The earliest behavioural interventions utilised teacher approval, disapproval and ignoring inappropriate behaviour. This was followed by the realisation that teacher behaviour itself was not always sufficient to bring about behavioural change and that providing concrete rewards for targeted behaviour using token economies was effective (Stage and Quiroz, 1997). A token economy is where children receive tokens such as stars, points, plastic counters, tickets for good behaviour. These tokens are exchanged later at a previously agreed level of exchange for some concrete reward that the children value, e.g. extra playtime, a class outing or sweets. The focus here was on positive behaviour only, and misbehaviour was ignored. Later, however, it was recognised that contingency measures that used only positive reinforcement were often not sufficient, and that adding response cost procedures worked better (Pfiffner and O'Leary, 1993; Rapport, Murphy and Bailey, 1980). Response cost involves removing tokens for misbehaviour.

Studies of behavioural management approaches are usually carried out in real classrooms, often with pre-existing class groups, rather than participants being randomly allocated to intervention conditions, with teachers attempting to bring about change to the real-life problems they face on a daily basis. While these elements contribute to the ecological validity of such studies, you will see in this chapter and throughout this book that carrying out real-world research brings its own particular problems of design and interpretation of findings. One research design often used for pre-existing groups is the time-series design where baseline measures are taken (Phase A), then the intervention is implemented and measures are again taken (Phase B). This single-case experimental design (see Chapter 3) allows one to observe from baseline the pattern of change when implementing and removing the intervention. A well-designed study will repeat this so that there is a baseline and then at least three more phases: $A_1 B_1 A_2 B_2$. Multiple baselines may also be employed by comparing different intervention groups as they undergo the baseline, treatment and reversal phases (see Figure 4.1).

Preventive interventions

Good teaching practice encourages teachers to set up their classroom systems and management strategies in a way that is proactive so that the focus is on avoiding behavioural problems occurring. Such a strategy does not focus on individual children but on the whole class. An example of this was the Cool Tool, a social skills

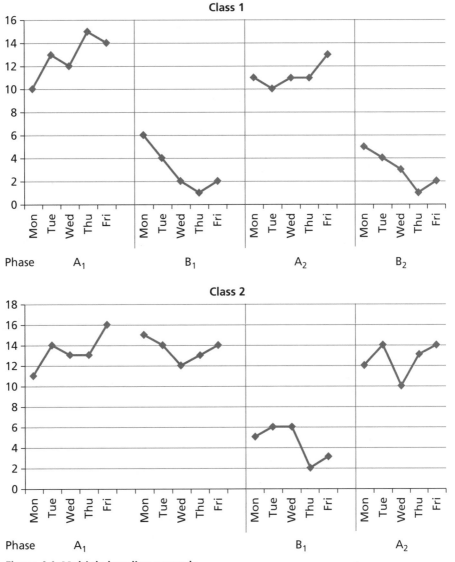

Figure 4.1 **Multiple baseline example**

programme designed to encourage prosocial behaviours in primary- and early-secondary-school-aged children through lessons with scenarios and activities that aimed to teach skills and expectations of social behaviour (Sugai, Geisen and Fernandez, 1995). Examples of skills addressed by this programme were 'being ready to learn', 'managing anger', 'being respectful'. Langland, Lewis-Palmer and Sugai (1998) evaluated this approach using an AB case study design (see Chapter 3) in two classrooms which were known to have high levels of disruptive behaviour. The A phase involved baseline problem behaviours measured in the two classes at different times so that one class had started on the B phase four days before the other. The B phase was the intervention phase when the Cool Tool lessons were delivered. Because two classrooms were used with two baselines, this is referred to as a multiple baseline study. The authors reported a reduction in disruptive behaviours in both classrooms, which included behaviours described as 'severe disruptions', 'verbal abuse', 'harassment' and 'defiance'. These fell in the first classroom from an average of 0.25 per minute to 0.07, and in the second from 0.11 to 0.04. Indeed the average level of disruptive behaviours in the second classroom actually dropped marginally before it had begun on the B phase of intervention, perhaps as a spillover effect of the intervention in the first classroom. After the Christmas holidays, two months after implementation of the B phase, the intervention effects had still been maintained. It is possible, however, that the effect in both classes might have been due to a factor other than the Cool Tool that might have been operating across both classrooms. As discussed in Chapter 3, Campbell and Stanley (1966) referred to 'history' as a possible threat to internal validity in quasi-experimental studies like this. For example, the teachers involved in the study might have carried out their work with renewed vigour and enthusiasm, knowing that they were to be involved in an intervention that might change the disruptive behaviour in their classrooms. Thus, the second class teacher may have unintentionally changed her teaching style in some way before the B phase began.

 Group activity (for 2–6 people)

Join up with some friends to discuss.

A head teacher at a school has heard about the Cool Tool and has asked you, the local educational psychologist for your opinion as to whether she should implement it in her school. Based on your critical evaluation (See Chapter 3) of the evidence provided in the Langland *et al.* (1998) paper, what do you advise?

In the Langland *et al.* (1998) study above, the teachers used a technique called **pre-correction**, by which students are prompted in a situation where problematic behaviour might occur, *before* the undesirable behaviour occurs (Colvin, Sugai and Patching, 1993). Pre-correction could involve reminding students of the rules, modelling appropriate behaviour, gesturing, or allowing them to practise the desired behaviour. Approaches like this that are proactive, rather than responsive, are sometimes referred to as 'antecedent-based'. Active supervision is another form of proactive, antecedent-based intervention. In active supervision, teachers circulate the classroom, scanning the room and checking for appropriate and inappropriate behaviours, engaging with students, and providing positive reinforcement when they see examples of appropriate academic and social behaviour (DePry and Sugai, 2002). De Pry and Sugai (2002) evaluated a daily intervention programme which applied these two antecedent-based methods to a social studies class of 26 primary school students, and where the teacher was trained to review daily data on behaviours to establish how to target her teaching of these in the intervention phase. The authors reported decreases in minor behavioural incidents: not academically engaged, eating in the classroom, not following directions, note-passing, out-of-seat behaviour, and copying another person's work. There were, however, a number of design limitations of the study in terms of possible confounding variables that may have contributed to behavioural outcomes other than the intervention itself. For example, the study was carried out with one class only and a very experienced teacher who had volunteered to take part. It was the end of the school year when staff and students may have been in particularly positive mood, looking forward to the holidays. Could proximity to the break, or the enthusiasm of this teacher, have contributed to the outcome rather than the intervention itself? These are questions you might ask yourself in weighing up the evidence presented for the effectiveness of this intervention approach. Remember Campbell and Stanley's (1966) concept of 'history' from Chapter 3. This means that a rival event happening at the same time as the intervention may be a threat to the internal validity of the study making it difficult to conclude unequivocally from the results that there is a causal relationship between the intervention and the outcome.

QUISSET *Now go beyond the text ... look it up yourself!*

Explore your library's electronic databases to investigate 'threats to internal validity'.

- Some of Campbell and Stanley's (1966) threats to internal validity were outlined in Chapter 3. Research threats to validity in more detail through the library databases and internet resources that are available to you so that you are satisfied you understand them.
- Which threats to internal validity might apply to interpretation of the findings of DePry and Sugai's (2002) study?

Interventions using contingency management

In the previous section we looked at evaluations of some proactive, preventive intervention approaches. More commonly evaluated, however, are contingency management approaches which are reactive, rather than proactive. The emphasis in contingency management is on reinforcing desirable behaviour *once it has occurred*.

A key question here is who should receive reinforcement. As we know from the prevalence data earlier in this chapter, in any class it is only a percentage of children who present with problematic behaviour and whose behaviour requires careful management by the teacher. So should reinforcement be at the level of the individual or the group? Should management programmes with individual targets and rewards only be applied to those children whose behaviour is problematic in class? A system that focuses on individuals is often perceived by teachers as cumbersome to administer. They also sometimes feel it is unfair to provide extrinsic rewards only for the poorly behaved pupils who require behavioural support when their peers who routinely behave well and get on with their work quietly do not have the opportunity to gain any additional rewards. In any case, evidence suggests both individual and group contingency management are equally effective (Axelrod, 1973; Rosenbaum, O'Leary and Jacob, 1975). Universal interventions that target the whole class or whole school, rather than targeting only selected individuals, are viewed as a way of developing a positive social environment within an educational establishment (Sugai, Sprauge, Horner, and Walker, 2000).

Group contingency management interventions have been found to be effective in addressing behaviour problems in the classroom (Stage and Quiroz, 1997). At the group level, there are three different levels at which contingency may be administered (Litow and Pumroy, 1975). Should it be *independent*, where children are reinforced individually when they achieve group criteria, regardless of the performance of the rest of the class? An example of this would be the award of 10 minutes' extra break time to pupils who achieved 60% of their behavioural targets. Here the same targets, assessment criteria and rewards are applied to everyone in the group but contingency reinforcement, i.e. allocating the reward, applies independently to each individual based on their own performance. Or should reinforcement be *dependent*, in which those members of the class with behavioural problems and targets determine the rewards of the whole class? By this method, the whole class will be awarded 10 minutes' extra break time depending on specific pupils achieving 60% of their goals. Social ostracism may be a problem with this method, with the rest of the class annoyed that the targeted individuals did not achieve their goals, blaming them for the class not receiving the reward. A third option is *interdependent* contingency. With this collaborative approach, rewards are dependent on the class as a whole meeting agreed class target behavioural criteria, i.e. 60% in this illustration. This means all students in the class are required to play their part to ensure that everyone receives their reward.

EXAMPLES Studies on interdependent group dependency

1 In Lohrmann and Talerico's (2004) study, a differential reinforcement procedure for omitting disruptive behaviour was used. With this method, reinforcement is contingent on target behaviours being below an agreed rate within a specified time period. The target behaviours were out-of-seat, incomplete assignments, and talking out of turn. Ten pupils in a learning support classroom took part in 'Anchor the Boat', an intervention in which pictures of a boat and an anchor were attached to the wall at a distance from each other. The group's objective was to join the anchor to the boat through their good behaviour. The group was given a paper clip for every lesson with fewer than 50 examples of disruptive

behaviour, until it had collected 10 paperclips, which were enough to link the boat and the anchor. Each participant then selected an individual reward from a list (e.g. toys, bookmarks, games). Using a multiple baseline design, the authors reported a decrease in talking-out-of-turn behaviour, although findings were less clear-cut for the other two target behaviours.

2 Luiselli, Putnam, Handler and Feinberg's (2005) study targeted disruptive behaviour at the whole-school level rather than at the level of the class over a three-year period. This involved forming a behaviour support team, refining their data management system to record discipline referrals and suspensions more accurately; revising school policy to clarify positive behavioural expectations, then introducing a token reinforcement system (independent group contingency). At the level of the classroom, positive behaviour was reinforced. The authors reported a decrease in mean levels of behaviour referrals to the head teacher (which fell from 1.3 per 100 students at pre-intervention to 0.54 at follow-up) and suspensions (dropping from 0.31 in pre-intervention to 0.2 in follow-up). This was a quasi-experimental study design, though, with resultant problems in attributing a causal relationship between the intervention and behavioural outcomes. Also, while levels of suspensions and referrals fell overall during the course of the intervention, they actually increased during the second year of the intervention.

3 Christ and Christ (2006) used a digital scoreboard to implement a differential reinforcement procedure with three disruptive high-school classes. The scoreboard automatically scored each two-minute interval in which the teacher perceived no disruption and the class gained one point. With 17 points the group was given free time. Independent observers rated the target behaviours. When disruptive behaviour occurred, the digital timer was reset and no score was obtained for that time interval. The authors reported an increase in engaged academic behaviour and a decrease in the number of disruptive verbalisations.

Evidence is not clear-cut as to which of the universal methods, interdependent, dependent or individual, is most effective, particularly when practical considerations are taken into account (Kelshaw-Levering, Sterling-Turner, Henry and Skinner, 2000). Kelshaw-Levering et al. (2000) further noted that dependent group reinforcement could be randomised by ensuring that random pupils, not known to the class, were selected for rewards being contingent on these pupils meeting behavioural criteria. With this randomised dependent contingency, the members of the class were required to work interdependently in any case, as only the teacher knew on which pupils the achievement of reward depended (Gresham and Gresham, 1982). By use of randomisation, dependent contingency reinforcement then could also share the collaborative benefits of interdependent contingency reinforcement.

Kelshaw-Levering et al. (2000), however, noted that as well as randomising the target pupils, there may be benefits if other elements of the intervention were randomised. For example, one limitation of contingency management is that when it is the group that is rewarded, not all group members may experience the selected reward as reinforcing. We know what is reinforcing to one child may not be so for another. This can be addressed by 'mystery motivators' (Rhodes, Jensen and Reavis, 1992) which are unknown, randomised reinforcers. Murphy, Theodore, Aloiso, Alric-Edwards and Hughes (2007) used this method with a small group of eight pre-school children who were part of a Head Start programme for disadvantaged children. If every child reached the criterion for the disruptive target behaviour, the whole class was given a mystery reward from a possible twelve, including tossing a bean-bag, games, singing or a sticker. In Kelshaw-Levering *et al.*'s (2000) study with school-aged children, when the group achieved the target a randomly selected pupil drew a reinforcer from a jar containing slips of paper with a selection of possible reinforcers such as extra playtime or an edible reward.

Kelshaw-Levering *et al.* (2000) further recognised that the reinforcement used was not the only limitation on effective behaviour change using contingency management in the classroom. For example, once the specified time limit had elapsed within which good behaviour was to occur, children might resort to the target misbehaviour again. Furthermore there could be a reduction only in the specific behaviours that were being targeted while other behaviours remained problematic. To deal with these concerns, Kelshaw-Levering *et al.* utilised a multi-phase contingency management intervention in which all elements were randomised: target behaviours, target students, reinforcers, and where criteria for rewards were unknown. Their study suggested that randomising all elements was possibly more effective than randomising only the reinforcers.

QUISSET *Now go beyond the text . . . look it up yourself!*

Explore your library's electronic databases to investigate 'randomised contingency management'.

- Kelshaw-Levering *et al.* (2000) and Murphy *et al.* (2007) discuss limitations to their respective studies. Identify what these are, and then evaluate your position on randomisation in contingency management.

What works? Results from meta-analyses

We have so far focused on some examples of behavioural management evaluations to give a sense of universal approaches teachers can use in their classrooms, and the inherent problems there are in designing and interpreting such studies. You can see that, while these studies suggest that the interventions are effective, because of possible confounding variables it is sometimes difficult to make a confident decision about whether these interventions would work as well in another school setting. If you were an educational psychologist or a teacher trying to determine which approach to take with a disruptive class, you might still be a little unsure as to how to proceed. Meta-analyses can help with this decision by quantitatively reducing related studies in the field to a common metric, effect size, so that the findings of all credible studies can be compared, even though their methods were different. This method can help identify what are the key features of effective programmes and for whom they are likely to work best. Here is a simple way of thinking about meta-analysis. The author has a research question in mind, e.g. 'How effective is this intervention?'. Instead of surveying individual participants to see what changes occurred through their participation in the intervention programme or comparison group, the author of a meta-analysis surveys the results of different studies, to determine the answer to this research question, (e.g. Cordray, 1990). Chapter 2 showed meta-analysis to be at the top of the hierarchy of evidence. You might want to revisit this chapter just now to remind yourself of the relative strengths and weaknesses of the different sources of evidence.

KEY CONCEPTS

What is meta-analysis?

Using the example of interventions to tackle classroom behaviour problems, even a cursory search of the literature will show you that there have been many, many studies carried out in this area. Some may claim better success than others. If you are trying to determine which interventions work, how do you find your way through all the different evidence? Clearly you would want to review relevant work, but then how do you weigh up what may appear to be conflicting findings? How do you integrate the various studies in order to synthesise findings sufficently to enable you to reach a conclusion to your question about which interventions work? Meta-analytic reviews allow this by quantifying the strength and statistical signfiicance of the effect of an intervention. Thus a meta-analysis will explain what databases were searched over which period, and what criteria were used for inclusion in the review. It will also identify exclusion criteria which are likely to conclude poorly designed studies, e.g. those with no comparison group or which used measurements of questionable reliability. Rather than simply accepting an author's interpretation of the importance of their findings, readers of a meta-analysis can then make their own judgments based on the statistical evidence presented. Furthermore they can do this by considering not just one study about the intervention's effectiveness, but instead can gain an overview by examining the findings from a range of studies on the topic, some with less impressive findings than others.

A meta-analysis, then, might also include studies with higher, less significant p-values and smaller effect sizes. This could mean examining those published in less prestigious journals (Rosenthal, 1995). The reason for this is that major journals tend to publish only significant findings, therefore a search of major journals could suggest that the only findings on the effectiveness of the intervention you are interested in, show it to be significant. But perhaps other studies with less significant p-values, less strong effect sizes have also been carried out and published. If you take into account their findings too, you now have some studies that show the intervention to be highly effective, while others, maybe in lesser journals, show it to be not quite so effective. Clearly if you are an educational psychologist deciding on which intervention to invest your time, your energies and your district's teaching staff resources, you will want to know about the less impressive results as well, to weigh up whether the proposed intervention is likely to work.

Meta-analysis provides a quantitative means of doing this. Effect size is the key component of a meta-analysis that allows you to do this, so much so that Rosenthal (1995) referred to effect size as 'the meta-analytic coin of the realm'. For each study that is referred to in a meta-analysis there should be an effect size given. This is quite different from significance, by which we mean statistically significant where a p-value tells you the extent to which any differences found could have occurred by chance, small, i.e. $p < .05$ or less, being viewed as significant and less likely to be a chance finding. Effect size, however, tells you what size that difference is. So it may be that a difference is statistically significant but has a small effect size. That means that there was a significant difference, say between the intervention and comparison groups, but that it's not much of a difference and might not be perceived as worth the resources to bring about such a small change. The meta-analysis then will provide a mean effect size for the intervention you are interested in. As a guide, where Cohen's d is used as a measure of effect size, 0.8 is a large effect size, 0.5 is medium and 0.2 is small (Cohen, 1988).

Stage and Quiroz (1997) carried out a meta-analysis of 99 studies designed to reduce disruptive behaviour in classrooms. Alongside behavioural programmes they considered more specialist and targeted interventions that may be carried out in schools, such as cognitive-behavioural therapy, e.g. anger management programmes, counselling, parent training programmes. They included only those studies with a non-treatment control group or where there was a baseline phase so that all studies provided a valid measure against which intervention change could be compared. They argued that often time-series data (see earlier section on Behavioural Interventions to remind yourself what this is) were omitted from meta-analyses and that this could constitute a loss of important data. Within their meta-analysis the authors used a particular statistical methodology that allowed them to calculate effect size from these time-series data, which addressed some of the challenges in interpretation of results presented in this design. The authors did not, however, include studies that reported appropriate classroom behaviour as they reasoned that improved positive behaviour does not necessarily mean that there has been a reduction in disruptive behaviour.

They reported that interventions carried out in school settings were generally effective in reducing disruptive behaviours for 78% of pupils. They found no clear differences between the various interventions which covered the range of possible treatments described above. It should be noted though that group contingency, differential reinforcement methods and self-management reduced disruptive behaviours in 85% of pupils. The first two methods have already been discussed. Self-management approaches may be considered a response to these externally managed interventions by aiming to help pupils learn to manage their own behaviour to a greater extent. Stage and Quiroz did, however, note that outcome measures that relied on teacher reports were less likely to demonstrate change than behavioural observations. The authors suggested that this may be because even though a particular pupil has reduced their disruptive behaviour, the teacher may still perceive that pupil as disruptive and problematic relative to the others in the class.

More recently, Wilson and Lipsey (2007) conducted a meta-analysis of experimental or quasi-experimental classroom intervention studies since 1950 that used aggressive or disruptive behaviour as an outcome variable. This included studies with children who had been diagnosed with an emotional or behavioural disorder as well as with children who presented with disruptive behaviour in the classroom and did not have any specific condition. The authors reported an overall mean effect size of 0.21 for reduction in aggressive/disruptive behaviour, which is small, according to Cohen's (1988) classification (see Key Concepts Box). For universal programmes which were delivered to all children in the classroom, the mean effect size was also 0.21. However, as Wilson and Lipsey pointed out, such an effect size can represent a reduction in disruptive behaviour that is of practical significance in the classroom. The authors found that children from low socio-economic groups showed larger effect sizes than those with higher socio-economic status. Most of the universal programmes reported in this study were cognitive, focusing on e.g. anger management, problem-solving in social situations, changing hostile thinking. Others involved social skills training or counselling. Only four universal studies used behavioural strategies, perhaps because time-series designs were not included in this meta-analysis which set as a criterion the requirement of a comparison group. It should be noted though that many of the cognitive programmes also used behavioural components.

For selected programmes in which the intervention was delivered only to those pupils who required it, Wilson and Lipsey reported a similar mean effect size of 0.29. These were mainly 'pull-out' programmes where only those children who required the intervention received it, either individually or in small groups, outside their usual classroom setting. Again, most of the selected interventions were cognitive, although this time there was also a substantial number of behavioural, social skills and counselling interventions, as well as peer-mediated interventions. Wilson and Lipsey found higher effect sizes in selected programmes for behavioural treatments than for other types of intervention. Importantly, they also identified fidelity of intervention as a significant predictor of outcome. Where programmes were implemented better, they were more effective. This suggests that schools should only take on an intervention programme that they feel they can commit to carrying out properly.

What interventions work for children with ADHD?

So far in this chapter we have focused on the evidence for the effectiveness of interventions for improving behaviour in children who do not have diagnosed conditions, i.e. general disruptive behaviour that occurs in classrooms. Let us now move to examining classroom interventions for ADHD. Not only is ADHD the most common developmental disorder but it is also the most commonly studied (Rowland *et al.*, 2002). This is helpful for our purposes as it means there is a rich source of data to mine for evidence as to how best to manage behaviour in the classroom. Indeed the problems presented by children with ADHD may be considered a more extreme form of the lower-level disruptive behaviours that routinely require teacher management.

Stimulant medication has been commonly prescribed for ADHD and has been shown to be effective (e.g. Pelham, 1993), but there are concerns about possible long-term effects (Pelham, 2008). Even though ADHD is thought to have a biological basis, the psychosocial context is also viewed as important (NICE, 2008) and it is well established that behavioural approaches are also effective (e.g. Pelham and Fabiano, 2008), having been used successfully for over 30 years (O'Leary, Pelham, Rosenbaum and Price, 1976). There is evidence for a combination of behaviour modification and medication together (American Academy of Pediatrics, 2001). UK guidelines recently stated that drug treatment should not be the first-line treatment for ADHD in school-aged children but that the first-line should be psychosocial methods and that teachers should implement behavioural interventions in the classroom (NICE, 2008). Pelham (2008) similarly argued the case that behavioural treatments should be the first approach. It is not our concern here to enter the debate as to which of medication, behavioural methods or a combination of both is most effective for ADHD treatment. Instead our focus is firmly on the application of behavioural approaches, with a view to examining the evidence in order to establish effect sizes, and which of the available approaches have been shown to work best in the classroom.

DuPaul and Eckert's (1997) meta-analysis examined the effect sizes of 63 studies that used school-based interventions, which they classified into contingency management, cognitive-behavioural, or academic. Academic interventions mainly focused on manipulating antecedent conditions in the classroom. They found that contingency management and academic interventions were more effective than cognitive-behavioural in addressing disruptive classroom behaviour with effect sizes in the moderate to high range at 0.5 and above. The authors reported no differences between programmes delivered in special education settings and those in mainstream classes – a finding which has important implications as children with ADHD tend to be educated in inclusive mainstream settings. A more recent meta-analysis carried out by Fabiano, Pelham, Coles, Gnagy, Chronis-Tuscano and O'Connor (2009) reported similar findings. Like DuPaul and Eckert, they decided to include both single-case time series and also within-group studies where each participant operates as its own control. They argued that examining only randomised between-group studies not only omitted potentially important sources of evidence but that also there were concerns about what results of randomised controlled trials meant in practice for individual cases. Their meta-analysis also included studies of ODD and CD, but only where a majority of children in the sample were diagnosed with ADHD. A large effect size (.83) for between-group studies where there was a no-treatment control group was obtained, and even larger effect sizes for within-group and single-case studies.

This suggests that behavioural treatments have a consistently robust effect in improving behaviour in children with ADHD across different settings, and that these findings are generalisable to other classroom settings. So we know that contingency management approaches work with children with ADHD in school settings. These include a combination of antecedent-based and consequent-based strategies, both of which rely on external teacher feedback, and internally based self-management strategies where pupils learn to monitor and reinforce their own behaviour without being dependent on the teacher for this (DuPaul and Stoner, 2003). Antecedent-based strategies for ADHD pupils include modifying the learning task by breaking it into smaller parts to aid on-task activity, active teaching of classroom rules, and allowing pupils to make choices of which task s/he wants to do next from a menu selected by the teacher (DuPaul and Weyandt, 2006). Consequent-based approaches typically include reward, token and points systems for targeted behaviour, daily report card, and judicious use of response-cost and time-out for disruptive behaviour (Pelham and Fabiano, 2008).

Furthermore, clinical behaviour therapy may be considered as a less intensive behavioural approach (Pelham and Murphy, 1986) as with this approach teachers are trained simply to give the class clear instructions, and to give praise or rewards contingent on appropriate behaviour, compared to more intense contingency management strategies that are used in special educational settings. Even though they differ in level of intensity of teacher input, both clinical behaviour therapy and contingency management have been reported as effective for improving behaviour in children with ADHD (DuPaul and Eckert, 1997; Pelham and Fabiano, 2008). Fabiano, Pelham, Gnagy, Burrows-MacLean, Coles, Chacko et al. (2007) were interested in following up this issue of intervention intensity because if the lower-intensity clinical behaviour therapy was just as effective as the more staff-intensive, time-consuming and therefore costly contingency management approach, then this would seem to be more appropriate to implement. Their study compared lower-(LBM) and higher-intensity behaviour modification(HBM) with three different doses of medication intervention, all known to be efficacious treatments, as well as looking at combined effects to try to tease out the optimal approach and intensity. In terms of behaviour modification, they found both LBM and HBM significantly improved classroom behaviour as measured by a reduction in breaking classroom rules, and improved academic productivity as measured by children sitting in their seat and completing their classwork. There was no significant difference between the two levels of intervention. The study further replicated the already well-established effects of medication. Importantly though, Fabiano et al.'s study found that effect sizes of LBM alone were equal to all interventions, except for HBM + medication, and except for interventions that included the highest doses of medication. Indeed LBM combined with a low dose of medication had the same effect as a high dose of medication. This finding of the effects of basic low-level contingency management procedures combined with low doses of medication is a potentially important one for the efficient use of teaching staff resources and for avoiding side effects from higher doses (MTA Cooperative Group, 2004). While these results seem to conflict with those reported by the MTA study (MTA Cooperative Group, 1999a, 1999b), Fabiano *et al.* suggested that this may be because previous studies may have had low levels of behaviour modification present as a confounding variable, and that their study was the first to separate out the effects of behaviour modification from medication. This research track clearly has important implications for the management of ADHD both within and outside the classroom. Indeed the American Psychological Association identified as a priority the investigation of the extent to which effective psychological interventions could be used as an alternative to, or in combination with, pharmacological interventions (Levant, 2005).

QUISSET *Now go beyond the text . . . look it up yourself!*

Explore your library's electronic databases to investigate 'intensity of contingency management/intensity of medication'.

- What are the effect sizes in the Fabiano *et al.* (2007) study?
- Fabiano *et al.* (2007) discuss limitations to this study. Identify what these are.
- These results seem to conflict with those from the MTA studies (MTA Cooperative Group, 1999a and 1999b). Have a look at the MTA findings, and taking account of both MTA findings and Fabiano *et al.* findings and the design of these studies, evaluate your position on intensity of contingency management and its relationship to medication.

Disappointingly, however, DuPaul and Eckert (1997) reported that there was little evidence of longer-term benefits beyond the end of the intervention programme. Few studies seem to evaluate this and, of those which have, very little of the observed improvement in behaviour had continued (e.g. Barkley, Shelton, Crosswait, Moorehouse, Fletcher, Barrett *et al.*, 2000; Shelton, Barkley, Crosswait, Moorehouse, Fletcher, Barrett *et al.*, 2000). Indeed, if you think about it, as single case studies, where reversal effects without the intervention are measured in the short term, are possible, this would seem to indicate behavioural programmes do not maintain their effects beyond the intervention in the short term (Pelham and Fabiano, 2008). To continue any behavioural improvements, programmes might require to build in a focus on maintenance (DuPaul and Eckert, 1997; Fabiano *et al.*, 2007). More promising was Reddy, Newman, De Thomas and Chun's (2009) report of what they referred to as 'sleeper' effects in later follow-up studies. Also results of a 10-month follow-up study by the MTA Cooperative Group (MTA Cooperative Group, 2004), followed up again at 22 months (Jensen *et al.*, 2007) with randomly assigned behavioural and medication groups, found that while the medication groups showed larger effect sizes at the first data point, by follow-up this effect was diminished so that by 22 months there were no differences between groups receiving behavioural and medication interventions.

While the evidence for the effectiveness of behavioural programmes for children with ADHD is convincing, you should note, however, that there is little evidence that cognitive-behavioural classroom interventions are effective in reducing disruptive behaviour in children with ADHD (DuPaul and Eckert, 1997; Pelham, Wheeler and Chronis, 1998). Typically these are self-instruction, self-control strategies that encourage children to reflect on a task and use cognitive rehearsal to guide them through the task. Anger management programmes are an example of a cognitive-behavioural classroom strategy. There is some suggestion, though, that cognitive-behavioural methods may be effective for academic outcomes, rather than behavioural (DuPaul and Eckert, 1997).

IN FOCUS

Task Force Standards

Pelham, Wheeler and Chronis (1998) reviewed classroom-based interventions for ADHD and concluded that cognitive-behavioural interventions did not meet American Psychological Association (APA) Task Force Criteria (Lonigan, Elbert, and Johnson, 1998) for a well-established treatment, in comparison with behaviour contingency management which clearly met criteria. They also concluded that there was not sufficient evidence to support the use of interventions that focus on social skills training to improve relationships with peers. In their more recent review, including all studies published between the last review and 2008, Pelham and Fabiano (2008) drew similar conclusions, this time using Nathan and Gorman's (2002) guidelines for evaluating treatments in conjunction with APA Task Force criteria. For more about Task Force Standards see Chapter 2.

What about other emotional/behavioural disorders?

In this chapter we have so far examined research evidence for management of low-level disruptive behaviours and management of the behaviour of children with ADHD in the classroom. Studies suggest, though, that diagnosed anti-social behaviours such as ODD and CD may similarly respond well to behavioural interventions.

Fossum, Handegård, Martinussen and Mørch (2008) carried out a meta-analysis that included children who had a diagnosis of CD or ODD, i.e. disruptive or aggressive behaviours within the clinical range. They reported large effect sizes of 0.95, and evidence of the effectiveness of behavioural approaches in reducing disruptive and aggressive behaviours in this group too. Reddy, Newman, De Thomas and Chun's (2009) meta-analysis was targeted at children with a diagnosed emotional disturbance or perceived to be at risk of emotional disturbance. The majority of the sample comprised children with ADHD and/or ODD, but it also included children identified as having adjustment disorders, Tourette's disorder, learning disabilities and language impairments, as well as internalising (rather than externalising) disorders. They included both school-based prevention and intervention programmes in their analysis, and reported large effect sizes of 1.00 post-test and 1.35 at follow-up with intervention studies generally reporting more successful results than prevention studies, although prevention programmes were better at improving active engagement and adaptive functioning. Reddy *et al.* noted, though, that children in intervention studies have more severe and chronic symptoms and so may be more likely to show a more dramatic improvement than those in prevention programmes. For intervention programmes, the largest school effects were in externalising behaviour, social skills and general academic skills. No conclusions can be drawn here, though, about which interventions were most effective as the meta-analysis was not classified in this way, but the study certainly suggests that school-based interventions can be effective in managing behaviour even with this most challenging population.

Summary and conclusions

This chapter has discussed a range of classroom behaviours that teachers experience as troublesome in the classroom. These range from low-level general problem behaviours such as talking in class, which all children engage in, to more severe and persistent behaviours that lead to diagnosed conditions such as ADHD in individual children. The view taken in this chapter and throughout this book is that both diagnosed and non-diagnosed behaviour problems are not solely characteristics of the child but that they result from an interaction between the child and his/her environmental context. Interventions reviewed in this chapter therefore involve changes to the teacher's management of the learning environment, often directed towards the whole class or group, rather than at an individual level. The chapter offered compelling evidence of the effectiveness of classroom-based behavioural intervention programmes for improving behaviours that teachers find troublesome in class.

Further study

Go to the website www.pearsoned.co.uk/markswoolfson **for the following starter articles:**

Fabiao, G., Pelham, W., Coles, E., Gnagy, E., Chronis-Tuscano, A., and O'Connor, B. (2009). A meta-analysis of behavioral treatments for attention-deficit/hyperactivity disorder. *Clinical Psychology Review, 29*(2), 129–40.

Kelshaw-Levering, K., Sterling-Turner, H., Henry, J., and Skinner, C. (2000). Randomized interdependent group contingencies: group reinforcement with a twist. *Psychology in the Schools, 37*, 523–33.

Langland, S., Lewis-Palmer, T., and Sugai, G. (1998). Teaching respect in the classroom: An instructional approach. *Journal of Behavioral Education, 8*, 245–62.

References

American Academy of Pediatrics (2001). Clincal practice guideline: Treatment of the school-aged child with attention-deficit/hyperactivity disorder. *Pediatrics, 108*, 1033–44.

American Psychiatric Assocation (1994). *Diagnostic and Statistical Manual of Mental Diseases (DSM-IV) 4th edition.* Washington, DC: American Psychiatric Association.

Arbuckle, C. and Little, E. (2004). Teachers' perceptions and management of disruptive classroom behaviour during the middle years (years five to nine). *Australian Journal of Educational and Developmental Psychology, 4*, 59–70.

Axelrod, S. (1973). Comparison of individual and group contingencies in two special classes. *Behavior Therapy, 4*, 83–90.

Barkley, R., Shelton, T., Crosswait, C., Moorehouse, M., Fletcher, K., Barrett, S., *et al.* (2000). Multi-method psychoeducational intervention for preschool children with disruptive behavior: Preliminary results at post-treatment. *Journal of Child Psychology and Psychiatry and Allied Disciplines, 41*, 319–32.

Beaman, R. and Wheldall, K. (1997). Teacher perceptions of troublesome classroom behaviour: A review of recent research. *Special Education Perspectives, 6(2)*, 49–55.

Beaman, R., Wheldall, K., and Kemp, C. (2007). Recent research on troublesome classroom behaviour: A review. *Australasian Journal of Special Education, 31*, 45–60.

Brophy, J. (1985). Classroom organisation and management. *Phi Delta Kappa, 5*, 2–17.

Campbell, D. and Stanley, J. (1966). *Experimental and quasi-experimental designs for research.* Chicago: Rand McNally.

Christ, T. and Christ, J. (2006). Application of an interdependent group contingency mediated by an automated feedback device: an intervention across three high school classrooms. *School Psychology Review, 35*, 78–90.

Cohen, J. (1988). *Statistical power analysis in the behavioral sciences.* (2nd ed). Hillsdale, NJ: Erlbaum.

Colvin, G., Sugai, G., and Patching, B. (1993). Precorrection: An instructional approach for managing predictable problem behaviours. *Intervention in School and Clinic, 28*, 143–50.

Cordray, D. (1990). Strengthening causal interpretations of non-experimental data: The role of meta-analysis. In L. Sechrest, E. Perrin, and J. Bunker (eds). *Research methodology: Strengthening causal interpretations of non-experimental data* (pp. 151–72). Washington, DC: US Department of Health and Human Services.

Department of Children, Schools and Families (2008). *Permanent and fixed exclusions from schools and exclusion appeals in England 2006/7*, SFR 14, 1–19. http://www.dcsf.gov.uk/rsgateway/DB/SFR/s000793/SFR_14Revised.pdf

DePry, R. and Sugai, G. (2002). The effect of active supervision and pre-correction on minor behavioral incidents in a sixth grade general education classroom. *Journal of Behavioral Education, 11(4)*, 255–67.

Ding, M., Li, Y., Li, X., and Kulm, G. (2008). Chinese teachers' perceptions of students' classroom misbehaviour. *Educational Psychology, 28*, 305–24.

DuPaul, G. and Eckert, T. (1997). The effects of school-based interventions for attention deficit hyperactivity disorder: A meta-analysis. *School Psychology Review, 26(1)*, 5–27.

DuPaul, G. and Stoner, G. (2003). *ADHD in the schools: Assessment and intervention strategies*, 2nd edn. New York: Guilford.

DuPaul, G. and Weyandt, L. (2006). School-based intervention for children with attention deficit hyperactivity disorder: Effects on academic, social and behavioural functioning. *International Journal of Disability, Development and Education, 53(2)*, 161–76.

Fabiano, G., Pelham, W., Gnagy, E., Burrows-MacLean, L., Coles, E., Chacko, A., *et al.* (2007). The single and combined effects of multiple intensities of behavior modification and multiple intensities of methylphenidate in a classroom setting. *School Psychology Review, 36*, 195–216.

Fabiano, G., Pelham, W., Coles, E., Gnagy, E., Chronis-Tuscano, A., and O'Connor, B. (2009). A meta-analysis of behavioral treatments for attention-deficit/hyperactivity disorder. *Clinical Psychology Review, 29*(2), 129–40.

Fossum, S., Handegård, B., Martinussen, M., and Mørch, W. (2008). Psychosocial interventions for disruptive and aggressive behaviour in children and adolescents: A meta-analysis. *European Child and Adolescent Psychiatry, 17*, 438–51.

Gresham, F. and Gresham, G. (1982). Interdependent, dependent and independent group contingencies for controlling disruptive behaviour. *Journal of Special Education, 16*, 101–10.

Hinshaw, S. (2001). Is the inattentive type of ADHD a separate disorder? *Clinical Psychology Science and Practice, 8*, 498–501.

Hinshaw, S. and Park, T. (1999). Research problems and issues: Towards a more definitive science of disruptive behaviour disorders. In H. Quay and A. Hogan (eds), *Handbook of disruptive behaviour disorders*. New York: Kluwer Academic (pp. 593–620).

Ho, C. and Leung, J. (2002). Disruptive classroom behavours osecondary and primary school students. *Educational Research Journal, 17*, 219–33.

Houghton, S., Wheldall, K., and Merrett, F. (1988). Classroom behaviour problems which secondary school teachers say they find most troublesome. *British Educational Research Journal, 14*, 297–312.

Jacob, A. (2005). Behaviour – whose choice? *Australasian Journal of Special Education, 29(1)*, 4–20.

Jensen, P., Arnold, L., Swanson, J., Vitiello, B., Abikoff, H., Greenhill, L. *et al.* (2007). 3-year follow-up of the NIMH MTA study. *Journal of the American Academy of Child and Adolescent Psychiatry, 46*, 989–1002.

Jenson, W., Olympia, D., Farley, M., and Clark, E. (2004). Positive psychology and externalising students in a sea of negativity. *Psychology in the Schools, 41(1)*, 67–79.

Jones, K., Charlton, T., and Wilkin, J. (1995). Classroom behaviours which first and middle school teachers in St Helena find troublesome. *Educational Studies, 21*, 139–53.

Kazdin, A. (1995). *Conduct disorders in childhood and adolescence*, 2nd edn. Thousand Oaks, CA: Sage.

Kelshaw-Levering, K., Sterling-Turner, H., Henry, J., and Skinner, C. (2000). Randomized interdependent group contingencies: group reinforcement with a twist. *Psychology in the Schools, 37*, 523–33.

King, S., Waschbusch, A., Frankland, B., Andrade, B., Thurston, C., McNutt, L., Terrio, B., and Northern Partners in Action for Child and Youth Services (2005). Taxonomic examnation of ADHD and Conduct Problem comorbidity in elementary school children using cluster analyses. *Journal of Psychopathology and Behavioral Assessment, 27*, 77–88.

Lahey, B., Miller, T., Gordon, R., and Riley, A. (1999). Developmental epidemiology of the disruptive behavior disorders. In H. Quay and A. Hogan (eds), *Handbook of disruptive behaviour disorders*. New York: Kluwer Academic (pp. 23–48).

Langland, S., Lewis-Palmer, T., and Sugai, G. (1998). Teaching respect in the classroom: An instructional approach. *Journal of Behavioral Education, 8*, 245–62.

Lawrence, J. and Steed, D. (1986). Primary school perception of disruptive behaviour. *Educational Studies, 12*, 147–57.

Leung, J. and Ho, C. (2001). Disruptive behaviour perceived by Hong Kong primary school teachers. *Educational Research Journal, 16*, 223–37.

Levant, R. (2005). *Report of the 2005 Task Force on evidence-based practice*. American Psychological Association.

Litow, L. and Pumroy, D. (1975). A brief review of classroom group-oriented contingencies. *Journal of Applied Behaviour Analysis, 8*, 341–7.

Little, E. (2005). Secondary school teachers' perceptions of students' problem behaviours. *Educational Psychology, 25*, 369–77.

Lohrmann, S. and Talerico, L. (2004). Anchor the boat: A classwide intervention to reduce problem behavior. *Journal of Positive Behavior Interventions, 6,* 113–20.

Lonigan, C., Elbert J., and Johnson, S. (1998). Empirically supported psychosocial interventions for children: An overview. *Journal of Clinical Child Psychology, 27,* 138–45.

Luiselli, J., Putnam, R., Handler, M. and Feinberg, A. (2005). Whole-school positive behaviour support: effects on student discipline problems and academic performance, *Educational Psychology, 25,* 183–98.

Meltzer, H., Gatward, R., Goodman, R., and Ford, T. (2000). *Mental health of children and adolescents in Great Britain.* London: HMSO.

Merrett, F. and Wheldall, K. (1984). Classroom behaviour problems which junior primary school teachers find most troublesome. *Educational Studies, 10,* 87–92.

MTA Cooperative Group. (1999a). 14-month randomized clinical trial of treatment strategies for attention deficit hyperactivity disorder. *Archives of General Psychiatry, 56,* 1073–86.

MTA Cooperative Group. (1999b). Moderators and mediators of treatment response for children with attention-deficit-hyperactivity disorder: The multimodal treatment study of children with ADHD. *Archives of General Psychiatry, 56,* 1088–96.

MTA Cooperative Group. (2004). National Institute of Mental Health multimodal treatment study of ADHD follow-up: 24-month outcomes of treatment strategies for attention-deficit-hyperactivity disorder. *Pediatrics, 113,* 754–61.

Murphy, K., Theodore, L., Aloiso, D., Alric-Edwards, J., and Hughes, T. (2007). Interdependent group contingency and mystery motivators to reduce preschool disruptive behavior. *Psychology in the Schools, 44,* 53–63.

Nathan, P. and Gorman, J. (2002). Preface. In P. Nathan and J. Gorman (eds), *A guide to treatments that work,* 2nd edn. New York: Oxford University Press (pp. 3–4).

NICE (2008). *Attention deficit hyperactivity disorder. Diagnosis and management of ADHD in children, young people and adults. NICE Clinical Guideline 72.* London: National Institute for Health and Clinical Excellence.

Nock,M., Kazdin, A., Hiripi, E., and Kessler, R. (2006). Prevalence, subtypes and correlates of DSM-IV conduct disorder in the National Comorbidity Replication. *Psychological Medicine, 36(5),* 699–710.

O'Leary, K., Pelham, W., Rosenbaum, A., and Price, G. (1976). Behavioral treatment of hyperkinetic children. *Clinical Pediatrics, 15,* 510–15.

Oswald, M. (1995). Difficult to manage students: A survey of children who fail to respond to student discipline strategies in government school. *Educational Studies, 21,* 265–276.

Pelham, W. (1993). Pharmacotherapy of children with attention-deficit hyperactivity disorder. *School Psychology Review, 22,* 199–227.

Pelham, W. (2001). Are ADHD-I and ADHD-C the same or different? Does it matter? *Clinical Psychology: Science and Practice, 8,* 502–6.

Pelham, W. (2008). Against the grain: a proposal for a psychosocial-first approach to treating ADHD – the Buffalo Treatment Algorithm. In K. Burnett, L. Pfiffer, R. Schachar, G. Elliott, J. Nigg (eds) *Attention deficit hyperactivity disorder: A 21st century perspective.* New York, NY: Informa Healthcare (pp. 301–16).

Pelham, W. and Fabiano, G. (2008). Evidence-based psychosocial treatment for ADHD. *Journal of Clinical Child and Adolescent Psychology, 37,* 184–214.

Pelham, W. and Murphy, H. (1986). Attention deficit and conduct disorder. In M. Hersen (ed.), *Pharmacological and behavioural treatment: An integrative approach.* New York: Wiley (pp. 108–48).

Pelham, W., Wheeler, T., and Chronis, A. (1998). Empirically supported psychosocial treatments for ADHD. *Journal of Clinical Child Psychology, 27,* 189–204.

Pfiffner, L. and O'Leary, S. (1993). School-based psychological treatments. In J. Matson (ed.) *Handbook of hyperactivity in children*. Boston, MA: Allyn and Bacon (pp. 234–55).

Polanczyk, G., De Lima, M., Horta, B., Biederman, J., and Rohde, L. (2007). The worldwide prevalence of ADHD: A systematic review and metaregression analysis. *American Journal of Psychiatry, 164(6)*, 942–48.

Polanczyk, G. and Rohde, L. (2007). Epidemiology of attention-deficit/hyperactivity disorder across the lifespan. *Current Opinion in Psychiatry, 20(4)*, 386–92.

Rapport, M., Murphy, A., and Bailey, J. (1980). The effects of a response cost treatment tactic on hyperactive children. *Journal of School Psychology, 18*, 98–111.

Reddy, L., Newman, E., De Thomas, C., and Chun, V. (2009). Effectiveness of school-based prevention and intervention programs for children and adolescents with emotional disturbance: a meta-analysis. *Journal of School Psychology, 47*, 77–99.

Rhodes, G., Jensen, W., and Reavis, H. (1992). *The tough kid book: Practical classroom management strategies*. Longmont, CO: Sopris West.

Rosenbaum, A., O'Leary, K., and Jacob, R. (1975). Behavioral intervention with hyperactive children: group consequences as a supplement to individual contingencies. *Behaviour Therapy, 6*, 315–23.

Rosenthal, R. (1995). Writing meta-analytic reviews. *Psychological Bulletin, 118(2)*, 183–92.

Rowland, A., Lesesne, C., and Abramowitz, A. (2002). The epidemiology of attention deficit/hyperactivity disorder (ADHD): A public health view. *Mental Retardation and Developmental Disabilities Research Reviews, 8*, 162–70.

Scottish Government (2009). Statistics publication notice. Exclusions from schools 2007/8. http://www.scotland.gov.uk/Resource/Doc/258163/0076560.pdf

Shelton, T., Barkley, R., Crosswait, C., Moorehouse, M., Fletcher, K., Barrett, S., *et al*. (2000). Multimethod psychoeducational intervention for preschool children with disruptive behavior. Two-year post-treatment follow-up. *Journal of Abnormal Child Psychology, 28*, 253–66.

Shen, J., Zhang, N., Zhang, C., Caldarella, P., Richardson, M.J., and Shatzer, R.H. (2009). Chinese elementary school teachers' perceptions of students' classroom behaviour problems. *Educational Psychology, 29*, 187–201.

Stage, S. and Quiroz, D. (1997). A meta-analysis of interventions to decrease disruptive classroom behaviour in public education settings. *School Psychology Review, 26(3)*, 333–68.

Sugai, G., Geisen, C., and Fernandez, E. (1995). *The Cool Tool: A social skills teaching format*. Behavioral Research and Teaching. University of Oregon, Eugene.

Sugai, G., Sprauge, J., Horner, R., and Walker, H. (2000). Preventing school violence: The use of office discipline referrals to assess and monitor school-wide discipline interventions. *Journal of Emotional and Behavioral Disorders, 8*, 94–101.

Turnuklu, A. and Galton, M. (2001). Students' misbehaviours in Turkish and English primary classrooms. *Educational Studies, 27*, 291–305.

Wentzel, K. (1993). Does being good make the grade? Social behaviour and academic competence in middle school. *Journal of Educational Psychology, 85*, 357–64.

Wheldall, K. and Merrett, F. (1988). Which classroom behaviours do primary school teachers say they find most troublesome? *Educational Review, 40*, 13–27.

Wilson, S. and Lipsey, M. (2007). School-based interventions for aggressive and disruptive behavior: update of a meta-analysis. *American Journal of Preventive Medicine, 33(S2)*, 130–43.

Wolfendale, S. (1996). Accounting a network of services for EBD: a description of the DECP working party and beyond. *Educational and Child Psychology, 13(1)*, 5–12.

Autism spectrum disorders

In this chapter we will examine current research on autism. You already probably know something about this. Issues around the provision of appropriate education of children with autism, or the special talents of 'autistic savants' seem to be regularly represented by the news media. The more considered, academic approach taken in this chapter should allow you to take a more informed position in any such debates.

Learning outcomes

By the end of the chapter you should be able to:

- Understand the terms autism, autism spectrum disorder, high-functioning autism, Asperger syndrome and their relationship to each other
- Understand the main theoretical perspectives in this area – theory of mind, executive dysfunction, weak central coherence, enactive mind – and the methods used to study them
- Critically evaluate the evidence base for different explanatory theories of autism
- Integrate different theoretical perspectives
- Identify unresolved issues and new research areas
- Evaluate evidence for the effectiveness of commonly used classroom intervention approaches.

How was autism first identified?

In the 1940s Leo Kanner, a child psychiatrist working in Baltimore, published a paper describing 11 cases presenting what he perceived as a rare pattern of strange behaviour that he referred to as 'early infantile autism'. One year later Hans Asperger in Vienna reported 'autistic psychopathy', which 40 years later Lorna Wing referred to as Asperger's Syndrome (Wing, 1981). Indeed Kanner's and Asperger's case studies were not the first records of children displaying unusual behaviours – the wild boy of Aveyron in the eighteenth century may have been an early example of a child with autistic behaviours (Frith, 2003).

Kanner and Asperger separately employing the term 'autistic' may not have been total coincidence. This term was first used by Bleuler in 1911, and by the 1940s appears to have been in common use in psychiatry to describe a narrowing of relationships with the outside world that was so extreme that the only relationship that remained was with oneself (Frith, 2003). Actually, the term 'autism' may even have been unnecessarily misleading as it implied a link with schizophrenia and thus suggested a withdrawal from social relationships and a retreat into fantasy life, rather than a failure to engage appropriately in relationships and poor imagination (Rutter, 1978).

Kanner's paper was published in English and Asperger's paper was published in German, and if different languages were not enough of a barrier, this took place during World War II when the English-speaking world and Germany were on opposing sides. It is likely then that only a very few researchers were even aware of the similarities between both papers until the late 1970s when Wing brought the German publication to the attention of the English-speaking world (Sharma, Woolfson and Hunter, submitted manuscript).

It has been suggested that our explanations of autism have mirrored the zeitgeist of their times (Rajendran and Mitchell, 2007). It is not then surprising that early notions of causality of autism in the 1950s were influenced by attachment theory and built on the now discredited idea of the 'refrigerator mother' (Bettelheim, 1967). This described a situation where the mother was perceived as having 'caused' the autistic behaviour observed in her child, because she displayed a lack of maternal warmth towards the child. In the present day we have moved away from this to very different explanations of autism, which you will see are more in keeping with the zeitgeist of our own times. These explanations are discussed below.

So what is autism?

Autism is a developmental disability, one of a group of pervasive developmental disorders, whose signs are apparent before the age of three years. It typically presents as a 'triad of impairments' first identified by Wing and Gould (1979).

The description of the three affected domains has evolved since then, with core features:

- social interaction
- communication
- behavioural flexibility which shows itself in restricted, repetitive behaviours, and lack of imagination.

See, for example, Boucher (2009).

As mentioned in Chapter 4, the Diagnostic and Statistical Manual of Mental Disorders (DSM-IV) and the International Classification of Diseases (ICD-10) are used by medical and health professionals for diagnosis. They provide clear criteria for clinicians for identification of autism. You will see studies referring to autism spectrum disorders (ASD) that cover a wide range of children who present with autism-like symptoms. In considering the concept of a spectrum of autism disorders, at one end of the spectrum will be children who present with severe social, communication and behavioural impairments and have low IQ. At the other end of the spectrum are children whose IQ is in the average or above-average range and these children are viewed as having high-functioning autism (HFA). Also at this end of the spectrum are those who have Asperger Syndrome. While these children show autistic impairments, their early language development and other milestones are the same as their typically developing peers, in many cases even superior. When reading studies, then, it is important to check carefully to determine what the characteristics were of the ASD sample.

Is there 'more' autism now than there used to be?

We seem to hear a lot more about autism these days. When I trained as an educational psychologist in the UK in the late 1970s, we considered it a rare condition that we were unlikely to experience in our work. Today most teachers and all educational psychologists are aware of autism and many teachers are likely to have had some direct experience of a child with autism in their mainstream classrooms. So is there 'more' autism now than before?

To answer this question we must look at prevalence and incidence data. Prevalence data from the 1960s through to the 1980s certainly bears out what we were being taught then as newly qualified psychologists, with a rate of 4.5 in 10,000 children reported by Lotter (1966) and Wing and Gould (1979) in the UK. Indeed, similarly low rates were reported in Ireland (McCarthy, Fitzgerald and Smith, 1984); US (Burd, Fisher and Kerbeshian, 1987); France (Cialdella and Marmelle, 1989); Germany (Steinhausen, Göbel, Breinlinger and Wohllebhen, 1984); Denmark (Brask, 1972); Sweden (Gillberg, 1984), and Japan (Hoshino *et al.*, 1982), although other Japanese studies reported a higher rate of 16 per 10,000 for autism (Ishi and Takahashi, 1983; Matsuishi *et al.*, 1987).

KEY CONCEPTS

Do I understand the difference between 'prevalence' and 'incidence'?

Prevalence and incidence are terms that are highly familiar to medical students but less so to psychology students. It is important, however, for psychology students to understand these concepts in order to understand the arguments about whether there is currently an increased rate of autism.

The terms prevalence and incidence refer to statistical numerical information. Autism prevalence figures tell us the proportion of children who have autism during a specified time period compared to the total number of children examined for the prevalence study. Prevalence is usually expressed as a percentage or as a number of cases with the condition per 10,000 of the child population and so is a measure of how common the condition is within the general population.

Incidence on the other hand refers to the frequency of occurrence of new diagnoses of autism during a particular time period compared to the total number of children in the population. Incidence is also usually expressed per 10,000 or per 100,000 of the population.

To consider how prevalence and incidence might differ from each other, let's consider a common illness like 'flu. Almost everybody catches it, so the incidence will be high during the time period of interest as many, many new cases are diagnosed. Fortunately 'flu lasts only for a short period, so prevalence for the year will be lower than incidence as only some people will actually have it at any particular time.

On the other hand, a chronic condition like autism does not go away, so prevalence of autism will be higher than incidence, as incidence only records the numbers of newly diagnosed cases while prevalence reflects all children with autism. Thus autism prevalence figures will include both those newly diagnosed during that reporting period (incidence), as well as those who were diagnosed in earlier years, who of course still present as autistic during the reporting period for data collection.

So have the numbers increased since then? More recent studies in UK, Hong Kong, China, Finland and US have recently reported in the 8–20 per 10,000 range, the lower end of which is not too dissimilar to the rates from the 1960s, 1970s and 1980s reported above (Croen, Grether, Hoogstrate and Selvin, 2002; Kielinen, Linna and Moilanen, 2000; Lin, Lin and Wu, 2009; Lingam *et al.*, 2003; Wong and Hui, 2008). Fombonne's (2009) recent review also suggested a prevalence rate of about 20 per 10,000. However, other studies have reported higher rates of autism with 39.2 (Australia; Icasiano, Hewson, Machet, Cooper and Marshall, 2004) and 100 in every 10,000 (Baird *et al.*, 2006; Baron-Cohen *et al.*, 2008). A Norwegian study reported an even higher rate of 2.7% (i.e. 270 per 10,000; Posserud *et al.*, 2006).

It's not straightforward, is it? Let's consider how to interpret this. In order to compare different data sources referred to in the literature, you need to be clear how autism has been defined for the study. Increased prevalence then may *partly* reflect recent broader conceptualisations of autism as a spectrum of disorders, rather than only as classic autism at the severe end of the spectrum. Rather than increased occurrence, it may also reflect professionals who are now better trained to identify and diagnose autism, as well as improved referral procedures and assessment measures, and heightened public awareness of the condition (Fombonne, 2009; Rutter, 2005). Thus some studies using the broader conceptualisation of autism spectrum disorder have previously reported approximately 50 to 60 cases in every 10,000 children but within these they report a much smaller number of 10 to 30 per 10,000 who have classic autism (e.g. Bertrand *et al.*, 2001; Gillberg, Cederlund, Lamberg and Zeijlon, 2006; Gurney *et al.*, 2003; Scott, Baron-Cohen, Bolton and Brayne, 2002).

To add to the complexities of this question, we now need to remember that so far we have only discussed prevalence; we are yet to consider incidence. Even taking into account the procedural changes outlined above, it is still possible that the incidence of autism has increased. So the question is: Are there more children now receiving diagnoses of autism spectrum disorders than there were? Examining incidence is of particular relevance, for example, for those seeking evidence to support or disconfirm the hypothesis that modern-day hazards in our environment are the cause of an autism 'epidemic'. We need to look at incidence figures to see if there is such an 'epidemic'.

In examining the literature we can see that most studies reported an incidence of less than 10 per 10,000 (e.g. Barbaresi *et al.*, 2005; Powell *et al.*, 2000; Williams *et al.*, 2005). This should make sense to you as you expected incidence rates for autism to be lower than prevalence rates (see Key Concepts Box). Higher incidence rates (but still lower than prevalence) were obtained in Hertz-Piciotto and Delwiche's (2009) study, which reported an incidence of 42.5 per 10,000 in 2001, and Honda *et al.* (2005), who reported 27.2 per 10,000 children for the period 1988–1991. Whatever the incidence rates, though, these studies do seem to suggest increased incidence over the years. For example, the US incidence reported by Barbaresi *et al.* (2005) had risen from 0.55 per 10,000 in the 1980s to 4.5 per 10,000 in the 1990s. Hertz-Piciotto and Delwiche (2009) reported a rise also in California from 6.2 in 1990 with the biggest change in children aged 2–3. Powell *et al.* (2000) in the UK also reported an increase in numbers from 3.5 per 10,000 in the 1991–2 period to 13.1 per 10,000 in the 1995–6 period. In Hong Kong, Wong and Hui (2008) reported an incidence rate of 5.2 between 1986 and 1990, which increased to 7.9 for the period 2001–5. While the same explanations for the increase in prevalence may partly explain this increase in incidence, it is nevertheless still a strong possibility that there has been a real increase in the numbers of children with autism over the last forty years.

QUISSET   *Now go beyond the text . . . look it up yourself!*

Explore your library's electronic databases to investigate 'prevalence/incidence'.

- What explanations have been offered in the literature for differing rates across different countries?
- How might differences in current rates be explained?
- Identify a question of your own to consider here.

Group activity *(for 2–6 people)*

Join up with some friends to discuss.

Having read the chapter and worked through the QUISSETS, you now have some understanding of the arguments about the occurrence of autism. So here's the question for you to consider as a group . . .

'Has the rate of autism increased over the years?' Support your arguments with evidence.

Divide the group in half. Half the group (one person/pair/group of three) is to research and present the argument that autism has indeed increased and provide evidence from studies to support this. The other half (person/pair/group of three) is to present the arguments that there are other explanations for any apparent increase and that there are no changes in the numbers of children with autism.

Hint: Make sure you have studied original journal papers to see how studies were carried out, how autism was defined, what age groups were studied, and what tools were used for diagnosis. Are there differences in these between studies? Your QUISSET research should help here. What are the unresolved issues here?

Now a final numbers question . . . are more boys or girls diagnosed with autism?

The answer to this question is less contentious than the rate of autism issue as it has been consistently found that there are more boys with autism than girls. What the prevalence figures are depends on how these are calculated, of course. For example, a boy:girl ratio of 4:1 was reported by both Fombonne (1999) and Scott, Baron-Cohen, Bolton and Brayne (2002). These ratios change, however, depending on whether you are looking at the ratio of boys to girls in mainstream or in special schools. In mainstream the ratio seems to be higher (8:1), while in special schools the boy:girl proportions become less dissimilar (3:1). This seems to be because girls diagnosed with autism tend to have more severe learning difficulties than boys and therefore are more likely to be educated in special schools (e.g. Gillberg, Steffenburgh and Shaumann, 1991). It may also be that girls' impairments have to be more severe for the problem to be recognised by parents or teachers. As mentioned earlier in the chapter, restricted repetitive behaviour such as repeatedly opening and shutting a door, or a preoccupation with dinosaurs, is a core feature of autism. It has been suggested that symptoms of autism are less recognisable in girls, perhaps because the condition presents differently in girls who engage in these restricted interests to a lesser degree than boys and also show less impairment in social development (Wolff and McGuire, 1995). This idea also fits with Baron-Cohen's (2002) *extreme male brain* explanation, which will be discussed later in this chapter.

Theories of autism

A variety of accounts have been offered to explain autism. We will now examine some of the key theoretical approaches that are currently stimulating research studies.

Impaired theory of mind

The idea here is that children with autism have a specific cognitive impairment in that they lack a *theory of mind*. Theory of mind is not only the recognition that other people have a mental state, a set of beliefs, that may be different from your own, but also the ability to understand what these beliefs may be. We use theory of mind to understand how another person feels in a situation or how it looks to them from their physical or emotional perspective, which may differ from how it seems to us. This is also referred to as a deficit in 'mentalising' or 'mind-reading'. Some people consider that this cognitive impairment may underlie the social impairment associated with autism. This ability to understand another's intentions and beliefs is best illustrated by the classic study carried out by Baron-Cohen, Leslie and Frith (1985).

They used the Sally–Anne test, a first-order false-belief paradigm developed by Wimmer and Perner (1983) (see In Focus box). They found that 80% of children with autism, whose intelligence was within the normal range, answered that Sally thought the marble was in Anne's box even though Sally had left the room and could not know that the marble had been moved. The conclusion was that they seemed to be using their own perspective rather than Sally's perspective as the basis for response. Baron-Cohen *et al.* (1985) found that children with autism were more likely to answer using their own perspective than their control groups of typically developing 4-year-olds and of children with Down Syndrome, both of which groups had lower mental ages than the autism group. This deficit in first-order belief attribution has been replicated with people as well as with dolls (Leslie and Frith, 1988).

Bloom and German (2000), however, argued that the false-belief task was more complex than it appeared and that in order to answer correctly children required to have more than just an understanding of false beliefs. They also needed to be able to follow the plot of what the dolls were doing. They needed to remember where the chocolate was before Anne moved it, as well as where it was after being moved. Bloom and German further pointed out that children also needed to fully

IN FOCUS

What is the Sally–Anne false-belief task?

The original task was developed by Wimmer and Perner (1983) to examine false beliefs in young children. Baron-Cohen *et al.* (1985) then modified its use for children with autism and obtained exciting results.

In this task the child who is being tested watches a sequence of events acted out by two dolls, Sally and Anne, who have a basket and a box respectively. The child observes Sally put a chocolate in her basket and then sees Sally leave the room. In Sally's absence, i.e. without Sally seeing, Anne removes the chocolate from Sally's basket and hides it in her own box. Sally returns and the child is asked the 'belief' question, 'Where does Sally think the chocolate is?' The correct response in order to pass this test is of course that Sally thinks it's in her basket (as that was where she left it and she didn't see Anne move it out).

This response indicates theory of mind operating at the simplest level and is known as first-order belief attribution (Wimmer and Perner, 1985). This is the understanding that another person holds a different belief to your own, and then the ability to use that understanding of their belief to predict how that person will respond in a particular situation that relies on that belief.

understand the question being asked, for example that the question was not about where Sally *should* look for the chocolate but where she *will* look. Thus they claimed that the Sally–Anne task may not only be tapping into theory of mind. They furthermore argued that theory of mind may indeed be a bigger concept than passing or failing the false-belief task. While older children with autism may fail this task because they do not have a theory of mind, younger typically developing children may fail rather because of these other task demands. Bloom and German suggested that the younger typically developing children could even fail the task because they don't have an understanding of false belief but yet still have a theory of mind. Normal preschoolers could not engage in the imaginative play that is so characteristic of this age group, without a theory of mind that allows them to pretend to carry out the daily living tasks of the significant adults in their lives.

Deficit or delay?

As discussed above, 80% of children with autism failed the first-order false-belief task. This meant, though, that 20% of children with autism actually passed it. This suggested that it could not be a deficit because some children with autism were successful in the task. A new second-order belief task was developed on the understanding that if the poor performance of autistic children here indicated a delay in developing a theory of mind, rather than a deficit, then the autistic subgroup who had passed the first-order false-belief task might be expected to fail in tackling a more complex belief task. And indeed, using a more advanced theory of mind task (I think she thinks he thinks) (see In Focus Box below), Baron-Cohen (1989) found that nine out of the ten children in the autism sample pointed to where they knew the van to be, rather than to where Mary believed John thought the van was. In contrast 90% of the typically developing 7-year-olds and 60% of the children with Down Syndrome, both groups with a lower mental age than the children with autism, passed the second-order belief question. This led Baron-Cohen (1989) to reconceptualise the issue as a specific cognitive *delay* rather than as a deficit.

A subsequent meta-analysis by Happé (1995) provided further support for cognitive delay rather than deficit. She found there was a significant correlation between children's verbal mental age (see Key Concepts Box) and their performance on the Sally–Anne task. Happé's results suggested that in order to succeed on this task children had to have reached a particular verbal mental age and that acquiring a theory of mind would be delayed until that verbal mental age was reached. Some of the typically developing children in her study began to pass this theory of mind task at a verbal mental age of 2 years 10 months. However, the threshold for passing seemed to be higher for the autistic children in the sample, who were unable to pass before reaching a verbal mental age of 5 years 6 months.

KEY CONCEPTS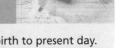

Chronological age is the child's actual age as dated from date of birth to present day.

Mental age is a score obtained by using a standardised age-related scale to evaluate child performance on a set of cognitive tasks. These cognitive tasks may be verbal tasks which would yield a **verbal mental age**, or they may be tasks that do not rely on language skills and thus give a **nonverbal mental age**.

IN FOCUS

Baron-Cohen's (1989) second-order false-belief task

The second-order false-beliefs test involved a toy village, with houses, a church, two dolls, John and Mary, and an ice-cream van. Again this was a paradigm that had been initially developed by Perner and Wimmer (1985).

The scenario is that John and Mary are in the park and John wants to buy ice cream but has no money, having left it at home. The ice-cream man says he'll be there all day so John can buy it later. John goes to his house for the money and sees the ice-cream man moving his van. The ice-cream man explains he is moving his van to outside the church to sell ice cream there.

Now Mary goes home to her house and then goes to John's house looking for him. She is told by his mother that he has gone to buy ice cream. The second-order belief question asks the child where Mary thinks John has gone to buy the ice cream.

In the first-order belief task, then, the child is asked 'What does Sally think?' In the second-order task, the child is asked 'What does Mary think John thinks?'

QUISSET   *Now go beyond the text ... look it up yourself!*

Explore your library's electronic databases to investigate 'advanced theory of mind'.

In investigating theory of mind, researchers have moved from first- and second-order beliefs to more advanced theory of mind tasks.

● What tasks have been used to study advanced theory of mind in children?

● What were their findings?

Hint: Happé's Strange Stories (Happé, 1995); Reading the Mind in the Eyes task with adults (Baron-Cohen, Joliffe, Mortimore and Robertson, 1997; see example of task below); Faux Pas task (Baron-Cohen *et al.*, 1999).

● Next step is to find more recent studies that have used these advanced theory of mind tasks. What were their findings? To what extent do they support/extend/challenge the initial findings on these tasks? What conclusions can you now draw about theory of mind and autism?

Support your answer with evidence from your reading.

IN FOCUS

'Reading the mind in the eyes': an adult advanced theory of mind (mentalising) test

In this test, an adult participant is shown 25 pictures of actors' eyes. In the original task (Baron-Cohen *et al.*, 1997) s/he then had to select, from a choice of two, which word best described what the person in the picture is feeling. The idea behind this is that to respond accurately you need to be able to put yourself into the mind of the other person to tune in to what they are feeling, i.e. their mental state. Baron-Cohen, Wheelwright, Hill, Raste and Plumb (2001) pointed out that while the 'Reading the Mind in the Eyes' test is viewed as an advanced theory of mind test, in comparison with the children's ice-cream van task, it only involves the first stage of theory of mind, attributing the right mental state to the person in the picture. It does not, however, involve the second stage of inference. Baron-Cohen *et al.* (2001) revised the orginal task to eliminate the possiblity that chance responses explained the findings because of the restricted choice of one out of two possible response words and because the test had too narrow a range of scores and could not distinguish well enough between people who had some autistic tendencies and people who had the condition. To deal with this they increased the number of pictures presented, increased the number of choices from two to four for each picture, and restricted the pictures to more complex mental states rather than simple happy/sad states to make the task more challenging.

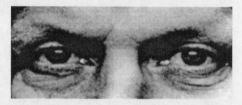

(a) An example of a (male) stimulus used: in the first version word choices were serious (correct) vs. playful. In the revised version the word choices were serious (correct), ashamed, alarmed, and bewildered.

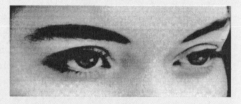

(b) A second (female) example from the Eyes test: in the first version the word choice was reflective (correct) vs. unreflective. In the revised version the word choice was reflective (correct), aghast, irritated, and impatient.

Source: Baron-Cohen *et al.* 2001, reproduced by permission of John Wiley & Sons Inc.

Could theory of mind deficit/delay be part of a broader empathy deficit?

Another way of thinking about theory of mind is that it involves cognitive empathy – the ability to tune into another person's thoughts and respond to them in an appropriate way. However, alongside the idea of cognitive empathy is that of emotional empathy, being able to tune into another's emotions and respond appropriately (Baron-Cohen, 2008). Baron-Cohen suggested that the vast body of research that exists on theory of mind work addresses cognitive empathy only, and that in addition affective (emotional) empathy is worthy of investigation in children with autism. This is a newer area of research interest. Baron-Cohen and Wheelwright (2004), however, argue that cognitive and affective aspects cannot always be readily separated out as some situations involve both aspects of empathy.

Empathy deficit

There is a general consensus that in a typically developing population, females are better at empathising than males (e.g. Davis, 1994; Hastings Zahn-Waxler, Robinson, Usher and Bridges, 2000; Karniol, Gabay, Ochion and Harari, 1998). We know that women are better than men at sustaining conversation (McMullen, Vernon and Murton, 1995); girls' speech is more facilitative and reinforcing than boys' speech (Austin, Salehi and Leffler, 1987); women's relationships in their social networks are more likely to show intimacy, personal disclosure and empathy than men's (Turner, 1994); and women's online communication is higher in empathic commentary than men's (Preece, 1999).

Lawson, Baron-Cohen and Wheelwright (2004) carried out a study with three groups: a group of males with Asperger syndrome, a group of males without Asperger syndrome and a group of females without Asperger syndrome. As well as demonstrating that females empathised better than males, this study also showed that the male Asperger syndrome group was poorer at empathising than the group of males without Asperger syndrome. Lombardo, Barnes, Wheelwright and Baron-Cohen (2007) reported a similar deficit for the autism group. However, Yirmiya, Sigman, Kasari and Mundy (1992) demonstrated with a child sample that although the high-functioning autism group scored lower than the controls on identifying which emotions were displayed in video clips, they did still demonstrate affective empathy in response to the emotions they observed. Indeed in their study, Rogers, Dziobek, Hassenstab, Wolf and Convit (2007) further challenged the notion of an empathy deficit when they found that after controlling for cognitive empathy and theory of mind, the Asperger syndrome group were not found to perform significantly more poorly than the control group on Davis's (1983) empathic concern scale. In this study the children with Asperger syndrome actually performed even better than the controls on the personal distress subscale, although this may have been due to the generally heightened levels of anxiety reported in autistic samples, rather than due to empathy itself. This was a study with a small sample size that relied on self-reports, but the findings suggest that children with autism could have as much concern for others as do typically developing children and that further study of affective empathy in autism is needed.

In addition to difficulties in tuning into the emotions of others, i.e. *interpersonal affective empathy*, there is evidence emerging that individuals with ASD may also have an *intrapersonal* impairment, a difficulty in recognising emotion within themselves (Lombardo *et al.*, 2007). Participants in this study had to indicate how well adjectives described themselves (self-reference), a friend who was similar to them, and Harry Potter, a character in a book/film dissimilar to them. The results suggested that self-referencing was impaired in the autism group. This was viewed by Lombardo *et al.* as further support for Frith's (2003) notion of the 'absent self' in autism.

A recent study by Minio-Paluello, Baron-Cohen, Avenanti, Walsh and Aglioti (2009) further suggested an absence of *embodied empathy* in individuals with Asperger syndrome. This is where when an individual sees someone experiencing pain, the viewer's body demonstrates an empathic, neuro-physiological response to the observed pain in the other person. In Minio-Paluello *et al.*'s study, participants observed video clips in which they saw pain inflicted on someone. The expected reaction then is that, by imagining the pain, the viewer will show vicarious reduction of motor-evoked potential in the same muscle as that which is subject to pain on the video. This is what happens in typically developing adults. Minio-Paulello *et al.* found no evidence of this effect in the sample of people with Asperger syndrome, leading them to conclude that there is a sensorimotor impairment that also contributes to the empathic deficits that have been previously noted in this population.

Hypersystemising, hypoempathising and the extreme male brain theory

While males may be poorer at empathising than females, and autistic individuals poorer still at empathising, i.e. *hypoempathising*, it is suggested, however, that males demonstrate a particular strength in systemising and autism may be an extreme example of this. Systemising is the ability to note the detail of the nature of the relationships between object or items in order for the purpose of establishing laws that will allow prediction (Baron-Cohen, 2002). Baron-Cohen (2006) suggested that every individual has a systemising mechanism set at a particular level. Some are set high, some low. Where an individual's systemising mechanism is set high, s/he will look for a logical pattern everywhere, whether or not this is likely or appropriate. This is *hypersystemising* which is common in autistic individuals, who prefer change that is highly predictable, or indeed no change. This insight provides the potential for a new way of thinking about the higher numbers of males that are diagnosed with autism compared to females.

Systemising uses 'if–then' rules – if this happens then that will follow. Baron-Cohen (2008) illustrated the concept of systemising with examples of systems that are totally lawful, switching on a light switch, or calculating using a mathematical formula. These allow you to predict outcomes using 'if–then' rules with 100% security that you will be correct. A little less reliable is the computer and even less reliable but still not totally unpredictable is the weather. On the other hand, Baron-Cohen points out, relationships in the social world are much more difficult to predict. They do not obey 'if–then' clear laws. *If* I say 'Hi' to you as we pass in the corridor, *then* what will follow? Could be nothing other than a reciprocal 'Hi' is expected. Could be that I expect to stop and chat. Could be that I expect a huge smile and a warm hug as we haven't seen each other in ages and are good friends. You can see from this example that systemising is not a useful skill for engaging with the social world. Empathising is.

Like empathising, there are also sex differences reported in systemising. However, while empathising favours girls, systemising favours boys. Consider, for example, subjects such as engineering, mathematics and physics that are heavily male-dominated. In most countries for which data are available the proportion of women researchers in science and engineering fields is less than 30% (UNESCO, 2007). These differences cannot be explained only by socialisation as Connellan, Baron-Cohen, Wheelwright, Ba'tki and Ahluwalia (2001) reported that one-day-old boys looked longer at cot mobiles than at faces, i.e. they preferred looking at systems whose movements can be predicted. Baby girls were reported as doing exactly the opposite.

In addition, hypersystemising can facilitate high achievement in these fields. Baron-Cohen, Wheelwright, Stone and Rutherford (1999) reported people with Asperger syndrome performed well in areas such as computer science, mathematics and physics. There is evidence that children with autism are likely to have relatives who work in systemising fields like engineering and mathematics, and that their parents are good at systemising (Baron-Cohen and Hammer, 1997; Baron-Cohen, Wheelwright, Stott, Bolton and Goodyer, 1997). Systemising may be part of a picture of autism-type symptoms in people who are not diagnosed with an ASD but show milder versions of some of the characteristic features. This is referred to as a broader autism phenotype (Baron-Cohen, Wheelwright, Burtenshaw and Hobson, 2007).

There are conflicting views on the exact nature of the relationship between systemising and empathising. Are these constructs on two separate unrelated dimensions? Or are they correlated in some inverse way such that deficits in one are associated with strengths in the other (Jarrold, Butler, Cottington and Jimenez, 2000)? An extension of the empathising–systemising theory is the extreme male brain theory of autism (Baron-Cohen, 2002; Baron-Cohen and Hammer, 1997). Think back also to our earlier discussion about how autism may present differently in boys and girls, with boys showing social impairment and restricted interests to a greater extent. The extreme male brain theory proposed that the very features that distinguish individuals with ASD may be considered as a more extreme version of the differences that commonly occur between males and females. Autistic features then may be thought of as extreme versions of the male brain. There is some neuroanatomic evidence for this theory as it has been suggested that some features of autistic neuroanatomy such as an enlarged cerebral cortex and greater growth of the amygdalae are an exaggeration of the differences between male and female brains (Baron-Cohen, Knickmeyer and Belmonte, 2005). There was, however, no evidence of higher prenatal testosterone in the autism spectrum group, which may provide a challenge to the extreme male brain theory (Falter, Plaisted and Davis, 2008).

QUISSET *Now go beyond the text . . . look it up yourself!*

Explore your library's electronic databases to investigate 'extreme male brain critical analysis'.

Read the Falter *et al.* (2008) paper. Then read Knickmeyer, Baron-Cohen, Auyeung and Aschwin's (2008) response study in which they identify methodological limitations in the Falter *et al.* study that challenge their conclusion.

● To what extent do you think Falter *et al.*'s study provides a challenge to the extreme male brain theory?

Work is ongoing by Baron-Cohen and colleagues at the University of Cambridge's Autism Research Centre to continue to investigate the relationship between systemising and empathy in individuals with autism. The centre has a useful website with a wealth of research information for those studying the area: www. autismresearchcentre.com.

QUISSETS *Now go beyond the text . . . look it up yourself!*

Explore your library's electronic databases to investigate 'hypoempathising/hypersystemising'.

● To what extent are the constructs 'theory of mind' and 'cognitive empathy' similar/different?

● Is hypoempathy a better explanation than a specific theory of mind deficit/delay for the difficulties autistic children experience? Provide evidence to support your answer.

● What is the evidence for a relationship between hypoempathising and hypersystemising in children with autism?

Enactive mind model

Klin, Jones, Schultz and Volkmar (2003) offered an alternative way of thinking about the deficits associated with autistic spectrum disorder. They were puzzled by the discrepancy between the high performance of individuals with autism in structured tasks of social reasoning, compared to their behaviour in real-world settings. Remember that while theory of mind difficulties are associated with autism, some children with autism do pass the first-level Sally–Anne task, to the extent that it was argued that development of theory of mind might be better considered a delay rather than a deficit. Success on the Sally–Anne task by individuals with autism required a higher-order theory of mind task (the ice-cream van) to be constructed. Klin *et al.* noted that even though success may be achieved on this sophisticated social reasoning task, poor social skills in the activities of daily life were universal across children with autism.

Klin (2000) argued that while theory of mind might be considered *necessary* for social competence as explained above, theory of mind alone might not be *sufficient* to explain the observed phenomena fully, and that other explanations might be required. For example, he noted that even very young infants with autism already show social disabilities, and that these difficulties precede the development of theory of mind. Perhaps theory of mind deficits are caused by early social disabilities rather than vice versa. Klin also queried whether theory of mind could in any case be considered specific to autism when children with other developmental disabilities showed theory of mind deficits.

Examination of eye movements of adults with autism showed that they tracked less relevant aspects of social situations and thus were missing out on important social cues. In particular they focused on the mouth rather than the eyes (Klin, Jones, Schultz, Volkmar and Cohen, 2002; Spezio, Adolphs, Hurley and Piven, 2007). For example, in a film clip showing a look of surprise on a man's face, the typical viewer scans the man's eyes, to try to understand what is happening. The viewer with autism tends to scan the man's mouth from which there is almost no information to be gathered. Even where the mouth was not shown and even where

(a) Viewer with autism

(b) Normal comparison viewer

Visual focus of an autistic man and normal comparison subject shown a film clip containing the face of a shocked young man

Klin *et al.* 2002, reprinted with permission from the *American Journal of Psychiatry*, American Psychiatric Association

Point light display

Source: Klin *et al.* 2009 'Two-year-olds with autism orient to non-social contingencies rather than biological motion', *Nature* 459, figure 1a, pp. 257–261, reproduced by permission from Macmillan Publishers Ltd

faces were inverted, autistic adults still fixed their eye gaze in the mouth area, suggesting they used an abnormal strategy for abstracting meaning from faces (Neumann, Spezio, Piven and Adolphs, 2006). Similar findings have been obtained with children where autistic 2-year-olds gazed at the mouth more and the eyes less, than did the control-group children (Jones, Carr and Klin, 2008). Indeed Jones *et al.* found that the extent to which autistic individuals preferred to orient towards adults' mouths rather than their eyes was a predictor of the severity of their social disability.

Individuals with autism then may build up their knowledge of the social world in quite a different way from typically developing individuals. Taking account of this, Klin *et al.* (2003) proposed an alternative conceptualisation of autism – the *enactive mind*. This relates to the predisposition to recognise the salience of social stimuli, and respond to them. The *enactive mind* framework proposes that the mind is active in its attempts to make sense of the social world in which it finds itself and that individuals differ in what they tune into in the social environment. If people are looking for different things in their social world then this could explain how people with autism have such different understandings and representations of the social world compared to typically developing individuals. Klin's approach has stimulated research on the development of social understanding, compared to Baron-Cohen's theory of mind hypothesis which stimulated study of cognitive abilities.

In their efforts to study the salience of social meaning in trying to make sense of visual stimuli, Klin and colleagues have made use of a methodological paradigm originally developed by Heider and Simmel in the 1940s. In the Social Attribution Task, moving geometric shapes are shown interacting with each other in a silent animated film. When typically developing adolescent viewers described what they saw, they told a story about the animation that attributed social relationships to the display. For example, they referred to the large triangle *bullying* the other shapes; a small triangle being *shy* and *scared* until other shapes came along to *protect* him; other shapes were described as *happy* and *playing*. Adolescents with autism produced narratives for the animation too but without any social dimension. They used physical relationships rather than social relationships to tell the story, e.g. 'The big triangle went into the little triangle' (Klin, 2000).

Klin and his research team have also investigated understanding of 'biological motion' in children with autism. This is where we attend more to human or animal motion, i.e. biological motion, than to the movement of inanimate objects, for example a leaf falling from a tree. Biological motion is more important to us as it could indicate a predator, or someone bringing us food, and thus is likely to have implications for our survival. Klin's team studied this using point light displays, where a moving human body is represented by a few spots of light at the body's joints. This method separates movement from the actual human form of the body.

We are able to attribute simple human social actions such as fighting or hugging, say, to figures that are represented just by points of light. With a point light display showing figures clapping 'pat-a-cake', Klin, Lin, Gorrindo, Ramsay and

Jones (2009) found that 2-year-olds with autism focused on non-social aspects of the display: in particular they focused on the audiovisual synchrony between the clapping movement and the sound of clapping. This was different from the control group of typically developing infants who attended to the clapping itself, i.e. biological motion with social meaning. Klin *et al.* suggested that this finding may also help explain why individuals with autism prefer to focus on mouths when they look at faces. It may be the audiovisual synchrony between the mouth and the speech sound that draws their attention.

Problems in abstracting social meaning from situations could help explain why autistic children experience such difficulties in social situations. In the playground there is such an array of complex facial, gestural and postural social cues to be tuned into in deciding whether you can join a group of children and how best to do this – does this group look friendly/hostile, open to a new person coming up? Or does their body language suggest they are a tight-knit group that isn't likely to want anyone else joining in? If social elements are not salient for you, then you may not be tuning into the appropriate features of this situation – for example, you need to know to attend to people's faces rather than physical features such as how the football is bouncing. You also need to know what part of the face is likely to give you the social information you seek – the eyes rather than the mouth. Klin and the research team at Yale University thus see investigation of the search for social meaning in situations as the way forward in the study of autism.

Executive dysfunction

Executive function refers to behaviours such as planning (e.g. thinking ahead to achieve a goal); inhibition of dominant but irrelevant responses (e.g. not acting on impulse); memory; and flexibility of thought (e.g. moving from one task, topic or idea to another without getting stuck or perseverating). These are all abilities that are required for effective problem-solving to achieve a goal. Unlike the studies we have discussed above, executive dysfunction studies with autistic samples were stimulated by cognitive neuropsychological work with atypical populations. Ozonoff, Pennington and Rogers (1991) noted in their work that some of the symptoms of autism appeared highly similar to symptoms shown by patients who had brain damage that resulted in executive function deficits.

From this, there developed a research stream examining executive function in autism. Children with autism were indeed found to have deficits in working memory (Goldberg *et al.*, 2005); in inhibition (Corbett, Constantine, Hendren, Rocke and Ozonoff, 2009; Hughes, Russell and Robbins, 1994); cognitive flexibility (Corbett *et al.*, 2009; Ozonoff, Strayer, McMahon and Filloux, 1994) and in planning (Hughes, 1996; Ozonoff *et al.*, 1991). The 'Stockings of Cambridge' task has been used, for example, to evaluate planning. This is a computerised task, which is a version of the Tower of Hanoi, a mathematical puzzle often used in psychological research on problem-solving. In the Tower of Hanoi task, you have to plan how to move disks from one rod to another within a set of prescribed rules. Similarly in the 'Stockings of Cambridge' task, individuals are shown two displays on the screen, each of which contains three coloured balls in a column that looks as though the balls are held in a hanging stocking. They have to move the balls into a new sequence as instructed by the examiner, and they have to plan it so that they complete the task in as few moves as possible. Children with autism spectrum disorders have been found to be impaired on this planning task relative to comparison groups.

There is, however, a problem with executive dysfunction theory as an explanation for autism because similar impairments of executive functioning are observed in other neurodevelopmental disorders, so these are not specific to autism (Pennington and Ozonoff, 1996). Nor has executive dysfunction been universally observed in everyone with autism (Hill, 2004a; Hill, 2004b). There does, however, seem to be some evidence of a distinct executive functioning profile that distinguishes autism from attention deficit hyperactivity disorder and pursuit of identification of differential executive dysfunction profiles has been suggested as a potential avenue for diagnosis (Hill, 2004a; Hill, 2004b; Ozonoff and Jensen, 1999). Thus, while there is not yet convincing support for executive dysfunction as an explanation for autistic spectrum disorders, it would seem that it cannot yet be ruled out.

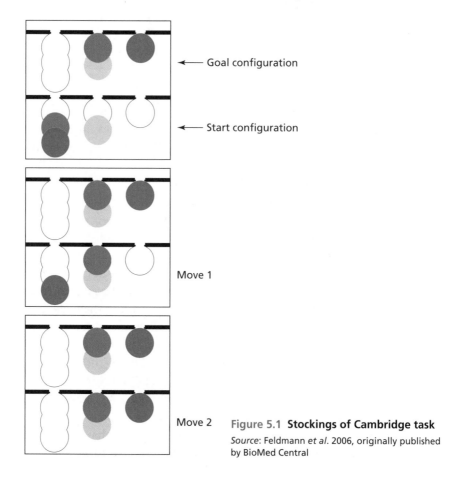

Figure 5.1 **Stockings of Cambridge task**
Source: Feldmann *et al*. 2006, originally published by BioMed Central

Weak central coherence

Social deficits are clearly central to the triad of communication, social interaction and behaviour flexibility impairments that identify autism. While theory of mind is currently viewed as the most influential explanation for autistic behaviours, neither it nor the enactive mind model can provide a strong explanation for cognitive strengths such as enhanced mental and calendar calculation abilities, recall of meaningless detail, exceptional spatial skills, and absolute pitch, reported in individuals with ASD (Hermelin and O'Connor, 1986; Rimland and Fein, 1988; Snyder and Mitchell, 1999; Treffert, 2006). There is, however, a line of research that pursues the idea that there may be a perceptual deficit in autistic individuals, potentially affecting all domains. Frith's (1989) *weak central coherence* theory proposed that the core deficit in autism was perceptual rather than social. The hypothesis was that individuals with autism were unable to integrate pieces of information into a global whole. This is a skill which is automatic in typical development and is important because it allows rapid, automatic interpretation of events within their context. It constitutes a search for meaning of the whole, the *gestalt*, rather than attending to the small details that make up this whole. Frith (1989) referred to this tendency to search for the meaning of the whole as *central coherence*. It was hypothesised then that individuals with autism show *weak central coherence*.

In the twenty years since this theory was originally proposed, Happé and Frith (2003) have adapted it in three key ways: (1) The central processing deficit in extracting meaning is now seen as a secondary problem rather than the primary problem. The focus on processing local details is viewed as a possible strength in people with autism. (2) The theory now proposes that autistic people have a *bias* towards processing details, rather than a *deficit*. This is because studies have shown that they can carry out abstraction of global meaning when they are explicitly asked to do so. (3) It is now likely that weak central coherence may operate alongside a theory of mind deficit rather than explaining it.

QUISSET *Now go beyond the text . . . look it up yourself!*

Explore your library's electronic databases to investigate 'weak central coherence'.

- Why did Happé and Frith (2003) change their theory to view children with autism as having a bias towards weak central coherence rather than a deficit?

  Hint: Have a look at *reduced generalisation* theory (Plaisted, O'Riordan and Baron-Cohen, 1998a, 1998b); *hierarchisation deficit* theory (Mottron and Belleville, 1993).

Shah and Frith's (1983) study (see In Focus box) provided evidence for the weak central coherence in autism when it demonstrated that the autism group outperformed controls on the Children's Embedded Figures Test, a task which required processing and matching parts of a figure, rather than integration of the whole.

IN FOCUS

A test for central coherence

Embedded Figures Test (Witkin, Oltman, Raskin, and Karp, 1971). This task involves being able to identify a simple target shape from a confusing background. Shah and Frith (1983) used the Children's Embedded Figures Test in a study with 20 children with autism, 20 typically developing, and 20 children with learning difficulties but without autism. All children were matched for mental age. Children were shown two cardboard shapes, a triangle and an irregular shape comprising a rectangle with a triangle added to its left top edge. These were referred to as a 'tent' and a 'house' for ease of communication and understanding. Children were then shown in sequence 25 complex shapes which had either the 'tent' or the 'house' hidden (embedded) in them. Children had to point to the embedded figure or place the cut-out shape over it. The autism group performed significantly better than the other two groups on this, both in terms of accuracy and in speed of response. It may be considered that children with autism show a superior ability here to break down 'the whole' so that the component parts can be seen clearly. Or it may be considered that due to information-processing difficulties, 'the whole' is less dominant or has less meaning for the autistic group and it is the individual parts that are dominant.

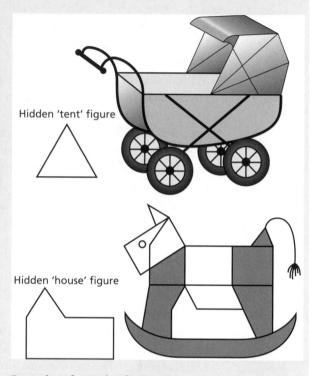

Examples of complex figures

Source: Shah and Frith, 1983, reproduced by permission of John Wiley & Sons Inc.

This is known as 'weak central coherence'. In another study, Joliffe and Baron-Cohen (1997) used the standard adult Embedded Figures Test with 17 adults with high-functioning autism, 17 with Asperger syndrome, and 17 adults without autism. The adult test comprised 12 cards each with a complex coloured design, each of which had a simple target shape hidden within. Participants were shown the complex design, then the simple shape which was on the other side of the card, then the card was turned over to show the complex design again. They were asked to trace the simple shape within the complex design. They could ask to see the simple shape again as often as they liked if they had forgotten it. In this study the groups did not differ in accuracy but they did in speed of response, with the two autistic groups faster than the non-autistic group. This study replicated Shah and Frith's (1983) finding of superior speed of performance by individuals with autism on the embedded figures task.

Shah and Frith's finding was supported by Morgan, Maybery and Durkin's (2003) study where the autism group were faster than the control groups on the embedded figures test, but not more accurate. However, findings on autism group strengths in this area are inconsistent as there are other studies that have not reported autistic superiority on this task (e.g. Joliffe and Baron-Cohen, 1997; Ozonoff, Pennington and Rogers, 1991; Ropar and Mitchell, 2001). Happé and Frith (2006) provided a useful overview of studies investigating weak central coherence and their findings, and highlight the inconsistency of findings here.

Universality and specificity

In evaluating how useful any theory is for explaining autism, the two concepts of **universality** and **specificity** are helpful. When you are considering studies investigating any theoretical model ask yourself to what extent the findings are universal for all individuals with autism. Does everyone with autism show this strength/deficit? None of the explanations put forward in this chapter applies to all children with autism. They don't all show weak central coherence or theory of mind deficits or executive dysfunction, so none of these explanations provides an explanation that extends to the whole autism spectrum population.

Specificity is the twin issue to universality in that while universality asks you to consider whether all those with autism show the deficit, specificity asks you to consider whether it is *only* those with autism who show the deficit or whether children, with ADHD for example, also show this impairment. Rajendran and Mitchell's (2007) paper provides a good summary of theory of mind, executive dysfunction and weak central coherence studies in terms of the universality and specificity of their findings to autism samples.

It may be that no one theory can account for the heterogeneity of autism and that multiple deficit accounts provide a better explanation. Such accounts would allow us to view autism as a complex combination of disorders of executive function, central coherence and theory of mind. It may be more useful now to try to identify sub-groups of children with autism, depending on their profiles of strengths and weaknesses on these different cognitive tasks (Baron-Cohen and Sweetenham, 1997; Happé and Frith, 2006).

QUISSET   *Now go beyond the text . . . look it up yourself!*

Explore your library's electronic databases to investigate 'other cognitive theories of autism'.

We have discussed evidence for three key cognitive theories that have been advanced to explain autism: theory of mind, executive dysfunction and weak central coherence.

- What other cognitive explanations of autism are there?

- What are their strengths and weaknesses?

Now reflect on what you have read. Synthesise your findings to produce your own arguments to answer the following question:

- How can we explain autism?

Research into memory

Another strand of current research investigates the role of memory in explaining deficits observed in children with autism. Episodic memory is the memory we have for events we have actually experienced ourselves. Semantic memory is the memory we have for factual information. The hypothesis here is that children with autism have a deficit in episodic memory and semantic memory that can explain some of the deficits associated with autism (Boucher, 2009). Early studies found a deficit in free recall of semantically related words in children with autism compared to controls, and furthermore, unlike controls, they did not show improved performance with semantically related compared to unrelated words (Boucher and Warrington, 1976; Hermelin and O'Connor, 1967). Weak central coherence theory may contribute to explaining this in that the focus of individuals with autism on details may mean that they do not perceive relationships between semantically related words that could aid recall of these items (Smith, Gardiner and Bowler, 2007). However, Boucher and colleagues have further proposed that impaired memory may in the future explain language and intellectual impairments observed in individuals at the lower end of the autistic spectrum. Additionally Boucher (2009) noted that individuals with autism have a poor sense of the passage of time and episodic memory impairment may be linked to a difficulty in grasping the temporal nature of events (Boucher, Pons, Lind and Williams, 2007). Boucher (2009) has proposed that impaired neural timing mechanisms could impact on connectivity in both the areas of memory and time processing. This research is ongoing.

Genetic and neurological research

We discussed earlier that children with autism often had relatives who worked in occupations such as science and engineering. Is there then a genetic component? Twin studies in UK and Scandinavia have shown a genetic component (Bailey *et al.*, 1995; Folstein and Rutter, 1977; Steffenburg *et al.*, 1989). Although it seems that no single chromosome is responsible for autism, several studies have reported that a particular chromosome, 7q, is likely to be one of the chromosomes involved (Bailey, 1998; International Molecular Genetic Study of Autism Consortium, 2001). A large-scale project involving DNA analysis, recently carried out at the Centre of Applied Genomics at the Children's Hospital of Philadelphia, has found gene abnormalities between genes CDH9 and CDH10, that are responsible for encoding information crucial to nerve cell communication (Wang *et al.*, 2009). From the same study, Glessner *et al.* (2009) identified duplications or deletions of DNA in two neural pathways. This looks like an important area of research for the future.

In terms of neural mechanisms, researchers have been examining abnormalities in particular neural pathways such as the magnocellular pathway (from the retina to the brain), and in particular regions of the brain, e.g. right posterior parietal lobe (Happé and Frith, 2006). Given the complex nature of autism spectrum conditions and the possibility of different profiles of autism rather than a unitary disorder, it is likely that they will find multiple pathways and a number of brain regions that contribute to the impairments we have identified in this chapter. Furthermore, the study of developmental disorders needs to allow for the brain's plasticity in a developing child, rather than considering autism as if it were a missing function in a fully grown adult brain (Johnson, Halit, Grice and Karmiloff-Smith, 2002).

Interventions

So what does all this mean for helping children with autism in educational settings? In the final section of this chapter some of the teaching methods currently used with children with autistic spectrum disorders will be outlined and evidence for their effectiveness presented.

TEACCH

TEACCH (Treatment and Education of Autistic and Communication-Handicapped Children) is a general teaching approach in which teachers structure and organise their classrooms to make them more understandable and predictable for children with autistic spectrum conditions, both in terms of the physical classroom organisation, as well as curriculum delivery and teaching methods. Probst and Leppert (2008) showed that 10 teachers from special schools who were trained to use structured education techniques with 10 pupils with autism, reported improvements. Limitations of this study, however, included its small sample size and its reliance on teacher self-report. Panerai *et al.* (2009) also reported success using the TEACCH method in the classroom. When 34 children with either an ASD or severe learning difficulties were given one of three treatment measures, residential TEACCH, TEACCH at home and in the mainstream classroom, or a non-specific intervention in a mainstream school, for three years, a significant difference in performance was found on adaptive behaviour for both TEACCH groups, but not for the non-specific education group.

The Lovaas method

Early intensive behaviour intervention, also known as applied behaviour analysis, was developed in California by Dr Ole Ivar Lovaas. This is an intensive home-based behaviour modification programme which should ideally begin when the child is a preschooler. It is one-to-one programme delivered to the child by a team of trained people, five days a week for approximately eight hours a day, for two years. Parental involvement is a central element to ensure generalisation to the home setting of the skills the child is learning. The Lovaas programme targets social and play skills as well as language, education and self-help, through application of behaviour modification principles. It breaks all targets into small, achievable steps and utilises reinforcement such as praise, hugs, food to encourage the desired behaviours.

Lovaas (1987) reported on a study comparing three groups of 20 children: an experimental group who received the Lovaas programme, a comparison group who received some behavioural intervention and special education; and a control group who received no behavioural treatment. Lovaas claimed that 47% of the experimental group achieved normal functioning, while another 40% made progress although still presented with autistic-type problems. It was further reported in a follow-up study that these gains were maintained into adolescence (McEachin, Smith and Lovaas, 1993).

QUISSET   *Now go beyond the text . . . look it up yourself!*

Explore your library's electronic databases to investigate 'intervention effectiveness'.

Read Lovaas's (1987) paper and the McEachin *et al.* (1993) paper referred to above. Using the principles of critical analysis outlined in Chapter 2, identify any methodological problems that may be associated with drawing conclusions from this study about programme effectiveness. Then look at Shea's (2004) paper.

● A parent of a child with autism asks your advice about undertaking a Lovaas programme. What would be your response? Support your answer with evidence.

Cohen, Amerine-Dickens and Smith (2006) replicated Lovaas's earlier study and acknowledged the limitations of one or both studies' key problems, that of non-random allocation to groups. That is to say, the studies compared pre-existing groups, a methodology known as quasi-experimental design and one commonly used in research in real-world settings. It does mean, however, that there may have been something different about the groups to begin with, that could explain any differences obtained post-intervention. Cohen *et al.* reported improvement in IQ and adaptive behaviour for the experimental group, although the IQ gains were only observed in the first year of what was a three-year study.

Eikeseth, Smith, Jahr and Eldevik (2002) evaluated a Lovaas-based treatment in mainstream schools in which children aged 4–7 years received 20 hours per week of one-to-one behavioural training with a special education teacher and an assistant. Outside treatment, the children were in their regular mainstream classrooms. A comparison group received the same intensity and amount of an eclectic treatment made up of different elements of best educational practice, including components of TEACCH. The authors reported that after one year, the treatment group showed good progress although the only significant difference was on adaptive behaviour. A follow-up study of the same sample (Eikeseth *et al.*, 2007) and another similar school-based intervention study by the same authors (Eldevik, Eikeseth,

Jahr and Smith, 2006) similarly reported progress for the intervention group but did not provide compelling evidence of statistically or clinically significant findings of differences between the two groups. These studies had small sample sizes and used comparison groups whose eclectic intervention programmes may have also comprised a high proportion of applied behaviour analysis and therefore shared a higher degree of similarity with the Lovaas programme than was intended. Matson and Smith (2008) and Reichow and Wolery (2009) have also recently examined the effectiveness of the Lovaas method and similarly concluded that there are difficulties in interpretation of studies due to factors such as severity of autism and composition of control group that have not been adequately controlled for. It is likely that this is an effective intervention method but studies have not so far demonstrated convincingly its superiority over other special education interventions.

Social stories

Social stories is a behavioural method used by teachers in classroom settings. These stories, written in the first person, were first developed by Gray and Garrand (1993). They explain how to act in a given social situation, situations that children with autism might find confusing or difficult to understand. In the story a typical school situation is described simply but with attention to the social details and the expected responses from the child. Its aim is to address theory of mind difficulties by explaining through the story what the others are doing, thinking and what the child with autism needs to do. The story should match the social skill that the teacher is trying to teach the child, e.g. what the child is to do at break time. In this case, the story might explain what happens when classes end, what the other children in the class will do (eat crisps, go out to the playground) and what s/he should do (get up from chair, eat snack, go outside).Teachers found this an easy intervention to implement and thought the method was effective (Reynhout and Carter, 2009). Rust and Smith (2006), reviewing the literature on the effectiveness of this method, concluded that while the effects appear to be positive, there have not yet been any adequately controlled studies to provide sufficient evidence for the effectiveness of this approach.

Interactive software approaches

Baron-Cohen's research group at Cambridge University have been developing animation DVD software, through a series known as *The Transporters*, depicting vehicles with faces, with some level of success. When Golan, Baron-Cohen, Chapman and Granader (2009) presented children with autism aged 4–7 years with at least three five-minute episodes of *The Transporters* each day, over a four-week period, they showed a significantly higher improvement in emotion recognition at three levels of increasing generalisation than did the control group of typically developing children and the group with ASD who had not taken part in the intervention. Research on using interactive software to aid learning in children with autism is in its early stages and not yet as widely utilised in schools as the other approaches mentioned in this section. However, these offer considerable promise for classroom intervention in the future.

Summary and conclusions

This chapter has outlined key theories that attempt to explain autism spectrum disorders, as well as examining the evidence base for the effectiveness of current intervention approaches. The purpose of the chapter was to synthesise key theoretical issues and debates in the area to try to clarify what is currently known and what is still unresolved. This should provide you with a sound basis for going forward with your own reading of research papers.

The section on universality and specificity suggests that there is indeed much that is unresolved in this regard. We may not yet have theoretical explanations that explain autism in all individuals, nor explanations that are unique to autism and not equally explanatory of other developmental disorders. Theoretical explanations of autism may in future become more complex to account for its heterogeneity, and interventions too will need to take account of this.

Further Study

Go to the website www.pearsoned.co.uk/markswoolfson **for the following starter articles:**

Baron-Cohen, S., O'Riordan, M., Stone, V., Jones, R., and Plaisted, K. (1999). Recognition of faux pas by normally developing children and children with Asperger syndrome or high functioning autism *Journal of Autism and Developmental Disorders, 29*(5), 407–18.

Happé, F. and Frith, U. (2003). The week coherence account: Detail-focused cognitive style in autism spectrum disorders. *Journal of Autism and Developmental Disorderes, 36*(1), 5–25.

Rajendran, G. and Mitchell, P. (2007). Cognitive theories of autism. *Developmental Review, 27,* 224–60.

References

Austin, A., Salehi, M., and Leffler, A. (1987). Gender and developmental differences in children's conversations. *Sex Roles, 16,* 497–510.

Bailey, A., Le Couteur, A., Gottesman, I., Bolton, P., Simonoff, E., Yuzda, E., and Rutter, M. (1995). Autism as a strongly genetic disorder: Evidence from a British twin study. *Psychological Medicine, 25,* 63–77.

Bailey, A. (1998). International Molecular Genetic Study of Autism Consortium. A full genome screen for autism with evidence for linkage to a region on chromosome 7q. *Human Molecular Genetics, 7*(3), 571–78.

Baird, G., Simonoff, E., Pickles, A., Chandler, S., Loucas, T., Meldrum, D., and Charman, T. (2006). Prevalence of disorders of the autism spectrum in a population cohort of children in South Thames: the Special Needs and Autism Project (SNAP). *Lancet, 368,* 210–15.

Barbaresi, W., Katusic, S., Colligan, R., Weaver, A., and Jacobsen, S. (2005). The incidence of autism in Olmsted County, Minnesota, 1976–1997: results from a population-based study. *Archives of Pediatric and Adolescent Medicine, 159,* 37–44.

Baron-Cohen, S. (1989). The autistic child's theory of mind – a case of specific developmental delay. *Journal of Child Psychology and Psychiatry and Allied Disciplines, 30*(2), 285–97.

Baron-Cohen, S. (2002). The extreme male brain theory of autism. *Trends in Cognitive Science*, 6, 248–54.

Baron-Cohen, S. (2006). The hypersystemising, assortative mating theory of autism. Progress in *Neuro-Psychopharmacology and Biological Psychiatry, 30,* 865–72.

Baron-Cohen, S. (2008). Autism, hypersystemizing and truth. *The Quarterly Journal of Experimental Psychology, 61*(1), 64–75.

Baron-Cohen, S. and Hammer, J. (1997). Parents of children with Asperger syndrome: What is the cognitive phenotype? *Journal of Cognitive Neuroscience, 9,* 548–54.

Baron-Cohen, S., Knickmeyer, R., and Belmonte, M. (2005). Sex differences in the brain: Implications for exploring autism. *Science, 310,* 819–23.

Baron-Cohen, S., Leslie, A., and Frith, U. (1985). Does the autistic child have a 'theory of mind'? *Cognition, 21,* 37–46.

Baron-Cohen, S., Jolliffe, T., Mortimore, C., and Robertson, M. (1997). Another advanced test of theory of mind: evidence from very high functioning adults with autism or Asperger syndrome. *Journal of Child Psychology and Psychiatry, 38*(7), 813–22.

Baron-Cohen, S., O'Riordan, M., Stone, V., Jones, R., and Plaisted, K. (1999). Recognition of faux pas by normally developing children and children with Asperger syndrome or high functioning autism *Journal of Autism and Developmental Disorders, 29*(5), 407–18.

Baron-Cohen, S., Scott, F., Allison, C., Williams, J., Bolton, P., Mathews, F. E., and Brayne, C. (2008). *Estimating autism spectrum prevalence in the population: A school based study from the UK.* Poster presented at the 7th Annual International Meeting for Autism Research, (IMFAR), May 2008, London UK.

Baron-Cohen, S. and Sweetenham, J. (1997). Theory of mind in autism: Its relation to executive function and central coherence. In D. Cohen and F. Volkmar (eds) *Handbook for autism and pervasive developmental disorders.* New York: Wiley, (pp. 880–93).

Baron-Cohen, S. and Wheelwright, S. (2004). The empathy quotient: An investigation of adults with Asperger Syndrome or high functioning autism and normal sex differences. *Journal of Autism and Developmental Disorders*, 34, 163–75.

Baron-Cohen, S., Wheelwright, S., Burtenshaw, A., and Hobson, E. (2007). Mathematical talent is genetically linked to autism. *Human Nature*, 18(2), 125–31.

Baron-Cohen, S., Wheelwright, S., Hill, J., Raste, J., and Plumb, I. (2001) The 'Reading the mind in the eyes' test revised version: A study with normal adults and adults with Asperger syndrome or high-functioning autism. *Journal of Child Psychology and Psychiatry*, 42(2), 241–51.

Baron-Cohen, S., Wheelwright, S., Stone, V., and Rutherford, M. (1999). A mathematician, a physicist, and a computer scientist with Asperger syndrome: Performance on folk psychology and folk physics test. *Neurocase, 5,* 475–83.

Baron-Cohen, S., Wheelwright, S., Stott, C., Bolton, P., and Goodyer, I. (1997). Is there a link between engineering and autism? *Autism: An International Journal of Research and Practice,* 1, 153–63.

Bertrand, J., Mars, A., Boyle, C., Bove, F., Yeargin-Allsopp, M., and Decoufle, P. (2001). Prevalence of autism in a United States population: The Brick Township investigations. *Pediatrics, 108,* 1155–61.

Bettelheim, B. (1967). *The empty fortress: Infantile autism and the birth of the self.* London: Collier-Macmillan.

Bloom, P. and German, T.P. (2000), Two reasons to abandon the false belief task as a test of theory of mind, *Cognition,* 77, 25–31.

Boucher, J. (2009). *The autistic spectrum: Characteristics, causes and practical issues.* London: Sage.

Boucher, J., Pons, F., Lind, S., and Williams, D. (2007). Temporal cognition in children with autistic spectrum disorders: Tests of diachronic thinking. *Journal of Autism and Developmental Disorders,* 37, 1413–29.

Boucher, J. and Warrington, E. (1976). Memory deficits in early infantile autism: Some similarities to the amnesic syndrome. *British Journal of Psychology,* 67, 73–87.

Brask, B. (1972). A prevalence investigation of childhood psychoses. In *Nordic Synaposium on the Comprehensive Care of the Psychotic Children*. Oslo: Barnepsykiatrist Forening, (pp. 145–53).

Burd, L., Fisher, W., and Kerbeshian, J. (1987). A prevalance study of pervasive developmental disorders in North Dakota *Journal of the American Academy of Child and Adolescent Psychiatry, 26*, 704–10.

Cialdella, P. and Marmelle, N. (1989). An epidemiological study of infantile autism in a French Department (Rhône): A research note. *Journal of Child Psychology and Psychiatry, 30*, 165–76.

Cohen, H., Amerine-Dickens, M., and Smith, T. (2006). Early intensive behavioral treatment: Replication of the UCLA model in a community setting. *Journal of Developmental and Behavioral Pediatrics, 27*, 145–55.

Connellan, J., Baron-Cohen, S., Wheelwright, S., Ba'tki., A., and Ahluwalia, J. (2001). Sex differences in human neonatal social perception. *Infant Behaviour and Development, 23*, 113–18.

Corbett, B., Constantine, L., Hendren, R., Rocke, D., and Ozonoff, S. (2009). Examining executive functioning in children with autistic spectrum disorder, attention deficit hyperactivity disorder, and typical development. *Psychiatry Research, 166*, 210–22.

Croen, L.A., Grether, J.K., Hoogstrate, J., and Selvin, S. (2002). The changing prevalence of autism in California. *Journal of Autism and Developmental Disorders, 32*, 207–15.

Davis, M. (1983). Measuring individual differences in empathy: Evidence for a multidimensional approach. *Journal of Personality and Social Psychology, 44*(1), 113–26.

Davis, M. (1994). *Empathy: A social psychological approach*. Boulder, CO: Westview Press.

Eikeseth, S., Smith, T., Jahr, E., and Eldevik, S. (2002). Intensive behavioral treatment at school for 4–7-year-old children with autism: A 1-year comparison controlled study. *Behavior Modification, 26*, 49–68.

Eikeseth, S., Smith, T., Jahr, E., and Eldevik, S. (2007). Outcome for children with autism who began intensive behavioral treatment between ages 4 and 7: A comparison study. *Behavior Modification, 31*, 264–78.

Eldevik, S., Eikeseth, S., Jahr, E., and Smith, T. (2006). Effects of low-intensity behavioural treatment for children with autism and mental retardation. *Journal of Autism and Developmental Disorders, 36*(2), 211–24.

Falter, C., Plaisted, K., and Davis, G. (2008). Visuo-spatial processing in autism – testing the predictions of extreme male brain theory. *Journal of Autism and Developmental Disorders, 38*, 507–15.

Folstein, S., and Rutter, M. (1977). Infantile autism: A genetic study of 21 twin pairs. *Journal of Child Psychology and Psychiatry, 18*, 297–321.

Fombonne, E. (1999). The epidemiology of autism: a review. *Psychological Medicine, 29*, 769–86.

Fombonne, E. (2009). Epidemiology of pervasive developmental disorders. *Pediatric Research*, Epub ahead of print.

Frith, U. (1989). *Autism: Explaining the enigma*. London: Blackwell.

Frith, U. (2003). *Autism: Explaining the enigma*, 2nd edn. London: Blackwell.

Gillberg, C. (1984). Infantile autism and other childhood psychoses in a Swedish urban region: Epidemiological aspects. *Journal of Child Psychology and Psychiatry, 25*, 35–43.

Gillberg, C., Cederlund, M., Lamberg, K., and Zeijlon, L. (2006). Brief report: "The Autism Epidemic": The registered prevalence of autism in a Swedish urban area. *Journal of Autism and Developmental Disorders, 36*, 429–35.

Gillberg, C., Steffenburg, S., and Schaumann, H. (1991). Is autism more common now than ten years ago? *The British Journal of Psychiatry, 158*, 403–9.

Glessner J., Wang, K., Cai, G., Korvatska, O., Kim, C., Wood, S., Zhang, H., Estes, A. *et al.* (2009). Autism genome-wide copy number variation reveals ubiquitin and neuronal genes. *Nature*, advance online publication.

Golan, O., Baron-Cohen, S., Chapman, E., and Granader, Y. (2007). *Facilitating emotional understanding and face-processing in young children with autism spectrum conditions, using animations of vehicles with faces*. Poster presented at the 6th Annual International Meeting For Autism Research, Seattle, Washington, May 2007.

Goldberg, M., Mostofsky, S., Cutting, L., Mahone, E., Astor, B, Denckla, M. *et al.*, (2005), Subtle executive impairment in children with autism and children with ADHD. *Journal of Autism and Developmental Disorders, 35,* 279–93.

Gray, C. and Garrand, J. (1993) Social stories: Improving responses of students with accurate social information, *Focus on Autistic Behaviour, 8,* 1–10.

Gurney, J., Fritz, M., Ness, K., Sievers, P., Newschaffer, C., and Shapiro, E. (2003). Analysis of prevalence trends of autism spectrum disorder in Minnesota. Archives of Pediatric and Adolescent Medicine, 157, 622–7.

Happé, F. (1995). The role of age and verbal-ability in the theory of mind task – performance of subjects with autism. *Child Development, 66,* 843–55.

Happé, F. and Frith, U. (2006). The weak coherence account: Detail-focused cognitive style in autism spectrum disorders. *Journal of Autism and Developmental Disorders, 36*(1), 5–25.

Hastings, P. (2000). The development of concern for others in children with behavior problems. *Developmental Psychology, 36,* 531–46.

Hastings, P., Zahn-Waxler, C., Robinson, J., Usher, B., and Bridges, D. (2000). The development of concern for others in children with behaviour problems. *Developmental Psychology, 36*(5), 531–46.

Hermelin, B. and O'Connor, N. (1967). Remembering of words by psychotic and subnormal children. *British Journal of Psychology, 58,* 213–18.

Hermelin, B., and O'Connor, N. (1986). Idiot savants calendrical calculators: rules and regularities. *Psychological Medicine, 16,* 885–93.

Hertz-Piciotto, I., and Delwiche, L. (2009). The rise in autism and the role of age at diagnosis. *Epidemiology, 20,* 84–90.

Hill, E. (2004a). Evaluating the theory of executive dysfunction in autism. *Developmental Review, 24,* 189–233.

Hill, E. (2004b). Executive dysfunction in autism. *Trends in Cognitive Sciences, 8,* 26–32.

Honda, H., Shimizu, Y., Imai, M., and Nitto, Y. (2005). Cumulative incidence of childhood autism: a total population study of better accuracy and precision. *Developmental Medicine and Child Neurology, 47,* 10–18.

Hoshino, Y., Yashima, Y., Ishige, K., Tachibana,R., Watanabe, M., Kancko, M., Kumashiro, H., Ueno, B., Takahashi, E., and Furukawa, H. (1982). The epidemiological study of autism in FukushimaKen. *Folia Psychiatrica et Neurologica Japonica, 36,* 115–24.

Hughes, C. (1996). Brief report: Planning problems in autism at the level of motor control. *Journal of Autism and Developmental Disorders, 26*(1), 99–107.

Hughes, C., Russell, J., and Robbins, T. (1994). Specific planning deficit in autism: evidence of a central executive dysfunction. *Neuropsychologia, 3,* 477–92.

Icasiano, F., Hewson, P., Machet, P., Cooper, C., and Marshall, A. (2004). Childhood autism spectrum disorder in the Barwon region: a community based study. *Journal of Paediatrics and Child Health, 40,* 696–701.

International Molecular Genetic Study Group of Autism Consortium (IMGSAC). (2001). A genomewide screen for autism: Strong evidence for linkage to chromosomes 2q, 7q, and 16p. *American Journal of Human Genetics, 69,* 570–81.

Ishi, T. and Takahashi, O. (1983). The epidemiology of autistic children in Toyota, Japan: Prevalence. *Japanese Journal of Child and Adolescent Psychiatry, 24,* 311–21.

Jarrold, C., Butler, D., Cottington, E., and Jiminez, F. (2000). Linking theory of mind and centreal coherence bias in autism and the general population. *Developmental Psychology, 36,* 126–38.

Johnson, M., Halit, H., Grice, S., and Karmiloff-Smith, A. (2002).Neuroimaging of typical and atypical development: a perspective from multiple levels of analysis. *Development and Psychopathology, 14*(3), 521–36.

Joliffe, T. and Baron-Cohen, S. (1997). Are people with autism and Asperger syndrome faster than normal on the Embedded Figures Test? *Journal of Child Psychology and Psychiatry, 38,* 527–34.

Jones, W., Carr, K., Klin, A. (2008). Absence of preferential looking to the eyes of approaching adults predicts level of social disability in 2-year-olds with autism. *Archives of General Psychiatry, 65,* 946–54.

Karniol, R., Gabay, R., Ochion, Y., and Harari, Y. (1998). Is gender or gender-role orientation a better predictor of empathy in adolescence? *Behavioural Science, 39,* 45–59.

Kielinen, M., Linna, S., and Moilanen, I. (2000). Autism in Finland. *European Child and Adolescent Psychiatry, 9,* 162–7.

Klin, A. (2000). Attributing social meaning to ambiguous visual stimuli in higher functioning autism and Asperger syndrome: The social attribution task. *Journal of Child Psychology and Psychiatry, 41(7),* 831–46.

Klin, A., Jones, W., Schultz, R., and Volkmar, F. (2003). The enactive mind, or from actions to cognition: lessons from autism. *Philosophical Transactions of the Royal Society of London, B, 358,* 345–60.

Klin, A., Jones, W., Schultz, R., Volkmar, F., and Cohen, D. (2002). Defining and quantifying the social phenotype in autism. *American Journal of Psychiatry, 159,* 895–908.

Klin, A., Lin, D., Gorrindo, P., Ramsay, G., and Jones, W. (2009). Two-year-olds with autism orient to non-social contingencies rather than biological motion. *Nature, advance online publication.*

Knickmeyer, R., Baron-Cohen, S., Auyeung, B., and Ashwin, E. (2008). How to test the extreme male brain theory in terms of foetal androgens. *Journal of Autism and Developmental Disorders, 38(5),* 995–6.

Lawson, J., Baron-Cohen, S., and Wheelwright, S. (2004). Empathising and systematising in adults with and without Asperger syndrome. *Journal of Autism and Developmental Disorders, 34,* 301–10.

Leslie, A. and Frith, V, (1988). Autistic children's understanding of seeing, knowing and believing. *British Journal of Developmental Psychology, 6,* 315–24.

Lin, J., Lin, L., and Wu, J. (2009). Administrative Prevalence of autism spectrum disorders based on national disability registers in Taiwan. *Research in Autism Spectrum Disorders, 3,* 269–74.

Lingam, R., Simmons, A., Andrews, N., Miller, E., Stowe, J., and Taylor, B. (2003). Prevalence of autism and parentally reported triggers in a north east London population. *Archives of Disease in Childhood, 88,* 666–70.

Lombardo, M., Barnes, J., Wheelwright, S., and Baron-Cohen, S. (2007). Self-referential cognition and empathy in autism. *PLoSONE 2(9):* e883.

Lovaas, O. (1987). Behavioral treatment and normal educational and intellectual functioning in young autistic children. *Journal of Consulting and Clinical Psychology, 55,* 3–9.

Lotter, V. (1966). Epidemiology of autistic conditions in young children: I. Prevalence. *Social Psychiatry, 1,* 124–37.

Matson, J. and Smith, K. (2008). Current status of intensive behavioral intervention for young children with autism and PDD-NOS. *Research in Autism Spectrum Disorders, 2,* 60–74.

Matsuishi, T., Shiotsuki, Y., Yoshimura, K., Shoji, H., Imuta, F. and Yamashita, F. (1987). High prevalence of infantile autism in Kurume City, Japan. *Journal of Child Neurology, 2,* 268–71.

McCarthy, P., Fitzgerald, M., and Smith, M. (1984). Prevalence of childhood autism in Ireland. *Irish Medical Journal, 77,* 129–30.

McEachin, J., Smith, T., and Lovaas, O. (1993) Long-term outcome for children with autism who received early intensive behavioral treatment, *American Journal on Mental Retardation, 97,* 359–72.

McMullen, L., Vernon, A., and Murton, T. (1995). Division of labor in conversations: Are Fishman's results replicable and generalizable? *Journal of Psycholinguistic Research, 24(4),* 255–68.

Mestre, M., Samper, P., Frias, M., and Tur, A. (2009). Are women more empathetic than men? A longitudinal study in adolescence. *The Spanish Journal of Psychology, 12(1),* 76–83.

Minio-Paluello, L., Baron-Cohen, S., Avenanti, A., Walsh, V., and Aglioti, S. (2009). Absence of embodied empathy during pain observation in Asperger syndrome. *Biological Psychiatry, 65,* 55–62.

Morgan, B., Maybery, M., and Durkin, K. (2003). Weak central coherence, poor joint attention, and low verbal ability: Independent deficits in early autism. *Developmental Psychology, 39(4),* 646–56.

Mottron, L. and Belleville, S. (1993). A study of perceptual analysis in a high-level autistic subject with exceptional graphic abilities. *Brain and Cognition, 23*, 279–309.

Neumann, D., Spezio, M., Piven, J., and Adolphs, R. (2006). Looking you in the mouth: Abnormal gazed in autism resulting from impaired top-down modulation of visual attention. *Social Cognitive and Affective Neuroscience, 1*(3), 194–202.

Ozonoff, S. and Jensen, J. (1999). Brief report: Specific executive function profiles in three neuro-developmental disorders. *Journal of Autism and Developmental Disorders, 29*(2), 171–7.

Ozonoff, S., Pennington, B., and Rogers, S. (1991). Executive function deficits in high functioning autistic individuals – relationship to theory of mind. *Journal of Child Psychology and Psychiatry and Allied Disciplines, 32*, 1081–105.

Ozonoff, S., Strayer, D., McMahon, W., and Filloux, F. (1994). Executive function abilities in autism and Tourette syndrome: An information processing approach. *Journal of Child Psychology and Psychiatry, 35*, 1015–32.

Panerai, S., Zingale, M., Trubia, G., Finocchiaro, M., Zuccarello, R., Ferri, R., and Elia M. (2009). Special education versus inclusive education: the role of the TEACCH program. *Journal of Autism and Developmental Disorders, 39*, 874–82.

Pennington, B. and Ozonoff, S. (1996). Executive functions and development psychopathologies. *Journal of Child Psychology and Psychiatry Annual Research Review, 37*, 51–87.

Perner, J. and Wimmer, H. (1985). "John thinks that Mary thinks that" . . . : attribution of second-order beliefs by 5-year-old to 10-year-old children. *Journal of Experimental Child Psychology, 39*(3), 437–71.

Plaisted, K., O'Riordan, M., and Baron-Cohen, S. (1998a). Enhanced discrimination of novel, highly similar stimuli by adults with autism during a perceptual learning task. *Journal of Child Psychology and Psychiatry, 39(5)*, 765–75.

Plaisted, K., O'Riordan, M., and Baron-Cohen, S. (1998b). Enhanced visual search for a conjunctive target in autism: a research note, *Journal of Child Psychology and Psychiatry, 39*(5), 777–83.

Posserud, M., Lundervold, A., and Gillberg, C. (2006). Autistic features in a total population of 7–9-year-old children assessed by the ASSQ (Autism Spectrum Screening Questionnaire). *Journal of Child Psychology and Psychiatry, 47*, 167–75.

Powell, J., Edwards, A., Edwards, M., Pandit, B., Sungum-Paliwal, S., and Whitehouse, W. (2000). Changes in the incidence of childhood autism and other autistic spectrum disorders in pre-school children from two areas of the West Midlands, UK, *Developmental Medicine and Child Neurology, 42*, 624–8.

Preece, J. (1999). Empathy online. *Virtual Reality, 4*, 74–84.

Probst, P. and Leppert, T. (2008). Brief report: Outcomes of a teacher training program for autism spectrum disorders. *Journal of Autism and Developmental Disorders, 38*, 1791–6.

Rajendran, G. and Mitchell, P. (2007). Cognitive theories of autism. *Developmental Review, 27*, 224–60.

Reichow, B. and Wolery, M. (2009). Comprehensive synthesis of early intensive behavioral interventions for young children with autism based on the UCLA young autism project model. *Journal of Autism and Developmental Disorders, 39*, 23–41.

Reynhout, G. and Carter, M. (2009). The use of social stories by teachers and their perceived efficacy. *Research in Autism Spectrum Disorders, 3*, 232–51.

Rimland, B. and Fein, D. (1988) Special talents of autistic savants. In L. Obler and D. Fein (eds) *The exceptional brain: neuropsychology of talent and special abilities* (pp. 472–92). New York: The Guilford Press.

Rogers, K., Dziobek, I., Hassenstab, J., Wolf, O., and Convit, A. (2007). Who cares? Revisiting empathy in Asperger syndrome. *Journal of Autism and Developmental Disorders, 37*, 709–15.

Ropar, D. and Mitchell, P. (2001). Susceptibility to illusions and performance on visuospatial tasks in individuals with autism. *Journal of Child Psychology and Psychiatry, 42*, 539–49.

Rust, J. and Smith, A. (2006). How should the effectiveness of social stories to modify the behaviour of children on the autism spectrum be tested? *Autism, 10*, 125–38.

Rutter, M. (1978). Diagnosis and definition of childhood autism. *Journal of Autism and Developmental Disorders, 8(2)*, 139–61.

Rutter, M. (2005). Incidence of autism spectrum disorders: Changes over time and their meaning. *Acta Paediatrica, 94*, 2–15.

Scott, F., Baron-Cohen, S., Bolton, P., and Brayne, C. (2002). Brief report: Prevalence of autism spectrum conditions in children aged 5–11 years in Cambridgeshire, UK. *Autism, 6*, 231–7.

Shah, A. and Frith, U. (1983). An islet of ability in autistic children: A research note. *Journal of Child Psychology and Psychiatry, 24(4)*, 613–20.

Sharma, S., Woolfson, L., and Hunter, S. (submitted manuscript). *Asperger Syndrome and high functioning autism: 30 years of research on diagnostic confusion*.

Shea, V. (2004). A perspective on the research literature related to early intensive behavioral intervention (Lovaas) for young children with autism, *Autism, 8(4)*, 349–67.

Smith, B., Gardiner, J., and Bowler, D. (2007). Deficits in free recall persist in Asperger's syndrome despite training in the use of list-appropriate strategies. *Journal of Autism and Developmental Disorders, 37*, 445–54.

Snyder, A. and Mitchell, J. (1999). Is integer arithmetic fundamental to mental processing? The mind's secret arithmetic. *Proceedings of the Royal Society of London B, 266*, 587–92.

Spezio, M., Adolphs, R., Hurley, R., and Piven, J. (2007). Abnormal use of facial information in high-functioning autism. *Journal of Autism and Developmental Disorders, 37(5)*, 929–39.

Steffenburg, S., Gillberg, C., Hellgren, L., Andersson, L., Gillberg, I., Jakobsson, G., and Bohman, M. (1989). A twin study of autism in Denmark, Finland, Iceland, Norway, and Sweden. *Journal of Child Psychology and Psychiatry, 30*, 405–16.

Steinhausen, H., Göbel, D., Breinlinger, M. and Wohllebhen, B. (1986). A community survey of infantile autism. *Journal of the American Academy of Child Psychiatry, 25*, 186–9.

Treffert, D. (2006). *Extraordinary people: Understanding savant syndrome*. New York: Ballantine Books.

Turner, H. (1994). Gender and social support: taking the bad with the good? *Gender Roles, 30*, 521–41.

UNESCO (2007). *Science, Technology and Gender: An international report*. Paris: UNESCO.

Wang, K., Zhang, H., Ma, D., Bucan, M., Glessner, J., Abrahams, B., Salyakina, D., Imilelinski, M. *et al.* (2009). Common genetic variants on 5p14.1 associate with autism spectrum disorders. *Nature*, advance online publication.

Williams, K., Glasson, E., Wray, J., Tuck, M., Helmer, M., Bower, C., and Mellis, C. (2005). Incidence of autism spectrum disorders in children in two Australian states. *Medical Journal of Australia, 182*, 108–11.

Wimmer, H. and Perner, J. (1983) Beliefs about beliefs representation and constraining function of wrong beliefs in young children's understanding of deception *Cognition, 13*, 103–28.

Wing, L. (1981). Asperger's Syndrome.: A clinical account. *Psychological Medicine, 11*, 115–29.

Wing, L. and Gould, J. (1979). Severe impairments of social interaction and associated abnormalities in children: Epidemiology and classification. *Journal of Autism and Childhood Schizophrenia, 9*, 11–29.

Witkin, H., Oltman, P., Raskin, E., and Karp, S. (1971). *A manual for the Embedded Figures test*. Palo Alto, Ca: Consulting Psychologists Press, Inc.

Wolff, S. and McGuire, R. (1995). Schizoid personality in girls: A follow-up study – what are the links with Asperger's syndrome? *Journal of Child Psychology and Psychiatry, 36*, 793–817.

Wong, V. and Hui, S. (2008). Epidemiological study of autism spectrum disorder in China. *Journal of Child Neurology, 23*, 67–72.

Yirmiya, N., Sigman, M., Kasari, C., and Mundy, P. (1992). Empathy and cognition in high-functioning children with autism. *Child Development, 63(1)*, 150–60.

School refusal behaviour

Absence from school is a serious problem and is linked with delinquent behaviour, poor academic achievement and poor adult outcomes. This means that it is an issue that not only affects non-attending individuals and their families but also has an impact on our wider society. This chapter will attempt to unravel conceptualisations of different patterns of absentee behaviour, and will propose how assessment might proceed in a way that articulates with subsequent intervention strategies. We will then consider evidence for the efficacy of intervention approaches used to tackle school refusal behaviours.

Learning outcomes

By the end of this chapter you should be able to:

- Distinguish problematic and non-problematic absenteeism
- Understand the distinctions and overlaps between school refusal, truancy, separation anxiety and school phobia
- Demonstrate awareness of the relative strengths of assessment of form and function of school refusal
- Understand key assessment approaches used and the evidence for their efficacy
- Demonstrate awareness of the efficacy of different intervention approaches.

To start us thinking about this topic, let's consider a case example.

 Group activity (for 2–6 people)

Join up with some friends to discuss.

Tom is 12 years old and has recently started secondary school. His attendance at primary school was good and he was seen as a good pupil. Recently though, he has been missing school. Establish a list of possible reasons.

What are school refusal behaviours?

Absence from school due to excessive anxiety was first described by Broadwin (1932) and was subsequently referred to as 'school phobia' (Johnson, Falstein, Szurek and Svendsen, 1941). Hersov (1977) provided a classic description of the problem:

> The problem often starts with vague complaints about school or reluctance to attend, progressing to total refusal to go to school or to remain in school in the face of persuasion, entreaty, recrimination and punishment by parents and pressures from teachers, family doctors and education welfare officers. The behaviour may be accompanied by overt signs of anxiety or even panic when the time comes to go to school and most children cannot even leave home to set out for school.

It seemed though to early psychodynamic theorists, with their particular interest in the parent–child relationship, that rather than an actual fear of school itself as implied by the term 'school phobia', the problem could be better explained by 'separation anxiety'. Thus, they viewed the child as unwilling to leave home to go to school because of an excessively strong mother–child attachment (Blagg, 1987). Nowadays, however, the mother–child relationship is seen as only one possible contributory factor alongside other child and family factors and, importantly, factors within the school itself, each of which will be discussed in the chapter.

It might be helpful next, though, to clarify how different non-attendance terms are currently understood in the research literature and how they contribute to our present-day definitions of absentee behaviour.

School phobia

School phobia nowadays usually refers to absence from school based on an irrational fear of a specific feature of school (Kearney, 2008a; Paccione-Dyszlewski and Contessa-Kislus, 1987). However, 'school' itself is not a specific stimulus and as such cannot really be the source of a phobic response (Kearney, Eisen and Silverman, 1995). It is more likely that the source of 'school phobia' would be some more specific aspect of school such as the gym, the fire alarm or the school bus

(Chitiyo and Wheeler, 2006). School phobia is nowadays viewed as rare (Hanna, Fischer and Fluent, 2006).

Separation anxiety disorder

Separation anxiety disorder (SAD) is the most common diagnosis for school refusal behaviour with 23% of young people with problems in school non-attendance receiving this diagnosis (Kearney and Bensaheb, 2006). The problem here is a reluctance to attend school because of excessive anxiety about separating from the parent or leaving home (Hanna *et al.*, 2006). Anxiety may be about actually separating, or even about anticipating separation (American Psychiatric Association, 2000). Such school refusal behaviour can contribute to the child receiving a diagnosis of SAD as defined by the Diagnostic and Statistical Manual of Mental Disorders (DSM-IV, American Psychiatric Association, 1994). You should note, however, that school phobia is not a DSM-IV diagnostic condition, although simple phobia and social phobia are, and consequently are often used as convenient diagnoses for school refusers (Elliot, 1999). Anxiety can have an impact on educational outcomes for the child; children with SAD were found to have difficulties with learning and memory tasks (Toren, Sadeh, Wolmer, Eldar, Koren, Weizman *et al.*, 2000). SAD may also be associated with adult psychiatric disorders (Eisen and Schaefer, 2005).

Truancy

UK law requires that children receive education, normally at school. Unexplained, unexcused absences from school with no documented justification, or for no legitimate reason, may be considered as truancy (Kearney, 2008a; Reid, 1999; Stoll, 1990). Links have been reported between truancy, excessive alcohol consumption and illegal use of drugs, and it has been suggested that these counter-conformity variables may in fact interact with, and reinforce, each other (Best, Manning, Gossop, Gross and Strang, 2006; Duarte and Escario, 2006). Furthermore, there is evidence to suggest truancy is also associated with criminal behaviour, as well as marital and job instability in adult life (Dryfoos, 1990). Truancy tends to be associated with externalising behaviour disorders such as antisocial, rule-breaking behaviour, rather than internalising disorders such as anxiety and depression (Henry, 2007). Experience of critical life events, such as bereavement, stress, family conflict, may also be more common among truants than among children who are absent from school for other reasons (Huffington and Sevitt, 1989). In recent years, strict government policies have been implemented to try to address this problem: parents may be fined or prosecuted if they are not seen to be actively trying to prevent their children truanting from school (Claes, Hooghe and Reeskens, 2009).

QUISSET *Now go beyond the text ... look it up yourself!*

Explore your library's electronic databases to investigate 'truancy'.

- What recent prevalence figures for truancy are mentioned in the literature for the UK and the US?
- How is truancy defined in these studies?
- Is there variability in the criteria used to identify truants across different studies?

Excusable and inexcusable absenteeism

The problem of school absenteeism has attracted researchers and professionals from different fields and from different theoretical backgrounds, including not only psychology and education, but also social work, law, psychiatry, family therapy and nursing (Kearney, 2008b). This has resulted in a rather disparate literature and disparate terminology. When reading journal papers it is important to be clear about the definition of non-attendance used by the author and which participants are the subjects of the study, as lack of precision about terms used makes it difficult to compare findings across different studies (Kearney, 2008b). Kearney (2008a) provided a useful explanation of key concepts here and how they relate to each other. Figure 6.1 provides a diagrammatic illustration of this. The areas highlighted in blue are those that will be discussed in this chapter.

According to Kearney (2008a, 2008b), the term 'absenteeism' may refer to *'excusable'* absence from school such as sickness or religious holidays, or it may refer to *'inexcusable'* absences. Kearney (2008a) suggested that *'inexcusable'* absences may be caused by:

- *School refusal behaviour* where the child is not motivated to attend school. This can range from complete absence from school for an extended period of time to simply missing particular classes, or begging parents to be allowed not to go to school on particular days.
- *Child mental health problems.* Recent studies have consistently found depression, anxiety and disruptive behaviour disorders to be the most common diagnoses associated with problematic absenteeism.
- *School withdrawal* where parents keep the child home from school on purpose, perhaps to babysit younger children so that the parent can get out to work, or perhaps to hide evidence of abuse such as bruises from teachers and peers, or to protect the child from bullying, or because the parent is unwell and wants the child's help and support at home to look after the sick parent or attend to the housework.

It is 'inexcusable', rather than 'excusable', absences that are of interest to psychologists researching school absenteeism, and in particular school refusal behaviour

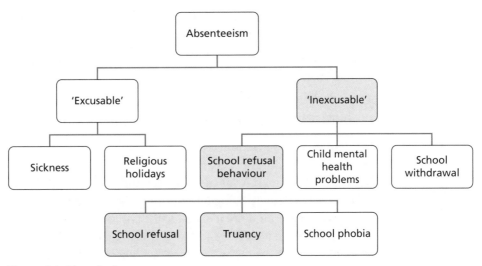

Figure 6.1 **Absenteeism**

which is often used as an overarching term that subsumes school refusal and school phobia as well as truancy. In this regard, *school refusal* is viewed as a narrower term than *school refusal behaviour*, and refers to anxiety-based school absenteeism (Kearney, 2008a). However, you will see when you study the literature that these three terms, school refusal, truancy and school phobia, are often used interchangeably, or have been defined differently in different studies (Elliott, 1999; Lauchlan, 2003; Pellegrini, 2007).

> **Remember:** When reading around this topic check the individual author's definition of school refusal behaviour so that you are clear who the study's participants are and therefore are in a better position to evaluate how that study's findings relate to the findings of other studies on school absentee behaviour.

This chapter's main focus will be on school refusal and truancy, rather than the rarer condition of school phobia. Let us look next then at how truancy and school refusal may be distinguished and how they overlap.

Some studies (Berg, Nichols and Pritchard, 1969; Elliott, 1999 and Kearney, 2008a) have noted that school refusers usually:

● experience severe anxiety in attending school, often separation anxiety

● complain they feel ill when it is expected that they will go to school

● are absent from school with their parents' knowledge

● do not have any anti-social disorders such as delinquency or conduct disorder.

On the other hand, truants generally:

● do not experience anxiety about attending school

- are not at school because they are not interested in their schoolwork , and often have academic problems

- do not want to conform to the school's rules and would rather do other things than be at school

- are likely to conceal absence from parents

- are likely to engage in disruptive, delinquent acts in company of anti-social peers.

Differences between school refusal and truancy, though, are not always as clear-cut as the above might imply. A small proportion of absentees show features of both truancy and school refusal (Berg, Butler and Franklin, 1993). For example, school refusers may begin by being absent from school without their parents' knowledge which is a behaviour more like that of the typical truant (Werry, 1996). On the other hand, in a French study Brandibas, Jeunier, Clanet and Fourasté (2004) studied a sample of young people in technical schools, which they reported as being well known for high truancy and deviant behaviour. They found anxiety, usually perceived as a key distinguishing feature of school refusers, was also associated with truancy in their sample. These findings suggest there is overlap between school refusal and truancy, in terms of the symptoms, or form, of these behaviours.

The idea presented above of truants as individuals who experience problems in their schoolwork was developed further by Southwell (2006). Southwell suggested that the problems of truancy may not reside within the child nor within the family but may rather be a marker that the school is not adequately meeting the young person's special educational needs. This suggests that intervention would target the school. We will return to the role of the school later in the chapter.

 Debate

Join up with some friends to discuss.

To what extent do different school refusal behaviours share underlying features, i.e. can school refusal behaviour be considered a unitary concept?

Function rather than form?

Like school phobia, children cannot actually be diagnosed with 'school refusal' as it is not itself a psychiatric diagnosis referred to in DSM-IV (American Psychiatric Association, 1994), and its symptoms do not fall neatly into available DSM categories. Nor is it referred to in ICD-10, the World Health Organization's 1992 diagnostic classification system. It has long been recognised that it is a heterogeneous rather than a unitary disorder (Elliott, 1999) and that its aetiology is complex (e.g. Berg and Nursten, 1996). It has not, however, been straightforward to identify the nature of this heterogeneity by attempting to distinguish between the forms of clinical symptoms of different school refusal behaviours for diagnostic purposes (Kearney, 2007). As we have seen in the above section, attempts to distinguish sub-groups of non-attendance behaviours based on, for example, parental knowledge of the absence or the presence of anxiety or other symptoms were found to lack empirical support and, perhaps even more importantly, such distinctions did not lead directly to intervention strategies and so were of little use to practitioner psychologists (Elliott, 1999; Kearney and Silverman, 1990).

For these reasons, in 'what can be considered the most comprehensive conceptualisation of school refusal behaviour' (Pina, Zerr, Gonzales and Ortiz, 2009, p. 11), Kearney and Albano (2004) suggested that as well as focusing on form (symptoms), assessment could usefully investigate the functions served by the absentee behaviour. That is to say, identification of the nature of the problem should assess not only what behaviours are present (form), but more importantly why the child is engaging in these behaviours (function). This would help to distinguish the different factors that maintain that behaviour and might usefully complement a focus on the form of the clinical symptoms. Kearney and Albano proposed four categories of function:

1 *Avoidance of specific stimuli in the school setting.* Examples of stimuli in the school setting that cause fear and anxiety might be particular teachers, the toilets, the corridors, or the school bus.

2 *Escape from aversive social situation.* This refers to absenteeism to escape social relationships with teachers or with peers where there is some evaluation of social or academic performance that is perceived as threatening, e.g. teachers commenting on classwork or on oral presentations, evaluation in exam situations, the cafeteria at lunchtime.

3 *Engaging in behaviour that will result in attention from parents or teachers.* Complaining about aches and pains or having a tantrum in order to remain at home to get parental attention. The school itself then is not the problem here for the child but rather that the child prefers to be receiving parental attention at home.

4 *Engaging in more rewarding experiences outside school.* The child might be at home watching TV or hanging out with friends at the shopping mall or engaging in delinquent activities.

It should be noted that the first two points relate to negative reinforcement where the child is reinforced by removing him/herself from an unpleasant school situation, while the second two points identify activities that result in positive reinforcement with children being rewarded for being away from school (Pelligrini, 2007).

This focus on the functions of the absentee behaviour has a number of advantages. Firstly these four functions cover all absentee behaviour and so can be applied to truancy as well as to anxiety-induced school refusal and to the less common condition of school phobia. They have been shown to be useful in predicting absenteeism (Kearney, 2007). Furthermore, assessment of function leads well to inform intervention planning as you will see below, while diagnosis of symptoms (form) does not articulate so readily with treatment. School refusers can change the form of their behaviour from missing an occasional class to missing whole days, but the function of that behaviour is likely to remain stable in terms of whether the refuser is seeking positive or negative reinforcement by their behaviour (Kearney, 2007). Assessment of function, of these factors that are maintaining the behaviour, would seem to be a useful addition to diagnosis of the form of school refusal behaviour to help the practitioner determine intervention approaches (Kearney, 2007; King and Bernstein, 2001).

EXAMPLE Case study

Katie had been in the top half of her class throughout the first few years of primary schooling and had almost perfect attendance. Over the summer between Years 5 and 6, her family moved from a rural Yorkshire school to an urban Leeds primary school, a move necessitated by her father's promotion at work. Katie was an adaptable girl and seemed to settle in well to the school, making new friends quickly.

Dad, however, had two concerns within a few months: firstly that Katie seemed to having some difficulties in completing her homework, and secondly that the new friends she had made were not quite what he would have chosen for her himself. They seemed rather old for their age in the way they dressed and how they behaved, and were allowed rather more freedom outside school than Katie. Dad had a lot on his plate, what with the new job and his wife's illness. Katie's mother had had muscular sclerosis now for four years and had shown significant deterioration since the move to Leeds. Katie was a great help to her with the housework and in looking after her younger brother and sister.

At parents' evening Dad took the opportunity to speak to the head teacher after a less than satisfactory meeting with the class teacher, who seemed inexperienced and unconcerned about the issues Dad raised. The class teacher viewed Katie as a child who struggled with much of the work but who was 'doing her best'. The head teacher did indicate that Katie's friends were part of 'the lowest common denominator' in the class but that the Year 5 teacher last year had maintained a tight control on the class and these girls had responded very well to her. The head teacher said that unfortunately this year their behaviour with their new teacher had not been quite so good, but in their favour they were good friends to Katie and their friendship had meant Katie wasn't being bullied so much.

Two months later Katie's friends' behaviour resulted in their being suspended from school. One week after this, Katie's mother phoned the school to say Katie was unwell and wouldn't be at school. Katie returned to school after a week's absence but her work was noticeably poorer. Instead of lunching in the cafeteria or going to the shops for a snack, she began to go home for lunch and often did not return in the afternoon. Attendance records showed that her friends were absent from school at the same times.

Mum had to go into hospital for a short spell and the school noted that Katie was now also often late for school. The head teacher observed that the class teacher's system of punishment exercises did not seem to be having an effect on Katie as she was still regularly late even though she had received several of these.

By the end of the school year attendance records showed that Katie had not been at school at all for four weeks.

- List the different factors that made it less likely that Katie would attend school.
- What do these imply for intervention?

In the above section we have examined what should be assessed in order to understand problems of school refusal behaviour, with the case having been argued for the assessment of form as well as function. Let's move on now to consider what instruments might be used for this, and then we will go on to discuss how these inform subsequent approaches to intervention.

Assessment

Traditional assessment of form involves reviewing the extent of child's non-attendance and aiming to identify any patterns using school attendance records, child report, parent report, and teacher report. Where there may be comorbid psychiatric conditions, there are also likely to be diagnostic interviews and assessment of externalising problems such as aggression and rule-breaking, and internalising problems such as fear, anxiety and depression (Kearney, 2008a; King and Bernstein, 2000). Tools such as the Anxiety Disorders Interview Schedule for DSM-IV, Child Version or the Self-Efficacy Questionnaire for School Situations (Heyne *et al.*, 1998) may be used for this (King and Bernstein, 2000; King, Tonge, Heyne and Ollendick, 2000). Assessment of family functioning may also be carried out (Kearney and Silverman, 1995; King and Bernstein, 2001).

To complement these measures, the School Refusal Assessment Scale-Child (SRAS-C; Kearney, 2002; Kearney and Silverman, 1993) is a particularly important instrument that may be utilised to assess the functions of these behaviours.

IN FOCUS

School Refusal Assessment Scale–Child (SRAS–R–C; Kearney, 2002; Kearney and Silverman, 1993)

The SRAS was constructed by Kearney and Silverman (1993) to provide a means of assessment of the four functions of refusal behaviours (see earlier in this chapter). The original scale comprised 16 items, four on each of the four functional conditions, avoidance of stimuli in the school that cause fear, escape from evaluative social situations, quest for attention, and engaging in more rewarding alternative activities. It was then revised to further strengthen its already strong psychometric properties. Additional items resulted in a 24-item scale, with six items for each function, and with versions for completion by the child (SRAS-R-C) and by the parent (SRAS-R-P). The first two functions, which both reflect negatively reinforced refusal behaviour, were associated with internalising behaviour problems, while the second two, positive reinforcement functions, were associated more with externalising behaviours. Good reliability and validity have been reported as well as confirmatory factor analysis supporting the four factor scale (Brandibas *et al.*, 2004; Kearney, 2002; Kearney, 2006).

Respondents are asked about their reasons for staying off school, and asked to rate on a 7-point Likert scale ranging from 0 'never' to 6 'always' the extent to which different reasons apply, e.g. preferring to be with their parents than go to school, or feeling embarrassed in front of others, or being afraid of things at school. Profiles of the functions of the school refusal can then be obtained from these responses for the individual child.

Intervention

An important feature of the SRAS-R-C is that it attempts to map assessment directly on to a treatment plan for the child, although more research is required to demonstrate that this link actually results in treatment outcomes that are successful. For example, for rewarding activities outside school ((4) in Table 6.1) the educational psychologist might negotiate increased incentives for school attendance and penalties for non-attendance aiming to make school attendance more rewarding.

Table 6.1 **SRAS-R-C functions and intervention**

Function	Primary diagnosis	Treatment
1	Specific fearfulness	Relaxation training and systematic desensitisation to encourage gradual return to anxiety-provoking school setting
2	Escape from aversive social situation	Modelling, role-play and cognitive interventions to increase coping skills and reduce cognitive distortions
3	Attention-getting, separation-anxious behaviour	Parent and/or teacher contingency management to reinforce school approach rather than school absentee or tantrum behaviours
4	Reinforcement by other rewarding activities	Add incentives to school attendance to make attending school more rewarding

Source: Adapted using data from Kearney and Silverman, 1993 and King *et al.*, 2000

? *Debate*

Join up with some friends to discuss.

How useful is a distinction between school refusal and truancy in addressing school absentee problems?

Let's now examine some of the main treatment approaches to see how they might operate and what the evidence is for their effectiveness.

Behavioural approaches

Behavioural programmes for school refusers are usually based on exposing the refuser to the school. Although behavioural approaches have been widely used by school psychologists for treating school absenteeism, probably because they are time-efficient (Kearney and Beasley, 1994), there is a lack of controlled empirical study of their efficacy (Elliott, 1999; Tranah and Yule, 1997). This is partly because there is often more than one reason for the absenteeism, so multiple strategies are required. Generally then a multi-modal intervention is tailored for the individual child to address an interaction of differing elements (King and Bernstein, 2001). It is difficult then to evaluate such a complex individualised treatment programme (King and Ollendick, 1997). How does the researcher untangle which elements are necessary to make this work?

Let's look at some examples of behavioural approaches.

Systematic desensitisation

Gradual return

One way of exposing the absentee to the school is by gradual return using small, manageable steps that the child has agreed and feels able to cope with. This approach, also known as counter-conditioning is based on classical conditioning (Farris and Jouriles, 1993). It is thought to be suitable regardless of the severity and complexity of the problem and can be used even for chronic school absentee behaviours (King and Ollendick, 1989). The first step could just be getting into the car in school uniform with schoolbooks as if to go to school, but not actually going any further than that. The second step might be to drive the child to the school building but not expect her to go in. The next step could be for her to spend a brief amount of time working alone in a quiet resource base and then to return home. These small steps continue until the child is now able to return to attend some of the class activities that she is least anxious about, progressing in small agreed steps until she can manage a full-time return to regular classes without requiring any special arrangements. If it is the PE class that was the key stimulus for the child's fear and anxiety then attending that would be at the final step of the hierarchy of progressive steps. The principle here is for the child to develop a relaxed state that gradually reduces and finally eliminates her anxiety response to allow her to approach the aspect of school that she finds threatening. Houlihan and Jones (1989), for example, reported a single case study with a 13-year-old boy using graduated exposure first in the 'homeroom', then at lunch and then finally into the regular classes. While improvement was reported relative to baseline measures, problems were still reported. In any case it is more common for more than one intervention approach to be used. For example, Pina *et al.* (2009) reported evidence for 15 different school refusal intervention studies, the majority of which used a combination of procedures. Here we see the nature of the problem in this area is being confident about conclusions of intervention effectiveness. Ollendick and King (1998) suggested that systematic desensitisation using graduated exposure was likely to be one of the treatments that was successful for school refusal problems but that more rigorous studies were needed to establish this more conclusively. This still seems to be the case more than ten years on.

QUISSET   *Now go beyond the text . . . look it up yourself!*

Explore your library's electronic databases to investigate 'systematic desensitisation'.

- Carry out a literature search to find studies that have used systematic desensitisation as an intervention for school refusal, either alone, or in tandem with other approaches. What conclusions can you draw from these studies?

Relaxation

Relaxation training is a particular form of systematic desensitisation that is viewed as highly suitable for the reduction of anxiety in school refusal behaviour and is a popular intervention approach for practitioners (Kearney and Bensaheb, 2006). The child learns here how to deal with feelings of anxiety by relaxing his body, often accompanied by suitable imagery to help relaxation. As there is a lack of carefully controlled studies of relaxation training, the evidence base for this is still weak, however (Elliott, 1999; Lauchlan, 2003). Barnes, Bauza and Treiber (2003) conducted a relaxation study using transcendental meditation. Children in two schools took part and one school was allocated to the relaxation training programme while the comparison group received a health education programme. Although Barnes *et al.* reported that the relaxation group demonstrated improved attendance compared to the control group, these differences could have been due to sample bias, that is to say, because of pre-existing groups, the two school groups were not in fact equivalent.

In a recent study Hughes, Gullone, Dudley and Tonge (2009) introduced the dimension of 'emotion regulation' into the field of research with anxious school refusers. Their interest was in the association between school refusal behaviour and children's poor management and regulation of their emotions. They proposed that school refusers may be poorer at emotion regulation than controls. Emotion regulation relates to awareness, understanding, monitoring, evaluating and managing your emotions so that you have some degree of control over which emotions are expressed, when, and how (Gross, 1998). If you make a mistake in class over something that you should have known you might feel emotions of shame or guilt at this action because you see yourself as someone who has done a stupid thing and you think everyone is laughing at you. Better, more adaptive emotion regulation might be to manage this by reappraising your thinking about it so that instead you say to yourself, 'Everyone makes mistakes. If you don't make mistakes you don't learn,' thus regulating your emotions so that you feel neither shame nor guilt. Hughes *et al.* were particularly interested in such cognitive re-appraisal as recent studies had indicated anxious children may have a tendency to utilise negative cognitions like the above, and then tend to persist with these interpretations. Given this current research interest in the relationship between emotion regulation and anxiety and that it is well-established that there is a high prevalence of anxiety in school refusers, Hughes *et al.* felt it made good sense to apply these new research ideas to the particular area of school refusal. They did indeed find that the school refusers reported less adaptive emotion regulation, with less use of cognitive reappraisal strategies than the matched non-clinical sample. They also used the strategy of suppression of expression of emotion to a greater extent. This focus on emotion regulation in school refusers is a new area of work and it is likely that there are also other emotion regulation strategies that could be examined. This work could have important implications for enhancing the efficacy of other treatment strategies such as cognitive behavioural therapy which we will discuss below. It may be that developing better emotion regulation strategies needs to be built in to these treatment programmes for optimal effect.

QUISSET   *Now go beyond the text . . . look it up yourself!*

Explore your library's electronic databases to investigate 'emotion regulation'.

- Carry out a literature search to investigate what other emotion regulation strategies might usefully be studied with respect to school refusal behaviour.

Rapid return

In contrast to the gradual exposure of a systematic desensitisation programme, exposure can utilise the behavioural principle of extinction using a rapid return to school procedure which involves exposure to the feared stimulus all at once. This is also based on classical conditioning and is a variation of the extinction technique, also referred to as 'flooding'. The principle is that immersing the child totally in the threatening school situation causes the anxiety to dissipate (Doobay, 2008; Farris and Jouriles, 1993). Not surprisingly it is viewed as somewhat controversial as it can be very stressful for the child and the parent (Elliott, 1999). In its favour though, the rapidity of this intervention can help to minimise secondary problems of prolonged absence from school, such as falling behind in schoolwork, missing out on the social culture of the school, or losing friends. These secondary problems themselves begin to require intervention and support as they can help maintain the absentee behaviour in addition to the primary problems that caused the child to remove himself from school in the first place. Rapid return also ensures that the child is not being reinforced for being at home rather than at school. It is most suitable where the school refusal is acute rather than chronic, and where the nature of the problem is simple such as anxiety about test-taking, rather than comprising a complex combination of multiple functional reasons for absence and the presence of comorbid conditions such as depression (Kearney and Beasley, 1994; Kearney and Tillotson, 1998). Assuming ethical arrangements can be made at the school to ensure that the child remains there when he may prefer to go home, this intervention was found to be quick to implement successfully (the authors reported an improvement in two and a half weeks), with good outcomes still reported at eight-year follow-up (Blagg and Yule, 1984). Perhaps because of the difficulties and stresses involved in this, Kearney and Beasley's (1994) survey of US practitioners found that only 11.6% of cases used rapid return to school. In the cases where it was used, however, an impressive 100% success rate of school attendance without further problems was reported.

Contingency management

Contingency management involves the psychologist enlisting the support of parents and teachers to manipulate the consequences of the refusal behaviour in order to provide positive reinforcement for the child's attendance at school. This can involve training parents how to establish 'house rules' for the behaviours they expect, training them how to set up routines for the child leaving home in the morning to go to school, and on identifying a system of suitable rewards and punishments for behaviours around school attendance (Kearney, Lemos and Silverman, 2006). It is not easy for parents to stay firm on instructing their child to go to school when the child is becoming very upset and fearful. Parent training can also involve learning how to give clear, unambivalent instructions about going to school without the parents showing any anxiety themselves, learning how to recognise appropriate behaviours in the child and how to reward them while at the same time ignoring tantrums, child complaints about headaches or stomach pains, or any other inappropriate behaviours that lead to maintenance of the school refusal behaviour. Rewards can range from praise, to tangible rewards, to tokens, as appropriate for the particular young person. Indeed good use can even be made of naturally occurring reinforcers such as going home at the end of the day after the child has successfully attended afternoon classes, social reinforcement in terms of peer approval, being awarded good marks in schoolwork (Elliott, 1999).

Again evaluation studies reported tend to be case studies. For example, Brown, Copeland and Hall (1974) described a study using contingency management where an 11-year-old boy was reinforced for spending time in the hall, then the library and then for attending class. Note that the behavioural principle of 'shaping' is used here, where approximations to the desired goal are reinforced. This study reported that the boy's behaviour improved beyond the baseline measure. One important exception to the case study approach was Blagg and Yule's (1984) study in which a treatment group of 30 children aged 10–16 years received a behaviour therapy programme consisting of a rapid return to school, contingency management both at home and school, and a variation of systematic desensitisation using humour and imagery. The use of humour and imagery in systematic desensitisation was developed by Ventis (1973). Using this technique participants might, for example, be asked to create humorous statements and images about the feared situation. These can then be used in the behaviour therapy programme by having programme participants pair imagining the feared situation with the humourous images. In Blagg and Yule's study, the behaviour therapy group was compared with 16 hospitalised children at an adolescent psychiatric unit, and 20 children who received home tuition with psychotherapy. After one year, 93.3% of the behaviour therapy group had successfully returned to full-time schooling. The other groups made less progress, 37.5% for inpatient group, and only 10% success for the home tuition group. Although groups were not randomly allocated, they were found to have no differences on a number of variables, such as gender, social class and intelligence. While the findings do suggest behaviour therapy was effective, group differences could not be ruled out as contributing to the reported outcomes because groups were not randomly allocated.

QUISSET *Now go beyond the text . . . look it up yourself!*

Explore your library's electronic databases to investigate 'school refusal'.

- As well as school attendance, what other outcome measures have been assessed in school refusal evaluation studies?
- Were gains in these other measures also found?
- Are these the most appropriate outcome measures?

Cognitive behavioural therapy

Behaviour management approaches outlined above focus on the key symptom of school absenteeism, that of non-attendance at school, with the aim of directly changing this behaviour. There are other psychological interventions that focus rather on the child's symptoms such as anxiety and depression. They use psychoeducational approaches such as cognitive restructuring, coping and relaxation training to help the child better manage their anxiety (Kearney, 2008b). Cognitive behavioural therapy (CBT) has been used in this regard. It is a structured approach based on the idea that the child holds distorted, negative thoughts about the feared school situation that contribute to and maintain the anxiety. The premise of CBT is that such maladaptive thoughts and images can be modified, and that changed cognitions about school will lead to behavioural change in school attendance. A child who will not attend school might believe 'If I go to school today, I'll have to take the maths test and I'll do so poorly everyone will think I'm really stupid.' This belief could be changed to something more realistic like 'If I go to school today, I'll have to take the maths test and I might not do too well on it but I won't be the only one as it's really hard, and no one will particularly notice how I did.' This can be applied to the child's parents as well, where they can learn to recognise their own cognitive distortions about their children's school attendance and substitute these with more appropriate ones. For example replacing 'He can't go to school, he's got a bad headache' with the more appropriate 'He's got a bit of a headache but he's fine, it'll go away at school as it normally does when he stays at home.'

Alongside cognitive restructuring, behavioural interventions are usually also used in the treatment of school refusal. This means that as well as working on modifying unhelpful beliefs and teaching the child to be aware of and monitor her anxiety-provoking self-talk (statements that she makes to herself about the threats of school attendance), a behavioural action plan is also devised to increase the amount of time the child is exposed to school. As with other studies of school refusal, there are often design limitations in CBT evaluations that restrict the conclusions that can be drawn. For example, in their review of CBT in school refusal, King, Tonge, Heyne and Ollendick (2000) found only two studies (King *et al.*, 1998; Last, Hansen and Franco, 1998) that met the APA Task Force guidelines that were current at the time of their study, on criteria for research to demonstrate that a particular treatment was supported by empirical evidence. While pointing out the limitations of these guidelines, and the likelihood that CBT is an effective intervention for school refusers, King *et al.* advised exercising caution in advocating CBT until further research can confirm this.

EXAMPLES Evaluations of interventions using CBT

- Last, Hansen and Franco (1998) randomly allocated 56 school refusers, aged 6–17 years, to 12 sessions of either a CBT group or an educational support therapy group. The CBT group received graduated exposure, training in cognitive restructuring and coping. The educational support group functioned as a control group who received a placebo that offered them a similar amount of attention. They kept diaries to note down their fears and received general educational and emotional support, but were not provided with help in dealing with the school situations that they were afraid of, or taught how to modify their cognitions as in CBT. At programme end, both groups showed improved school attendance with no differences. This was maintained after a four-week follow-up. So while in this study CBT was shown to be effective, it was no more so than the placebo condition. A support group itself seemed to have been sufficient to bring about the required change for this sample with anxiety-based school refusal problems.

- King *et al.* (1998) randomly assigned 34 school refusers aged 5–15 years to CBT or on to a waiting-list control group, which neatly addressed possible ethical concerns about a control condition requiring the withholding of a possibly successful treatment from a needy group. The CBT group received CBT for the child along with parent and teacher management training over four weeks. The treatment comprised six sessions with the child, five with the parent, and one with the teacher over a four-week period, in a manualised, multi-treatment intervention that utilised exposure, training in coping skills, and parent and teacher involvement. King *et al.* reported that 88.2% (15 out of 17) of the treatment group participants showed a 90% improvement in their attendance while only 29.4% (5 out of 17) of the waiting list control group showed this level of improvement. Gains were still maintained at three month follow-up. However, because this was a multi-modal treatment, it cannot be concluded with confidence that it was CBT that was effective here. Perhaps parent involvement rather than CBT might have been the important element in the treatment success reported.

- King *et al.* (2001) followed up the children from their 1998 study three to five years later, managing to carry out telephone interviews with parents and teachers of 16 out of the 17 children in the original treatment group. There was no comparison group for this follow-up as the original comparison group who had been on a waiting list for intervention were offered intervention after the first study. Of these 16, 13 were reported as having normal attendance (defined as at least 90%) with no new psychological problems. These results seemed to indicate the long-term efficacy of the original CBT programme although it should be noted that the children themselves were not interviewed and no clinical assessments were undertaken.

- Heyne *et al.* (2002) randomly allocated 61 7–14-year-olds to a CBT group, a parent and teacher training group, or a group combining the two elements. One of their concerns was the the possibility that child involvement alone or caregiver involvement alone might be the key feature of intervention, and that this design limitation had not been sufficiently addressed by previous studies. Heyne *et al.*'s design took account of this by having a group with each of these as the key elements, as well as a combined group with both elements. Heyne *et al.* predicted that the combined group would show the best outcomes, as fits with the view of school refusal problems as generally complex and requiring a multi-stranded approach. All treatments were manualised but allowed for some flexibility of delivery. Child therapy comprised eight sessions of systematic desensitisation, relaxation, cognitive therapy, and social skills training. Parent/teacher training also comprised eight sessions advising on contingency management and cognitive therapy for the parents, dealing with beliefs about their role, and helping them to manage their own anxiety. The combined group used both these procedures and made parents and teachers aware of what the child CBT group was attempting to do so that they could reinforce strategies the child tried to implement as a result of the CBT programme. All children showed improvements as a result of the interventions but no differences were found between the treatment groups on any of the measures.

From the studies discussed above it would seem that CBT is likely to be an effective treatment for school refusal, but that it is not necessarily more successful than parent and teacher training. Heyne *et al.*'s (2002) study suggests there could be a number of workable options available for practitioners and that perhaps the more time-consuming combined approach is not always required. It is likely though that exposure of the child to the feared situation of school is a common denominator in all successful outcomes.

 Debate

Join up with some friends to discuss.

Research your library databases to find other studies that evaluate the effectiveness of CBT in school absenteeism.

Based on these and on the studies presented in this chapter, evaluate the evidence currently available to discuss to what extent CBT is necessary for improvement in school attendance, and to what extent it is sufficient or requires to be complemented by other approaches.

The role of the family

The involvement of parents in contingency management training has already been discussed above. From the CBT evaluations discussed we can see that it is still unclear whether working with parents alone might even be sufficient to bring about a change in the child's refusal behaviour. Indeed Berg (1992) suggested that it is only when the child realises that the parents are no longer going to tolerate and support absentee behaviours that progress can be made on return to school.

Family factors therefore are generally viewed as important to take into account. Family dynamics are often evaluated as these could have implications for the success of the intervention plan (Elliott, 1999). Is this family isolated, conflictual, interdependent, or detached from each other? There is evidence that such family problems are associated with school refusal (Kearney and Silverman,1995; Lagana, 2004). McShane, Walter and Rey (2001) found that 43% of the school refusers in their Australian study reported that they experienced conflict at home, and 39% of the sample lived in a single-parent family, supporting earlier findings by Corville-Smith, Ryan, Adams and Dalicandro (1998). Lyon and Cotler (2007) further argued that discussion of the role of families in the school refusal literature had not previously addressed cultural differences to any extent. In particular they argued that the focus of the literature has traditionally been on children with clinical levels of depression and anxiety, and did not specifically include examination of school absentee problems in low-income groups whose family relationships might be quite different from those in clinic-referred samples.

QUISSET *Now go beyond the text . . . look it up yourself!*

Explore your library's electronic databases to investigate 'family involvement in school refusal intervention'.

● Other than supporting contingency management, how have families been involved in intervention for school refusal? What is the evidence for the effectiveness of these approaches?

The role of the school

Researchers in the area of school absenteeism tend to come from non-educational fields such as clinical psychology and psychiatry and so they focus their analysis on child and family, rather than school factors. However, a more systemic view of absentee problems considers the child's difficulties in attending school in relations to the environmental context that the school system provides. The functions that the absentee behaviours fulfil for the child relate to how he experiences the school environment and therefore how he chooses to behave to avoid or escape from these experiences that he perceives as threatening. One way of looking at this is to consider the response as extreme and particular to this individual child. Another way of looking at this is to consider how the school environment may be perceived as threatening or unrewarding to the school refuser and indeed to the larger group of children who may be less sensitive to the school environment and who do not respond by refusing to attend but who nonetheless perceive the school as a hostile and unsatisfying place. Indeed Blagg (1987) suggested that schools with impersonal teacher–pupil relationships and poor supervision of public areas would be likely to see high levels of school refusal in their pupils. This implies attention should be paid to the school and classroom environment to try to determine how these might sustain absentee behaviour.

School climate is a measure that has been utilised in the extensive literature on school effectiveness, a body of research that aims to identify what factors contribute to learning and behavioural outcomes. School climate varies considerably across schools, even within schools located side by side in the same neighbourhood and socio-economic area. The concept of school climate incorporates measures of the learning environment including teacher norms, values and beliefs about pupil learning; school processes and policies; school ethos such as teacher–pupil relationships; and a focus on good behaviour and fair discipline (Dronkers and Robert, 2008; Heck and Marcoulides, 1996; Lee and Smith, 1999; Papanastasiou, 2008a; Rutter and Maughan, 2002). Kearney (2008a) further includes within the concept of school climate the extent to which students feel connected to, respected by, and supported by their school. Pupils have shown sensitivity to, and awareness of, their school's social climates with those pupils in schools with poorer social climates perceiving more friction and difficulty than those in schools with climates recognised by their school districts as 'exemplary' (Waxman, Garcia and Read 2008). The school climate, as measured by an orderly learning climate and the quality of relationships between teachers and pupils, has been found to have an effect on pupil effort and achievement outcomes (Opdenakker and Van Damme, 2007), and these are consistent across a range of different countries (Dronkers and Robert, 2008).

More importantly, however, for the purposes of our focus in this chapter, school climate has been shown to be moderately correlated to school absenteeism (e.g. Brookmeyer, Fanti and Henrich, 2006; Mortimore, Lewis, Stoll, Sammons and Ecob, 1988; Smyth, 1999). It has further been demonstrated that the effect of school social climate operates at the level of the individual classroom (Papanastasiou, 2008a, 2008b; Rutter and Maughan, 2002). That is to say, an 'effective' school is not evenly effective across all departments and classes. The child's day-to-day experience of school is for the most part at the level of the specific classes they attend and the teachers and peers that they engage with, within these classes. Classroom climate has been shown to influence school absenteeism (e.g. Claes *et al.*, 2009). As explained in the introduction to Part 2, educational psychologists as a profession are often committed to working in a systemic way (Woolfson, Whaling, Stuart and Monsen, 2003) and therefore, alongside interventions to instigate behavioural change in the child where the school staff will be involved in contingency management as discussed above, they may work with school staff on changing problematic aspects of the classroom climate that have contributed to the onset and maintenance of the presenting school refusal behaviours. It has been suggested that this could perhaps happen to a greater extent (Elliott, 1999; Lauchlan, 2003).

Summary and conclusions

School refusal behaviours are complex, multi-causal and can have long-term effects both on the individuals and on wider society. Assessment and intervention methods need to reflect the complexity of factors that contribute to absentee behaviours. Combining assessment of form with assessment of function would seem to point a constructive way forward. Further research is still needed to demonstrate the efficacy of current assessment and intervention approaches.

Further study

Go to the website www.pearsoned.co.uk/markswoolfson for the following starter articles:

Elliott, J. (1999). Practitioner review: school refusal: issues of conceptualisation, assessment and treatment. *Journal of Child Psychology and Psychiatry, 40*(7), 1001–12.

Kearney, C. (2008a). School absenteeism and school refusal behaviour in youth: a contemporary review. *Clinical Psychology Review, 28*, 451–71.

References

American Psychiatric Association (1994). *Diagnostic and statistical manual of mental disorders* 4th edition. Washington, DC: APA.

American Psychiatric Association (2000). *Diagnostic and statistical manual of mental disorders* 4th edition – text revision. Washington, DC: APA.

Barnes, V., Bauza, L., and Treiber, F. (2003). Impact of stress reduction on negative school behaviour in adolescents. *Health and Quality of Life Outcomes, 1*, 10.

Berg, I. (1992). Absence from school and mental health. *British Journal of Psychiatry, 161*, 154–66.

Berg, I., Nichols, K., and Pritchard, C. (1969). School phobia – its classification and relationship to dependency. *Journal of Child Psychology and Psychiatry, 10*, 123–41.

Berg, I., Butler, A., and Franklin, J. (1993). DSM-III disorders, social factors and management of school attendance problems in the normal population. *Journal of Child Psychology and Psychiatry, 34*(7), 1187–203.

Berg, I. and Nursten, J. (eds). (1996). *Unwillingly to school.* London: Gaskell.

Best, D., Manning, V., Gossop, M., Gross, S., and Strang, J. (2006). Excessive drinking and other problem behaviours among 14–16 year old schoolchildren. *Addictive Behaviour, 31*, 1424–35.

Blagg, N. (1987). *School phobia and its treatment.* London: Croom Helm.

Blagg, N. and Yule, W. (1984). The behavioural treatment of school refusal: a comparative study. *Behaviour, Research and Therapy, 22*, 119–27.

Brandibas, G., Jeunier, B., Clanet, C., and Fourasté, R. (2004). Truancy, school refusal and anxiety. *School Psychology International, 25*, 117–26.

Broadwin, I. (1932). A contribution to the study of truancy. *American Journal of Orthopsychiatry, 2*, 253–9.

Brookmeyer, K., Fanti, K., and Henrich, G. (2006). Schools, parents, and youth violence: A multi-level, ecological analysis. *Journal of Clinical child and Adolescent Psychology, 35*, 504–14.

Brown, R., Copeland, R., and Hall, R. (1974). School phobia: Effects of behaviour modification treatment applied by an elementary school principal. *Child Study Journal, 4*, 125–33.

Chitiyo, M. and Wheeler, J.(2006). School phobia: Understanding a complex behavioural response. *Journal of Research in Special Educational Needs, 6*(2), 87–91.

Claes, E., Hooghe, M., and Reeskens, T. (2009). Truancy as a contextual and school-related problem. *Educational Studies, 35*(2), 123–42.

Corville-Smith, J., Ryan, B., Adams, G., and Dalicandro, T. (1998). Distinguishing absentee students from regular attenders: The combined influence of personal, family, and school factors. *Journal of Youth and Adolescence, 27*, 629–40.

Doobay, A. (2008). School refusal behaviour associated with separation anxiety disorder: A cognitive-behaviour approach to treatment. *Psychology in the Schools, 45*, 261–72.

Dronkers, J. and Robert, P. (2008). Differences in scholastic achievement of public, private, government-dependent, and private independent schools: A cross-national analysis. *Educational Policy, 22*, 541–77.

Dryfoos, J. (1990). *Adolescents at risk: Prevalence and prevention.* Oxford: Oxford University Press.

Duarte, R. and Escario, J. (2006). Alcohol abuse and truancy among Spanish adolescents: A count-data approach. *Economics of Education Review, 25*, 179–87.

Eisen, A. and Schaefer, C. (2005). *Separation anxiety in children and adolescents: An individualized approach to assessment and treatment.* New York: Guilford Press.

Elliott, J. (1999). Practitioner review: school refusal: issues of conceptualisation, assessment and treatment. *Journal of Child Psychology and Psychiatry, 40*(7), 1001–12.

Farris, A. and Jouriles, E. (1993). Separation anxiety disorder. In A Bellack and M. Hersen (eds), *Handbook of behaviour therapy in the psychiatric setting* (pp. 407–26). New York: Plenum Press.

Gross, J. (1998). The emerging field of emotion regulation: An integrative review. *Review of General Psychology, 2*, 271–99.

Hanna, G., Fischer, D., and Fluent, T. (2006). Separation anxiety disorder and school refusal in children and adolescents. *Pediatrics in Review, 27,* 56–63.

Heck, R. and Marcoulides, G. (1996). School culture and performance: Testing the invariance of an organizational model. *School Effectiveness and School Improvement, 79*(1), 76–95.

Henry, K. (2007). School-related risk and protective factors associated with truancy among urban youth placed at risk. *Journal of Primary Prevention, 28,* 505–19.

Hersov, L. (1977). School refusal. In M. Rutter and L. Hersov (eds), *Child and adolescent psychiatry: Modern approaches,* 2nd edn. Oxford: Blackwell (pp. 382–399).

Heyne, D., King, N., Tonge, B., Rollings, S., Young, D., Pritchard, M., and Ollendick, T. (2002). Evaluation of child therapy and caregiver training in the treatment of school refusal. *Journal of American Academy of Child and Adolescent Psychiatry, 41,* 687–95.

Houlihan, D. and Jones, R. (1989). Treatment of a boy's school phobia with in vivo systematic desensitization. *Professional School Psychology, 4,* 285–93.

Huffington, C. and Sevitt, M. (1989). Family interaction in adolescent school phobia. *Journal of Family Therapy, 11,* 353–75.

Hughes, E., Gullone, E., Dudley, A., Tonge, B. (2009). A case-control study of emotion regulation and school refusal in children and adolescents. *The Journal of Early Adolescence* OnlineFirst.

Johnson, A., Falstein, E., Szurek, S., and Svendsen, M. (1941). School phobia. *American Journal of Orthopsychiatry, 11,* 702–12.

Kearney, C. (2002). Identifying the function of school refusal behaviour: A revision of the School Refusal Assessment Scale. *Journal of Psychopathology and Behavioural Assessment, 24,* 235–45.

Kearney, C. (2006). Confirmatory factor analysis of the School Refusal Assessment Scale-Revised: Child and Parent Versions. *Journal of Psychopathology and Behavioural Assessment, 28*(3), 139–44.

Kearney, C. (2007). Forms and functions of school refusal behaviour in youth: an empirical analysis of absenteeism severity. *Journal of Child Psychology and Psychiatry, 48*(1), 53–61.

Kearney, C. (2008a). School absenteeism and school refusal behaviour in youth: a contemporary review. *Clinical Psychology Review, 28,* 451–71.

Kearney, C. (2008b). An interdisciplinary model of school absenteeism in youth to inform professional practice and public policy. *Educational Psychology Review, 20,* 257–82.

Kearney, C., and Albano, A. (2004). The functional profiles of school refusal behaviour: Diagnostic aspects. *Behaviour Modification, 28,* 147–61.

Kearney, C. and Beasley, J. (1994). The clinical treatment of school refusal behaviour: a survey of referral and practice characteristics. *Psychology in the Schools, 31,* 128–32.

Kearney, C. and Bensaheb, A. (2006). School absenteeism and school refusal behaviour: A review and suggestions for school-based health professionals. *Journal of School Health, 76*(1), 3–7.

Kearney, C., Eisen, A., and Silverman, W. (1995). The legend and myth of school phobia. *School Psychology Quarterly, 10*(1), 65–85.

Kearney, C., Lemos, A., and Silverman, J. (2006). School refusal behaviour. In R. Mennuti, A. Freeman, and R. Christner (eds) *Cognitive-behavioural interventions in educational settings: A handbook for practice.* New York: Routledge (pp. 89–106).

Kearney, C. and Silverman, W. (1990). A preliminary analysis of a functional model of assessment and treatment of school refusal behaviour. *Behaviour Modification, 14,* 340–66.

Kearney, C. and Silverman, W. (1993). Measuring the function of school refusal behaviour: The School Refusal Assessment Scale. *Journal of Clinical Child Psychology, 22,* 85–96.

Kearney, C. and Silverman, W. (1995). Family environment of youngsters with school refusal behaviour: A synopsis with implications for assessment and treatment. *American Journal of Family Therapy, 23,* 59–72.

Kearney, A. and Tillotson, C. (1998). School attendance. In D. Watson and M. Gresham (eds) *Handbook of child behaviour therapy.* New York: Plenum Press (pp. 143–61).

King, N. and Bernstein, G. (2001). School refusal in children and adolescents: A review of the past ten years. *Journal of the American Academy of Child and Adolescent Psychiatry, 40*(2), 197–205.

King, N. and Ollendick, T. (1989). School refusal: Graduated and rapid behavioural treatment strategies. *Australian and New Zealand Journal of Psychiatry, 23*(2), 213–23.

King, N. and Ollendick, T. (1997). Annotation: treatment of childhood phobias. *Journal of Child Psychology and Psychiatry, 38*(4), 389–400.

King, N., Tonge, B., Heyne, D., and Ollendick, T. (2000). Research on the cognitive-behavioural treatment of school refusal: A review and recommendations. *Clinical Psychology Review, 20*(4), 495–507.

King, N., Tonge, B., Heyne, D., Young, D., Myerson, N., Rollings, S., Pritchard, M., and Ollendick, T. (1998). Cognitive-behavioural treatment of school refusing children: A controlled evaluation. *Journal of the American Academy of Child and Adolescent Psychiatry, 37*, 375–403.

King, N., Tonge, B., Heyne, D., Turner, S., D., Pritchard, M., and Young, D., Rollings, S., Myerson, N., and Ollendick, T, (2001). Cognitive-behavioural treatment of school refusing children: Maintenance of improvement at 3- to 5-year follow-up. *Scandinavian Journal of Behaviour Therapy, 30*, 85–9.

Lagana, M. (2004). Protective factors for inner-city adolescents at risk of school dropout: Family factors and social support. *Children and Schools, 26*, 211–20.

Last, C., Hansen, M., and Franco, N. (1998). Cognitive-behavioural treatment of school phobia. *Journal of the American Academy of Child and Adolescent Psychiatry, 37*, 404–11.

Lauchlan, F. (2003). Responding to chronic non-attendance: A review of intervention approaches. *Educational Psychology in Practice, 19*(2), 133–46.

Lee, V. and Smith, J. (1999). Social support and achievement for young adolescents in Chicago: The role of school academic press. *American Educational Research Journal, 36*(4), 907–45.

Lyon, A. and Cotler, S. (2007). Toward reduced bias and increased utility in the assessment of school refusal behavior: The case for diverse samples and evaluations of context. *Psychology in the Schools, 44*, 551–65.

McShane, G., Walter, G., and Rey, J. (2001). Characteristics of adolescents with school refusal. *Australian and New Zealand Journal of Psychiatry, 35*, 822–6.

Mortimore, P., Lewis, D., Stoll, L., Sammons, P., and Ecob, R. (1988). *School matters: The junior years*. London: Paul Chapman.

Ollendick, T. and King, N. (1998). Empirically supported treatments for children with phobic and anxiety disorders: Current status. *Journal of Clinical Child Psychology, 27*, 156–67.

Opdenakker, M. and Van Damme, J. (2007). Do school context, student composition and school leadership affect school practice and outcomes in secondary education? *British Educational Research Journal, 33*(2), 179–206.

Paccione-Dyszlewski, M., and Contessa-Kislus, M. (1987). School phobia: Identification of subtypes as a prerequisite to treatment intervention. *Adolescence, 22*, 377–84.

Papanastasiou, C. (2008a). Factors distinguishing most and least effective school in terms of reading achievement: a residual approach. *Educational Research and Evaluation, 14*(6), 539–49.

Papanastasiou, C. (2008b). A residual analysis of effective school and effective teaching in mathematics. *Studies in Educational Evaluation, 34*, 24–30.

Pellegrini, D. (2007). School non-attendance: Definitions, meanings, responses interventions. *Educational Psychology in Practice, 23*(1), 63–77.

Pina, A., Zerr, A., Gonzales, N., and Ortiz, C. D. (2009). Psychosocial interventions for school refusal behaviour in children and adolescents. *Child Development Perspectives, 3*, 11–20.

Reid, K. (1999). *Truancy and schools*. New York: Routledge.

Reynolds, D. (1996). School factors. In I. Berg and J. Nursten (eds) *Unwillingly to school*, 4th edn. London: Gaskell (pp. 38–56).

Rutter, M. and Maughan, B. (2002). School effectiveness findings 1979–2002. *Journal of School Psychology, 40*(6), 451–75.

Smyth, E. (1999). Pupil performance, absenteeism, and school drop-out: A multi-dimensional analysis. *School Effectiveness and School Improvement, 10*, 480–502.

Southwell, N. (2006). Truants on truancy – a badness or a valuable indicator of unmet special educational needs. British Journal of Special Education, *33*(2), 91–7.

Stoll, P. (1990). Absent pupils who are officially present. *Education Today, 4*(3), 22–5.

Toren, P., Sadeh, M., Wolmer, L., Eldar, S., Koren, S., Weizman, R., *et al.* (2000). Neurocognitive correlates of anxiety disorders in children: A preliminary report. *Journal of Anxiety Disorders, 14*, 239.

Tranah, T. and Yule, W. (1997). Treatment strategies in children with anxiety disorders. In J. den Boer (ed.) *Clinical management of anxiety* New York: Marcel Dekker, (pp. 399–420).

Ventis, W. (1973). Case history: The use of laughter as an alternative response in systematic desensitization. *Behavior Therapy, 4*, 120–2.

Waxman, H., Garcia, A., and Read, L. (2008). Classroom learning environment and student motivational differences between exemplary, recognized and acceptable urban middle level schools. *Middle Grades Research Journal, 3*(2), 1–21.

Werry, J. (1996). Psychiatric diagnosis. In I Berg and J. Nursten (eds) *Unwillingly to school*, 4th edn. (pp. 211–27). London: Gaskell.

Woolfson, L., Whaling, R., Stewart, A., and Monsen, J. (2003). An integrated framework to guide educational psychologist practice. *Educational Psychology in Practice, 19*(4), 283–302.

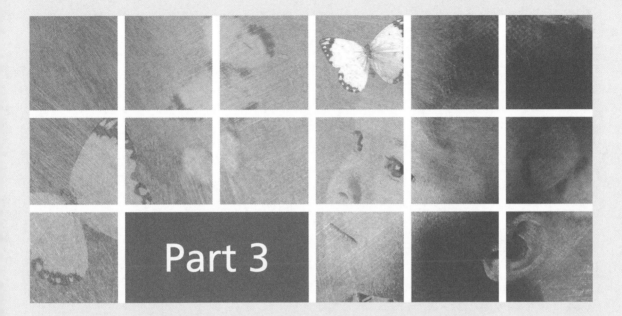

PSYCHOLOGY RESEARCH AT SCHOOL LEVEL

As explained in Part I, I have structured the parts of this book to align with different ecological levels of analysis, using Bronfenbrenner's (1979) social ecological model as an overall conceptual framework. In Part 2 we focused on issues at the level of the classroom microsystem.

In Part 3 our focus now moves outwards from the class subsystem to examine some key topics that tend to be addressed rather at a whole-school level. These are:

- Chapter 7 Improving literacy
- Chapter 8 Bullying
- Chapter 9 Inclusive education of children with special needs.

Reference

Bronfenbrenner, U. (1979). *The ecology of human development*. Cambridge, MA: Harvard University Press.

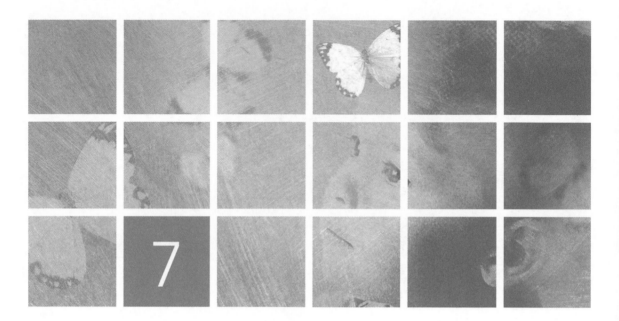

Improving literacy

'Too many cannot read and write' ran a January 2009 BBC News report on the unacceptably high levels of illiteracy in adults. Literacy problems have certainly been shown to be remarkably persistent and to continue not only through the school years but also when followed up 30 years later (Maughan, Messer, Collishaw, Pickles, Snowling, Yule and Rutter, 2009).

Reading is a multifaceted skill made up of a number of underlying sub-skills and knowledge. It does not develop naturally like walking or talking, but instead requires instruction, repetition, and lots of experience of print. Children then need to engage in regular reading activities in order to develop this skill, a skill which our increasingly complex society demands and on which other activities depend. There is, however, a problem with this because the more difficult an activity is, the less children are likely to engage in it regularly. Stanovich (1986) referred to this as the 'Matthew effect in literacy' where good readers get better at reading because of increased exposure to print and poor readers get poorer at reading because they read less. This effect takes its name from the biblical gospel of Matthew, where it was expounded that those who have get more and those who have little get that little taken away.

Frequent reading leads to increased vocabulary, which leads to increased comprehension of reading material and therefore a more efficient, easier and more enjoyable reading experience. This then means we have a reciprocal relationship in which the greater amount of time children spend on reading the better they are at it, and the better they are at it the more they read (e.g. Lonigan, Burgess and Anthony, 2000).

Children who have had rich early educational experiences are able to make better use of subsequent experiences and children who have not, are less able to benefit. Avoiding the 'Matthew effect' argues for the importance of addressing early deficits in the development of reading skills. But what might these deficits and underlying skills be?

Learning outcomes

By the end of this chapter you should be able to:

- Appreciate the role of phonological skills in reading
- Understand the role of rhyme, onset-rime, analogy and phonemic awareness
- Show awareness of the relative strengths of analytic and synthetic phonics
- Show awareness of the range of theories and models that have been used to explain difficulties in reading in general and dyslexia in particular
- Appreciate how classroom effects might influence literacy interventions
- Understand the contribution of parents in promoting literacy.

What do children have to do to learn to read fluently?

1 *Print awareness* Children need to have print awareness, a knowledge of the purposes of print. Through experiences in their daily lives, they learn that print conveys meaning and that it is not only in books, but instead print is all around them, with information that they need day to day. When they are out and about, they see that street signs tell adults when they have arrived in the right place, shop signs provide information about special offers on goods they might want to buy; posters and advertisements tell them about activities in their area; destination information tells the family which train platform to go to, which bus to board or which direction to head in; menus list what to choose to eat; writing on packaging shows which one contains their favourite biscuits; newspapers, magazines, television all provide printed information about what is going on around us locally and in the wider society. Environmental print awareness can be measured by asking children to name logos or signs that they might see in their local environment (Molfese *et al.*, 2006).

2 *Awareness of words* In order to engage with reading, there needs to be understanding of a word as a unit of language as early reading often starts with the assumption that children will learn to recognise familiar words one at a time, and it would be difficult for teachers not to use the word 'word' to teach this (Adams, 1990). If a child does not understand what is meant by 'word' they are already struggling before having even attempted to learn how to read anything at all. Printed word units are signified clearly by the spaces between

words. Exposure to print is likely to be the main way children learn about the word as a unit in language and reading (Ehri, 1976; Lomax and McGee, 1987). Understanding what a word is and learning by sight a vocabulary of common words are part of the task of learning to read.

3 *Awareness of parts of words* Beyond the level of the word, children must understand that the spoken word unit can be further broken down into sound segments, the smallest of which in any particular language are referred to as phonemes (see Glossary). Longitudinal studies carried out in the 1970s provided convincing evidence that awareness of sounds at school start influenced later literacy skills (e.g. Bradley and Bryant, 1983; Bryant and Bradley, 1985; Fox and Routh, 1976; Lundberg, Olofsson and Wall, 1980).

4 *Grapheme–phoneme matching* The task of reading requires being able to pair up a grapheme (a printed letter) with the right phoneme (sound) that it represents. Children therefore have to be aware of the alphabetic system and be able to decode words that they have never seen before.

QUISSET | *Now go beyond the text ... look it up yourself!*

Explore your library's electronic databases to investigate 'models of literacy'.

In the simple outline above of some of the required basics there has been no suggestion of any particular order or sequence. However, many of the activities outlined are very similar to those represented in Lomax and McGee's (1987) model, which does propose a sequence of stages.

● What stages do Lomax and McGee's (1987) model propose?

● What problems might sequential stage models present in their application to real-life situations?

Causal connection theory

Goswami and Bryant's (1990) causal connection theory proposed that three sets of separate but interlinked causal connections need to be in place for children to develop literacy. These are connections:

● between preschool awareness of rhyme and alliteration and later reading

● between instruction about phonemes and phonemic awareness

● between reading and spelling development (reciprocal).

Let's now examine the first of the causal connections in Figure 7.1, the relationship between preschool awareness of rhyme and later reading, as this has been the focus of some debate and has significant implications for how we teach reading to new readers (Goswami, 1999).

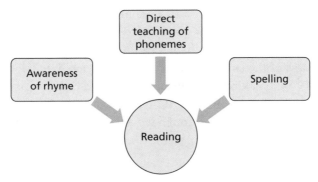

Figure 7.1 Causal connection theory (Goswami and Bryant, 1990)
Source: Goswami and Bryant, 1990, reproduced by permission of Taylor & Frances

The importance of rhyme

Bradley and Bryant (1978, 1983) first showed that awareness of rhyme in pre-schoolers predicted reading and spelling skills. They showed that poor readers lacked this awareness of rhyme compared to younger, age-appropriate readers whose reading was at the same level. The importance of rhyme for reading has been demonstrated since then in a number of studies (see Examples Box).

> **EXAMPLES Studies showing influence of rhyme on reading skills**
>
> 1 Maclean, Bryant and Bradley (1987) assessed knowledge of common nursery rhymes such as 'Humpty Dumpty' and 'Baa, Baa, Black Sheep' in 66 children aged 3 years. They then assessed their progress on pre-reading and then reading tasks every four months. Early familiarity of these nursery rhymes was found to be related to the development of phonological skills and to later reading, but not to the development of arithmetic skills.
>
> 2 In following up the same sample, Bryant, Maclean, Bradley and Crossland (1990) showed that there was a relationship between knowledge of nursery rhymes in these preschool children aged 3 years and their reading and spelling in school at ages 5 and 6 years. IQ and social background factors were controlled for in this study.
>
> 3 In their study of 95 children, Cronin and Carver (1998) found a relationship between rhyme at age 5 years and reading at age 6, when controlling for vocabulary and age.

Onset-rime

Goswami (1999) suggested that the value of rhyme as an early predictor of reading lay in its being an early phonological skill, albeit that understanding of rhyme utilises large segments of sound, but that this may be as fine-tuned to sound segments as a young preschooler can manage. Thus we have here the idea of phonological awareness being on a developmental continuum that starts with knowledge of nursery rhymes, moves to understanding of other large sound units such as syllables, splitting syllables up into *onset* and *rime* (see Glossary), and then to awareness of the smallest sound units, *phonemes* (see Glossary) (Goswami and Bryant, 1990). Breaking a syllable into onset and rime (e.g. s-un) is an easier and more natural task than breaking it into its component *phonemes* (e.g. s-u-n) (Adams, 1990; Treiman, 1985). Children have a natural predisposition to the first while teaching is seen as being required for the latter (Goswami, 1999; Lenneberg, 1967).

Analogy

Children make use of onset-rime skills with the use of analogies in reading. This is where the child reads a word such as *sit* and by using the rime pattern as an analogy, by awareness of similarity is then able to read the word *pit*. Or the child may use the onset as an analogy, so by reading the word *ship*, can also read the word *shut*. Analogy too is seen as a natural strategy that the child brings to the reading task but it is also one that can be developed through teaching (Goswami and Bryant, 1990). Teachers should first present to beginning readers words with large 'rime neighbourhoods' as these are easier for them to learn (Leslie and Calhoon, 1995). The rime neighbourhood refers to the number of words that end with the same rime so where there are lots of words with the same rime, i.e. a large 'rime neighbourhood', then a child who can read one of these, *shop*, can by analogy read them all, *drop, mop, pop, top*. . . . It seems also that the larger the child's reading vocabulary, the better use she can make of analogy, as she has more words on which to base these analogies (Duncan, Seymour and Hill, 1997; Goswami, 1986).

QUISSET   *Now go beyond the text . . . look it up yourself!*

Explore your library's electronic databases to investigate 'analogy in reading'.

Goswami and Bryant (1990) proposed that children are naturally predisposed to analogy and that they bring this with them to the task of learning to read, so

- what is the evidence then that early readers use analogy as Goswami and Bryant claim?

Also, if children can make use of analogy to help them read new words with the same rime pattern as a familiar word, does this have practical implications for teaching, i.e.

- what is the evidence that training in analogy improves reading skills?

Phonemic awareness

As early as the 1960s, Bond and Dykstra (1967) reported the finding that the ability to discriminate phonemes was an important predictor of reading development in early readers. Phonemic awareness has been studied in a number of different ways:

Phonemic segmentation tasks

Phonemic segmentation refers to how well children can break up a syllable into its component phonemes. Liberman, Shankweiler, Fischer and Carter (1974), for example, carried out a tapping task where children were asked to tap with a stick on the table to indicate the number of phonemes in a word, e.g. for cat they should tap three times, one each for /c/, /a/, and /t/. Performance on the tapping task was found to be related to children's later reading performance on the Wide Range Achievement Test (Liberman, Shankweiler, Liberman, Fowler and Fischer, 1977). Nation and Hulme (1997) asked children in the early school years to segment a single syllable non-word into phonemes, e.g. /gat/ into /g/ /a/ /t/. Their performance on this task was found to be a significant predictor of reading ability as measured on the British Ability Scales Word Reading Test.

Phonemic manipulation

Phonemic manipulation tasks involve the child having to carry out operations on words or syllables at the level of the phoneme typically involving the addition or deletion of phonemes.

- **Phoneme deletion task.** Muter *et al.* (1998) used a phoneme deletion task in which they showed children a picture of, for example, a bus. They then asked children to say the word deleting the initial phoneme, i.e. 'bus' without the /b/ says...., 'us' being the correct response with the phoneme /b/ deleted. Phoneme deletion can also involve deleting the end phoneme, rather than the initial phoneme, i.e. 'bus' without the /s/ says...., 'bu' being the correct response. Muter, Hulme, Snowling and Stevenson (2004) found these two types of deletion tasks were correlated with each other, suggesting a common underlying difficulty in phoneme deletion. Phoneme deletion has emerged as a key skill for development of reading; Muter and Snowling (1998) found that phoneme deletion was one of the best long-term predictors of reading both in the short term at school start and longitudinally at age 9. Indeed they found it to be an even better predictor than rhyming ability.

- **Phoneme addition task.** The opposite activity may also be carried out where a phoneme is to be added to a syllable (instead of deleted) to make a new word (Morais, 1991). Illiterate adults struggled with phoneme addition compared to literate adults (Morais, Gary, Alegria and Bertelson, 1979), suggesting an important relationship between this phonemic manipulation task and literacy.

- **Spoonerisms.** Children have to swap round the initial phonemes of two words, e.g. 'bones and joint' would be 'jones and boint'. Older children who had difficulties with this phonemic manipulation task were poor at spelling (Perin, 1983).

These studies suggest that in the early stages of pre-reading and reading, it is important to draw children's attention to phonemic segments in speech. They need this awareness that words are made up of individual sounds to be able later to learn to map these individual sounds to printed words as required for developing reading skills.

Relationship between onset-rime and phoneme awareness

While many children arrive at school with some knowledge of some nursery rhymes and some awareness of rime, their awareness of phonemes is limited: this pattern changes in the early school years due to direct teaching of phonemes (Goswami and Bryant, 1990). Sensitivity to rhyme is associated with sensitivity to phonemes, and to ease of tackling grapheme–phoneme correspondence, suggesting a continuum of phonological awareness in reading. Goswami (1999) proposed then that the first causal connection in Figure 7.1, knowing nursery rhymes, might impact on reading in two ways.

These two routes are shown in Figure 7.2. Firstly children might use rhyme and analogy to make use of the patterns of letter strings that are repeated in English as already described. Using this method they recognise groups of words that share the same rimes and can all be read and spelled in the same way. The second connection between rhyme and reading as shown on the right-hand side of Figure 7.2 addresses the relationship between rhyme awareness and phoneme awareness, suggesting that those children who are aware of rhyme will be more responsive to learning about phonemes and their better-developed phoneme awareness will contribute to their development of reading skills.

Some studies have provided evidence questioning the importance of onset-rime relative to phonemic awareness and indeed have shown phoneme skills to be better predictors of early reading than onset-rime skills (e.g. Muter *et al.*, 2004; Muter, Hulme, Snowling and Taylor, 1998; Nation and Hulme, 1997). Goswami (1999) argued, however, that Goswami and Bryant's (1990) model of causal connections did not suggest that children should be taught onset and rime *instead* **of** phonemes, but rather argued that teaching should include both onset-rime and

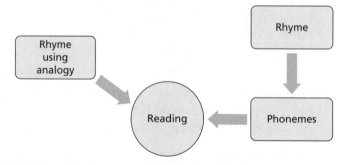

Figure 7.2 **Relationships between rhyme and reading** (Based on Goswami, 1999)

grapheme–phoneme relationships. Awareness of large syllable sound segments and rime awareness was shown to predict later phoneme awareness in preschool children (Carroll, Snowling, Hulme and Stevenson, 2003). This suggests a developmental progression from awareness of large sound units to small phoneme units. Carroll *et al.*'s study also provided evidence that onset-rime and phoneme awareness are distinct skills.

The nature of the relationship between awareness of phonemes and reading is not clear-cut, though. It may be that phonemic awareness has a direct causal influence on word recognition skills (Muter *et al.*, 2004). Causality could, however, perhaps operate in the opposite direction with children developing phonemic understanding once they have acquired knowledge of letters or begun to recognise words (e.g. Read, Zhang, Nie and Ding, 1986). Or, more likely, the relationship between phonemic awareness and word recognition may be a reciprocal one in which each influences the other (Burgess and Lonigan, 1998; Muter *et al.*, 2004).

 Debate

Join up with some friends to discuss.

Discuss the evidence presented in Nation and Hume's (1997) paper that 'phonic segmentation is a better predictor of reading than onset-rime segmentation'. Bring in arguments from your wider reading to support your case.

How best to teach phonics

A phonics intervention has the purpose of directing children's attention to the relationship between letters and sounds and as such will have some overlap with teaching designed to develop phonemic awareness as both phonics and phonemics deal with phoneme segmentation and blending of letters to read and spell words (Ehri *et al.*, 2001). There is now a large body of evidence on the importance of phonological skills in teaching children to read (e.g. Rack, Hulme and Snowling, 1993). Furthermore, the systematic teaching of phonics has been found to be more effective than less direct methods. Ehri, Nunes, Stahl and Willows (2001) found this in a study commissioned by US Congress to review which of the available reading approaches were most effective for teaching reading. They carried out a meta-analysis of 38 studies that compared systematic phonics with indirectly teaching phonics (unsystematic), or not teaching it at all. For inclusion in Ehri *et al.*'s study these had to be interventions that were actually used in schools, rather than laboratory-based studies that investigated a single aspect of phonology training. Another US review was carried out by Camilli, Vargas and Yurecko (2003), who began their analysis with the same 38 studies as Ehri *et al.* but added three more which met their meta-analysis inclusion criteria, and deleted one which did not because closer examination revealed there was no comparison group. Their results also found effects for systematic phonics, although Camilli *et al.*

argued that those developing reading policy should not infer that phonics alone was sufficient as their analysis indicated that language activities and individual tutoring were also important influences on reading outcomes. Torgerson, Brooks and Hall (2006) reported similar findings in a systematic UK review of 20 randomised controlled trials, of which only one study, Johnston and Watson (2004) took place in the UK. We will return to this study shortly.

Phonics intervention also covers practising reading skills using sound units larger than phonemes including units as large as words. Knowing that systematic phonics instruction is recommended still leaves a major question to be addressed in translating this research into policy and practice in the classroom. What form should this systematic teaching take? Analytic and synthetic phonics are two key methods that have been used in classrooms (see Table 7.1).

As can be seen from Table 7.1, analytic phonics uses the analysis of sounds in whole words to learn about phonemes, while synthetic phonics works in the opposite direction synthesising from phoneme part to whole word. In terms of Goswami and Bryant's (1990) causal connection theory, analytic phonics is often seen as mainly utilising rhyme and analogy, while synthetic phonics is perceived as emphasising the teaching of phonemes. However, the reading approaches that schools use are often hybrids of these, and indeed analytic and synthetic phonics

Table 7.1 **Methods of teaching phonics**

Method	*Description*
Analytic phonics	Whole-word recognition is encouraged for beginning readers using a graded reading book. This is the look-and-say approach to learning to read. The aim is to help children develop a reading vocabulary, and to use analogy to read new words by recognising word-family patterns from known words. Children can then infer new words from the onset-rime patterns of known words, without having to sound each phoneme separately. Initial sounds are usually introduced next, after children have achieved a sizeable whole-word vocabulary. Children learn one initial sound at a time, e.g. /c/, by teaching them words that begin with that initial sound, e.g. cat, cup, car. They will then learn final sounds in the same way, e.g. /t/, as in hat, met, pot, and similarly with middle sounds. New sounds are typically taught at the pace of one per week. Children learn about sounds using whole words.
Synthetic phonics	Emphasis here is on sounding and blending to build up parts (phonemes) into whole words. Children learn to decode graphemes into phonemes and to blend these phonemes to make words. Sets of common sounds (e.g. /a/, /i/, /p/, /n/, /s/, /t/) which together make up a large number of three-letter words (pan, tin, sat, etc.) may be taught together. This is likely to take place even before children are given books. Children also use magnetic letters to help them learn how to blend individual sounds into words.

Source: Adapted using data from Ehri *et al.*, 2001 and Johnston and Watson, 2005

may be considered as lying on a continuum of phonic activities from the analytic to the synthetic, rather than being completely different approaches to reading (Ehri et al., 2001, Johnstone and Watson, 2005).

How should schools interpret the research evidence to decide which approach they should use in the teaching of reading? Recent US and Australian government-commissioned reviews of the evidence addressed these questions for teachers in their respective countries and each concluded that systematic phonics produced better results than indirect methods, recommending teachers to implement systematic teaching of phonics as a central element in their teaching of reading. An English review, the Rose Report (Rose, 2006), however, went further in recommending systematic phonics in particular as the method of teaching phonics. As we discussed in Chapter 3, randomised controlled trials (RCTs) and meta-analyses are the most compelling sources of evidence for attributing outcomes to specific interventions. While there are a number of studies that have compared analytic and synthetic phonics (e.g. Hatcher, Hulme and Snowling, 2004; O'Shaughnessy and Swanson, 2000; Savage and Carless, 2005; Walton, Walton and Felton, 2001), only modest differences in effect sizes have been reported and most of these studies did not use RCT methodology (Savage, Abrami, Hipps and Deault, 2009). Similarly Torgerson et al.'s (2006) review for the Department for Education and Skills in England found only three studies that used RCTs to compare analytic and synthetic phonics which did not provide them with sufficient evidence to conclude which method was better. Wyse and Goswami (2008) also concluded that the evidence for the superiority of synthetic phonics is not currently available.

More recently, Savage et al. (2009) further added an RCT study to this literature although in this study both these analytic and synthetic phonics programmes were delivered by a computer programme ABRACADABRA to examine whether computer-based technology might be effective in the development of literacy skills. In this study, 144 children who had just started school were taught for 20 minutes a day for four days a week for 12 weeks. In the intervention groups, four children worked together with a single computer, while the control-group children worked on literacy in their usual classroom setting. The results of the study showed that both interventions had a significant effect on literacy measures both immediately and seven months after the intervention had finished. At immediate post-test, letter awareness had improved in the analytic phonics programme and phonological awareness, listening comprehension and reading comprehension in the synthetic phonics programme. At the delayed post-test, effects of the synthetic phonics programme (increased phonological awareness and reading fluency) were maintained. Savage et al. concluded the effect sizes of the two methods were similar, with each method having different strengths in terms of specific literacy sub-skills. Currently it seems that neither RCTs nor meta-analyses can offer strong evidence in favour of synthetic over analytic phonics.

IN FOCUS

The Clackmannanshire studies

In the UK the work of Johnstone and Watson was influential in persuading educators of the benefits of synthetic phonics. These studies were considered in the Rose Report that advocated synthetic phonics.

Johnstone and Watson carried out a series of studies comparing analytic and synthetic phonics in Clackmannanshire in Scotland. They focused on 300 children in their first year of schooling and their progress was regularly followed up and reported on the Scottish government website (Johnstone and Watson, 2003, 2005; Watson and Johnstone, 1998) and in a peer-reviewed journal (Johnstone and Watson, 2004). The study comprised three groups, synthetic phonics, a typical analytic phonics group which was the standard teaching method in Scottish schools at study start, and a third analytic phonics + phonological awareness group. Children in the study received 16 weeks of 20 minutes' training each day. Watson and Johnstone (1998) initially reported that the synthetic phonics group was reading seven months ahead of the other two groups and ahead of their chronological age, and were spelling eight to nine months ahead. This group also read irregular words better and could read previously unseen words by analogy. By the end of their primary schooling, with 95 boys and 84 girls still in the sample they reported that the group, now in Primary 7, were now reading three years six months ahead of their chronological age and spelling one year nine months ahead.

? Debate

Join up with some friends to discuss.

Read the reports by Johnstone and Watson on the Clackmannanshire studies. Consider the arguments presented by Wyse and Goswami (2008). Argue the case for and against the superiority of synthetic phonics.

Phonological linkage theory (Hatcher, Hulme and Ellis, 1994)

In considering the overwhelming evidence base of the relationship between phonological awareness skills and later reading development, Hatcher, Hulme and Ellis (1994) proposed that it might not be training in phonological skills alone that was most effective but instead phonological training linked explicitly with reading experiences. Hatcher *et al.* called this the phonological linkage hypothesis and tested it out in an experimental study that assigned children who were experiencing difficulties in reading to three different intervention programmes:

- Reading only
- Phonological training only
- Phonological training linked with reading.

A fourth group was assigned as a control group.

Hatcher *et al.* found that only the phonology with reading group showed consistently larger improvements than the control group on each of the reading measures used and this improvement was still maintained over the longer term when the children were followed up again nine months later. While the phonological-only group made significant improvements in their phonological skills, they did not improve more than the controls in learning to read, suggesting that phonology only is less effective than phonology explicitly linked with reading. Furthermore Hatcher *et al.*'s study showed that the intervention effects were specific to reading as the children did not similarly improve in their arithmetic skills, suggesting that it was the phonology + reading approach itself that was effective for reading, rather than teacher enthusiasm and motivation for a new teaching method having a generally enhancing effect on all class activity. In a later study, Hatcher, Hulme and Snowling (2004), however, found no benefits for the phonological linkage group over the other groups when this intervention was extended to whole classes of children who were just beginning to learn to read, rather than the older (7-year-old) weaker readers in the Hatcher *et al.* (1994) study.

IN FOCUS

Hatcher, Hulme and Ellis (1994) study

The study compared four groups of 7-year-olds who had been identified as poor readers through a county-wide screening process. There were three intervention groups which each received 40-half hour sessions over 20 weeks with a teacher who had been specially trained for the purpose. There were 32 children in each group.

1 *Phononological training only* This condition consisted of recognising rhyming words, identifying words as units in sentences, manipulating syllables, identifying sounds in words, building up sounds into words, deleting and substituting sounds in words.

2 *Phonological training linked with reading* This group used a modified version of Clay's (1985) teaching methods with phonological training added as described above. They had less phonological training than the phonology-only group because their programme time was taken up with activities linking reading and phonology which derived from individualised issues arising from the children's own reading and writing activities. Reading from easy books and graded reading programmes was combined with phonological awareness training for this group. Phonological linkage activities included practising letter–sound associations, using plastic letters to relate spelling to sounds, and writing out words paying attention to letter-sound associations.

3 The *reading only* group experienced the same intervention but without any explicit phonology teaching or phonological linkage activities.

4 The *control group* received their regular classroom teaching and additional support.

While both groups that received phonological training improved on phonological skills only, it was only the phonological training linked with reading group that showed improved progress on reading measures. This study showed that for poor readers, phonological skills interventions were most effective in improving reading if they were integrated into the teaching of reading rather than delivered separately.

A further study then compared the sound-linkage reading intervention with the *Early Literacy Support* (ELS) programme which was the National Literacy strategy devised by the Department for Education and Skills for children who were slow in developing reading skills, (DfES, 2001) (Hatcher, Götz, Snowling, Hulme, Gibbs and Smith, 2006). The ELS intervention was similar in literacy content to the reading intervention (RI) that had been evaluated by Hatcher *et al.* (1994) as described, with both making use of phonological linkage strategies. RI, however, also involved tailored, individual work, and was thus a more expensive and time-consuming intervention than ELS. Study participants were children with reading difficulties in their second year of school. Children in both groups showed equivalent gains in spelling and reading, placing them at the average level of reading for their age, with effects maintained at follow-up.

Because there was no control group in the above study, limiting the conclusions that could be drawn, Hatcher, Hulme, Miles, Carroll, Hatcher, Gibbs *et al.* (2006) devised an RCT study. They adapted RI so that it comprised both one-to-one reading with a teaching assistant and also group phonological training, with children working on letter identification, phoneme awareness, and phonological linkage exercises. Seventy-seven children, identified as being in the bottom 8% for reading development from 14 schools, took part in the intervention. One group received the RI for two 10-week sessions, while the other group only received it for the second 10-week block. The intervention group made more progress than the control group on letter knowledge, single-word reading and phoneme awareness after the first block. By the end of the second block, however, the children who had been in the control group for the first block who only received 10 weeks of intervention had effectively reached the same level of reading attainment as the group who had been in the intervention for 20 weeks, suggesting the possibility of a 'plateau' effect in the first group after 10 weeks. In addition the results demonstrated that teaching assistants could deliver an effective daily intervention to improve the performance of struggling readers. Nonetheless there still remained a group of children who required more intensive tuition than this to show improvements in literacy.

Bowyer-Crane, Snowling, Duff, Fieldsend, Carroll, Miles *et al.* (2008) reported similar findings with 4-year-olds who had difficulties in vocabulary and verbal reasoning. They compared a phonology + reading (P+R) intervention with an Oral Language (OL) intervention, which contained vocabulary and comprehension activities. P+R was again found to be more successful in improving scores on literacy and phonological measures, while OL was more effective in improving vocabulary and grammar abilities. Post-intervention though, more than half of the children had still not reached age-appropriate levels in literacy.

Because of this continuing problem of children who fail to respond to intervention, Duff, Fieldsend, Bowyer-Crane, Hulme, Smith, Gibbs and Snowling (2008) investigated further twelve 8-year-old children who had previously responded poorly to the RI intervention implemented by Hatcher, Hulme *et al.* (2006). This further nine-week intervention was delivered on a one-to-one basis by specially trained teaching assistants. It comprised two 15-minute sessions, the first of which included reading, vocabulary instruction, and writing, and the second of which was adapted from RI and contained phonological training linked to the target vocabulary where possible. Post-intervention these children showed improvements in measures of reading, phonological awareness and language skills, which were maintained at six-month follow-up although were still mostly below chronological age. This study provided further evidence that trained non-professionals can aid in literacy development activities, which is cost-effective for schools.

 Debate

Join up with some friends to discuss.

Discuss the evidence presented by Hulme and colleagues on interventions building on the phonological linkage hypothesis.

- How convincing is the research evidence on the effectiveness of RI?
- How convincing is the research evidence on non-teachers delivering literacy training?

A note of caution

It should be noted that the aspect of reading that we are focusing on in this chapter is word recognition. Reading comprehension skills are, however, also required for developing fluency in reading. It is through comprehension skills that children reflect on what they have read, relate it to their experience, make inferences about implied meanings, and interpret the text in order to abstract from it what the author's overall message is. This involves different, non-phonological, language-based skills compared to word-by-word reading and assumes greater importance during the middle primary school years by which time it is hoped that basic decoding skills are established. Reading comprehension skills are not addressed here. We are focusing only on how to help early readers establish word recognition.

Developmental dyslexia

We can see from the above that there are clearly significant individual differences in how children learn to read, and that some children experience significant and enduring problems in this, despite receiving considerable instruction in literacy skills. The British Psychological Society (BPS, 1999) defined dyslexia as severe and persistent reading difficulties in spite of the provision of appropriate learning opportunities. You should note that many view this as a controversial definition because it does not distinguish dyslexics from other poor readers.

Other definitions of dyslexia, however, view dyslexia as a specific learning difficulty that is unexpected in relation to an individual's other cognitive abilities and attainments (Lyon, Shaywitz and Shaywitz, 2003; Snowling, 2000). This is often referred to as a *discrepancy* model, because dyslexia is perceived as occurring when there is a discrepancy between the child's actual reading ability and his expected reading ability as predicted by tests of cognitive ability. A discrepancy definition is often used in research as it allows tighter specification of the study sample as those who have no neurological, sensory or learning difficulties other than a specific reading difficulty. Within the UK, however, practitioner educational psychologists may use the BPS definition in which classroom interventions target literacy difficulties experienced by children irrespective of their IQ level or the extent to which they may also have problems in other areas of learning.

For a majority of dyslexic children, their reading difficulty primarily manifests itself as a core phonological deficit with difficulty in reading non-words, i.e. nonsense words, alongside better skills at reading familiar, exception words (see Glossary at end of chapter) (Frith, 1997; Snowling, 2000). Even so, most researchers acknowledge that reading is such a complex task that it is probable that reading disorders must be similarly complex and are unlikely to present in only one form with a unitary profile of impairment (Castles, Datta, Gayan and Olson, 1999). As a result there have been attempts to categorise dyslexic difficulties into different subtypes.

Phonological v surface dyslexia

Research with adult brain-damaged patients found that while some patients indeed presented with *phonological dyslexia* as described above, others with *surface dyslexia* could no longer read words that they had once known well but were still able to sound out words using phonic skills. Castles and Coltheart (1993) used regression methods to identify these subtypes in dyslexic children, finding 55% phonological and 30% surface subtypes. This study was devised to provide support for dual-route models of reading which propose that there are two separate strategies that children use to read. One route is a direct, visual, lexical strategy which they can use to read words that are already familiar to them from their sight vocabulary. The other route is non-lexical and requires the application of phonological grapheme–phoneme correspondence rules to read unfamiliar words. Both these routes must be accessible to the child for successful reading. Conversely, if these are two separate systems then they would develop separately and there would therefore also be two distinct patterns of reading disorder evident, one pattern for each system (Castles and Coltheart, 1993). The phonological subtype would have problems with the phonological route and the surface subtype would have problems with the visual, lexical route.

Supporting evidence for these subtypes has been found in other studies (e.g. Castles *et al.*, 1999; Manis, Seidenberg, Doi, McBride-Chang and Peterson, 1996; Rapcsak, Henry, Teague, Carnahan and Beeson, 2007), although studies using reading-age-matched controls rather than chronological age-matched controls have reported reduced incidence of surface subtypes. This leads us to the conclusion that surface dyslexia may be caused by a *delay* in reading development perhaps due to lack of experience of print, while phonological dyslexia is due to a reading *disorder* (Manis *et al.*, 1996; Stanovich, Siegel and Gottardo, 1997). The suggestion that the surface subtype may not be a distinct subtype has, however, been challenged by McDougall, Borowsky, Mackinnon and Hymel (2005), who employed a different subtyping procedure and did indeed find children who displayed pure surface dyslexia.

QUISSET   *Now go beyond the text ... look it up yourself!*

Explore your library's electronic databases to investigate 'phonological and surface dyslexia subtypes'.

Compare the methodology used in Castles and Colheart (1993), Manis *et al.* (1996), and Castles *et al.* (1999) for classifying readers into phonological and surface subtypes.

● What are the differences between their approaches?

In any case, we can see that the majority of dyslexic children do not readily fall into one or other of these categories but rather constitute a mixed subtype (Snowling, 2000). Indeed the incidence reported above for Castle and Coltheart's (1993) subtyping study used 'soft' subtypes where children had difficulties outside the normal range for both nonword and exception word reading from sight vocabulary, but more so for one of the two component skills, from which the 'soft' subtyping classification was then derived.

Models of reading that help explain mixed dyslexia subtypes

Connectionist models

Our interest is with children who are learning to develop reading skills. One cannot necessarily infer from a model of skilled reading, though, how reading develops to that point of skillfulness (Plaut, McClelland, Seidenberg and Patterson, 1996). Furthermore, the dual-route model was based on studies of acquired dyslexia in adults; the same principles may not apply to developmental dyslexia. Another issue to be addressed is whether two mechanisms are actually required for learning to read as proposed by the dual-route model or whether a single mechanism can better explain the development of reading (Ehri, 1995; Seidenberg and McClelland, 1989).

KEY CONCEPTS

- **Acquired dyslexia** is a reading difficulty that has been acquired due to brain damage in an individual who had learned to read.
- **Developmental dyslexia** refers to where children experience difficulties in acquiring reading skills in the first place.

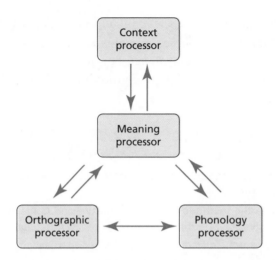

Figure 7.3 **Connectionist model** (Based on Seidenberg and McClelland, 1989)

We use connectionist models, which are also referred to as *Parallel Distributed Processing (PDP)* models, to help explain the development of other cognitive skills including language acquisition and production as well as reading. These are computer models that simulate how humans would behave under conditions predetermined by a particular theoretical formulation of the underlying processes. With respect to reading, a connectionist model (see Figure 7.3) is not then the strategy that a reader consciously adopts in learning to read, but is a computer simulation of the processes that might be involved.

Seidenberg and McClelland's (1989) connectionist model shows how a unified phonological-processing mechanism that is lexically based might evolve through experience with print. We can see from this that reading a word is based not just on processing its visual appearance (orthography), but also coordinating this with processing the sounds that make up the word (phonology) as well as its meaning (semantics).

The connectionist model does not view these as separate systems, but instead as highly interactive processes. The orthographic visual processor is the first part of the system and the only part to receive input directly from the printed word on the page. The word's visual image then sends signals to units in the meaning processor which sends back signals relating to which meanings might be appropriate. The semantic processor also sends signals to, and receives them from, the context processor to help ensure the word selected is appropriate to the context of the sentence. The arrows that run between the orthographic and phonological processors indicate that as the word's string of letters is being processed visually by the orthographic processor, signals are also being sent to the phonological processor which is also connected to the meaning processor. This means that activating the sounds and pronunciation of the word activates its meaning, and vice versa – activating its meaning activates the phonological units that specify how to pronounce that word. Both the orthographic and phonological processors receive input from outside the system, but while the orthographic receives information from the printed page, the phonological processor receives its external information from speech. The connectionist model then assumes that reading knowledge is built up by associations between these elements, learned through experience.

While the model can simulate, and therefore offer an explanation to us, as to why words that are encountered more frequently are recognised and read more quickly, it should be noted that children's learning of associations in reading in real life does not actually take place in the same way as in the model (Plaut *et al.*, 1996). Connectionist models provide a way of testing out our hypotheses about reading processes and allow us to simulate the building up of associations to help us understand how children may similarly learn these associations. The ultimate goal of connectionist modelling is to develop an integrated theory of reading and the underlying brain systems (Seidenberg, 2005). Magnetic resonance imaging and electroencephalogram studies have used scans to compare the brain structure and brain activity of dyslexics with those who do not have dyslexia and have provided evidence for the connectionist perspective assumption that a single unified mechanism underlies dyslexia (Grigorenko, 2001). We shall return to these studies in Chapter 12 when we examine the application of neuroscience research to education.

QUISSET *Now go beyond the text… look it up yourself!*

Explore your library's electronic databases to investigate 'connectionist modelling'.

Search for papers that critique connectionist models, e.g. Powell, Plaut and Funnell (2006).

- What differences are there between reading as simulated by connectionist models and how children actually learn to read?

Dual-route cascaded model

The dual-route cascaded model (DRC) (Coltheart, Rastle, Perry, Langdon and Ziegler, 2001) was a later version of the dual-route model that was influenced by connectionist models but which still has the two routes (lexical and non-lexical) as for the original dual-route model. The DRC, however, makes greater use than the dual-route model of feedback loops that direct our attention to interactions between the different systems. For example, in a study with French dyslexic children, Ziegler, Castel, Pech-Georgel, George, Alario and Perry (2008) were able to use the DRC to go beyond the single deficit explanation that is typically used to explain developmental dyslexia, e.g. a phonological deficit, to find evidence of heterogeneity. They investigated processes within the four interactive levels of the DRC model: the letter units, the orthographic lexicon, phonological lexicon, and the phoneme system. Children in their sample showed combinations of deficits in

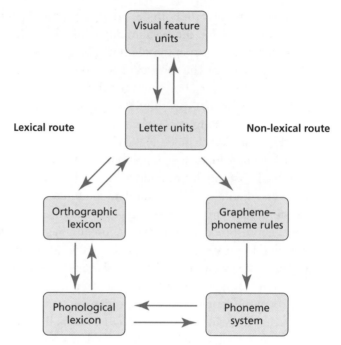

Figure 7.4 Dual-route cascaded model

Source: Coltheart *et al*., 2001, published by the American Psychological Association (APA), adapted with permission

these core components of the reading system that predicted success and failure in reading. It should be noted, though, that most of the dyslexics in the sample did indeed show phonological deficits, as well as other deficits.

In addition to the theoretical explanations presented above, there are other research streams that have generated evidence for explanations that suggest there may be other dyslexia subtypes linked to impaired functioning in different regions of the brain. Possible subtypes include magnocellular (Stein, 2001), cerebellar (Nicolson and Fawcett, 2008), short-term memory (Kibby, in press). It should be noted that these each still acknowledge a core phonological deficit. For an outline see the Key Concepts box.

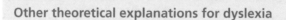

KEY CONCEPTS

Other theoretical explanations for dyslexia

1 **The magnocellular hypothesis** proposes that dyslexic difficulties are caused by problems in the visual magnocellular pathway. This work focuses on the visual aspects of dyslexia rather than on language, and offers evidence that, for example, binocular fixation is unstable in dyslexic children. This means that when they are reading, letters in a word may seem as if they are moving around and crossing over each other. Having dyslexic readers use only the right eye by occluding the left one with a patch has been shown to result in improved reading performance (e.g. Stein, Richardson

and Fowler, 2000), to the extent that children caught up with the reading age of their peers compared with a control group who remained two years behind their chronological age (Stein, 2001).

2 **Cerebellar deficit hypothesis** proposes that dyslexic children have difficulties in the automatisation of skills so that reading cannot take place without making a conscious effort. This difficulty in performing skills in an automatic way was noted by Nicolson and Fawcett (1995) when they observed that dyslexic children wobbled if they were distracted in a balancing task. This suggested that they required to compensate actively in order to maintain balance and more importantly that they struggled to perform this automatically. These automatisation deficits, and therefore the core phonological deficit, are thought to be caused by a cerebellar abnormality. The implication for intervention is to retrain the cerebellum by balance exercises. These then should not only improve automatic motor skills but also improve cognitive skills and literacy. There is mixed evidence as to the effectiveness of this intervention approach which is also proposed to benefit children with dyspraxia and attentional problems (Rack, Snowling, Hulme and Gibbs, 2007; Reynolds and Nicolson, 2007).

3 **Working memory deficit** There is general agreement that phonological impairments underlie dyslexia. The issue for researchers then may be to determine the nature of this phonological deficit. In relation to this challenge, much of what has been discussed earlier in this chapter pertains to the development of phonological awareness skills. Although it may not contribute as strongly to word reading difficulties as does phonological awareness (Bowey, Cain and Ryan, 1992), there has also been a considerable research focus on the role of phonological processing in dyslexia, and in particular the component known as phonological short-term memory. Children with dyslexia are thought to have verbal short-term memory difficulties with nonsense word reading (van Ijzendoorn and Bus, 1994) and also in repeating nonsense words verbally (Snowling, Goulandris, Bowlby and Howell, 1986). Underlying difficulties in temporal processing of auditory stimuli may contribute with dyslexic children possibly needing more time to discriminate sounds and remember phonologically complex words (Tallal, Miller, Jenkins and Merzenich,1997). The primary memory deficit for children with dyslexia seems to be restricted to phonological short-term memory with their visual short-term memory and long-term memory both similar to controls (Kibby, in press). As well as for reading, studies with typically developing children suggest that phonological memory skills may also be needed for learning new vocabulary (Gathercole, Hitch, Service and Martin, 1997).

? Debate

Join up with some friends to discuss.

After considering the different theoretical models and their supporting evidence, discuss the following question: Is dyslexia a unitary syndrome?

Tackling literacy is usually addressed at a whole-school level, with schools developing a literacy policy that applies to all teachers and classes in the school in order to inform their teaching, not only of reading, which we have focused on so far, but also writing and spelling. While we would certainly infer, from the research presented in this chapter, that activities to develop phonological skills would form a central part in such a policy, another question we might ask is: What is the influence of classroom and teacher factors on literacy? If a good intervention programme is in place, does little else matter?

Classroom effects and literacy

Factors at the level of the classroom do indeed have an influence. It's not just which intervention is carried out, but how it is carried out in the individual classroom, that has an influence. Both the amount of time allocated to activities and teacher effectiveness are important factors in determining reading outcomes (Connor, Morrison and Underwood, 2007; Foorman, Schatschneider, Eakin, Fletcher, Moates and Francis, 2006). Cameron, Connor, Morrison and Jewkes (2008) found higher reading scores where teachers had initially spent time on classroom organisation. This suggests that teachers should establish an orderly, well-organised classroom as early as possible with their classes and, having done this, can then devote their class time more productively to reading and other academic intervention activities. Perhaps also those pupils who understand classroom procedures for learning early ontake greater responsibility for their own learning. It is also possible that teachers who have an organised classroom from the outset may be more effective teachers overall.

The issue of how well teachers actually take on board the implementation of intervention programmes may be a crucial one. When Connor, Piasta, Fishman, Glasney, Schatschneider, Crowe *et al.* (2009) set out to test the efficacy of individualised instruction, they indeed found that the individualised intervention improved children's literacy. More importantly, though, they found that the more closely the teacher followed the intervention programme, the larger were the treatment gains for the children. It is not then simply sufficient for teachers to be implementing a programme – it is thorough implementation of the programme that may be important here, i.e. implementation fidelity.

Parents and child literacy

Addressing literacy is not just down to schools, however. Parents have an important role to play in promoting an interest in literacy and in actively supporting their children in their attempts to learn to read. Myrberg and Rosén (2009) found that children's literacy levels varied according to parent level of education. As well as this direct effect of parent education level on reading, their results indicated an indirect effect that was mediated by, for example, the number of books at home, and early literacy activities undertaken in the home which supported previous findings (e.g. White, 1982). They suggested that these early parent–child activities can result in expectations and values about literacy being transmitted through which young children perceive themselves as readers before they are actually able to read, and which then can encourage further development of reading skills.

So what kind of reading activities can parents engage in with their children? Just reading with them may not be sufficient. Activities directed at helping children actually understand print conventions are important. Direct parental coaching on letter names and sounds was found to be related to the development of reading, rather than just parent–child reading (Evans, Shaw and Bell, 2000; Levy, Gong, Hessels, Evans and Jared, 2006). Print convention activities make children aware, for example, that a scribble is not a word; that a word has to have letters all in a line, oriented in a particular direction, not upside-down or backwards; a word needs to have vowels and a variety of letters rather than the same letter repeated. Reading books with their children should not then be a passive activity for parents. To impact on their children's reading skills, parents need to actively direct their child's attention towards these specific elements of print.

Further support for the importance of active direction from parents in reading with their children came from a study with an electronic storybook (Gong and Levy, 2009). Ninety-six kindergarten children were assigned to one of four groups:

- In Group 1 the book was read passively just as a parent might normally read a story to their child.

- In Group 2 a bouncing ball followed every word to focus the child's attention on the word that was being read.

- In Group 3 the bouncing ball would occasionally stop when it can across an unreadable word, the voice would say 'Oh-oh' before the word was corrected by the computer and the corrected version read by the voice.

- In Group 4 the procedure was the same as for Group 3, except that the children themselves had to click the computer mouse to make the correction for the unreadable word, before the voice would continue.

Children were tested on reading ability and print knowledge before the week in which the e-book reading took place. After the intervention, reading ability was significantly better in Groups 2, 3 and 4, where the child's attention had been drawn to the word–sound correspondence. The Levy *et al.* and Gong and Levy studies further highlight that while phonological awareness and letter knowledge are important precursors for reading they are not the only skills required. Knowledge of print conventions is important too and parents have an important role to play in this.

The above studies of parent involvement in reading have focused specifically on reading skills outcomes but it should be noted that these are not the only outcomes for parent–child reading. Language development, both receptive and expressive, is also influenced by home literacy practices and this enhanced language ability can then allow children to take better advantage of literacy teaching at school (e.g. Deckner, Adamson and Bakeman, 2006; Saracho and Spodek, 2009).

Furthermore, it seems that even the reading abilities of adolescent children might be influenced by their parents, especially with regards to their motivation to read, with parents sharing books and discussing emergent issues with their adolescent children (Klauda, 2009). Outside the child's formal reading activities in school, then, the experiences of the literacy environment provided by parents are crucially important. Developing literacy is not only a cognitive process to be engaged in as part of learning at school, but it is also a social and cultural process that occurs in the home (Myrberg and Rosén, 2009; Whitehurst and Lonigan, 1998).

QUISSET *Now go beyond the text . . . look it up yourself!*

Explore your library's electronic databases to investigate 'parental involvement in early literacy'.

Some recent studies indicating the influence of the early home literacy environment have been described above. Using your library database find other studies of the effects of the home literacy environment. What home factors do these suggest are important?

Synthesise your findings to produce your own arguments to answer the following questions:

- How does the home literacy environment influence children's reading?
- How can parents best help their children develop literacy skills?

Summary and conclusions

In this chapter we have focused on early reading and the skills children need to learn in order to read words. We have seen that while there is compelling evidence that phonological skills are central in learning to read and that a core phonological deficit underlies dyslexia, the nature of the processes involved in reading reflects complex interactions between a variety of component skills with differing implications for intervention approaches at the level of the school, the class, and the family. We will learn more about the nature of such processes in Chapter 12 when we examine the impact of neuroscience on our understanding of reading difficulties.

Glossary

exception word – a real word that does not follow the usual phonological rules, e.g. busy

grapheme – written (or printed) alphabetic letter

grapheme–phoneme correspondence – matching of written symbols to sound segments

lexical – relating to words

logography – whole-word reading

nonword – nonsense word, e.g. gromp. Also referred to as pseudoword.

orthography – system of letter symbols used for writing down the sounds of the language

phoneme – smallest distinct segment of sound in any particular language e.g. /d/o/g/ are the three phonemes that make up the word 'dog'

phonological awareness or phonics – recognising patterns of sound in spoken words includes:
- **rhyming** dig with pig
- **onset-rime** onset is initial consonant of syllable, rime is vowel with consonants that follow it, e.g./c/ is onset and /at/ is rime in word cat, i.e. c-at
- **segmenting** breaking up words at level of syllable (large segment) or phoneme (small segment)
- **blending phonemes** to make words

syllable – word segment larger than phoneme. 'Bis-cuit' has two syllables.

Further Study

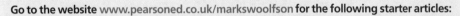

Go to the website www.pearsoned.co.uk/markswoolfson for the following starter articles:

Castles, A., Datta, H., Gayan, J., and Olson, R. (1999). Varieties of developmental reading disorder: Genetic and environmental influences. *Journal of Experimental Child Psychology, 72,* 73–94.

Lomax, R., and McGee, L. (1987). Young children's concepts about print and reading: Toward a model of word reading acquisition. *Reading Research Quarterly, 22,* 237–56.

Torgerson, C., Brooks, G., Hall, J. (2006). *A systematic review of the research literature on the use of phonics in the teaching of reading and spelling. Research Report No. 711.* London: Department of Education and Skills.

References

Adams, M. (1990). *Beginning to read: Thinking and learning about print.* Cambridge, MA: The MIT Press.

Bond, G. and Dykstra, R. (1967). The cooperative research program in first-grade reading instruction. *Reading Research Quarterly, 2,* 5–142.

Bowey, J., Cain, M., and Ryan, S. (1992). A reading-level-design study of phonological skills underlying fourth-grade children's word reading difficulties, *Child Development, 63,* 999–1011.

Bowyer-Crane, C., Snowling, M., Duff, F., Fieldsend, E., Carroll, J., Miles, J, Gotz , K., and Hulme, C. (2008). Improving early language and literacy skills, differential effects of an oral language versus a phonology with reading intervention. *Journal of Child Psychology and Psychiatry, 49,* 422–32.

Bradley, L. and Bryant, P. (1978). Difficulties in auditory organisation as a possible cause of reading backwardness. *Nature, 271,* 746–7.

Bradley, L. and Bryant, P. (1983). Categorising sounds and learning to read: A causal connection. *Nature, 301,* 419–521.

British Psychological Society (1999). *Dyslexia, literacy and psychological assessment. Report of a working party of the Division of Educational and Child Psychology.* Leicester: British Psychological Society.

Burgess, S. and Lonigan, C. (1998). Bidirectional relations of phonological sensitivity and pre-reading abilities: Evidence from a preschool sample. *Journal of Experimental Child Psychology, 70,* 117–41.

Bryant, P. and Bradley, L. (1985). Phonetic analysis capacity and learning to read. *Nature, 313,* 73–4.

Bryant, P. and Maclean, M., Bradley, L., and Crossland, J. (1990). Rhyme, alliteration, phoneme detection and learning to read. *Developmental Psychology, 26,* 429–38.

Cameron, C., Connor, C., Morrison, F., and Jewkes, A. (2008). Effects of classroom organization on letter-word reading in first grade. *Journal of School Psychology, 6*, 173–92.

Camilli, G., Vargas, S., and Yurecko, M. (2003). Teaching children to read: The fragile link between science and federal education policy. *Educational Policy Analysis Archives, 11*(15), 1–51.

Carroll, J., Snowling, M., Hulme, C., and Stevenson, J. (2003). The development of phonological awareness in preschool children. *Developmental Psychology, 39*(5), 913–23.

Castles, A. and Coltheart, M. (1993). Varieties of developmental dyslexia. *Cognition, 47*, 149–80.

Castles, A., Datta, H., Gayan, J., and Olson, R. (1999). Varieties of developmental reading disorder: Genetic and environmental influences. *Journal of Experimental Child Psychology, 72*, 73–94.

Clay, M. (1985). *The early detection of reading difficulties* (3rd edition). Tadworth, Surrey: Heinemann.

Coltheart, M., Rastle, K., Perry, C., Langdon, R., and Ziegler, J. (2001). DRC: A dual route cascaded model of visual word recognition and reading aloud. *Psychological Review, 108*, 204–56.

Connor, C., Morrison, F., and Underwood, P. (2007). A second chance in second grade? The independent and cumulative impact of first and second grade reading instruction and students' letter-word reading skill growth. *Scientific Studies of Reading, 11*, 199–233.

Connor, C., Piasta, S., Fishman, B., Glasney, S., Schatschneider, C., Crowe, E., *et al.* (2009). Individualizing student instruction precisely: Effects of child by instruction interactions on first graders' literacy development. *Child Development, 80*, 77–100.

Cronin, V. and Carver, P. (1998). Phonological sensitivity, rapid naming and beginning reading. *Applied Psycholinguistics, 19*, 447–61.

Deckner, D., Adamson, L., and Bakeman, R. (2006). Child and maternal contributions to shared reading: Effects on language and literacy development. *Applied Developmental Psychology, 27*, 31–41.

Department for Education and Skills (DfES). (2001). *The National Literacy Strategy Early Literacy Support Programme*. London: DfES Publications.

Duff, F., Fieldsend, E., Bowyer-Crane, C., Hulme, C., Smith, G., Gibbs, S., and Snowling, M. (2008). Reading with vocabulary intervention: evaluation of an instruction for children with poor response to reading intervention. *Journal of Research in Reading, 31*, 319–36.

Duncan, L., Seymour, P., and Hill, S. (1997). How important are rhyme and analogy in beginning reading? *Cognition, 63*, 171–208.

Ehri, L. (1976). Word learning in beginning readers and prereaders: Effects of form class and defining contexts. *Journal of Educational Psychology, 67*, 204–12.

Ehri, L. (1995). Phases of development in learning to read words by sight. *Journal of Research in Reading, 18*, 116–25.

Ehri, L., Nunes, S., Stahl, S., and Willows, D. (2001). Systematic phonics instruction helps students learn to read: Evidence from the National Reading Panel's meta-analysis. *Review of Educational Research, 71*, 393–447.

Evans, M., Shaw, D., and Bell, M. (2000). Home literacy activities and their influence on early literacy skills. *Canadian Journal of Experimental Psychology, 54*, 65–75.

Foorman, B., Schatschneider, C., Eakin, M., Fletcher, J., Moates, L., and Francis, D. (2006). The impact of instructional practices in grades 1 and 2 on reading and spelling achievement in high poverty schools. *Contemporary Educational Psychology, 31*, 1–29.

Fox, B. and Routh, D. (1976). Phonemic analysis and synthesis as word attack skills. *Journal of Educational Psychology, 68*, 70–4.

Frith, U. (1997). Brain, mind and behaviour in dyslexia. In C. Hulme and M. Snowling (eds), *Dyslexia: biology, cognition and intervention* (pp. 1–19). London: Whurr.

Gathercole, S., Hitch, G., Service, E., and Martin, A. (1997). Phonological short-term memory and new word learning in children. *Developmental Psychology, 33*, 966–79.

Gong, Z. and Levy, B. (2009). Four-year-old children's acquisition of print knowledge during electronic story book reading. *Reading and Writing, 22*(8), 889–905.

Goswami, U. (1986). Children's use of analogy in learning to read: A developmental study. *Journal of Experimental Child Psychology, 42*, 73–83.

Goswami, U. (1999). Causal connections in beginning reading: The importance of rhyme. *Journal of Research in Reading, 22*(3), 217–40.

Goswami, U. and Bryant, P. (1990). *Phonological skills and learning to read.* Hillsdale, NJ: Lawrence Erlbaum Associates.

Grigorenko. E. (2001). Developmental dyslexia: An update on genes, brains and environments. *Journal of Child Psychology and Psychiatry, 42*, 91–125.

Hatcher, P., Götz, K., Snowling, M., Hulme, C., Gibbs, S., and Smith, G. (2006). Evidence for the effectiveness of the Early Literacy Support programme. *British Journal of Educational Psychology, 76*, 351–67.

Hatcher, P., Hulme, C., and Ellis, A. (1994). Ameliorating reading failure by integrating the teaching of reading and phonological skills: The phonological linkage hypothesis. *Child Development, 65*(1), 41–57.

Hatcher, P., Hulme, C., Miles, J., Carroll, J., Hatcher, J., Gibbs, S., *et al.* (2006). Efficacy of small group reading intervention for beginning readers with reading-delay: A randomized controlled trial. *Journal of Child Psychology and Psychiatry, 47*, 820–7.

Hatcher, P., Hulme, C., and Snowling, M. (2004). Explicit phoneme training combined with phonic reading instruction helps young children at risk of reading failure. *Journal of Child Psychology and Psychiatry, 45*, 338–58.

Johnston, R. and Watson, J. (2003). *Accelerating reading and spelling with synthetic phonics: a five year follow up. Insight 4.* Edinburgh: Scottish Executive Education Department.

Johnston, R. and Watson, J. (2004). Accelerating the development of reading, spelling and phonemic awareness. *Reading and Writing: An Interdisciplinary Journal, 17*(4), 327–57.

Johnston, R. and Watson, J. (2005). *A seven year study of the effects of synthetic phonics teaching on reading and spelling attainment. Insight 17.* Edinburgh: Scottish Executive Education Department.

Kibby, M. (in press) Memory functioning in developmental dyslexia: An analysis using two clinical memory measures. *Archives of Clinical Neuropsychology.*

Klauda, S. (2009). The role of parents in adolescents' reading motivation and activity. *Educational Psychology Review, 21*, 325–363. doi: 10.1007/s10648-009-9112-0.

Lenneberg, E. (1967). *Biological foundations of language.* New York: Wiley.

Leslie, L. and Calhoon, A. (1995). Factors affecting children's reading of rimes: reading ability, word frequency and rime neighbourhood size. *Journal of Educational Psychology, 87*, 576–86.

Levy, B., Gong, Z., Hessels, S., Evans, M., and Jared, D. (2006). Understanding print: Early development and the contributions of home literacy experiences. *Journal of Experimental Child Psychology, 93*(1), 63–93.

Liberman, I., Shankweiler, D., Fischer, F., and Carter, B. (1974). Reading and the awareness of linguistic segments. *Journal of Experimental Child Psychology, 18*, 201–12.

Liberman, I., Shankweiler, D., Liberman, A., Fowler, C., and Fischer, F. (1977). Phonetic segmentation and recoding in the beginning reader. In A. Reber and D. Scarborough (eds) *Toward a psychology of reading* (pp. 207–25). Hillsdale, NJ: Erlbaum Associates.

Lomax, R. and McGee, L. (1987). Young children's concepts about print and reading: Toward a model of word reading acquisition. *Reading Research Quarterly, 22*, 237–56.

Lonigan, C., Burgess, S., and Anthony, J. (2000). Development of emergent literacy and early reading skills in preschool children: Evidence from a latent-variable longitudinal study. *Developmental Psychology, 36*, 596–613.

Lundberg, I., Olofsson, A., and Wall, S. (1980). Reading and spelling skills in the first school years predicted from phonemic awareness skills in kindergarten. *Scandinavian Journal of Psychology, 21*, 159–73.

Lyon, G., Shaywitz, S., and Shaywitz, B. (2003). A definition of dyslexia. *Annals of Dyslexia, 53*, 1–14.

Maclean, M., Bryant, P., and Bradley, L. (1987). Rhymes, nursery rhymes and reading in early childhood. *Merrill-Palmer Quarterly, 33,* 255–81.

Manis, F., Seidenberg, M., Doi, L., McBride-Chang, C., and Peterson, A. (1996). On the basis of two subtypes of developmental dyslexia. *Cognition, 58,* 157–95.

Maughan, B., Messer, J., Collishaw, A., Pickles, A., Snowling, M., Yule, W., and Rutter, M. (2009). Persistence of literacy problems: Spelling in adolescence and at mid-life. *Journal of Child Psychology and Psychiatry, 50*(8), 893–901.

McDougall, P., Borowsky, R., MacKinnon, G., and Hymel, S. (2005). Process dissociation of sight vocabulary and phonetic coding in reading: A new perspective on surface and phonological dyslexias. *Brain and Language, 92,* 185–203.

Molfese, V., Modglin, A., Beswick, J., Neamon, J., Berg, S., Berg, C., and Molnar, A. (2006). Letter knowledge, phonological processing, and print knowledge: Skill development in nonreading preschool children . *Journal of Learning Disabilities, 39,* 206–305.

Morais, J. (1991). Metaphonological abilities and literacy. In M. Snowling and M. Thomson (eds), *Dyslexia: Integrating theory and practice* (pp. 95–107). London: Whurr.

Morais, J., Gary, L., Alegria, J., and Bertelson, P. (1979). Does awareness of speech as a sequence of phones arise spontaneously? *Cognition, 7,* 323–31.

Muter, V., Hulme, C., Snowling, M., and Stevenson, J. (2004). Phonemes, rimes, vocabulary, and grammatical skills as foundations of early reading development: Evidence from a longirudinal study. *Developmental Psychology, 40,* 665–81.

Muter, V., Hulme, C., Snowling, M., and Taylor, S. (1998). Segmentation, not rhyming, predicts early progress in learning to read. *Journal of Experimental Child Psychology, 71,* 3–27.

Muter, V. and Snowling, M. (1998). Concurrent and longitudinal predictors of reading: The role of metalinguistic and short-term memory skills. *Reading Research Quarterly, 33*(3), 320–37.

Myrberg, E. and Rosén, M. (2009). Direct and indirect effects of parents' education on reading achievement among third graders in Sweden. *British Journal of Educational Psychology, 79*(4), 695–711.

Nation, K. and Hulme, C. (1997). Phonic segmentation, not onset-rime segmentation, predicts early reading and spelling skills. *Reading Research Quarterly, 32*(2), 154–167.

Nicolson, R. and Fawcett, A. (1995). Dyslexia is more than a phonological disability. *Dyslexia: An International Journal of Research and Practice, 1,* 19–37.

Nicolson, R. and Fawcett, A. (2008). *Dyslexia, learning and the brain.* Cambridge, MA: MIT Press.

O'Shaughnessy, T., and Swanson, H. (2000). A comparison of two reading interventions for children with reading disabilities. *Journal of Learning Disabilities, 33,* 257–77.

Perin, D. (1983). Phonemic segmentation and spelling. *British Journal of Psychology,* 74, 129–44.

Plaut, D., McClelland, J., Seidenberg, M., and Patterson, K. (1996). Understanding normal and impaired word reading: Computational principles in quasi-regular domains. *Psychological Review, 103*(1), 56–115.

Powell, D., Plaut, D., and Funnell, E. (2006). Does the PMSP connectionist model of single word reading learn to read in the same way as a child? *Journal of Research in Reading, 29*(2), 229–50.

Rack, J., Hulme, C., and Snowling, M. (1993) Learning to read: A theoretical synthesis. In H. Reese (ed.), *Advances in child development and behaviour.* (vol. 24, pp. 99–132). New York: Academic Press.

Rack, J., Snowling, M., Hulme, C., and Gibbs, S. (2007). No evidence that an exercise-based treatment programme (DDAT) has specific benefits for children with reading difficulties. *Dyslexia, 13,* 97–104.

Rapcsak, S., Henry, M., Teague, S., Carnahan, S., and Beeson, P. (2007). Do dual-route models accurately predict reading and spelling performance in individuals with acquired alexia and agraphia? *Neuropsychologia, 45,* 2519–24.

Read, C., Zhang, Y., Nie, H., and Ding, B. (1986). The ability to manipulate speech sounds depends on knowing alphabetic spelling, *Cognition, 24,* 31–44.

Reynolds, D. and Nicolson, R. (2007). Follow-up of an exercise-based treatment for children with reading difficulties. *Dyslexia: An International Journal of Research and Practice, 13,* 78–96.

Rose, J. (2006). *Independent review of the teaching of early reading*.Nottingham: DfES Publications.

Saracho, O. and Spodek, B. (2009). Parents and children engaging in storybook reading. *Early Child Development and Care*. doi:10.1080/03004430903135605.

Savage, R., Abrami, P., Hipps, G., and Deault, L. (2009). A randomised control trial study of the ABRACADABRA reading intervention program in grade 1. *Journal of Educational Psychology, 101*, 590–604.

Savage, R. and Carless, S. (2005). Phoneme manipulation but not onset-rime manipulation is a unique predictor of early reading. *Journal of Child Psychology and Psychiatry, 46*, 1297–308.

Seidenberg, M. (2005). Connectionist models of word reading. *Current Directions in Psychological Science, 14*(5), 238–242.

Seidenberg, M. and McClelland, J. (1989). A distributed, developmental model of word recognition and naming. *Psychological Review, 96*, 523–68.

Snowling, M. (2000). *Dyslexia*, 2nd edn. Oxford: Blackwell.

Snowling, M., Goulandris, N., Bowlby, M., and Howell, P. (1986). Segmentation and speech perception in relation to reading skill: A developmental analysis, *Journal of Experimental Child Psychology, 41*, 489–507.

Stanovich, K. (1986). Matthew effects in reading: Some consequences of individual differences in the acquisition of literacy. *Reading Research Quarterly, 21*(4), 360–407.

Stanovich, K. and Siegel, L., and Gottardo, A., (1997). Progress in the search for dyslexia subtypes. In C. Hulme and M. Snowling (eds), *Dyslexia: biology, cognition and intervention* (pp. 108–30). London: Whurr.

Stein, J. (2001). The magnocellular theory of developmental dyslexia. *Dyslexia, 7*, 12–36.

Stein, J., Richardson, A., and Fowler, M. (2000).Monocular occlusion can improve binocular control and reading in developmental dyslexics. *Brain, 1*, 2–3.

Tallal, P., Miller, S., Jenkins, W., and Merzenich, M. (1997). The role of temporal processing in developmental language-based disorders: research and clinical implications. In B. Blachman (ed.) *Foundations of reading acquisition and dyslexia: Implications for early intervention*. Mahwah, NJ: Lawrence Erlbaum (pp. 49–66).

Torgerson, C., Brooks, G., Hall, J. (2006). *A systematic review of the research literature on the use of phonics in the teaching of reading and spelling. Research Report No. 711*. London: Department of Education and Skills.

Treiman, R. (1985). Onset and rimes as units of spoken syllables: Evidence from children. *Journal of Experimental Child Psychology, 39*, 161–81.

van Ijzendoorn, M., and Bus, A. (1994). Meta-analytic confirmation of the nonword reading deficit in developmental dyslexia, *Reading Research Quarterly, 29*, 266–75.

Walton, P., Walton, L., and Felton, K. (2001). Teaching rime analogy or letter recoding reading strategies to prereaders: Effects on pre-reading skills and word reading. *Journal of Educational Psychology, 93*, 160–80.

Watson, J. and Johnston, R. (1998). Accelerating reading attainment: the effectiveness of synthetic phonics. *Interchange 57*, Edinburgh: SOEID.

White, K. (1982). The relation between socio-economic status and academic achievement. *Psychological Bulletin, 91*(3), 461–81.

Whitehurst, G. and Lonigan, C. (1998). Child development and emergent literacy. *Child Development, 69*, 848–72.

Wyse, D. and Goswami, U. (2008). Synthetic phonics and the teaching of reading. *British Educational Research Journal, 34*(6), 691–710.

Ziegler, J., Castel, C., Pech-Georgel, C., George, F., Alario, F., and Perry, C. (2008). Developmental dyslexia and the dual route model of reading: Simulating individual differences and subtypes. *Cognition, 107*, 151–78.

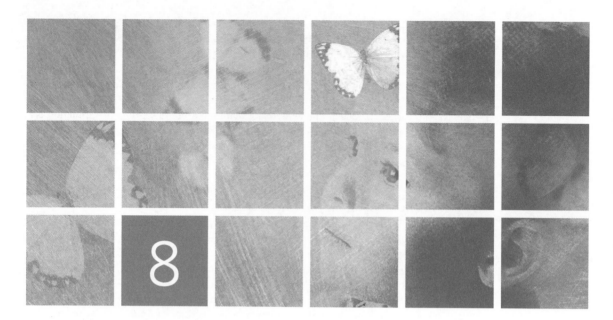

Bullying

Anyone who has been to school will intuitively understand what is meant by 'bullying' and is likely to be able to give examples from their own childhood, either of their own experiences or those of a classmate. You will have read in the press about children who have been on the receiving end of continued bullying and who have been forced to change school or who have sadly committed suicide as a result. You will also be aware of a new type of bullying using mobile phones and the internet, cyberbullying, that offers parents and teachers significant challenges to control because of the anonymity of the bullies and the extensive reach of electronic communications at the press of a button. We know that the experience of bullying can blight children's lives if not dealt with satisfactorily. All schools have a responsibility to take bullying seriously and put in place policies that tackle bullying. In this chapter we will examine explanations of bullying offered by different psychological theoretical perspectives, and then look at some school intervention programmes that build on these perspectives to address bullying.

Learning outcomes

By the end of this chapter you should be able to:

- Define bullying
- Recognise what different types of bullying behaviours look like
- Appreciate prevalence rates for bullying
- Evaluate the extent to which there are gender differences
- Evaluate the evidence for different theoretical explanations of bullying
- Understand how psychological theory has informed whole-school anti-bullying interventions
- Evaluate the evidence for intervention effectiveness
- Recognise the similarities and differences between cyberbullying and bullying.

What is bullying?

In Chapter 4 we mentioned aggressive and anti-social behaviour. Bullying behaviour may be viewed as a particularly common kind of aggressive behaviour which is directed at peers (Coie and Dodge, 1998). We can further distinguish between *reactive aggression* which occurs within a relationship that is governed by conflict, and *proactive aggression* which is engaging in coercive behaviour in order to dominate an individual (Dodge, 1991). Bullying is an instance of proactive aggression (Boulton and Smith, 1994). It is marked by an asymmetric relationship with the asymmetry in the relationship favouring the bully. Thus a quarrel between two children who are equal in strength and power is not considered as an instance of bullying (Olweus, 1993). Furthermore, the imbalance of power is not restricted to physicality, but can occur via the bully's popularity status, or through the size of the group they belong to, and can be demonstrated by the tone of voice and posture used by the bully (Atlas and Pepler, 1998; Hunter, Boyle and Warden, 2007). This imbalance of power can be real when the bully is actually stronger, or indeed it can even just be a perception that the bully is stronger (Hunter *et al.*, 2007).

Bullying has been defined as a systematic abuse of power (Smith and Sharp, 1994). This means that as well as the imbalance of power, bullying behaviour is both repeated over time and has the intention of causing physical or psychological harm or distress (Atlas and Pepler, 1998; Naylor, Cowie, Cossin, de Bettencourt and Lemme, 2006). But while bullying is viewed as being centred around an imbalance of power (Olweus, 1993), contrary to popular misconception this imbalance need not be the physical power of a bigger, stronger child resorting to violence against a smaller weaker one because it is the 'only way he knows how' (Sutton, Smith and Swettenham, 1999a). There is indeed the question of whether bullies show a deficiency at all but rather that they can bully because they are skilled in particular ways. We will explore the deficit versus skills approaches in this chapter.

Bullying occurs within the social context of the group and in particular within a dyad (i.e. between two children) (Atlas and Pepler, 1998; Veenstra, Lindenberg, Zijlstra, De Winter, Verhulst and Ormel, 2007). To be clear, the bully is the one who carries out the repetitive, negative behaviour, while the victim is the recipient of this repetitive, negative behaviour. Victims themselves may react, though, by engaging in aggressive, bullying behaviour when they perceive others to be hostile or threatening towards them. These bully/victims differ from 'pure' victims because they react aggressively to being bullied. They also differ from 'pure' bullies because their aggression is reactive in response to the provocation of being bullied and is not proactive with the intention of bullying (Olweus, 1978; Salmivalli, Lagerspetz, Bjorkqvist, Österman and Kaukiainen, 1996).

What does bullying behaviour look like?

Bullying may be **direct** or **indirect**.

- **Direct bullying** is where the victim knows which individual is doing the bullying. Direct bullying may be physical or verbal (Crick and Grotpeter, 1995; Pellegrini, 1998).
  - *Physical bullying* is an easy form of bullying to recognise as it is characterised by overtly aggressive behaviour such as hitting and kicking.
  - *Verbal bullying* on the other hand involves name-calling, teasing, and threatening behaviour.

- **Indirect or relational bullying** is where the individual who is carrying out the bullying may remain unidentified to the victim (Lagerspetz, Björkqvist and Peltonen, 1988).

Indirect bullying is rather more manipulative in intent than direct bullying, involving acts of social exclusion and damage to friendship by spreading rumours or encouraging other peers to ignore and not play with the victim (Crick and Grotpeter, 1995). Crick and Grotpeter (1995) used a peer nomination measure in a US study (see Key Concept Box) and found correlational evidence to suggest that direct and indirect forms of bullying are distinct but related.

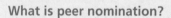

KEY CONCEPTS

What is peer nomination?

Peer nomination is a technique that is commonly used in studies of bullying as well as in studies of social relationships. It provides a means of identifying friendship preferences, sociometric status, and in the case of bullying studies the techique highlights children in the class who are aggressive or who engage in bullying behaviour within a class group. Many researchers see it as more reliable than pupil self-report because the information on who in the class is bullying or being bullied comes from multiple sources, rather than relying on children to report themselves if they experience bullying.

In peer nomination, children are typically asked to select up to three of their classmates who fit a particular description such as 'children who do nice things' or 'children who are mean', 'children who start fights', 'children who I most like to be with', 'children who get picked on', 'children who get pushed'. Crick and Grotpeter (1995) used their *Peer Nomination Instrument* to measure not only aggressive and prosocial behaviours but also to identify those individuals who were socially isolated.

An alternative to peer nomination is the forced-choice technique. With this method, instead of nominating the top three or the bottom three children in any category, children are given a list of all children in the class and are 'forced' to categorise each child in terms of the themes of interest. So for example while a peer nomination technique might ask 'Name three children who are aggressive,' which means the researcher then has no information on the extent to which the other 20+ un-nominated children are or are not aggressive, forced choice asks that a categorisation be made for each child as to whether they are aggressive or not, with a middle category for use if required. Forced choice also means that the researcher does not have to ask children to select only three negative examples from their class, such as 'children I don't like to play with', which could present ethical problems (Frederickson and Furnham, 2001).

Prevalence of bullying

Prevalence rates of bullying vary across different countries and also within countries depending on how bullying was defined and the methods used to elicit participant responses. When you read the original papers you will see that most studies used self-report questionnaires while some interviewed participants individually, e.g. Wolke *et al.* (2001). However, cross-national studies do suggest that there are real cultural differences in the prevalence of bullying. A comparison of health behaviour in school children over 28 countries was carried out by the World Health Organization (WHO; Due *et al.*, 2005). 123 227 children participated in this study which was concerned with victims of bullying, not bullies themselves. The authors found wide variations in the percentage of children who reported that they had been bullied in the preceding school term. This ranged from 5.1% for girls and 6.3% for boys in Sweden, to 38.2% for girls and 41.4% for boys in Lithuania. The average for the entire study was 15.2% (girls) and 18.4% (boys). As can be seen from Table 8.1, reported rates for the UK tended towards the lower end of this range. Table 8.2 provides us with some examples of UK bullying studies and their findings.

QUISSET *Now go beyond the text . . . Look it up yourself!*

Explore your library's electronic databases to investigate 'prevalence of bullying.'

- Critically examine literature reporting prevalence across a range of countries. To what extent can differences in rates of bullying across countries be explained by cross-cultural differences or methodological differences?

Table 8.1 **Prevalence rates of bullying in UK (WHO)**

	Scotland	*England*	*Northern Ireland*	*Wales*
Boys	9.3%	9.1%	10.7%	12%
Girls	9.5%	7.2%	8.7%	11.3%

Source: Based on data from Due *et al.*, 2005, Oxford University Press

Table 8.2 **Examples of UK studies**

Study	Place	Participants	Findings
Ahmad and Smith (1990)	South Yorkshire	2000 pupils	20% middle school children and 16% secondary school children reported being victims of bullying 'sometimes', 'now and then', or 'more often'. 6% of middle school children and 8% of secondary school children reported being victims of bullying 'once a week or more often'.
			8% of middle school children and 10% of secondary school children reported bullying other children 'sometimes', 'now and then', or 'more often,' and 2% of middle school children and 3% secondary school children reported bullying other children once a week or more often.
Whitney and Smith (1993)	Sheffield	6758 children	27% of junior/middle school children and 10% of secondary school children reported being bullied 'sometimes or more in a term', while 10% of junior/middle school children and 4% of secondary school children reported being bullied 'at least once a week'.
			12% of junior/middle school children and 6% of secondary school children reported bullying other children 'sometimes or more in a term'; and 4% of junior/middle school children and 1% of secondary school children reported bullying other children 'at least once a week'.
Wolke et al. (2001)	Hertfordshire	1072 6-year-olds (Year 2) and 1304 8-year-olds (Year 4)	Compared to German children a much larger 54.7% of Year 2 English children and 53.7% of Year 4 children had been bullied frequently, i.e. four or more times in the past six months.
			Smaller proportion of English children were bullies. 14% of Year 2 pupils and 18.9% of Year 4 pupils had bullied others frequently.
			Almost a quarter of the children in their study, 24.3% of Year 2 pupils and 24.7% of Year 4 pupils, had been bullied very frequently. On the other hand, only 1.9% of Year 2 pupils and 2.9% of Year 4 pupils bullied others very frequently.
Collins, McAleavy and Adamson (2004)	Northern Ireland	1079 Year 6 primary pupils and 1353 Year 9 post-primary pupils	40% of primary children and 30.2% of post-primary children were at least occasional victims of bullying, reporting that they had been bullied at least once or twice in the preceding school term.
			25% of primary pupils and 29% of post-primary pupils had bullied others occasionally.
			15% of primary children and 9.9% of post-primary children had been victims of bullying at least two or three times a month. 9% of primary and 6.5% of post-primary had been victims of bullying at least once a week, and 3% of both age groups admitted to bullying at least once a week.

Gender differences . . .

. . . in bullying

Although we will see later in this section that this is not a clear-cut finding, there is nonetheless a considerable body of evidence showing that boys are more likely to bully than girls. This was first reported by Olweus (1991) in a sample of Norwegian children, and subsequently supported by studies in other countries: with primary school pupils in England (Whitney and Smith, 1993); Germany (Wolke, Woods, Stanford and Schultz, 2001); Canada (Bentley and Li, 1996); and Northern Ireland (Collins, McAleavy and Adamson, 2004). Similar findings have also been reported with older pupils in England and Scotland (Siann, Callaghan, Glissov, Lockhard and Rawson, 1994; Whitney and Smith, 1993); USA (Bosworth, Espelage and Simon, 1999); and Germany (Scheithauer, Hayer, Petermann and Jugert, 2006). Moreover, studies using naturalistic observation carried out in the playground have estimated that over half the observed instances of bullying involved boys (Craig and Pepler, 1997; Craig, Pepler and Atlas, 2000). In their meta-analysis of gender differences, Card, Stucky, Sawalani and Little (2008) also found gender differences, specifically with boys engaging in direct aggression more than girls.

While the evidence certainly points to boys engaging in aggressive bullying behaviour more than girls. there is considerable evidence that when both direct and indirect forms of bullying (see below) are taken into account there may be indeed be less evidence of gender differences. On the other hand though, Siann *et al.* (1994) and Scheithauer *et al.*'s (2006) studies found there to be more male than female bullies, regardless of type of bullying.

. . . in victims

A similarly uncertain picture emerges when we consider the gender of victims. It may be that girls experience more indirect, covert forms of bullying compared to the more physical bullying experienced by boys (Crick and Grotpeter, 1995; Olweus, 1991; Pellegrini, 1998; Whitney and Smith, 1993), but that there is also considerable overlap in their experience of bullying (Smith, Cowie, Olafsson and Liefooghe, 2002). Studies have certainly reported more male than female victims of bullying (Collins *et al.*, 2004; Olweus, 1991; Olweus, 1993; Siann *et al.*, 1994).

There may, however, be subtleties to this assertion such as the location of the bullying, cultural differences across countries, and differences depending on how victims are classified. For example, while Craig *et al.* (2000) also reported more male victims in the classroom, they found that in the playground there was actually the same number of incidents involving male and female victims. In both England and Germany, Wolke *et al.* (2001) also found that more boys than girls were bully victims, and that more boys than girls were pure victims in Germany while in England the numbers of male and female pure victims were the same.

Other investigators too have reported similar numbers of male and female victims (Bentley and Li, 1996; Whitney and Smith, 1993), although, Scheithauer *et al.* (2006) also found there to be a higher number of male bully victims.

Perhaps then boys and girls experience bullying differently?

Gender differences in perceptions of what actually constitutes bullying (Siann *et al.*, 1994) could help explain any reported gender differences in bullying, although Smith, Cowie, Olafsson and Liefooghe (2002) did not in fact find any gender differences in an extensive study that covered 14 different countries in which they asked children to decide which of a series of cartoons showed 'bullying'.

Perhaps then boys and girls experience different types of bullying? There is certainly convincing evidence that boys experience more physical bullying than girls compared to relational or verbal bullying (Olweus, 1991; Olweus, 1993; Scheithauer *et al.*, 2006; Siann *et al.*, 1994). Nevertheless, while girls are more likely to be bullied indirectly than directly, indirect bullying is the most frequent form of bullying experienced by both genders, so boys actually also experience

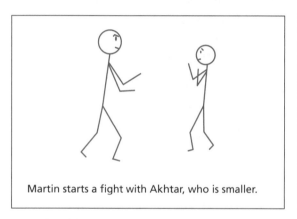

Martin starts a fight with Akhtar, who is smaller.

Jim forgot his pen, so Kirk lends him one of his.

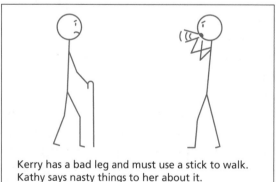

Kerry has a bad leg and must use a stick to walk. Kathy says nasty things to her about it.

Jenny and her friends won't let Claire play with them.

Examples of four cartoons

Source: Smith *et al*, 2002, reproduced by permission of John Wiley & Sons Inc.

indirect bullying, e.g. name calling and spreading lies, as well as physical bullying (Olweus, 1991; Olweus, 1993; Wolke *et al.*, 2001). Several studies have reported that female bullies favour indirect bullying and are more likely to use indirect methods of social exclusion than are male bullies (Collins *et al.*, 2004; Lagerspetz, Björkqvist and Peltonen, 1988; Whitney and Smith, 1993), but, although in their meta-analysis Card *et al.* (2008) also found this gender difference to be significant, they reported it as 'trivial' in size. Card *et al.*'s analysis suggested that this trivial gender difference remained consistent across age.

When we consider who bullies whom, we find that in general boys tend to bully boys (Bentley and Li, 1996; Collins *et al.*, 2004; Craig and Pepler, 1998; Craig *et al.*, 2000; Olweus, 1991, 1993; Seals and Young, 2003; Whitney and Smith, 1993; Wolke *et al.*, 2001) and girls tend to bully girls (Collins *et al.*, 2004; Wolke *et al.*, 2001). Conversely, there is also evidence that girls may be bullied by a combination of boys and girls (Bentley and Li, 1996; Collins *et al.*, 2004; Olweus, 1991, 1993; Wolke *et al.*, 2001) and that some of the bullying experienced by males is at the hands of a female bully (Craig *et al.*, 2000). Moreover, girl victims are more likely to seek support for bullying than boys by discussing the problem with a parent, friend or teacher (Collins *et al.*, 2004; Hunter, Boyle and Warden, 2004; Wolke *et al.*, 2001).

 Debate

Join up with some friends to discuss.

Discuss the following assertion:

'Boys bully more than girls: Girls are victims more than boys.'

Support your arguments with evidence from your extended reading.

Theoretical explanations for bullying behaviour

In this next section we will see that researchers have offered a variety of explanations for bullying behaviour from quite different theoretical perspectives. These have informed a plethora of studies and generated alternative formulations of how best to intervene to prevent bullying. We will discuss bullying interventions later in this chapter. First now, let us consider some influential theoretical explanations and examine the supporting evidence.

Participant role theory

Participant role theory considers not only the bully and the victim but also examines the role of other peers in supporting bullying. Do they also participate in some way? Olweus (1978), who was one of the first investigators to examine bullying in his studies of the characteristics of bullies and victims in Sweden, did not place much emphasis on the roles of the other children who were likely to be present when bullying occurred. Lagerspetz, Björkqvist, Berts and King (1982) in replicating Olweus's (1978) study in Finland also focused only on bullies and victims but noted that examining the roles played by the other group participants could permit greater understanding of the phenomenon of group aggression.

Salmivalli *et al.* (1996) thus decided to investigate all of the participant roles they perceived to be part of bullying behaviour as well as the relationship of these roles with social status. They reported that previous studies found a strong link between children's behaviour and social status, though this link was not for bullying behaviour itself. Salmivalli *et al.* studied a sample of 573 Finnish sixth grade children, aged 12–13 years. Participant roles were established through peer nomination questionnaires with hypothetical situations relating to five subscales:

- *bully*
- *reinforcer* of the bully
- *assistant* of the bully
- *defender* of the victim
- *outsider*.

Pupils had to rate their own behaviour in each situation, and also that of their peers. Victims identified as such by 30% of their peers on a separate part of the questionnaire were considered to be victims, regardless of their own self-report in the questionnaire. Social status was established by peer nomination; asking children to nominate the three children they most liked and the three they least liked.

Salmivalli *et al.* found that almost 90% of children could be classified into one of the participant roles using their Participant Role Questionnaire. The most common peer roles were *reinforcer*, *defender* and *outsider*. The role of the *reinforcer* is to provide the bully with positive feedback, the *defender* takes the side of the victim, the *outsider* is aware that bullying is in progress but does not take part and may try to ignore that it is happening. There are also *assistants* who support the bully. Their results highlighted a dramatic difference between boys and girls, with many more girls who were *defenders* (30.1%, compared to 4.5% of boys), and *outsiders* (40.2%, compared to 7.3% of boys), and many more boys who were *reinforcers* (37.3%, compared to 1.7% of girls, or *assistants* (12.2%, compared to 1.4% of girls).

The participants were reasonably accurate in representing their own roles, though they tended to underestimate their active participation in bullying behaviour, and overestimate the extent to which their behaviour was prosocial (caring about, and helping, others). *Victims* had lower social status than all of the other groups, and almost a quarter did not identify themselves as *victims*. *Defenders* had the highest social status. Only the most popular boys defended the victims. The authors suggested that, because in contrast to boys so many girls played this role, to do so may actually raise their social standing. While male bullies were of low social status, female bullies scored above the mean for both social acceptance and rejection. This may be because female bullies are more likely to bully verbally than physically, so girls may use their verbal taunts to amuse others in the classroom and be both popular and rejected. Guided by this evidence that most members of the class had a role to play in bullying, the authors inferred that any interventions to address bullying behaviour should be on a classroom scale (Salmivalli, 1999; Salmivalli *et al.*, 1996).

Social networks

In a questionnaire-based study of 459 Finnish 11–12-year-olds, Salmivalli, Huttunen and Lagerspetz (1997) found that children who shared the same participant role tended to be part of the same social network. This could be because bullies selected aggressive children like themselves as friends, and similarly for *reinforcers* and *defenders*. However, instead of active selection of friendships, an alternative explanation is that bullies may be limited to socialising with the only other pupils who were accepting of their behaviour.

Socialisation effects, rather than selection, could also explain participant role networks. Spending time together may lead to friends' behaviour becoming more similar to each other's. Additionally, the reputation of a certain network may cause other peers to view members of a network as more similar than they really are. In an attempt to unravel the effects of socialisation from those of selection, Salmivalli, Lappalainen and Lagerspetz (1998) conducted a follow-up study, this time testing 189 children from their original sample (Salmilvalli *et al.*, 1996), who were now in eighth grade. There was no correlation between their self-reported participant roles at these time points two years apart. That is to say, girls behaved more similarly to others in their current social network than to how they themselves had behaved two years before. It seemed that socialisation explained girls' participant role networks, more so than for boys' networks.

For both boys and girls though, victims remained victims, even when they had moved from one class to another. Interestingly, Salmilvalli *et al.* (1997) found that female victims were sometimes even part of the same social network as bullies, suggesting that it was so important to girls to be part of a social network that they preferred to be part of a network in which they were bullied than not to be part of a network at all. While for girls bullying was related to membership of social groupings, for boys bullying was a symbol of power (Salmivalli *et al.*, 1998). Among boys, however, there was greater stability in bullying behaviour over time with many boys playing the same role of bully or defender two years later. This suggested that male bullying could be explained by aggressive behaviour patterns as originally proposed by Olweus (1991).

While a degree of stability in bullying behaviour has been observed, some changes over time have also been noted. In a sample of 871 students aged 10–14 years at study start, studied over a seven-year period, four categories of bullying change over time were identified:

- *high* – frequent bullying across time
- *moderate* – moderate bullying across time
- *desisting* – moderate bullying at the beginning of the study but almost none by the end
- *never* – never or almost never bullied.

(Pepler, Jiang, Craig and Connolly, 2008)

While 41.6% reported that they never bullied, only 13.4% were in the *desisting* group, the group who changed their behaviour over the seven-year period from bullying to not bullying; 9.9% were in the *high* group and 35.1% in the *moderate* group, the two groups who continued bullying over the seven-year period at more or less the same level throughout. Pepler *et al.* found that these two groups who continued bullying differed from the never-bullying group in continuing to associate with peers who bullied, in being involved in peer conflict, and in being susceptible to peer pressure. The *desisting* group, on the other hand, were similar to the never group except for being susceptible to peer pressure. Perhaps they had bullied when they were younger to gain power and status, but no longer required these strategies as they grew into middle adolescence (14–17 years).

 Debate

Join up with some friends to discuss.

Pepler *et al.* (2008) acknowledge that their findings largely rely on self-reported data from the adolescents themselves.

- What are the problems with this?
- To what extent is this an issue of concern across the area of bullying studies as a whole?
- How could researchers address this when designing their studies?

Popularity

Networks of *bullies* and *reinforcers* were larger than those of *defenders* and *outsiders*. This is a rather surprising finding as defenders were rated as most popular by their peers (Salmivalli *et al.*, 1997). One explanation for this apparent discrepancy between popularity and size of network may be that these popular children have small networks that comprise very close friends, with whom they share a stronger bond.

A Dutch study of 10–13-year-olds examined the relationship between bullying and the desire to be liked (Olthof and Goossens, 2008). The researchers used the New Participant Role Scales (Goossens, Olthof and Dekker, 2006) to assess children's involvement in bullying. This was an adapted version of Salmivalli *et al.*'s (1996) procedure, with five subscales: *bully*, *follower* which combined *assistants* and *reinforcers*, *outsider*, *defender* and *victim*. In addition Olthof and Goosens measured children's desire to be accepted by each classmate, by asking them to rate on a five-point scale the importance of being liked by each classmate and how bad they would feel if that classmate did not like them. Their results showed a correlation in boys between *bully /follower* behaviour and a desire to be liked by *bully/follower* boys. In girls too there was a correlation between a desire to be liked by *bully/follower* boys and *bully/follower* behaviour (note: not a correlation with *bully/follower* girls). These data provided some support for the idea that bullying behaviour is motivated by a desire to be accepted by bullying children, rather than being explained by selection or socialisation. However, there was only a marginal positive correlation between the acceptance *bully/ follower* boys gave to girls who exhibited *bully/follower* behaviour, and indeed a negative correlation between the acceptance *bully/follower* boys gave to boys displaying this type of behaviour. Thus, these strategies were largely unsuccessful. Finally, girls who desired acceptance from boys in general were more likely to display *bully/follower* behaviour than girls who were not as concerned with acceptance from boys.

Social information processing

The social information processing model (SIP) proposed by Dodge and Crick (1990) and later reformulated by the same authors (Crick and Dodge, 1994) provides an explanation for bullying behaviour that has been useful in stimulating research. This six-step model assumes that aggressive behaviour is the result of a social skills deficit in processing information within a social context. Child A attends to particular cues in the social situation with which he is confronted, encodes these cues in Step 1 and then interprets them in Step 2. Child A now has a mental representation of this social situation that has been guided by *schemata*, the memories of previous experiences organised in a way that allows cognitively efficient understanding of new experiences by processing the extent to which they are consistent with previous experiences. But if Child A engages in biased processing that relies on aggressive schemata to interpret Child B bumping into him, then he may respond by enacting aggressive behaviour. When considering Child B's perspective, Child A may use biased attributions that attribute the cause of the bumping as aggressive on the part of Child B. SIP proposes that any of these biased interpretations will lead Child A to construct different goals at Step 3 compared to those if he had attributed the cause of the bumping as accidental or unintentional. At Step 3, then, Child A selects his goal or the outcome he would like. Where he is subject to biased processing, SIP suggests that the goal he settles on here might be anti-social, for example, to get even with Child B for bumping him, rather than to ignore, or give the benefit of the doubt. SIP then proposes that Child A accesses from his long-term memory in Step 4 previous behavioural responses to the situation or constructs new responses if it is indeed a new situation that he finds himself in. Finally, at Step 5 Child A evaluates and decides which of the Step 4 responses he will enact. An important factor here is self-efficacy, the extent to which Child A believes he can successfully perform the behaviour under consideration. It should be noted that Crick and Dodge's (1994) reformulation of SIP is not simply sequential but is a cyclical model that recognises the transactional and reciprocal nature of the relationships between these different steps.

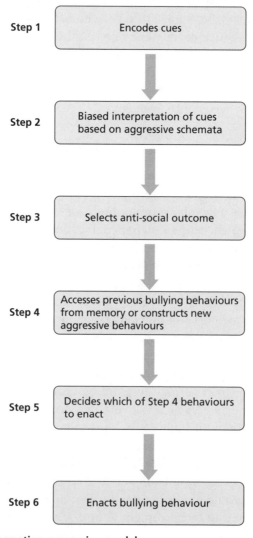

Figure 8.1 Social information processing model

EXAMPLE Applying social information processing model to studying bullying

Camodeca and Goossens (2005) wanted to examine whether children who bully process social information differently from children who do not bully. The study was carried out in 242 Dutch children (mean age 9 years 7 months). Using peer nominations on the Participant Role Questionnaire (Salmivalli, Lagerspetz, Björkqvist, Osterman and Kaukiainen,1996), children were identified either as bullies or as having another role. Steps 1–3 of the SIP model were examined using four stories and for Step 5 a self-efficacy questionnaire was used. Results showed a significant effect of role in Steps 1–3, with bullies attributing more hostile intentions to the perpetrator of an action in the story than did children who were identified as having other roles, with the exception of those identified as victims. In addition, bullies' responses indicated more anger than other peers. There was also a significant effect of role at Step 5, with bullies reporting that they found it easier to behave in an aggressive manner than did defenders and outsiders. Bullies also found it easier to encourage others to engage in bullying than did other peer roles. Salmivalli *et al.* concluded that bullies thus showed deficits in processing social information providing support for Crick and Dodge's proposal that cognitive biases in the interpretation of cues result in the enactment of aggressive bullying behaviour.

Superior theory of mind

Perhaps as bullying is carried out within a social context, rather than having a social deficit, bullies instead have advanced social cognitive skills. Could it be that bullies have a superior theory of mind and are highly sophisticated at understanding and interpreting others' behaviour? (See Chapter 5 for explanation of theory of mind.) This would certainly seem to be essential for indirect bullying in order for the bully to determine who to choose, how to manipulate others to participate, and how to bully in a subtle, indirect way that escapes detection by authorities (Sutton, Smith and Swettenham, 1999a, 1999b). However, Sutton *et al.* extended this further to argue that an advanced theory of mind is even required in bullies who engage in direct bullying. They found that more bullies compared to control children aged 6–7 years passed a standard theory of mind task (see Chapter 5 for Wimmer and Perner task), and that with children aged 7–10 years more bullies scored higher on an advanced theory of mind task using Happé's Strange Stories (see Chapter 5). Indeed they not only scored higher on cognitive measures on the Strange Stories but also on emotional measures. These results suggested that bullies do not have a deficit in their social skills, but instead are superior at detecting and interpreting social and emotional cues. This gives them a social advantage which allows them to be successful in manipulating both the victim and the social group. These findings were also supported by Gini (2006) in an Italian study.

Monks, Smith and Swettenham (2005) suggested that indirect bullying, where bullies are working with other children as assistants and reinforcers, evolves as children mature. This is because social interactions with peers have enhanced the bully's theory of mind skills and having now developed a more advanced theory of mind, the bully understands the importance of recruiting a group of peers to support the bullying behaviour. This suggestion receives support from a study by Perner, Ruffman and Leekam (1994), who found that a child's family size had a significant effect on their ability to pass the Wimmer and Perner false-belief task (see Chapter 5). As the number of siblings in a family increased, the ability to pass the theory of mind task also increased, such that children with one or more siblings in the family performed better than an only child. The authors proposed that this effect occurred because having a sibling provided more opportunities for interaction, thus creating a natural learning environment for pretend play and taking other roles and perspectives. Clearly then if this effect can be obtained by sibling interaction, then peer interaction is also likely to have the same effect (Sutton *et al.*, 1999a, 1999b).

Social identity theory

So far we have considered three different theoretical explanations of bullying: participant role theory, social information processing and superior theory of mind. Let's now examine a fourth explanation, social identity theory, which has been utilised by a series of recent studies to inform their study of bullying. Social identity theory was developed in the 1970s through the work of Tajfel and Turner (1979). It recognises the importance to the individual of belonging to a group and predicts how individuals use group membership to create a positive social identity for themselves by establishing group norms for behaviour and attitudes. All members of the group are expected to conform to these norms.

Ojala and Nesdale (2004) used social identity theory to build on Salmivalli *et al.*'s studies, which were discussed earlier in this chapter. The principle then is that if bullying is the group norm, then one would predict that members of that group would be more likely to bully, or to view bullying as acceptable. Ojala and Nesdale presented 120 boys aged 10–13 years with different versions of a story in which there were two characters, Paul and David, who belonged either to the 'dudes', the in-group (the preferred group to belong to) or the 'try hards', the out-group. The experimenters manipulated the behaviour and norms of the in-group, the extent to which the out-group was similar to the in-group, and the extent to which Paul's behaviour towards David was bullying or helpful. Some of their results provided support for social identity theory as an explanation for bullying. They found, for example, that the in-group character would be more likely to be judged to be part of the group if he engaged in behaviour that was consistent with the norm for the group. Bullying behaviour was also viewed as more acceptable when the out-group character was similar to the in-group and so perceived as a threat to the in-group's identity. Duffy and Nesdale's (2009) study of 351 8–13-year-olds, however, also reported within-group similarities on all bullying subscales, and that members of a group where bullying was the norm were more likely to be involved in bullying than members of other groups where this behaviour was not the norm. In a study of 4650 students in China, Chang (2004) also found that in classes where aggressive behaviour was the norm, it was more likely to be viewed as acceptable.

Age, however, seems to be an important factor in the development of group norms. In a study carried out at a UK summer school, Abrams, Rutland, Cameron and Ferrell (2007) found that bullying behaviour became more dependent on group norms as children matured. Children in this study rated the in-group, comprising peers who were complimentary about their own summer school, as more likely to be accepted by their peers than so-called deviant members, who expressed favourable opinions of both the in-group but also of the out-group, a nearby summer camp. This effect was more pronounced among the older children. Additionally, when the children were held accountable by being told that other children would be able to see their ratings, older children showed a stronger relationship between what they judged peer acceptance to be and their own ratings than did younger children. Abrams *et al.* suggested that, as children get older, their bullying behaviour may be more reliant on group norms and conformity.

As well as providing an explanation for the act of bullying, social identity theory may also help explain the role of victim. Cassidy's (2009) results showed that victims were less likely to identify with a network of friends, and that those victims who showed evidence of psychological distress had the lowest social identity. In contrast, bullies had more friends and indeed the likelihood of bullying increased by 12% with each friend they had (Barboza, Schiamberg, Oehmke, Korzeniewski, Post and Heraux, 2009).

Social dominance theory

This theoretical perspective developed from animal behaviourists' observation of the pecking order of chickens in which they noted that members of a group are ordered into a hierarchy to determine their access to resources and that this holds true for many animal species including primates (Dunbar, 1988). Thus social dominance must be considered as a relationship between peers in the context of a social group, where bullies choose less powerful, more vulnerable victims in order to maximise their own dominance status (Pellegrini, 1995). The resources that children are competing for here are not food or water, but rather social contact, such as love and attention, friends to interact with, and new experiences, games, and activities (Hawley, 1999). The purpose of bullying within this, then, is to gain higher status within the dominance hierarchy and also to achieve social approval (Hawley, 1999; Veenstra *et al.*, 2007). Furthermore, bullies preferred to achieve both dominance and popularity at the same time, achieving dominance by attacking a less dominant, less aggressive peer, and social approval/popularity from the bystanders, assistants and reinforcers of the bullying (O'Connell, Pepler and Craig, 1999). As a less dominant peer is less popular or even rejected by their peers, there was minimal risk to the bully's popularity when that child was the object of their bullying. Veenstra *et al.*, (2007) found positive correlations between being a bully and engaging in dominant aggressive behaviour. They also found that victims were less aggressive, vulnerable children who were rejected by their peers.

What characteristics does a bully need to possess in order to be able to bully, still be accepted and liked by peers? Vallancourt and Hymel (2006) found that individuals who were rated as high on perceived popularity, power and social status were also rated high on the peer-valued characteristic measures of style, attractiveness, good at sport, sense of humour, lots of possessions, toughness and talent; they found that the relationship between social dominance and aggression was moderated by these peer-valued characteristics.

At the toddler and preschooler stage, dominant children using coercive strategies such as bossing and fighting are liked by others and are seen as competent, popular and powerful. They have access to environmental resources, in this case toys, and other children want to learn from them and be associated with them (Hawley, 1999). While coercion works well in the preschool years when children are limited in the extent to which they can use verbal or negotiation skills, older children are less approving of coercion and aggressive children are less popular. Other strategies then are required to achieve both dominance and social approval, such as engaging others to help, directing others, and this requires dominant individuals to have a position of social centrality within the peer group (Hawley, 1999).

Rough-and-tumble play may be used as a way of exerting physical dominance in older children. In Pellegrini's (1995) study, rough-and-tumble play was categorised as either 'chase' or 'physically rough', each of which had a different function. Only 'physically rough' was used to provide an opportunity for exploiting a playful activity to establish physical dominance. Boys aged 12–13 years at the transition to adolescence were studied over two years. At the end of year one, 'physically rough' play correlated positively with aggression, and correlated negatively with popularity. By the second year, the dominance hierarchy was already established and 'physically rough' play decreased in frequency as there was less need for it.

Could bullying and aggressive behaviour be particularly important then in establishing dominance relationships during the emergence and formation of new social groups such as when children make the transition from primary to secondary school? Pellegrini and Long's (2002) longitudinal study over this transition period certainly suggested so. Using self-report, peer nominations, teacher measures, direct observations and diary entries, they measured bullying and dominance status and found that dominance was effected through bullying strategies, and that both bullying and aggressive behaviour increased during the primary to secondary transition, and then decreased. In a more recent study on this transition, instead of relying on information on dominance and vulnerability, assessed through teacher report, to infer status goals, Sijtsema, Veenstra, Lindenberg and Salmivalli (2009) investigated children's status goals directly by adding them as a new variable to their model and found direct status goals were positively linked to bullying behaviour in older male bullies, but not for older female bullies or younger bullies of either gender. It seemed that bullying is motivated by more specific goals among older children than younger children. Schafer, Kron, Brodbeck, Wolke and Schulz (2005) additionally suggested that in primary schools peer hierarchies are less stable and less driven by dominance hierarchies than secondary schools, and that hierarchy stability was associated with victims remaining in the victim role.

Regarding gender differences in the bullying methods utilised by children to establish themselves in dominance hierarchies, Leenar, Dane and Marini (2008) proposed an evolutionary theory that bullying is used to increase status in the dominance hierarchy in order to obtain a sexual partner. The sexual selection process, however, differs for males and females. Females want males to be able to provide them with resources for survival, e.g. food and shelter. In contrast, males choose on the basis of physical appearance for reproductive value, and thus seek attractive females. This results in females enhancing their physical appearance, and males illustrating their strength and athleticism, proving that they are capable of providing for the female. Consequently, males may engage in more physical bullying in order to move up the dominance hierarchy. In contrast, the authors found that for females, physical appearance interacted with indirect bullying. The more attractive a female was, the more likely they were to be seen by other females as a rival, therefore indirect aggression was used because they were perceived as being in competition. This indirect bullying resulted in attractive females moving down the dominance hierarchy, while the bullying females moved up, increasing their chance of obtaining their resource, the attractive male.

Social learning theory

Can social learning, i.e. learning by observation, modelling and reinforcement, explain bullying? Craig and Pepler (1997) noted that bullies mostly have an audience for their actions, with peers witnessing 85% of all bullying incidents. O'Connell, Pepler and Craig (1999) argued that peers watching bullying may then be passively reinforcing the behaviour of the bully by condoning their actions through lack of intervention; indeed Craig and Pepler (1995) found children were more friendly and respectful to bullies than to victims. A further concern here is that the bully is then modelling bullying behaviour and where peers who are witnessing this see that the bully is not stopped or punished in any way, this may lead them to learn that bullying does not have negative consequences. Furthermore, the authors suggested that witnesses can become desensitised to this bullying behaviour, which may make it more likely that they themselves will bully in the future. O'Connell *et al.* (1999) showed that peers spent 21% of each bullying incident reinforcing the bully by participating physically or verbally, and that this was reported more for older boys than for younger boys or older girls. In terms of time, 53.9% was spent just watching, without either intervening or participating. Although 41% of children in self-report claimed they would try to intervene on behalf of their classmates, peers only intervened for an average of 25.4% of incidents, with older and younger girls more likely to intervene than older boys.

Empathy and bullying

Another explanation for bullying is that bullies have low empathy, that is to say, poor understanding of emotions experienced by another person. Studies by Björkqvist, Österman and KauKiainen (2000) and Jolliffe and Farrington (2006) both provided evidence of an association between low total empathy and greater levels of bullying and aggressive behaviour. Further support for this view came from Caravita and Di Blasio's (2009) study which reported that cognitive and affective empathy were two different constructs, and that bullying behaviour was negatively associated with low affective empathy in particular. Gini (2006) extended this idea to examine the emotions of guilt and shame in 204 Italian children. The idea here is that these emotions are related to empathy through their role in regulating the conscience so that individuals who experience feelings of guilt and shame are less likely to engage in bullying behaviours. Peer nomination procedures were used in Gini's study to allocate children to the roles they assumed during bullying situations. They were presented with stories and assessed on their understanding of what the appropriate emotion in this bullying situation should be. The study found that bullies, reinforcers and assistants tended to use cognitive mechanisms such as justifying the use of aggressive behaviour, to allow them to disengage morally from their aggressive behaviour. They did this more so than outsiders, defenders and victims.

Heightened arousal

'Arousal' refers to a state of consciousness that differs according to activity and can vary across different situations (Eysenck and Gudjonsson, 1989). A young person listening to a boring lesson would be in a low state of arousal, but when about to sit an important exam would be in a high level of arousal. In addition though, individuals vary in their susceptibility to arousal, having their own predisposition to a particular arousal level. With respect to bullying, bully victims were found to have higher levels of arousal than neutral and uninvolved children (Woods and White, 2005). Their high arousal levels may make them particularly sensitive to signs of possible punishment and so make them both anxious bullies and, at the same time, provocative victims, i.e. bully victims provoke bullying by attracting attention because of their extreme anxiety and increased tension; as well as this they become anxious bullies in order to try to gain peer acceptance and avoid actually being bullied (Guerin and Hennessy, 2002).

Parental influences on bullying

Do parents turn their children into bullies? A number of parenting variables have been studied as possible contributors to bullying behaviour in children. For example, The Cambridge Study in Delinquent Development, which followed 411 boys from aged 8 years through into adulthood, found intergenerational continuity in bullying: that boys who were bullies tended to have children who were also bullies (Farrington, 1993). Let's look at some possible parenting influences on bullying.

Parenting style

Results from a 1986 survey of bullying with troubled secondary school-aged pupils in schools for children with emotional and behavioural difficulties, mainstream secondary schools and community homes found that there was a lack of parental discipline and poor parent–child relationships in families of children in this sample who were bullies, victims or bully victims (Stephenson and Smith, 1989).

Although Stephenson and Smith's study did not identify any differences between the families of children with different participant roles, later studies have. For example, in a longitudinal study of 198 boys, Schwartz, Dodge, Pettit and Bates (1997) showed aggressive victims to be slightly more likely to have experienced strict parental discipline than both passive victims and non-victimised aggressors. Curtner-Smith (2000) too found a correlation between inappropriate parental discipline (e.g. hitting, nagging) and high rates of bullying when she assessed bullying behaviour in 54 boys, aged from 10 to 13 years. More recent evidence of the role of authoritarian parenting in bullying behaviour was provided by Ahmed and Braithwaite (2004) from their study of 610 children aged 9–12 years. Parents of bully–victims and bullies were more likely to have used an authoritarian parenting style than were parents of victims or children completely uninvolved in bullying behaviour. Joussemet *et al.* (2008) too in a longitudinal study of 1993 Quebec children found that controlling parenting increased the risk of children showing aggression. Even with younger children in a sample of 44 parents enrolled in Head Start programme, Curtner-Smith *et al.* (2006) found that the parental need to exert control over their preschoolers was positively correlated with relational bullying in their children. Finally, focusing on victims rather than bullies, Georgiou (2008), in a study of 252 Cypriot older primary school children, reported that children of overprotective mothers were significantly more likely to be victims of bullying. These studies therefore suggest that authoritarian parenting style with an over-emphasis on parental discipline and control seems to be associated with aggressive, bullying behaviour in the child.

Family problems

Family problems in the home have also been linked to an increased risk of involvement in bullying behaviour in bullies, victims and bully victims when compared with unaffected children (Ahmed and Braithwaite, 2004; Stephenson and Smith, 1989), although in Ahmed and Braithwaite's study bullies actually experienced less, rather than more, family disharmony than victims and bully victims.

The marital relationship itself can be an important factor in bullying behaviour. Stephenson and Smith (1989), again reporting on their 1986 survey, showed that children from families with parental marital problems were more likely to have a participant role in bullying. Schwartz *et al.* (1997) revealed bully victims to be significantly more likely to come from homes of marital conflict than were passive victims or non-bullying children, but not more likely than were aggressive bullies; indicating that marital conflict is perhaps responsible for the aggression of these children, and not the victimisation. Curtner-Smith (2000) provided further evidence to support this assumption, in her finding that mothers' marital dissatisfaction was correlated with high bullying scores among their sons. Additionally, Joussemet *et al.* (2008) found that children from separated parents were also at an increased risk of displaying aggressive bullying behaviour in later years.

Parent–child relationship

Looking now more closely at the quality of the parent–child relationship there is evidence of greater maternal hostility in mother–son relationships of bully–victims than of non-bullies or non-victims (Schwartz *et al.*, 1997), and of bullies being less likely to have responsive mothers who displayed warmth, empathy, kindness and compassion, than non-aggressive children (Georgiou, 2008). Children who had mothers who treated them with less empathy were more likely to take part in both relational and overt bullying (Curtner-Smith *et al.*, 2006), which was also the case for children with mothers who had unreasonable developmental expectations and expected them to assume the role of caregiver at an early stage. It may be that these different factors are all indicative of a lack of parental understanding and it is this poor understanding of children's needs that contributes to participation in bullying in the child. Furthermore, parents of bullies may prefer to use physical discipline than other methods of discipline, and may encourage their children to respond to perceived provocation by fighting back (Loeber and Dishion, 1984). There is certainly evidence that bully victims and victims have experienced higher levels of physical abuse and violence than other peers (Duncan, 1999; Schwartz *et al.*, 1997). In addition, maternal depression may also be a factor with some evidence that bullies and victims are more likely to have depressive mothers than are non-bullying children (Curtner-Smith, 2000; Georgiou, 2008). Early motherhood and lack of social support for the mother from her family, friends and partner were both also related to bullying. Indeed, boys who were less involved in family social activities had higher bullying scores than those who participated more actively (Curtner-Smith, 2000; Joussemet *et al.*, 2008).

Genetic influences

The final parental influence to examine here is that of genetics. Ball, Arseneault, Taylor, Maughan, Caspi and Moffitt's (2008) US study on 1116 American families with 10-year-old twins showed that genetics accounted for 73% of the variability for victims and 61% for bullies. Some genetic factors were found to predict particular participant roles while approximately 14% of genes linked to bullying were also linked to victimisation. The authors concluded that in addition to environmental factors, genetics was also an important influence on whether children became bullies, victims or bully victims.

QUISSET *Now go beyond the text . . . Look it up yourself!*

Explore your library's electronic databases to investigate 'theoretical explanations for bullying.

● How well does participant role theory explain bullying? Are there aspects of bullying that are better addressed by other theoretical approaches?

Support your answer with evidence from your extended reading.

How has understanding bullying informed school intervention programmes?

It is important for schools to try to address bullying by putting into place anti-bullying intervention programmes. Being bullied has negative effects on the victims, who may display anxiety, depression and find it difficult to concentrate (Nansel *et al.*, 2001; Smith and Sharp, 1994). Even bystanders may experience stress-related problems (Kyriakides Kaloyiru and Lindsay, 2006). Bullies themselves may be more likely to be involved in violent or criminal behaviour in the future (Coie, 2004).

In this section we will look at programmes derived from two highly influential approaches to bullying.

The Olweus Bullying Prevention Programme (OBPP)

The OBPP was based on Olweus's work, and has been the prototype for subsequent anti-bullying programmes (Merrell, Gueldner, Ross and Isava, 2008). It emphasises the need to work at the level of the wholes-school community to create a warm school environment that is concerned about bullying and violence. The whole school is involved in creating an anti-bullying environment with school rules on bullying, increased levels of supervision at intervals, anonymous questionnaires to establish nature and extent of bullying, a whole-school committee to take overall responsibility for coordinating the programme. The OBPP also operates at the level of the class and at the level of individual bullies and victims. At the class level, there are class rules against bullying and class meetings to discuss this. At the individual level, talks are held with bullies and victims, and also with their parents. School staff play the major role in implementation, supported by additional staff such as counsellors, social workers and educational psychologists for training and for handling the most serious incidents of bullying.

Olweus evaluated this intervention from 1983 to 1985 in a sample of 2500 primary and secondary students aged 11–14 years in 42 schools in Bergen, Norway. He reported reductions in bullying, with the number of students who reported bullying or being bullied 'now and then' or more frequently, falling by approximately 50%. Olweus (1991) reported a reduction in new as well as existing cases of bullying, and an improvement in overall classroom discipline.

Roland (1989), however, collected data one year after Olweus's last data collection point which was three years after the start of Olweus's intervention programme and found that the number of bullies and the number of victims of bullying had now increased. Other evaluations of OBPP have also reported mixed findings (Bauer, Lozano and Rivara, 2007; Hawkins, Catalano and Arthur, 2002). Roland (2002) found that bullying was correlated with level of involvement in the intervention: those schools who had fully implemented the intervention showed decreased levels of bullying, while those who had been less conscientious in their implementation showed increased levels. This may relate to the point previously made at the end of Chapter 7 about the importance of implementation fidelity, that it is important not just to carry out an intervention programme, but to do this thoroughly and consistently. We will return to this point about intervention fidelity later in this chapter.

Bullying intervention using participant role theory

Based on Salmivalli *et al.*'s (1996) participant role theory, Salmivalli, Kaukiainen and Voeten (2005) devised a whole-school intervention. Through class discussions, the attention of pupils is drawn to group processes in bullying and how they tend to behave differently in a group. Children are encouraged to self-reflect upon the discrepancy between the negative attitudes they may have towards bullying and the role they actually play in reality. These discussions may also lead to role-plays, with pupils playing a different participant role from that which they usually play. These class discussions are set within the context of a whole-school approach to bullying, with school policies against bullying and guidelines a central part of this intervention. Discussions at the individual level based on the method of shared concern (Pikas, 1989), the no-blame approach (Maines and Robinson, 1998) or the Farsta method (Ljungström, 1990) are also conducted.

QUISSET *Now go beyond the text ... Look it up yourself!*

Explore your library's electronic databases to investigate 'bullying interventions'.
- Examine the literature to find out what is involved in:
  - Shared concern
  - No-blame approach
  - Farsta method.
- What are the strengths and weaknesses of these approaches?

Forty-eight classes from 16 schools in Finland were involved in Salmivalli *et al.*'s (2005) evaluation study which had 1220 9–12-year-old children participating. Teachers were trained in how to deliver the intervention in four training sessions over the course of a year. Intervention effects were measured after six months and after 12 months. Positive findings were found for self-reported data though not for peer-reported data indicating effects for the younger age group in the sample. Among these younger pupils, there were moderate effects of implementation across the five participant roles in schools who spent less time implementing the intervention, and high effects in those who spent more time on implementation. There were few overall effects for older children.

The KiVa approach is another recently evaluated bullying intervention that is also based on participant role theory (Kärnä, Voeten, Little, Poskiparta, Kaljonen, and Salmivalli, in press). This also targets at three levels, the whole school, the classroom and the individual. It provides theoretical ideas to the teachers as well as concrete materials, such as a computer game for them to use in the classroom. The aim is to explain group processes in bullying, create empathy for the victim and encourage peers to intervene on their behalf. Schools are provided with posters to advertise the intervention and also high-visibility jackets for playground supervisors, making it very clear to pupils that there is a high level of supervision and awareness of bullying. When bullying incidents do occur, a group of three teachers conducts discussions with the involved pupils, and also asks high-status students to support the victims. There are two training days, and networks of teachers are also created, who meet up with KiVa support staff three times a year for advice. An evaluation study was also carried out in Finland, with 8237 pupils aged 10 to 12 years. After four months of the intervention, children were more likely to defend victims, showed more anti-bullying attitudes and greater empathy towards the victim. After nine months, positive behavioural outcome measures were reported, with pupils in the intervention schools showing lower rates of victimisation, assisting and reinforcing, and higher levels of self-efficacy for defending and wellbeing at school.

QUISSET *Now go beyond the text . . . Look it up yourself!*

Explore your library's electronic databases to investigate 'bullying interventions'.

- Identify from the literature other intervention approaches that build on other theories of bullying explained in this chapter. Evaluate the evidence for their effectiveness.

Roland's (2002) finding, that there was a correlation between the success of the intervention in reducing levels of bullying and the extent to which the intervention had been fully implemented, highlights a key problem when delivering a whole-school intervention in a real-world setting: the issue of intervention fidelity. It is very difficult to ensure that the programme is implemented faithfully as intended, when there are many other competing demands on teacher time and energy, and therefore many other variables that may not have been accounted for. In their systematic review of bullying interventions from 1997 to 2007, Ryan and Smith (2009) raised this as an issue. In their attempts to try to ensure programme integrity, most of the programmes in Ryan and Smith's review mentioned that they had used a manual and that there was staff training, although few had provided any supervision for staff carrying out the intervention. Only just over one-third of the studies reported on the extent to which the programme was delivered as intended in the manual (programme adherence). This usually involved a record of the frequency with which the programme was delivered, or some note of attitudes towards the programme or responsiveness of participants. With a limited amount of monitoring information on the extent to which programmes were delivered as intended, it is difficult to separate out the effects of ineffective programmes from those which were poorly delivered.

In spite of possible implementation problems, many local councils choose to invest both economic and human resources into anti-bullying interventions because they recognise the necessity of trying to combat the harmful effects of bullying. Because of this huge investment of staff time and energies it is important to examine evidence of the effectiveness of these interventions. The best way to do this is by considering the findings of meta-analyses and systematic reviews (see Chapter 4).

1 Smith, Schneider, Smith and Ananiadou (2004) conducted a meta-analysis of whole-school bullying intervention studies in Australia, Europe or North America until 2003. Fourteen studies met their inclusion criteria. They found that 93% of the effect sizes for decreased self-reporting of victimisation were small, negligible, or even negative, indicating increased experience of victimisation. For self-reported bullying, 92% of effects were negative or negligible. Smith *et al.* concluded that there was not sufficient evidence to conclude that whole-school intervention strategies were effective.

2 Ferguson, San Miguel, Kilburn and Sanchez's (2007) meta-analysis focused on the years 1995 to 2006. They identified 42 studies and although all effect sizes reported were positive and significant, these were so small that the authors concluded they were of very little practical significance. They suggested that while victims may perceive it to be of benefit to them to take part in such programmes, there do not seem to be any particular benefits for bullies, who indeed may only stand to lose their social dominance advantage by participation.

3 Vreeman and Carroll's (2007) review findings were a little more positive. Of the ten whole-school interventions reviewed, eight had positive outcomes . Of the remaining two whole-school interventions, one had a negative outcome, and the other no significant effect. The evidence for classroom level interventions such as lessons on bullying or participating in social and behavioural skills groups was very weak. As a result the authors recommended whole-school interventions as the most effective approach, but qualified this with the comment that method of implementation and the motivation of staff were very important elements in their success.

4 Merrell, Gueldner, Ross and Isava (2008) conducted a meta-analysis of whole-school bullying intervention studies published between 1980 and 2004, including not only papers published in peer-reviewed journals but also studies from dissertations and chapters in books. The authors concluded, though, that they were unable to infer any pattern from the results. They noted that many studies concentrated on knowledge of bullying, rather than directly measuring bullying behaviour itself. When these more direct measures were used, they tended to show weaker, and sometimes even negative, effects. However, as only three of the studies used an experimental design, any conclusions should be treated with caution.

Considering the resources devoted to anti-bullying interventions, and that there have now been more than 20 years of research carried out, results appear somewhat disappointing. However, this is not to say that bullying interventions do not work, but that rather that there are two main problems for us when we try to draw conclusions from the literature. Firstly, as has already been discussed, there is the issue of promoting and verifying the integrity of the programme so that we can be sure that the intended programme was the programme that was actually delivered. Secondly, the design of the studies tend to lack the methodological rigour required to allow us to draw convincing conclusions, with few studies using standardised interventions, equivalent groups and trial environments, or qualitative data to provide a context for the intervention (Ryan and Smith, 2009).

Cyberbullying: new ways to engage in bullying?

With the ready availability of mobile phones, email and social networking websites, it seems that a new form of bullying has emerged. A website, set up in Canada in 2001 specifically to address this new phenomenon, may have been the first use of the term 'cyberbullying' (Belsey, 2008). Cyberbullying has been defined by Patchin and Hinduja (2006) as 'wilful and repeated harm inflicted through the medium of electronic text' (p.152). Thus young people may experience bullying outside the school environment by electronic means such as websites, blogs, text messaging, emails, instant messages, discussion groups and social networking sites (Willard, 2007). Cyberbullying then can take various forms such as flaming, sending rude electronic messages; harassment, repeatedly sending someone threatening, offensive messages; or exclusion, where someone is excluded from an online group in an intentionally hurtful way (Willard, 2007). Children who experience cyberbullying are more likely to feel unsafe at school, and to miss school due to feelings of insecurity (Marsh, McGee, Nada-Raja and Williams, in press; Raskauskas and Stoltz, 2007). They also report feelings of sadness, hopelessness and depression (Raskauskas and Stoltz, 2007).

Like traditional bullying, the prevalence of cyberbullying appears to vary across different countries and also within countries, depending on different definitions and methodologies used in studies. We can see an example of this disparity from two US studies: Finkelhor, Mitchell and Wolak (2000) reported 6% of adolescents had experienced cyberbulling at least once, while Juvonen and Gross (2008) reported a figure of 72% for this. As well as methodological differences, another explanation for the disparity could be that over the short time period between the two studies, use of electronic technology has greatly increased, so the frequency rate reported by Finkelhor *et al.* may also reflect its time. It is early days yet for this new area of research.

The relationship between gender and cyberbullying is similarly unclear at this stage. While some studies have found that more females have been victims of cyberbullying than males (Patchin and Hinduja, 2006; Smith *et al.*, 2008, Study 1; Wang, Ianotti and Nansel, 2009; Ybarra, Diener-West and Leaf, 2007), others have reported no differences (Fleming *et al.*, 2006; Li, 2006; Smith *et al.*, 2008, Study 2; Ybarra, Mitchell, Wolak and Finkelhor, 2006); most studies have found there to be no difference between the number of males and females who report engaging in cyberbullying as bullies (e.g. Li, 2007; Marsh *et al.*, in press; Patchin and Hinduja, 2006; Smith *et al.*, 2008; Williams and Guerra, 2007; Ybarra *et al.*, 2006).

There seems, however, to be a clearer association between traditional school bullying and cyberbullying. Being a victim of traditional bullying was correlated with being a victim of cyberbullying, and being a traditional bully correlated with the role of electronic bully (e.g. Juvonen and Gross, 2008; Katzer, Fetchenhauer and Belschak, 2009; Raskauskas and Stoltz, 2007; Riebel, Jäger and Fischer, 2009; Smith *et al.*, 2008, Study 2). Both cyber and traditional victims were reported low in popularity, with low self-concept and over-protective parents (Katzer *et al.*, 2009). Like traditional bullies, there is also evidence that cyberbullies have higher rates of delinquency (Ybarra and Mitchell, 2004). On the other hand there are ways in which cyberbullying can be viewed as quite distinct from traditional bullying. Unlike traditional school bullies, cyberbullies can easily remain anonymous (Katzer *et al.*, 2009; Li, 2008; Patchin and Hinduja, 2006), and can quickly spread offensive messages through copy-and-paste and forwarding functions (Li, 2007; 2008). Indeed cyberbullying was found to be a separate factor from overt and relational bullying in a factor analysis (Dempsey, Sulkowski, Nichols and Storch, 2009). Katzer *et al.* (2009) likewise reported that the school victimisation scale and the chat victimisation scale loaded on different factors.

Early implications for intervention suggest that it is important to ensure that young people feel able to report cyberbullying to their parents (Mishna, Saini and Solomon, 2009). They may be reluctant to report occurrences of online bullying because they are concerned that their parents might restrict their internet use (Juvonen and Gross, 2008). The connection between school and online bullying implies that educators should feel the same degree of responsibility for online bullying as for that which occurs on school grounds (Juvonen and Gross, 2008). This means that education professionals need to be trained in how to deal with incidents of online harassment just as they are trained in how to deal with bullying incidents in school itself (Wolak, Mitchell and Finkelhor, 2007). Whole-school bullying interventions should then be extended to apply to cyberbullying (Raskauskas and Stoltz, 2007; Williams and Guerra, 2007).

Summary and conclusions

Bullying continues to be a serious problem in schools for both boys and girls, and now operates not only inside school but through cyberbullying can now extend its reach to children's home lives too. Different theoretical explanations help explain underlying processes and have been used to inform intervention approaches. However, in spite of many years of large-scale research studies, evidence for the effectiveness of anti-bullying interventions in changing the behaviour of bullies is not yet compelling. It may well be that these interventions do work but that there are difficulties for schools in implementing them with the intensity and consistency required. Further studies may need to focus on documentation of details of programme adherence, frequency, attitudes and responsiveness, in order to demonstrate not only how effective the outcomes were, but also how effective was the programme delivery itself.

Further Study

Go to the website www.pearsoned.co.uk/markswoolfson **for the following starter articles:**

Kärnä, A., Voeten, M., Little, T., Poskiparta, E., Kaljonen, A., and Salmivalli, C. (in press). A large scale evaluation of the KiVa anti-bullying program. *Developmental Psychology*.

Patchin, J. and Hinduja, S. (2006). Bullies move beyond the schoolyard: A preliminary look at cyberbullying. *Youth Violence and Juvenile Justice*, *4*, 148–69.

Sutton, J., Smith, P., and Swettenham, K. (1999a). Social cognition and bullying: Social inadequacy or skilled manipulator. *British Journal of Developmental Psychology*, *17*, 435–50.

References

Abrams, D., Rutland, A., Cameron, L., and Ferrell, J. (2007). Older but wilier: In-group accountability and the development of subjective group dynamics. *Developmental Psychology, 43*, 134–48.

Ahmad, Y. and Smith, P. (1990). Behavioural measures review No. 1: bullying in schools. *Newsletter for the Association for Child Psychology and Psychiatry, 12*, 26–7.

Ahmed, E. and Braithwaite, V. (2004). Bullying and victimization: Cause of concern for both families and schools. *Social Psychology of Education, 7*, 35–54.

Atlas, R. and Pepler, D. (1998). Observations of bullying in the classroom. *The Journal of Educational Research, 92*(2), 86–99.

Ball, H., Arseneault, L., Taylor, A., Maughan, B., Caspi, A., and Moffitt, T.E. (2008). Genetic and environmental influences on victims, bullies, and bully-victims in childhood. *Journal of Child Psychology and Psychiatry, 49*, 104–12.

Barboza, G., Schiamberg, L., Oehmke, J., Korzeniewski, S., Post, L., and Heraux, C. (2009). Individual characteristics and the multiple contexts of adolescent bullying: An ecological perspective. *Journal of Youth and Adolescence, 38*, 101–21.

Bauer, N., Lozano, P., and Rivara, F. (2007). The effectiveness of the Olweus bullying prevention program in public middle schools: a controlled trial. *Journal of Adolescent Health, 40*(3), 266–74.

Belsey, B. (2008) *Cyberbullying: An emerging threat to the "always on" generation*. Retrieved December 4, 2009 from http://www.canadianteachermagazine.com/pdf/CTM_Spring08_Cyberbullying.pdf.

Bentley, K. and Li, A. (1996). Bullying and victim problems in elementary schools and students' beliefs about aggression. *Canadian Journal of School Psychology, 11*(2), 153–65.

Björkqvist, K., Österman, K., and KauKiainen, A. (2000). Social intelligence – empathy = aggression. *Aggression and Violent Behaviour, 5*(2), 191–200.

Bosworth, K., Espelage, D., and Simon, T. (1999). Factors associated with bullying behavior in middle school students. *Journal of Early Adolescence, 19*, 341–62.

Boulton, M. and Smith, P. (1994). Bully/victim problems in middle school children: Stability, self-perceived competence, peer perceptions and peer acceptance. *British Journal of Developmental Psychology, 12*, 315–29.

Camodeca, M. and Goossens, F. (2005). Aggression, social cognitions, anger and sadness in bullies and victims. *Journal of Child Psychology and Psychiatry, 46*(2), 186–97.

Caravita, S. and Di Blasio, P. (2009). Unique and interactive effects of empathy and social status on involvement in bullying. *Social Development, 18*(1), 140–63.

Card, N., Stucky, B., Sawalani, G., and Little, T. (2008). Direct and indirect aggression during childhood and adolescence: A meta-analytic review of gender differences, intercorrelations, and relations to maladjustment. *Child Development, 79*(5), 1185–29.

Cassidy, T. (2009). Bullying and victimisation in school children: the role of social identity, problem-solving style, and family and school context. *Social Psychology of Education, 12*, 63–76.

Chang, L. (2004). The role of classroom norms in contextualizing the relations of children's social behaviors to peer acceptance. *Developmental Psychology, 40*, 691–702.

Coie, J. (2004).The impact of negative social experiences on the development of antisocial behavior. In J. Kupersmidt and K. Dodge (eds) *Children's peer relations: From development to intervention* (pp. 243–67). Washington, DC: American Psychological Association.

Coie, J. and Dodge, K. (1998). Aggression and antisocial behaviour. In N. Eisenberg (ed.), *Handbook of child psychology* (vol. 3). New York: Wiley (pp. 779–62).

Collins, K., McAleavy, G., and Adamson, G. (2004). Bullying in schools: A Northern Ireland study. *Educational Research, 46*(1), 55–71.

Craig, W. and Pepler, D. (1995). Peer processes in bullying and victimization: an observational study. *Exceptionality Education Canada, 5*, 81–95.

Craig, W. and Pepler, D. (1997). Observations of bullying and victimization in the schoolyard. *Canadian Journal of School Psychology, 2*, 41–60.

Craig, W., Pepler, D., and Atlas, R. (2000). Observations of bullying in the playground and in the classroom. *School Psychology International, 21*, 22–36.

Crick, N. and Dodge, K. (1994). A review and reformulation of social information-processing mechanisms in children's social adjustment. *Psychological Bulletin, 115*(1), 74–101.

Crick N. and Grotpeter, J. (1995). Relational aggression, gender, and social-psychological adjustment. *Child Development, 66*, 710–22.

Curtner-Smith, M. (2000). Mechanisms by which family processes contribute to school-age boys' bullying. *Child Study Journal, 30*, 169–86.

Curtner-Smith, M., Culp, A., Scheib, C., Owen, K., Tilley, A., Murphy, M., *et al.* (2006). Mothers' parenting and young economically disadvantaged children's relational and overt bullying. *Journal of Child and Family Studies, 15*, 177–89.

Dempsey, A., Sulkowski, M., Nichols, R., and Storch, E. (2009). Differences between peer victimization in cyber and physical settings and associated psychosocial adjustment in early adolescence. *Psychology in the Schools, 46*, 962–72.

Dodge, K. (1991). The structure and function of reactive and proactive aggression. In D. Pepler and K. Rubin (eds), *The development and treatment of childhood aggression* Hillsdale, NJ: Lawrence Erlbaum, (pp. 201–18).

Dodge, K. and Crick, N. (1990). Social information-processing bases of aggressive behaviour in children. *Personality and Social Psychology Bulletin, 16*(1), 8–22.

Due, P., Holstein, B., Lynch, J., Diderichsen, F., Gabhain, S., Scheidt, P., Currie, C., and The Health Behaviour in School-Aged Children Bullying Working Group (2005). Bullying and symptoms among school-aged children: International comparative cross sectional study in 28 countries. *European Journal of Public Health, 15*, 128–32.

Duffy, A. and Nesdale, D. (2009). Peer groups, social identity, and children's bullying behavior. *Social Development, 18*, 121–39.

Dunbar, R. (1988). *Primate social systems*. Ithaca, NY: Cornell University Press.

Duncan, R. (1999). Maltreatment by parents and peers: The relationship between child abuse, bully victimization, and psychological distress. *Child Maltreatment, 4*, 45–55.

Eysenck, H. and Gudjonsson, G. (1989). *The causes and cures of criminality*. London: Plenum Press.

Farrington, D. (1993). Understanding and preventing bullying. In M Tonry (ed.) *Crime and justice: A review of research.* (vol. 17) Chicago: University of Chicago Press, (pp. 381–458).

Ferguson, C., San Miguel, C., Kilburn, J., and Sanchez, P. (2007). The effectiveness of school-based anti-bullying Programs: A meta-analytical review. *Criminal Justice Review. 32*, 401–14.

Finkelhor, D., Mitchell, K., and Wolak, J. (2000). *Online victimization: A report on the nation's youth by the Crimes against Children Research Center.* Retrieved December 1, 2010 from http://www.unh.edu.ccrc/pdf/jvg/CV38.pdf

Fleming, M., Greentree, S., Cocotti-Muller, D., Elias, K., and Morrison, S. (2006). Safety in cyberspace: Adolescents' safety and exposure online. *Youth and Society, 38*, 135–54.

Frederickson, N. and Furnham, A. (2001). The long-term stability of sociometric status classification: a longitudinal study of included pupils who have moderate learning difficulties and their mainstream peers. *Journal of Child Psychology and Psychiatry, 42*(5), 581–92.

Georgiou, S. (2008). Bullying and victimization at school: The role of mothers. *British Journal of Educational Psychology, 78*, 109–25.

Gini, G. (2006). Social cognition and moral cognition in bullying: What's wrong? *Aggressive Behaviour, 32*, 528–39.

Goossens, F., Olthof, T., and Dekker, P. (2006). The New Participant Role Scales: A comparison between various criteria for assigning roles and indications for their validity. *Aggressive Behavior, 32*, 343–57.

Guerin, S. and Hennessy, E. (2002). *Aggression and Bullying*, Oxford: Blackwell.

Hawkins, J., Catalano, R., Arthur, M. (2002). Promoting science-based prevention in communities. *Addictive Behavior, 27*, 951–76.

Hawley, P. (1999). The ontogenesis of social dominance: A strategy-based evolutionary perspective. *Developmental Review, 19*, 97–132.

Hunter, S., Boyle, J., and Warden, D. (2004). Help seeking among child and adolescent victims of peer aggression and bullying: The influence of school stage, gender, victimisation, appraisal and emotion. *British Journal of Educational Psychology, 74*(3), 375–90.

Hunter, S., Boyle, J., and Warden, D. (2007). Perceptions and correlates of peer victimization and bullying. *British Journal of Educational Psychology, 77*, 797–810.

Jolliffe, D. and Farrington, D.(2006). Examining the relationship between low empathy and bullying. *Aggressive Behaviour, 32*, 540–50.

Joussemet, M., Vitaro, F., Barker, E., Cote, S., Nagin, D., Zoccolillo, M., *et al.* (2008). Controlling parenting and physical aggression during elementary school. *Child Development*, 79, 411–25.

Juvonen, J. and Gross, E. (2008). Extending the school grounds? – Bullying experiences in cyberspace. *Journal of School Health, 78*, 496–505.

Kärnä, A., Voeten, M., Little, T., Poskiparta, E., Kaljonen, A., and Salmivalli, C. (in press). A large-scale evaluation of the KiVa anti-bullying program. *Developmental Psychology*.

Katzer, C., Fetchenhauer, D., and Belschak, F. (2009). Cyberbullying: Who are the victims? A comparison of victimization in internet chatrooms and victimization in school. *Journal of Media Psychology, 21*, 25–36.

Kyriakides, L., Kaloyirou, C., and Lindsay, G. (2006). An analysis of the revised Olweus Bully/Victim Questionnaire using the Rasch measurement model. *British Journal of Educational Psychology, 76*, 781–801.

Lagerspetz, K., Björkqvist, K., Berts, M., and King, E. (1982). Group aggression among school children in three schools. *Scandinavian Journal of Psychology, 23*, 45–52.

Lagerspetz, K., Björkqvist, K., and Peltonen, T. (1988). Is indirect aggression typical of females? Gender differences in aggressiveness in 11- to 12-year-old children. *Aggressive Behaviour, 14*, 403–14.

Leenar, L., Dane, A., and Marini, Z. (2008). Evolutionary perspective on indirect victimization in adolescence: The role of attractiveness, dating and sexual behaviour. *Aggressive Behaviour, 34*, 404–15.

Li, Q. (2006). Cyberbullying in schools: A research of gender differences. *School Psychology International, 27*, 157–70.

Li, Q. (2007). New bottle but old wine: A research on cyberbullying in schools. *Computers and Human Behavior, 23*, 1777–91.

Li, Q. (2008). A cross-cultural comparison of adolescents' experience related to cyberbullying. *Educational Research. 50*, 223–34.

Ljungström, K. (1990). Mobbning i skolan. Ett compendium om mobbning samt on mobbning-behandling enligt Farstametoden. (Bullying in schools: A handbook on bullying and its treatment by use of the Farsta method). Stockholm: Ordkällan/Pedaktiv.

Loeber, R. and Dishion, T. (1984). Boys who fight at home and school: Family conditions influencing cross-setting consistency. *Journal of Consulting and Clinical Psychology, 52*, 759–68.

Maines, B. and Robinson, G. (1998). The no blame approach to bullying. In D. Shorrocks-Taylor (ed.), *Directions in educational psychology*. London: Whurr Publishers Ltd. (pp. 281–95).

Marsh, L., McGee, R., Nada-Raja, S., and Williams, S. (in press). Brief report: Text bullying and traditional bullying among New Zealand secondary school students. *Journal of Adolescence*.

Merrell, K., Gueldner, B., Ross, S., and Isava, D. (2008). How effective are school bullying intervention programs? A meta-analysis of intervention research. *School Psychology Quarterly, 23*, 26–42.

Mishna, F., Saini, M., and Solomon, S. (2009). Ongoing and online: Children and youth's perceptions of cyber bullying. *Children and Youth Services Review*. 31, 1222–8.

Monks, C., Smith, P., and Swettenham, J. (2005). Psychological correlates of peer victimisation in preschool: Social cognitive skills, executive function and attachment profiles. *Aggressive Behaviour, 31*, 571–88.

Nansel, T., Overpeck, M., Pilla, R., Ruan, W., Simons-Morton, B., and Scheidt, P. (2001). Bullying behaviors among US youth: Prevalence and association with psychosocial adjustment. *Journal of the American Medical Association, 285*(16), 2094–100.

Naylor, P., Cowie, H., Cossin, F., de Bettencourt, R., and Lemme, F. (2006). Teachers' and pupils' definitions of bullying. *British Journal of Educational Psychology, 76*(3), 553–76.

O'Connell, P., Pepler, D., and Craig, W. (1999). Peer involvement in bullying: insights and challenges for intervention. *Journal of Adolescence, 22*, 437–52.

Ojala, K. and Nesdale, D. (2004). Bullying and social identity: The effects of group norms and distinctiveness threat on attitudes towards bullying. *British Journal of Developmental Psychology, 22*, 19–35.

Olthof, T. and Goossens, F. (2008). Bullying and the need to belong: early adolescents' bullying-related behavior and the acceptance they desire and receive from particular classmates. *Social Development, 17*, 24–46.

Olweus, D. (1978). *Aggression in the schools. Bullies and whipping boys.* New York: John Wiley and Sons.

Olweus, D. (1991). Bully/victim problems among schoolchildren: Basic facts and effects of a school based intervention program. In D. Pepler and K. Rubin (eds). *The development and treatment of children aggression* (pp. 411–48). Hillsdale, NJ: Lawrence Erlbaum.

Olweus, D. (1993). *Bullying at school: What we know and what we can do.* Oxford: Blackwell.

Patchin, J. and Hinduja, S. (2006). Bullies move beyond the schoolyard: A preliminary look at cyberbullying. *Youth Violence and Juvenile Justice, 4*, 148–69.

Pellegrini, A. (1995). A longitudinal study of boys' rough-and-tumble play and dominance during early adolescence. *Journal of Applied Developmental Psychology, 16*, 77–93.

Pellegrini, A. (1998). Bullies and victims in school: A review and call for research. *Journal of Applied Developmental Psychology, 19*(2), 165–76.

Pellegrini, A. and Long, J. (2002). A longitudinal study of bullying, dominance, and victimization during the transition from primary school through secondary school. *British Journal of Developmental Psychology, 20*, 259–80.

Pepler, D., Jiang, D., Craig, W., and Connolly, J. (2008). Developmental Trajectories of Bullying and Associated Factors. *Child Development, 79*, 325–38.

Perner, J., Ruffman, T., and Leekam, S. (1994). Theory of mind is contagious: you catch it from your sibs. *Child Development, 65*(4), 1228–38.

Pikas, A. (1989). The Common Concern method for the treatment of mobbing. In E. Roland, and E. Munthe (eds), *Bullying: An international perspective*. London: David Fulton, (pp. 91–104).

Raskauskas J. and Stoltz, A. (2007). Involvement in traditional and electronic bullying among adolescents. *Developmental Psychology, 43*, 564–75.

Riebel, J., Jäger, R., and Fischer, U. (2009). Cyberbullying in Germany – an exploration of prevalence, overlapping with real life bullying and coping strategies. *Psychology Science Quarterly, 51*, 298–314.

Roland, E. (1989). Bullying: The Scandinavian research tradition. In D.Tattum, and D. Lane (eds), *Bullying in schools*. London: Trentham Books (pp. 21–32).

Roland, E. (2002). Bullying, depressive symptoms and suicidal thoughts. *Educational Research, 4*, 55–67.

Ryan, W. and Smith, J. (2009). Antibullying in schools: How effective are evaluation practices? *Prevention Science, 10*, 248–59.

Salmivalli, C. (1999). Participant role approach to school bullying: implications for interventions. *Journal of Adolescence, 22*, 453–9.

Salmivalli, C., Huttunen, A., and Lagerspetz, K. (1997). Peer networks and bullying in schools. *Scandinavian Journal of Psychology, 38*, 305–12.

Salmivalli, C., Kaukiainen, A., and Voeten, M. (2005). Anti-bullying intervention: Implementation and outcome. *British Journal of Educational Psychology, 75*, 465–87.

Salmivalli, C., Lagerspetz, K.M.J, Bjorkqvist, K., Österman, K., and Kaukiainen, A. (1996). Bullying as a group process: Participant roles and their relations to social status within the group. *Aggressive Behaviour, 22*, 1–15.

Salmivalli, C., Lappalainen, M., and Lagerspetz, K. (1998). Stability and change of behavior in connection with bullying in schools. *Aggressive Behavior, 24*, 205–18.

Schäfer, M., Korn, S. Brodbeck, F., Wolke, D., and Schultz, H. (2005). Bullying roles in changing contexts: The stability of victim and bully roles from primary to secondary school. *International Journal of Behavioural Development, 29*, 323–35.

Scheithauer, H., Hayer, T., Petermann, F., and Jugert, G. (2006). Physical, verbal, and relational forms of bullying among German students: Age trends, gender differences, and correlates. *Aggressive Behavior, 32*, 261–75.

Schwartz, D., Dodge, K., Pettit, G., and Bates, J. (1997). The early socialization of aggressive victims of bullying. *Child Development, 68*, 665–75.

Seals, D. and Young, J. (2003). Bullying and victimization: Prevalence and relationship to gender, grade level, ethnicity, self-esteem, and depression. *Adolescence, 38*, 735–47.

Siann, G., Callaghan, M., Glissov, P., Lockhart, R., and Rawson, L. (1994). Who gets bullied? The effect of school, gender and ethnic group. *Educational Research, 36*, 123–34.

Sijtsema, J. Veenstra, R., Lindenberg, S., and Salmivalli, C. (2009). Empirical test of bullies' status goals: assessing direct goals, aggression, and prestige. *Aggressive Behavior, 35*, 57–67.

Smith, J., Schneider, B., Smith, P., and Ananiadou, K. (2004). The effectiveness of whole-school antibullying programs: A synthesis of evaluation research. *School Psychology Review, 33*, 547–60.

Smith, P., Cowie, H., Olafsson, R., and Liefooghe, A. (2002). Definitions of bullying: A comparison of terms used, and age and gender differences, in a fourteen country international comparison. *Child Development, 73*(4), 1119–33.

Smith, P., Mahdavi, J., Carvalho, M., Fisher, S., Russell, S., and Tippett, N. (2008). Cyberbullying: Its nature and impact in secondary school pupils. *Journal of Child Psychology and Psychiatry , 49*(4), 376–85.

Smith, P. and Sharp, S. (1994). *School bullying: Insights and perspectives.* London: Routledge.

Stephenson, P., and Smith, D., (1989). Bullying in the junior school. In D. Tattum and D. Lane, (eds), *Bullying in schools* (pp. 45–57). Stoke-on Trent: Trentham Books.

Sutton, J., Smith, P., and Swettenham, K. (1999a). Social cognition and bullying: Social inadequacy or skilled manipulator. *British Journal of Developmental Psychology, 17*, 435–50.

Sutton, J., Smith, P., and Swettenham, J. (1999b). Bullying and 'theory of mind': A critique of the 'social skills deficit' view of anti-social behaviour. *Social Development, 8*(1), 117–27.

Tajfel, H. and Turner, J. (1979). An integrative theory of intergroup conflict. In W.G. Austin, and S. Worchel (eds), *The social psychology of intergroup relations* (pp. 33–47). Monterey, CA: Brooks/ Cole.

Vallancourt, T. and Hymel, S. (2006). Aggression and social status: The moderating roles of sex and peer-values characteristics. *Aggressive Behaviour, 32*, 396–408.

Veenstra, R., Lindenberg, S., Zijlstra, B., De Winter, A., Verhulst, F.,and Ormel, J. (2007). The dyadic nature of bullying and victimization: testing a dual-perspective theory. *Child Development, 78*(6), 1843–54.

Vreeman, R. and Carroll, A. (2007). A systematic review of school-based interventions to prevent bullying. *Archives of Pediatrics and Adolescent Medicine, 161*, 78–88.

Wang, J., Iannotti, R., and Nansel, T. (2009). School bullying among adolescents in the United States: Physical, verbal, relational, and cyber. *Journal of Adolescent Health, 45*, 368–75.

Whitney, I. and Smith, P. (1993). A survey of the nature and extent of bullying in junior/middle and secondary schools. *Educational Research, 35*(1), 3–25.

Willard, N. (2007). *Cyberbullying and cyberthreats. Responding to the challenge of online social aggression, threats and distress.* Champaign, IL: Research Press.

Williams, K. and Guerra, N. (2007). Prevalence and predictors of Internet bullying. *Journal of Adolescent Health, 41*(6 suppl. 1), 14–21.

Wolak, J., Mitchell, K., and Finkelhor, D. (2007). Does online harassment constitute bullying? An exploration of online harassment by known peers and online-only contacts. *Journal of Adolescent Health, 41*, 51–8.

Wolke, D., Woods, S., Stanford, K., and Schulz, H. (2001). Bullying and victimization of primary school children in England and Germany: prevalence and school factors. *British Journal of Psychology, 92*, 673–96.

Woods, S. and White, E. (2005). The association between bullying behaviour, arousal levels and behaviour problems. *Journal of Adolescence, 28*, 381–95.

Ybarra, M. Diener-West, M., Leaf, P. (2007). Examining the overlap in internet harassment and school bullying: implications for school intervention. *Journal of Adolescent Health, 41*(suppl. 1), 42–50.

Ybarra, M. and Mitchell, K. (2004). Youth engaging in online harassment: associations with caregiver–child relationships, Internet use, and personal characteristics. *Journal of Adolescence, 27*, 319–36.

Ybarra, M., Mitchell, K., Wolak, J., and Finkelhor, D. (2006). Examining characteristics and associated distress related to Internet harassment: findings from the Second Youth Internet Safety Survey. *Pediatrics, 118*, 1169–77.

Inclusive education of children with special needs

Inclusive education was advocated at an international level through the United Nations Convention on the Rights of the Child 1989 and the Salamanca Statement (UNESCO, 1994). It has also been influenced by the European Social Charter, a human rights charter that addresses the right to be educated without experiencing discrimination. Closer to home it is also enshrined in UK legislation and government guidelines (e.g. Special Educational Needs and Disability Act 2001, Disability Discrimination Act 2005, Standards in Scotland's Schools Act 2000, Education (Additional Support for Learning) (Scotland) Act 2004.

While inclusion is underpinned by principles of social justice in terms of children's right to access a good education within their local community regardless of disability, this chapter explores the extent to which outcomes have been shown to be beneficial for the child. First we'll look at the history and key concepts here, and then we'll go on to discuss research evaluating inclusive education that examines the evidence for the effectiveness of inclusive education for children with additional support needs. We will also look at teacher views of inclusive education, as well as considering outcomes for typically developing peers.

Learning outcomes

By the end of this chapter you should be able to:

- Appreciate terminology, principles and key issues around the concepts of inclusive education and special needs
- Understand methodological difficulties in research evaluating effectiveness of inclusive education
- Evaluate research findings on academic and psychosocial outcomes in inclusive settings for children with special needs and for typically developing children.

From 'handicap' to 'learning difficulties'

In the late 1970s the dominant concept in the UK that was used for thinking about what is now referred to as 'learning difficulties' was then 'handicap'. 'Handicap' was viewed as something personal that belonged to the individual, a 'deficit' within the child. Children were categorised according to their 'handicap' and went to a special school for children with that 'handicap'. So children who were 'mentally handicapped' went to a school for 'the mentally handicapped'. There were different schools catering for different levels of severity of 'mental handicap' as assessed by IQ testing: mild, moderate, or severe. Similarly children who were 'physically handicapped' went to a school for 'the physically handicapped' and children with visual or hearing impairments went to schools for 'the deaf' or attended 'blind' schools. The educational psychologist's job then was to assess and categorise those children whose IQ was below 70 in order to determine which kind of separate segregated school was most appropriate for them, according to the nature and severity of the child's impairment. The role of an educational psychologist in the 1970s was often that of gatekeeper to special education; a child had to be 'ascertained' by the psychologist in order to be placed in a special school. The teacher's job at that time involved identifying children who were seen as having been wrongly placed in mainstream schooling. The notion of supporting diversity in mainstream did not exist, nor did the idea of adapting the curriculum. The curriculum was perceived as a fixed programme to be presented without adaptation to a homogeneous group of children who could learn from it. If a child wasn't able to cope with the curriculum then the problem was within the child, and that child was viewed as needing to be educated elsewhere. The educational psychologist was called in to assess the child by IQ test and thus categorise the child for the appropriate educational provision.

This sounds dreadful now but it was well-intentioned at the time because it was thought these measures ensured that the child received the special education that they needed. Bear in mind too that 'educational subnormality' and 'mental handicap' were improvements on the previous language of professionals that had referred to 'mental deficiency'. This new language had reflected a conceptual shift in professionals' understanding of the difficulties experienced by this population. In fact, even earlier categorisations using IQ testing employed the terms 'imbecile', 'idiot', and 'feeble-minded' for different levels of cognitive impairment. While this language is now perceived as highly derogatory and sounds shocking to modern ears, it was once was the vocabulary of medical discourse, educational terminology and legislation before it came to have these disparaging connotations (Norwich, 1999; Solity, 1991). Well-meaning professionals did not realise at the time that allocating a child to a segregated special school effectively categorised and labelled that child in a way that stigmatised them during their school life and beyond. Those children who had been assigned to the special education system were effectively excluded from subsequently achieving high-status occupations or social mobility (Tomlinson, 1982).

The thinking about how best to meet the needs of children who experience significant difficulties in learning or in accessing a mainstream curriculum has gradually changed over the last 30 years. Although the Warnock Report (1978) did not itself advocate inclusive education, it made a significant contribution to initiating an agenda that subsequently led to inclusive education policies as a human rights issue being advocated internationally with the UN Convention on the Rights of the Child 1989 and the UNESCO Salamanca Statement 1994. The Warnock Report recognised that saying someone had a particular mental or physical handicap said nothing about the kind of educational help that child required. It was not the case that all children with mild mental handicap required the same educational setting. So the issue was no longer about categorising the child but about careful identification of the child's special educational needs and working out how to meet these. Special needs could be cognitive, communication, behavioural, emotional, sensory or physical. This influential report was followed by educational legislation from 1981 onwards to enable children to access an education appropriate to their needs at their local neighbourhood school. Post-Warnock, children in the UK with special educational needs were referred to as having learning difficulties or learning disabilities, which could be moderate, severe or complex. Categories of handicap were replaced with new terminology about special educational needs (SEN), which directed attention away from the idea of a deficit within the child, to assessment of the impact of the impairment on the child's access to education and ensuring provision minimised this. Again, however well-intentioned the new language of impairment, it can be argued that one set of stigma-laden labels was simply replaced with another (Corbett, 1996; Norwich, 1999).

Inclusive education

In the 1980s and 1990s integration was the term used to describe the first efforts to introduce special school pupils into mainstream schools. This was also called mainstreaming in the US. Integration could range from very occasional visits of special school pupils to the mainstream school, to full-time placement in a mainstream class in the child's local school. Even so, that pupil could spend the whole day supposedly integrated, i.e. placed, in a mainstream class, without any interaction with their peers, effectively still quite segregated.

The concept of 'integration' implies 'additional arrangements within a system of schooling that remains largely unchanged'. Contrast this with inclusive education, where the aim is to restructure the school so that it can better respond to the diverse needs of all children in a way that facilitates their full and active participation in the life and activities of the school (Booth and Ainscow, 2000). With inclusive education you start from an assumption of student diversity and design a school system that attempts to address a wide range of different needs (e.g. Sebba and Ainscow, 1996). To use a Piagetian analogy of assimilation and accommodation, with inclusion the mainstream school reorganises its structures to accommodate children regardless of their needs. Integration on the other hand leaves the school structure unchanged and the child's task is to assimilate into an unchanged school environment (Avramidis and Norwich, 2002). With inclusion you bring additional support services to the child in the mainstream school rather than remove the child from the school because they require additional services (Smelter, Rasch and Yudewitz, 1994).

Inclusive education is not just another name for 'special education' and does not only apply to students with special needs but to any students who may be excluded or who are at risk of not engaging fully in the life of the school, e.g. traveller children, schoolgirls who become pregnant, children for whom English is an additional language. The term 'additional educational needs' (or 'additional support needs' in Scotland) is now being used to reflect this wider population with needs that now also require to be addressed by schools. Inclusive education is part of a broader UK government agenda of social inclusion by way of principles of comprehensive education and equal educational opportunities for all children, as well as human rights and social justice principles (Croll and Moses, 1994; Farrell, 1997; Lindsay, 1997). While this chapter's concern is with the subset of children with additional educational needs who have SEN, it should be noted that wider socio-cultural factors may interact with children being identified as having SEN. A disproportionate representation in the SEN population of some ethnic minority groups was noted early on by Croll and Moses (1985), and more recently by, for example, MacMillan and Reschly (1998) and Eitle (2002). Socio-economic disadvantage is certainly one factor that contributes to this ethnic disproportionality within special education (Skiba, Poloni-Staudinger, Simmons, Feggins-Azziz and Chung, 2005; Strand and Lindsay, 2009).

Research evaluating inclusion of children with SEN

There are convincing political, moral and philosophical arguments for inclusive education. However, values are only one aspect of policy formulation (Lindsay, 2003). There may be other good reasons for the benefits of inclusive education. Mainstream schools may devote more curriculum time to developing key literacy and numeracy skills and the typically developing peer group may provide a richer environment for the development of language, communication and social skills (e.g. Laws, Byrne and Buckley, 2000). For the main part of this chapter then, we will examine the key aspect of this for educational psychology: that is, answering the question 'Do children with special needs achieve better academic and psychosocial outcomes when they receive their education in an inclusive mainstream environment rather than in a segregated special school or class?'

Methodological issues

When we examine the literature there are a number of methodological issues that we should keep in mind.

1 What provision is being studied?

Older studies often compare the outcomes of what they refer to as 'integrated' and segregated schooling. When reading these studies it is necessary to identify exactly what is being compared because a separate unit in a mainstream school may be referred to as an integrated setting in some studies, while others would view this as a segregated setting. Certainly nowadays we would consider it as segregated, as our ideas about what inclusive education looks like have developed considerably over the last 30 years. Furthermore, synthesising findings from different countries can be a particular problem as the language of inclusion differs across countries (Booth, 1996; Farrell, 2000).

2 What variables define the intervention provision?

Even with studies conducted in the UK, stating that one group in a study receives its education in a mainstream school does not sufficiently distinguish which variables might be relevant to the study outcomes as this label in itself does not specify the features of the curriculum, teaching methods or relevant aspects of the school environment that might be the same as, or different from, those experienced by the special school group in the study. To what extent are elements of special school education such as a differentiated curriculum or special support staff or additional pull-out sessions offered in the inclusive placement, or is the mainstream provision being studied one that has no elements of special education at all with an emphasis on whole-group, undifferentiated teaching (Kavale, 2002)?

3 Which sample is being studied?

'Special needs' is an umbrella heading for developmental difficulties that impact on children's learning, social and emotional development, behaviour and communication (Lindsay, 2007), so children with special needs are not a homogeneous group. As we will see in this chapter, study findings from a sample of children with special needs, which comprises children with intellectual disabilities, are not necessarily generalisable to the inclusion of children with behavioural difficulties or to those with severe and complex needs. Indeed, even within a sample of children with intellectual disabilities there may be a wide range of problems, so unless the sample is very well specified, it is difficult to know the extent to which one can generalise to another sample of children with SEN (Farrell, 2000). The severity of the impairment is also an important variable to take into account, as well as the extent to which there are comorbid impairments. This means that even a sample that is defined as having intellectual disabilities is likely to be a heterogeneous one.

As discussed at the beginning of this chapter, the language of SEN has changed over time. Different language in different countries may be used not only to describe type of schooling as above, but also to describe the nature of the impairment. For example, 'learning disabilities' in the UK is taken to be the equivalent of learning difficulty, meaning an intellectual impairment, whereas in the US it refers to a specific learning difficulty such as dyslexia (MacKay, 2009). Even within the constituent countries of the UK, there are small differences in the language of SEN. In Scotland, the term 'social, emotional and behavioural difficulties' (SEBD) is used, while in England the same difficulties are referred to as 'behavioural, emotional and social' (BESD). And indeed even within the UK, health practitioners may use different language to characterise a sample compared to education practitioners, e.g. learning disabilities rather than learning difficulties (Lindsay, 2007).

4 What is the comparison group?

Studies make use of different comparison groups depending on the purpose of the study. In some studies that you read, you will find that there is an attempt to match the target group of children with special needs with similar children also with special needs – one group in a special school, and one who are being educated in mainstream school (but who may receive additional educational support within the mainstream setting). Here the comparison aims to study the differential effects of mainstream and special education on educational and social outcomes for that particular group of special needs. In other studies you may find that the special needs group is compared with typically developing peers. These are quite different comparisons which allow quite different conclusions to be drawn.

5 Problems in matching SEN samples

Given the heterogeneity in a group of children with SEN, it is almost impossible then to find a comparison group in another provision that matches an intervention group in age, gender, type of impairment, severity of impairment and comorbidity. Matching will usually try to address some of these variables. It is difficult to draw any useful conclusions about the effectiveness of inclusive education from a sample that has not been fully matched as the two groups in the study do not have exactly the same characteristics and any differences between groups may be due, not to the different education received, but to differences between the samples.

Not only is it necessary to consider how well the sample has been matched but it is also important to consider the extent to which even the teachers have been matched, as the effect may be at teacher level rather than at the level of the type of provision.

6 Research design

As discussed in Chapter 3, randomised controlled trials are viewed as the 'gold standard', the most stringent means of establishing whether an intervention actually caused the reported outcomes, as this design removes threats to the internal validity of the study which provide competing explanations for causality. Greater use of experimental design has not only been advocated in educational research in general but also specifically in the area of special education for answering the kinds of questions we are interested in, in this chapter, about what works best for children with SEN (Gersten, Fuchs, Compton, Coyne, Greenwood and Innocenti, 2005). However, RCTs are rarely used in this area and there are ethical implications regarding the withholding of an intervention from a group that needs this (Farrell, 2000; Lindsay, 2007). It is more usual for there to be non-random allocation to groups because pre-existing groups are being compared, e.g. children who attend one form of provision compared to children who attend another. This is a quasi-experimental design from which only cautious conclusions may be drawn about the extent to which the intervention caused the outcome (see Chapter 3).

To give a flavour of the problem in research on the effectiveness of inclusive education for children with SEN, let us consider Lindsay's (2007) review on the topic. Lindsay reviewed research studies in this area that were carried out between 2000 and 2005. From 1373 papers that were broadly on the effectiveness of inclusive education, he found only 14 that actually compared outcomes for children with SEN. None of these was an RCT design. Of the 14, two were not actually studies in themselves but were review papers of previous studies. Of the remaining 12, only nine compared children with SEN across special education and mainstream settings, the comparison of greatest interest for answering questions about the effectiveness of inclusive education. Two of these nine were actually comparisons of preschool provision for younger children with SEN, rather than school provision itself. You can see that from over 1000 studies that were in the subject area, Lindsay identified only a very limited amount of evidence from suitably tightly constructed studies on which we could base answers to our question, 'How effective is inclusive education for children with SEN?'

Effect of inclusion on pupils with SEN – academic outcomes

There are certainly studies that report positive effects of mainstreaming. For example, Baker, Wang and Walberg (1995) concluded from studying effect sizes across three meta-analyses that SEN pupils in mainstream classes did better academically than those in non-inclusive settings. Lipsky and Gartner (1996) similarly noted that many evaluations had found positive academic outcomes for pupils with disabilities, and in addition no adverse outcomes for their typically developing classmates. More recently, Markussen (2004) carried out a longitudinal study over five years which comprised more than 700 Norwegian pupils with mild SEN. The study found that children with SEN in mainstream classes achieved better academically than did their peers in the special setting. The academic outcome measure used in this study was 'achievement of formal competence', which was the school leaving certification used in Norwegian schools. Formal competence related to either study competence, the requirement for entry to higher education or further post-school study; vocational competence which included apprentice-ship training for trades such as plumbing and joinery; and competence at a lower level. This last competence was a new competence level introduced in 1994 for students with SEN to allow them to complete their schooling with certification that could help their entry into the labour market. Markusson's study reported that the mainstream SEN group were more likely to achieve formal competence at some level than the special school group. In another Norwegian study, Mykelbust (2007) too found better academic attainment outcomes for the pupils in inclusive education with more achieving formal qualifications than those in special edu-cation. Similarly Ruijs and Peetsma's recent (2009) review of the effectiveness of inclusion generally found inclusive settings to show better or similar outcomes compared to special educational settings. It should be noted, though, that most of the studies they reported were descriptive accounts of progress in mainstream, and many were without special education comparison groups, making drawing conclusions problematic.

There are, on the other hand, studies that have not reported advantages of inclusive education over special education for academic outcomes. Despite con-siderable teacher investment of time in planning, preparation and support for children with SEN, Zigmond et al. (1995) reported that in a series of studies, less than half the number of the pupils with learning disabilities showed gains in reading progress compared to their typically developing peers. Furthermore, Zigmond and Baker (1995) noted that many SEN pupils in inclusive settings did not receive the amount and intensity of direct, focused instruction on reading skill development, compared to that available in special education classes. The authors suggested that this meant they were unlikely to make good progress in the development of their reading skills in the general classroom environment. However, it should be noted that Ruijs and Peetsma's (2009) review of effective-ness studies carried out in the last ten years found only one study in which spe-cial education actually demonstrated superior outcomes to inclusive mainstream education. Like Zigmond et al.'s earlier (1995) study, this also concerned reading performance. It was, however, a small-scale, unpublished study that comprised only five young people with learning disabilities so cannot be considered as providing convincing evidence of the superiority of special education over main-stream education.

It is difficult, though, to determine to what extent one can generalise from studies where all types of SEN are grouped together in the sample: this design does not address the relationship between academic outcomes and the nature and severity of disability (Klingner, Vaughan, Hughes, Schumm and Elbaum, 1998; Ruijs and Peetsma, 2007). To illustrate how these effects can be lost, in a generic sample, let us consider Carlberg and Kavale's (1980) early meta-analysis that showed that for children with SEN there was a small effect size associated with mainstream educational provision compared to special school placement. However, when their findings were examined in closer detail, it could be seen that type of disability was a significant factor in this. Pupils with cognitive impairments indeed showed significantly better outcomes in mainstream general class placements, but pupils who had behavioural or emotional disorders or who had a learning disability showed better outcomes in special education provision (Carlberg and Kavale, 1980; Kavale, 2002). Leinhardt and Pallay's (1982) review also concluded that those with learning disabilities progressed better when they received their education in resource bases rather than the general classroom. To answer questions about whether inclusive education is effective, we need to be more specific regarding which group of children the question is being asked about.

Research that identifies participant disability more clearly has been carried out. For example, Laws *et al.* (2000) compared 22 children with Down syndrome who were educated in mainstream schools with 22 who attended special school. As impairments in language and memory are core features of Down syndrome, the research team was particularly concerned with examining the effect of mainstream and special educational settings on language and memory outcomes. Their results showed that the group who received the mainstream educational provision attained significantly higher scores in language measures assessed by their understanding of vocabulary and of grammar. In terms of development of memory abilities, children in the mainstream group also showed higher scores for both auditory and visual recall of digits, but not for recall of sequences of hand shapes or recall of faces, which were non-language-based memory measures. Peetsma, Vergeer, Roeleveld and Karsten (2001), too, reported positive results for SEN pupils in mainstream in a large-scale longitudinal study in the Netherlands with a sample of children identified as having mild 'learning and behavioural difficulties' or 'mild mental retardation'. Peetsma *et al.*'s study found that the children with SEN in the inclusive setting made greater progress in mathematics and language, as measured by standardised achievement tests, compared to the special education comparison group. Similar findings were obtained by Karsten, Peetsma, Roeleveld and Vergeer (2001), who further found that the gap between mainstream and special education outcomes increased as children grew older.

IN FOCUS

A Dutch study of the effectiveness of inclusion

Peetsma, Vergeer, Roeleveld and Karsten (2001) compared the development of matched pairs of primary-aged pupils in mainstream and special schools over four years. Data gathered included standardised achievement tests in language and mathematics, teacher assessments of psychosocial functioning, teacher reports of classroom characteristics such as differentiation of tasks and the extent of specialist support for the children with SEN, and qualitative data from pupil and teacher interviews on pupil self-image, wellbeing, behaviour, and their attitude to school work. The SEN sample had 'learning and behavioural difficulties' or were 'mildly mentally retarded'. Peetsma *et al.* identified the sample as having 'rather mild educational problems' (Peetsma *et al.*, 2001, p. 132). After four years, the SEN group who were in mainstream had made greater academic progress than their matched pairs whose educational placements were in special education.

But identifying provision as 'special' or 'mainstream' tells us little about what was actually going on in the classroom to result in the observed differences. The researchers were interested in what the specific characteristics were of classrooms that resulted in these positive outcomes for children with SEN. One possiblity that Peetsma *et al.* considered was that the observed progress might be linked to differentiation, the special adaptations to curriculum content and delivery of teaching, that teachers make for children who experience difficulties in class. Such differentiation is seen as good practice and could take place regardless of whether the setting was a mainstream or special school. However, the study found no relationship between the characteristics of education provided and child progress outcomes. Nor were there any clear findings from the qualitative data gathered in the study. It seemed that academic outcomes were associated with individual patterns of child, school and family characteristics.

QUISSET   *Now go beyond the text . . . look it up yourself!*

Explore your library's electronic databases to investigate 'effectiveness of inclusive education for children with SEN'.

Some studies comparing the effectiveness of inclusive and special educational settings have been discussed in this chapter. Carry out a literature search on this topic using the databases that are available to you in order to identify further studies on this topic.

State clearly which databases you have searched, over which years, and which search terms you have used.

- Evaluate the studies you have found in terms of their scientific quality (see Chapter 3 for guidelines).

- What conclusions can you draw about the effectiveness of inclusive educational settings for children with SEN?

- What problems have you encountered in trying to draw such conclusions?

- What are the implications for future research studies?

It has been suggested previously in this chapter that as well as specifying type of disability, severity of disability might also be an important factor that might differentially influence academic outcomes. Rafferty, Piscitelli and Boettcher's (2003) study indeed found severity to act as a moderator of the relationship between school setting (mainstream or special) and academic outcomes. There was an interaction effect between setting and severity of disability such that setting did not have an effect on children with a mild level of disability but children with severe disabilities showed better outcomes in the inclusive setting, although it was noted that in this study the inclusive setting comprised a high proportion of children with disabilities and so may not be a typical mainstream setting (Lindsay, 2007).

Because of the way inclusion effectiveness studies have been designed and because of the limited information in some studies on sample specification, it is difficult to draw strong conclusions about the relative effects of inclusive and special education settings, but the findings on academic outcomes for children with SEN seem promising in the extent to which they provide support for a social justice agenda.

In Myklebust's (2002) study it was noted that while the sample performed better academically in the inclusive setting than in special classes, there was a higher drop-out rate from the inclusive classroom. This leads us to the issue of social outcomes of inclusion.

Effect of inclusion on pupils with SEN – psychosocial factors

Along with the rights issue, one of the driving forces for inclusion has been that social benefits are anticipated for children with SEN in mainstream. Instead of attending segregated special schools which are both geographically and socially isolated from their communities, they attend the same local schools as their siblings and neigbourhood peers. The intention is that they have the opportunity to develop appropriate social skills and to engage in social relationships with peers in their community (e.g. Vaughn, Elbaum and Schumm, 1996). Let us next examine then the evidence for the effectiveness of inclusive education on these psychosocial outcomes.

Social competence

As well as positive academic outcomes for inclusive education as discussed earlier in this chapter, Baker et al.'s (1995) meta-analysis reported mainstream education as having a positive effect on the social development of SEN learners. Cole and Meyer (1991), for example, found that a mainstreamed group of children with severe learning difficulties, defined in their longitudinal study as IQ < 30, progressed on a social competence measure while a group of segregated children regressed. The authors suggested that the ability to generalise skills from one environmental context to another is usually a key deficit for children with severe cognitive impairments so it was likely that the mainstreamed group would have benefited from learning social interactional skills within the real-world settings in which they had to be applied. This was not the case for the special school group who were learning social skills within a restricted, managed environment rather than in a more naturalistic setting. In their recent Irish study, however, with a sample of learners with moderate intellectual impairment, i.e. less severely impaired than in Cole and Meyer's study, Hardiman, Guerin and Fitzsimons (2009) did not find type of placement to have a differential impact on social competence.

There seem, though, to be few well-designed studies that conclusively demonstrate benefits in social competence for pupils with SEN, that specify to which group of learners their findings apply, and that measure social competence outcomes beyond the classroom (Hardiman *et al.*, 2009). In any case the cause and effect relationship is unclear. Might we expect social skills to develop as a result of the inclusive placement or does the relationship between these factors operate in the opposite direction? Perhaps it is pupils with better social skills who are more likely to achieve successful inclusion in mainstream settings than those who are less competent socially. In effect it may be social competence rather than other factors that make or break an inclusive educational placement (Kemp and Carter, 2002).

Social relationships

If we now move our focus from social competence and social development to examine social relationships, social inclusion and social status of SEN pupils, we find that there is a wider range of evidence available for consideration.

In an effort to answer such questions, recent reviews have been carried out by Freeman and Alkin (2000) and Webster and Carter (2007). Freeman and Alkin's review focused specifically on children with intellectual disabilities and reported five quantitative studies that showed higher social interaction and more social contacts for learners with SEN in general class settings compared to special education settings. However, when instead of comparing with a matched group of children with SEN in a special educational setting, the children with SEN were compared with their typically developing (TD) peers, findings were less positive. Generally studies have found the SEN group to have lower social acceptance than their typically developing peers (Freeman and Alkin, 2000; Nowicky, 2003; Ochoa and Olivarez, 1995; Stone and La Greca, 1990). Two studies in Freeman and Alkin's review, though (Evans, Salisbury, Palombaro, Berryman and Hollowood, 1992; Hudson and Clunies-Ross, 1984), showed no differences in social acceptance between SEN and TD groups. In Webster and Carter's (2007) review, only some of the settings they reviewed were standard school settings, our focus of interest in this chapter. Others were preschool or early education or atypical settings such as universities, or groups specifically set up to study relationships. Lack of sample specification was again a problem in many studies, just as we noted earlier in this chapter to be the case for studies on academic outcomes. Webster and Carter concluded that findings were patchy and that there is a lack of research on social relationships in children with disabilities of high methodological quality to parallel the comprehensive existing literature on social relationships in typically developing children.

EXAMPLES Some recent studies on social status

In an Australian study, Kemp and Carter (2002) followed up the progress in mainstream schools of 22 pupils with moderate intellectual disabilities. They assessed social interaction by playground observation, and social status by teacher and parent ratings, as well as nomination procedures.

Kemp and Carter used a typical restricted nomination procedure to carry out sociometric analysis of a classroom. They asked each child in the class to nominate three children in the class with whom s/he liked to play at break time. They were then asked to use a 'smiley face' Likert rating scale with a smiling face (1), a neutral face (2) and a sad face (3), corresponding to 'really like', 'OK', and 'don't like'. For each of the children nominated, the child being interviewed was asked to point to one of the faces to indicate whether they really liked, didn't like the child or if they were neutral, i.e. that the person was 'all right'. Using these different measures of social interaction, Kemp and Carter found large differences between the target group of children with SEN and typically developing peers in the amount of time spent interacting with peers, with the typically developing peers spending more time with other peers than the students with intellectual disabilities.

Frederickson and Furnham (2001) investigated the stability of sociometric classifications over a two-year period in 8–10-year-olds in inclusive classrooms with children with moderate learning difficulties. Rather than the standard peer nomination approach described above, they used a 'forced choice' technique. This was because children with SEN tend to be classified as 'rejected' by the above restricted nomination approach because they weren't named in many pupils' top three friends. They may not however be 'rejected', just not in the top three, as the nomination method does not distinguish between the child who is rejected and the child who is mildly accepted, but not in many children's top three. With the forced choice technique, instead of just being asked to rate the three friends they have nominated, children have to rate every member of the class. Frederickson and Furnham (2001) used 'work with' and 'play with' questions for their rating questions and applied this to every child in the class. They found that pupils with SEN were significantly less likely to be classified as popular and more likely to be classified as rejected. Over the two-year period just over half the children, both SEN and typically developing, remained in the same category to which they had first been allocated. But the stability coefficients for the rejected and popular status groups were found to be higher in the included sample than in the mainstream sample. That is to say, once the child with SEN was rejected, s/he was more likely to remain rejected. Could this be due to peers' stereotypic responses to children with SEN?

Motivation and self-confidence

One disadvantage for children with SEN within inclusive classes is that there may be a lack of opportunities in which they can achieve success relative to peers. Always perceiving oneself as not doing well in schoolwork in relation to TD peers may result in loss of motivation for children with SEN (Bakker, Denessen, Bosman, Krijger and Boutts, 2007), a group for whom extra motivation may indeed be required in order to address their significant difficulties in the classroom (Peetsma *et al.*, 2001). However, this could equally well work the opposite way. With their high emphasis on academic achievement compared to special schools, mainstream schools could motivate all learners to achieve more, including those learners with SEN (Cole, Waldron and Majd, 2004; Mykelbust, 2007; Ruijs and Peetsma, 2009). Mixed results on motivation and self-confidence were obtained by Peetsma *et al.* (2001) with their sample of children with mild cognitive impairment. After two years the group in the special educational setting scored higher in motivation towards their schoolwork than their matched pairs in mainstream, suggesting that children with SEN in mainstream may indeed lack motivation. After four years, however, there were no differences between these groups, nor were there differences between the learning and behavioural difficulties groups in either their motivation or their self-confidence.

The findings on psychosocial outcomes seem at best mixed. If social inclusion as part of the school community is a key purpose of inclusive education for children with SEN, then perhaps we need to consider that we may be some way away from demonstrating convincingly that this target has been achieved.

 Debate

Join up with some friends to discuss.

Half the group should advance the case for the benefits for inclusive education and provide evidence to support these arguments.

Half the group should argue the case for special education, providing evidence to support these arguments.

Typically developing children and inclusive education

We have so far focused on the academic and social impacts of inclusive education on children with SEN. In this section we will turn to consider typically developing children, in terms of their attitudes to learners with SEN and also with respect to the outcomes that inclusive education has on this group of learners who do not have SEN.

Promoting positive attitudes in typically developing children

In a previous section of this chapter we examined the extent to which learners with SEN experienced social inclusion within mainstream schools. But how can schools best encourage positive attitudes in typically developing children? Early research suggested that it was important to ensure that there was contact between children with and without SEN and that the SEN group should be highly visible within the mainstream setting, rather than secluded and separated, and that it helped if the typically developing children saw similarities between themselves and the children with SEN (Furnham and Pendred, 1984; McConkey, McCormick and Naughton, 1983; Siperstein and Chatillon, 1982). Maras and Brown (2000) investigated what type of contact would encourage positive attitudes in typically developing children both towards learners with SEN in their school, and towards learners with SEN in general. They found that schools that downplayed the salience of the disability tended to have children with less biased attitudes towards disabled children and disability. Disappointingly, these attitudes were not more positive than those of children in the control schools where there were no children with disabilities, so this study's findings cannot be readily translated into policy for improving attitudes towards children with disabilities.

IN FOCUS

Maras and Brown's (2000) study of the relationship between contact and children's attitudes towards disability

Maras and Brown (2000) compared two different types of contact. 'Categorised contact' was where typically developing children were given specific information about the kinds of difficulties experienced by the children with SEN who attended the same school. The aim was to make them more aware of differences and similarities between themselves and children with SEN. 'Decategorised contact' was where group differences were not discussed and children with SEN within the school were not specifically identified as being part of a special group. In this condition, children with SEN were educated in a special unit within the mainstream school. For the 'categorised' condition, however, children with SEN were taught most or all of the time in a separate building from the mainstream school. Group differences were highlighted in the 'categorised' condition by, for example, teachers discussing disability with the typically developing children.

The study focused on children with hearing impairments, learning difficulties and physical disabilities. Children were shown photographs of unknown children with these conditions and also photographs of non-disabled children without any of these conditions. They were asked questions about how much they wanted to play with the children in the photos, how much they liked them and whether they were able to run fast, work hard and so on. 'Decategorised' contact where the salience of the disability was downplayed seemed to result in less biased attitudes towards children with disabilities than schools with 'categorised' contact, but this pattern of response was broadly similar to that in the control schools where children had no contact with children with disabilities. The authors point out that as this was a study involving pre-existing groups and not randomised allocation to groups, there may have been other variables operating other than 'categorised' or 'decategorised'.

Activity

Read Maras and Brown's (2000) paper.

As the authors pointed out, the study used pre-existing groups which might limit the extent to which the 'categorised' and 'decategorised' conditions might contribute to the attitude outcome measures.

What other confounding variables might contribute to the findings?

Maras and Brown's study examined the relationship between types of contact and attitudes to disability. We might ask, though, why it matters what attitudes children hold. We are interested in investigating attitudes because we understand there to be a link between children's attitudes and the behaviour they engage in. Roberts and Smith (1999) addressed this specifically by applying Ajzen's Theory of Planned Behaviour (TPB; Ajzen, 1988) to investigate the relationship between children's attitudes to disability in general and their behaviour towards peers with physical disabilities in their school. TPB has been used extensively in the area of health psychology to predict health-related behaviour from attitudes. With respect to interactional behaviour with peers with disabilities (see Figure 9.1), TPB proposes that behavioural intentions to befriend peers with disabilities predict actual interactional behaviour and further that behavioural intentions are influenced by (a) personal attitudes towards interacting with peers with disabilities (i.e. Does the child value this behaviour themselves?); (b) subjective norms regarding befriending peers with disabilities (Do their friends value this behaviour?); (c) perceived behavioural control (i.e. How easy or difficult will the performance of the behaviour be?). This latter relates to factors that may prevent a child from carrying out

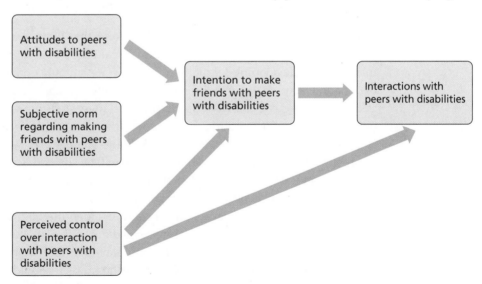

Figure 9.1 Theory of Planned Behaviour as applied to attitudes of typically developing children towards peers with disabilities

Source: Roberts and Smith, 1999, reprinted by permission of the publisher (Taylor & Francis Group, www.informaworld.com)

their intention to interact with disabled classmates, for example, lack of opportunities to interact with peers with disabilities because timetabling means they are not in same classes, or perhaps typically developing children feeling they don't have the skills to interact suitably with children with communication difficulties.

Roberts and Smith found, in support of TPB, that behavioural intentions predicted interactional behaviour with peers with disabilities. When children perceived interaction with disabled peers as difficult to engage in (perceived behavioural control), they expressed fewer intentions to interact, even where their attitude towards interaction with children with disabilities was positive. As with the Maras and Brown research, however, it is not straightforward to infer policy implications for schools from this study. In what circumstances do children perceive friendship behaviours as hard to enact? Roberts and Smith suggested these may be where children feel they lack understanding of disability, or perhaps where they perceive structural barriers such as not being in same group as the disabled child, so see themselves as not having any obvious opportunity for interaction.

 ## Debate

Join up with some friends to discuss.

Consider the findings of Roberts and Smith (1999) and Maras and Brown (2000).

- What do these findings suggest about how schools should proceed with typically developing children in order to encourage positive and supportive attitudes to learners with SEN?
- Do both studies suggest that the same approach should be taken?

Effects of inclusion on typically developing classmates

It often seems to teachers in mainstream schools that there is a tension between including a wide range of learners with special needs and continuing to ensure that typically developing learners in the class are suitably challenged (Ainscow, Booth and Dyson, 2006). What then are the effects of inclusive education on typically developing children? Some studies have suggested improved psychosocial outcomes such as increase in acceptance of difference and in caring relationships (e.g. Maras and Brown, 2000; Peltier, 1997; Staub and Peck, 1994). In their systematic review of the literature, Kalambouka, Farrell, Dyson and Kaplan (2007) established that in the majority of the 26 studies they reviewed, there were positive or neutral effects of inclusion of learners with SEN on academic or social outcomes for typically developing peers. While the authors identified limitations, including that most of the reviewed studies were carried out in the US, they concluded that local authorities need have no major concerns about the effect of inclusive education on learners who did not have disabilities. Furthermore, it should be noted that the study samples reviewed comprised learners with different types of SEN – cognitive, behavioural, sensory/physical and communication, so the review findings were not specific to any particular type of disability.

Activity

Kalambouka *et al.* (2007) identified limitations with their review.

- What were they?
- How do these affect the conclusions which might be drawn?

Teachers' attitudes to inclusion

As it is teachers who are ultimately responsible for implementing inclusive education policies on a day-to-day basis, researchers have been interested in investigating their views. For example, Scruggs and Mastropieri (1996) carried out a meta-analysis of studies that were carried out over a forty-year period from the late 1950s until 1995. They reported that although 65% of teachers agreed with inclusion as a general principle, only 40% thought it was actually realistic for most children and that it depended on the disability. Cognitive and physical disabilities were viewed as suitable for inclusion in mainstream classes (Forlin, 1995), with severity of disability perceived as an important factor in determining the appropriateness of full-time mainstream placement (Avramidis and Norwich, 2002; Forlin, 1995; Ward, Center and Bochner, 1994). Social and emotional behaviour disorders are the special educational need that teachers tend to find most problematic for inclusion: there has been a rise in school exclusions in the UK for children with this problem (Avramidis and Norwich, 2002).

In a recent study, mainstream teachers were less positive than special education teachers about the extent to which difficulties experienced by children with learning disabilities were amenable to change (Woolfson, Grant and Campbell, 2007). Also, teachers with less experience of teaching children with SEN attributed difficulties less to factors external to the child, which suggests less willingness on their part to adapt their teaching to take responsibility for learner progress, instead assuming difficulties were inherent within the child because of the child's SEN (Brady and Woolfson, 2008; Cook, Tankersley, Cook and Landrum, 2000; Jordan, Lindsay and Stanovich, 1997). These studies suggest that many mainstream teachers may hold attitudes and beliefs that could be more receptive to responding to learner diversity within inclusive educational settings.

There are conflicting findings, though, about what factors influence teachers' attitudes and beliefs about teaching learners with SEN in their classes. Some studies have found that teachers with fewer years' teaching experience held more positive views about the inclusion of children with SEN than those with more years of teaching (Forlin, 1995; Brady and Woolfson, 2008). This could relate to newer recruits to a profession being generally more idealistic, or it could be that more recently trained teachers studied on training courses that focused more on inclusive practices than teachers who were trained 15–20 years ago (Brady and Woolfson, 2008). Other studies, though, have not found length of teaching experience to be a significant factor (Avrimidis, Bayliss and Burden, 2000; Villa *et al.*, 1996; Woolfson and Brady, 2009), or found a relationship with training experiences (Brady and Woolfson, 2008; Tait and Purdie, 2000; Woolfson and Brady, 2009).

Perhaps it is not just experience that is needed in order for there to be an impact on teacher beliefs and attitudes. Perhaps it is specific experience of learners with SEN that is required. Some studies have certainly reported that when teachers had experience of inclusion, and perhaps had developed new professional skills, they were more positive about teaching learners with SEN (Avrimidis *et al.*, 2000; Brady and Woolfson, 2008; Cook *et al.*, 2000; Villa, Thousand, Meyers and Nevin, 1996). Other studies, though, reported the opposite (Leyser, Kapperman and Keller, 1994; Soodak, Podell and Lehman, 1998), i.e. that teachers became more hostile to inclusion with experience. Others have found no particular relationship between the two (Scruggs and Mastropieri, 1996). Worryingly, Talmor, Reiter and Feigin (2005) reported that the more positive teachers' attitudes were, the more they experienced burn-out.

Summary and conclusions

While there is a wide range of research literature on the topic of inclusive education for children with SEN, much of it constitutes opinion pieces. There is therefore a smaller available literature of well-designed studies from which to evaluate the effectiveness of mainstream education for this group of learners. What is more, results may differ depending on whether it is academic or social outcomes that are under examination, and depending on the nature and severity of the disability. The currently available educational and psychological evidence seems to vindicate a social justice agenda by providing evidence that inclusive education is at least as effective for included learners as special education and that typically developing children do not seem to be disadvantaged by this policy.

Further study

Go to the website www.pearsoned.co.uk/markswoolfson **for the following starter articles:**

Kalambouka, A., Farrell, P., Dyson, A., and Kaplan, I. (2007). The impact of placing pupils with special educational needs in mainstream schools on the achievement of their peers. *Educational Research, 49,* 365–82.

Lindsay, G. (2007). Educational psychology and the effectiveness of inclusive education/ mainstreaming. *British Journal of Educational Psychology, 77,* 1–24.

Roberts, C. and Smith, P. (1999). Attitudes and behaviour of children towards peers with disabilities. *International Journal of Disability, Development and Education, 46*(1), 35–50.

References

Ainscow, M., Booth, T., and Dyson, A. (2006). Inclusion and the standards agenda: Negotiating policy pressures in England. *International Journal of Inclusive Education, 10*(4), 295–308.

Ajzen, I. (1988). *Attitudes, personality and behaviour.* Milton Keynes, UK: Open University Press.

Avrimidis, E., Bayliss, P., and Burden, R. (2000). A survey into mainstream teachers' attitudes towards the inclusion of children with special educational needs in the ordinary school in one local educational authority. *Educational Psychology, 20*(2), 191–211.

Avramidis, E. and Norwich, B. (2002). Teachers' attitudes towards integration/inclusion: a review of the literature. *European Journal of Special Needs Education, 17*(2), 129–47.

Baker, K. and Donelly, M. (2001). The social experience of children with disability and the influence of environment: A framework for intervention. *Disability and Society, 16*(1), 71–85.

Baker, E., Wang, M., and Walberg, H. (1995). The effects of inclusion on learning. *Educational Leadership, 52*(4), 33–5.

Bakker, J., Denessen, E., Bosman, A., Krijger, E., and Boutts, L. (2007). Sociometric status and self-image of children with specific and general learning disabilities in Dutch general and special education classes. *Learning Disability Quarterly, 30*, 47–62.

Booth, T. (1996). Changing views of research on integration: the inclusion of children with 'special needs' or participation for all? In A. Sigston, P. Curran, A. Labram, and S. Wolfendale (eds) *Psychology in practice with young people, families and schools* London: David Fulton, (pp. 181–194).

Booth, T. and Ainscow. M. (2000). *Index on Inclusion.* Bristol: Centre for Studies on Inclusive Education.

Brady, K. and Woolfson, L. (2008). What teacher factors influence their attributions for children's difficulties in learning? *British Journal of Educational Psychology, 78*, 527–44.

Carlberg, C. and Kavale, K. (1980). The efficacy of special versus regular class placement for exceptional children: a meta-analysis. *The Journal of Special Education, 14*, 295–309.

Cole, C., Waldron, N., and Majd, M. (2004). Academic progress of students across inclusive and traditional settings. *Mental Retardation, 42*, 136–44.

Cole, D. and Meyer, L. (1991). Social integration and severe disabilities: A longitudinal analysis of child outcomes. *The Journal of Special Education, 25*, 340–51.

Cook, B., Tankersley, M., Cook, L., and Landrum, T. (2000). Teachers' attitudes toward their included students with disabilities. *Exceptional Children, 67*(1), 115–35.

Corbett, J. (1996). *Bad mouthing: The language of special needs.* London: Falmer.

Croll, P. and Moses, D. (1985). *One in five: The assessment and incidence of special educational needs.* London: Routledge and Kegan Paul.

Croll, P. and Moses, D. (1994). Policy making and special educational needs: a framework for analysis. *European Journal of Special Needs Education, 9*(3), 275–86.

Eitle, T. (2002). Special education or racial segregation: Understanding variation in the representation of Black students in educable mentally handicapped programs. *Sociological Quarterly, 43*, 575–605.

Evans, I., Salisbury, C., Palombaro, M., Berryman, J., and Hollowood, T. (1992). Peer interactions and social acceptance of elementary-age children with severe disabilities in an inclusive school. *Journal of the Association for Persons with Severe Handicaps, 17*, 205–12.

Farrell, P. (1997). *Teaching pupils with learning difficulties: Strategies and solutions.* London: Cassell.

Farrell, P. (2000). The impact of research on developments in inclusive education. *International Journal of Inclusive Education, 4*(2), 153–62.

Forlin, C. (1995). Educators' beliefs about inclusive practices in Western Australia. *British Journal of Special Education, 22*, 179–85.

Frederickson, N. and Furnham, A. (2001). The long-term stability of sociometric status classification: a longitudinal study of included pupils who have moderate learning difficulties and their mainstream peers. *Journal of Child Psychology and Psychiatry, 42*(5), 581–92.

Freeman, S. and Alkin, M. (2000). Academic and social attainments of children with mental retardation in general education and special education settings. *Remedial and Special Education, 21*(1), 3–20.

Forlin, C. (1995). Educators' beliefs about inclusive practices in Western Australia. *British Journal of Special Education, 22*, 179–85.

Furnham, A. and Pendred, J. (1984). Attitudes towards the mentally and physically disabled. *British Journal of Medical Psychology, 56*, 179–87.

Gersten, R., Fuchs, L., Compton, D., Coyne, M., Greenwood, C., and Innocenti, M. (2005). Quality indicators for group experimental and quasi-experimental research in special education. *Exceptional Children, 71*, 149–64.

Hardiman, S., Guerin, S., Fitzsimons, E. (2009). A comparison of the social competence of children with moderate intellectual disability in inclusive versus segregated school settings. *Research in Developmental Disabilities, 30*, 397–407.

Hudson, A. and Clunies-Ross, G. (1984). A study of the integration of children with intellectual handicaps into regular schools. *Australia and New Zealand Journal of Developmental Disabilities, 10*, 165–77.

Jordan, A., Lindsay, L., and Stanovich, P. (1997). Classroom teachers instructional interactions with students who are exceptional, at risk and typically achieving. *Remedial and Special Education, 18*, 82–93.

Kalambouka, A., Farrell, P., Dyson, A., and Kaplan, I. (2007). The impact of placing pupils with special educational needs in mainstream schools on the achievement of their peers. *Educational Research, 49*, 365–82.

Karsten, S., Peetsma, T., Roeleveld, J., and Vergeer, M. (2001). The Dutch policy of integration put to the test: Differences in academic and psychosocial development of pupils in special and mainstream education. *European Journal of Special Needs Education, 22*, 7–14.

Kavale, K. (2002). Mainstreaming to full inclusion: From orthogenesis to pathogenesis of an idea. *International Journal of Disability, Development and Education, 49*(2), 201–14.

Kemp, C. and Carter, M. (2002). The social skills and social status of mainstreamed students with intellectual disabilities. *Educational Psychology, 22*(4), 391–411.

Klingner, J., Vaughn, S., Hughes, M., Schumm, and Elbaum, B. (1998). Outcomes for students with and without learning disabilities in inclusive classrooms. *Learning Disabilities Research and Practice, 13*(3), 153–61.

Laws, G, Byrne, A., and Buckley, S. (2000). Language and memory development in children with Down syndrome at mainstream schools and special schools: A comparison. *Educational Psychology, 20*(4), 447–57.

Leinhardt, G. and Pallay, A. (1982). Restrictive educational settings: Exile or haven? *Review of Educational Research, 52*, 557–78.

Leyser, Y., Kapperman, G., and Keller, R. (1994). Teacher attitudes towards mainstreaming: A cross-cultural study in six nations. *European Journal of Special Needs Education, 9*, 1–15.

Lindsay, G. (1997). Are we ready for inclusion? In G. Lindsay and D. Thompson (eds) *Values into practice in special education* London: David Fulton, (pp. 89–103).

Lindsay, G. (2003). Inclusive education: A critical perspective. *British Journal of Special Education, 30*, 3–12.

Lindsay, G. (2007). Educational psychology and the effectiveness of inclusive education/mainstreaming. *British Journal of Educational Psychology, 77*, 1–24.

Lipsky, D. and Gartner, A. (1996). Inclusion, school restructuring and the remaking of the American society. *Harvard Educational Review, 66*, 762–96.

MacKay, T. (2009). Severe and complex learning difficulties: Issues of definition, classification and prevalence. *Educational and Child Psychology, 26*(4), 9–18.

MacMillan, D. and Reschly, D. (1998). Overrepresentation of minority students: The case for greater specificity and reconsideration of the variables examined. *Journal of Special Education, 32*, 15–24.

Maras, P. and Brown, R. (2000). Effects of different forms of school contact on children's attitudes towards disabled and nondisabled peers. *British Journal of Educational Psychology, 70*(3), 337–51.

Markussen, E. (2004). Special education: Does it help? A study of special education in Norwegian upper secondary schools. *European Journal of Special Needs Education, 19*, 33–48.

McConkey, R., McCormick, B., and Naughton, M. (1983). A national survey of young people's perceptions of mental handicap. *Journal of Mental Deficiency Research, 27*, 2113–34.

Myklebust, J. (2002). Inclusion or exclusion? Transitions among special needs students in upper secondary education in Norway. *European Journal of Special Needs Education, 17*, 251–63.

Mykelbust, J. (2007). Diverging paths in upper secondary education: Competence attainment among students with special educational needs. *International Journal of Inclusive Education, 11.* 215–31.

Norwich, B. (1999). The connotation of special education labels for professionals in the field. *British Journal of Special Education, 26*(4), 179–83.

Nowicky, E. (2003). A meta-analysis of the social competence of children with learning disabilities compared to classmates of low and average to high achievement. *Learning Disability Quarterly, 26*, 171–88.

Ochoa, S. and Olivarez, A. (1995). A meta-analysis of peer rating sociometric studies of pupils with learning disabilities. *The Journal of Special Education, 29*, 1–19.

Peetsma, T., Vergeer, M., Roeleveld, J., and Karsten, S. (2001). Inclusion in education: Comparing pupils' development in special and regular education. *Educational Review, 53*(2), 125–35.

Peltier, G. (1997). The effect of inclusion on non-disabled children: A review of the research. *Contemporary Education, 68*(4), 234–8.

Rafferty, Y., Piscitelli, V., and Boettcher, C. (2003). The impact of inclusion on language development and social competence among preschoolers with disabilities. *Exceptional Children, 69*, 467–79.

Roberts, C. and Smith, P. (1999). Attitudes and behaviour of children towards peers with disabilities. *International Journal of Disability, Development and Education, 46*(1), 35–50.

Ruijs, N. and Peetsma, T. (2009). Effects of inclusion on students with and without special educational needs reviewed. *Educational Research Review, 4*, 67–79.

Scruggs, T. and Mastropieri, M. (1996). Teacher perceptions of mainstreaming-inclusion, 1958–1995: A research synthesis. *Exceptional Children, 63*, 59–74.

Sebba, J. and Ainscow, M. (1996). International developments in inclusive schooling: Mapping the issues. *Cambridge Journal of Education, 26*(1), 5–18.

Siperstein, G. and Chatillon, A. (1982). Importance of perceived similarity in improving children's attitudes towards mentally retarded peers. *American Journal of Mental Deficiency, 86*(5), 453–8.

Skiba, R., Poloni-Staudinger, L. Simmons, A., Feggins-Azziz, L., and Chung, C. (2005). Unproven links: Can poverty explain ethnic disproportionality in special education? *Journal of Special Education, 39*, 130–44.

Smelter, R., Rasch, G., and Yudewitz, G., (1994). Thinking of inclusion for all special educational needs students? Better think again. *Phi Delta Kappan, 76*, 35–8.

Solity, J. (1991). Special needs: A discriminatory concept? *Educational Psychology in Practice, 7*(1), 12–19.

Soodak, L., Podell, D., and Lehman, L. (1998). Teacher, student and school attributes as predictors of teachers' responses to inclusion. *Journal of Special Education, 31*, 480–97.

Staub, D. and Peck, C. (1994). What are the outcomes for non-disabled students? *Educational Leadership, 52*(4), 36–40.

Stone, W. and La Greca, A. (1990). The social status of children with learning disabilities: A re-examination. *Journal of Learning Disabilities, 23,* 32–7.

Strand, S. and Lindsay, G. (2009). Ethnic disproportionality in special education: Evidence from an English population study. *Journal of Special Education, 43,* 174–90.

Tait, K. and Purdie, N. (2000). Attitudes towards disability: Teacher education for inclusive environments in an Australian university. *International Journal of Disability, Development and Education, 47,* 25–38.

Talmor, R., Reiter, S., and Feigin, N. (2005). Factors relating to regular education teacher burnout in inclusive education. *European Journal of Special Needs Education, 20*(2), 215–29.

Tomlinson, S. (1982). *A sociology of special education.* London: Routledge.

UNESCO. (1994). *The Salamanca Statement and framework for action on special needs education.* Paris: UNESCO.

Vaughn, S., Elbaum,B., and Schumm, J. (1996). The effects of inclusion on the social functioning of students with learning disabilities. *Journal of Learning Disabilities, 29,* 598–608.

Villa, R., Thousand, J., Meyers, H., and Nevin, A. (1996). Teacher and administrator perceptions of heterogeneous education. *Exceptional Children, 63,* 29–45.

Ward, J., Center, Y., and Bochner, S. (1994). A question of attitudes: Integrating children with disabilities into regular classrooms? *British Journal of Special Education, 21,* 34–9.

Warnock Report (1978). *Special educational needs: Report of the committee of enquiry into the education of handicapped children and young people.* London: HMSO.

Webster, A. and Carter, M. (2007). Social relationships and friendships of children with developmental disabilities: Implications for inclusive settings. A systematic review. *Journal of Intellectual and Developmental Disability, 32*(3), 200–13.

Woolfson, L. and Brady, K. (2009). An investigation of factors impacting on mainstream teachers' beliefs about teaching students with learning difficulties. *Educational Psychology, 29*(2), 221–38.

Woolfson, L., Grant, E., and Campbell, L. (2007). A comparison of special, general and support teachers' controllability and stability attributions for children's difficulties in learning. *Educational Psychology, 27*(2), 293–304.

Zigmond, N. and Baker, J. (1995). Full inclusion for students with learning disabilities – too much of a good thing? *Theory into Practice, 35*(1), 26–34.

Zigmond, N., Jenkins, J., Fuchs, L., Demo, S., Fuchs, D., Baker, J., Jenkins, L., and Couthino, M. (1995). Special education in restructured schools. *Phi Delta Kappan, 76,* 531–40.

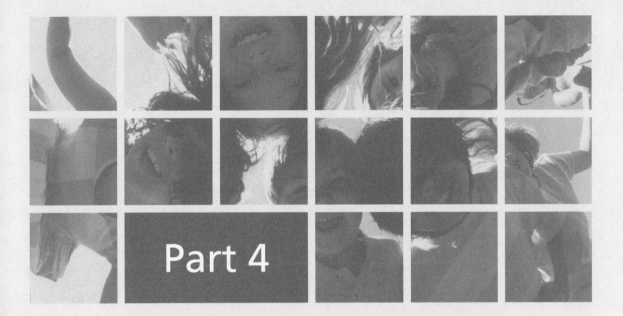

Part 4

EDUCATIONAL PSYCHOLOGY
RESEARCH BEYOND THE SCHOOL

Continuing with the framework we have adopted in this book, that of using an ecological systems structure, this final section now goes beyond the application of psychology research at the level of the individual and beyond that of the school system to consider the application of research to issues within the family and the wider community. Finally it will address new horizons by exploring possibilities offered by cognitive neuroscience research for investigating educational problems.

Part 4 then deals with three topics outside the school:

- Chapter 10 Eradicating disadvantage in preschoolers
- Chapter 11 Parenting children with developmental disabilities
- Chapter 12 Neuroscience and education.

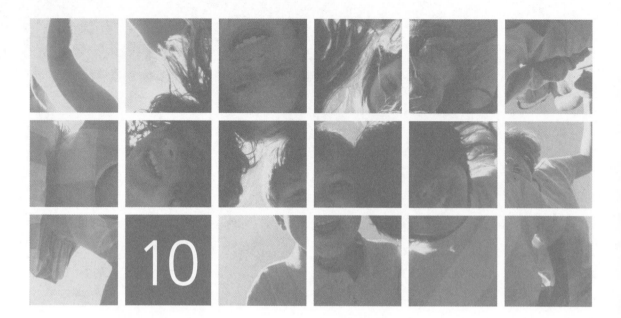

Eradicating disadvantage in preschoolers

This chapter examines issues around the educational and development impact of social disadvantage on preschool children. Children living in poverty are disproportionately represented among the children who are found to be experiencing difficulties even as early as at the preschool stage. Starting school already at a disadvantage can result in problems in the transition to formal schooling and then in subsequent difficulties all the way through school (Hauser-Cram, Sirin and Stipek, 2003). We will look at factors that contribute to this, examine psychological models that help explain child developmental outcomes, and consider how intervention programmes have attempted to eradicate early disadvantage and the extent to which they have met with success.

Learning outcomes

By the end of this chapter you should be able to:

- Demonstrate understanding of the concepts of risk and resilience
- Show awareness of models that explain child developmental outcomes
- Show awareness of major early intervention evaluation projects
- Appreciate short-term and long-term intervention project outcomes.

Risk

Children from low-income, low-socio-economic status households who live in urban environments face multiple and disproportionate risks that can impact on academic, emotional and behavioural outcomes (McLoyd, 1998). While socio-economic status (SES) and growing up as the child of a single parent are predictors of these developmental outcomes, they do not sufficiently unpack underlying factors of interest to educational psychology, factors that vary across different SES groups and individual single-parent families and that can affect child developmental outcomes. Examples of such risk factors are low occupational status, low maternal education, stressful life events, poor parent–child relationships, a large number of people living in the home, disadvantaged minority group status, and maternal depression and anxiety (Burchinal, Peisner-Feinberg, Pianta and Howes, 2002; McLoyd, 1998; Rutter, 1979; Sameroff, Seifer, Baldwin and Baldwin, 1993). In any case, although these single-risk factors can result in differences in developmental outcomes for children, even these factors tend to explain only a small amount of the variance. For more powerful explanations we look to the idea of cumulative risk (Sameroff *et al.*, 1993).

Cumulative risk effects

In a seminal study, Rutter (1979) examined six risk factors:

- low SES
- marital distress
- father's criminal record
- mother's psychiatric problems
- large family size
- being in local authority care.

Rutter's interest here was in child psychiatric disorder as an outcome measure and his finding was that it was not any of the particular risk factors individually that predicted this outcome, but instead it was the number of risk factors.

This idea of the cumulative effect of environmental risk factors on children's intelligence was examined by Sameroff, Seifer, Barocas, Zax and Greenspan (1987), and on social-emotional competences (Sameroff, Seifer, Zax and Barocas, 1987). A further study was then carried out by Sameroff *et al.* (1993) (Rochester Longitudinal Study) to follow up the children through the preschool years and on into adolescence. The study comprised 152 families who were studied from when the mothers were pregnant with the children who were to be followed up. Sameroff *et al.* examined ten risk variables, some of which were similar to those investigated in Rutter's study. Factors studied here were:

- parental perspectives on child development
- mother–child interaction during infancy

- maternal mental illness
- maternal anxiety
- maternal education
- occupation
- available family support,
- family size
- stressful life events
- disadvantaged minority status.

Sameroff, Seifer, Barocas, Zax and Greenspan (1987) found that each of the ten risk items *individually* was a significant predictor of lower IQ scores in the children at age 4 years, particularly minority status, occupation of the head of the household, and level of maternal education. Further, at age 13 years seven of these ten risk factors still showed a significant relationship to child IQ. These were again social status factors, parenting perspectives and maternal mental health (Sameroff *et al.*, 1993). Parent–child interaction was a risk factor for prediction of outcomes at age 4 years but not for age 13 years, perhaps suggesting the greater importance of interaction with peers rather than parents for this age group. Peer factors were not, however, measured in the Rochester study (Sameroff *et al.*, 1993).

Once Sameroff and colleagues took into account multiple environmental risk factors which were calculated from the factors above, they too found cumulative risk to be a better longitudinal predictor. Like Rutter's (1979) study, which had child psychiatric disorder as an outcome measure, it was still the number of risk factors that was important in these longitudinal studies with IQ and social competence as outcome measures, not which risk factors they were. Large differences in outcomes were found between children with low multiple-risk scores and those with high scores. With respect to intelligence scores this meant that children with no environmental risk gained IQ scores that were more than 30 points higher than children who had eight or nine risk factors. Children with the same number of risk factors, but with a pattern comprised of different risks, had similar outcome scores. This principle operated across each socio-economic level, rather than it being SES itself that was the key influence.

Rutter's and Sameroff *et al.*'s studies examined child psychiatric disorder, intelligence, and social competence outcomes. Similar findings on the importance of cumulative risk have also been reported with respect to behaviour problems where multiple-risk scores explained two-thirds of the variance in the longitudinal prediction of behaviour problems (Deater-Deckard, Dodge, Bates and Pettit, 1998). Moreover, the effects of early disadvantage seem to multiply, as these risk factors accumulate within the same children (Masten and Coatsworth, 1998). These children then unfortunately experience more problems and fall ever further behind their peers in their attainments as they get older (Entwhistle and Alexander, 1992). To take account of cumulative risk, Fergusson and Lynskey (1996) devised an adversity index that took account of 39 different measures of family functioning, covering, for example, parent–child separation, marital conflict, socio-economic disadvantage. A high family adversity index was associated with severe problem behaviour in adolescents.

These studies together then suggest that it is cumulative risk rather than individual risk factors that predicts poor child developmental outcomes. Implications for preschool intervention are that, as each child's cumulative risk is made up of a unique cluster of risks particular to them, universal interventions are unlikely to be effective but instead approaches more tailored to the package of individual needs are required (Sameroff and Fiese, 2000).

Resilience

Risk is just one of the factors that influence developmental outcomes. Not all vulnerable children who experience these risk factors have poor outcomes. This is because there are also protective factors that can have a positive impact on developmental outcomes. This more optimistic approach to the study of developmental trajectories is organised around this concept of 'resilience', the ability to recover from challenges, life stresses, setbacks or difficult circumstances. The study of resilience constitutes a challenge to deficit-focused models about children who grow up in disadvantaged communities (Masten, 2001). There are three broad ways resilience has been studied, each focusing on protective mechanisms:

1 Achievement of good developmental outcomes in children from high-risk backgrounds, e.g. socio-economic disadvantage, mental illness in a parent, child abuse/neglect.

2 Maintaining competence under specific stressors such as parental divorce.

3 Recovery from childhood trauma such as war or political violence.

(Werner, 2000)

It is the first of these that will be the focus of our interest in this chapter.

Protective factors

Werner (1984) carried out a longitudinal study in which she identified the following protective factors in resilient children who were able to make a good adjustment to adult life. These were:

- adaptable temperament
- realistic goals
- competent, supportive caregivers
- opportunities at school, or work, in the community that opened up new experiences to reinforced skills.

It can be seen that some may be characterised as internal resources of the child while others are external to the child, e.g. support systems. Another resilience study, known as Project Competence, gathered longitudinal data from families in the late 1970s, comparing 205 children who comprised three groups: competent children who had not experienced difficult circumstances, resilient children who had, and 'maladaptive' children who also had experienced adversity but who had not managed to recover sufficiently from it. This team was particularly interested in what competence criteria might be used to judge resilience, particularly with respect to age-appropriate developmental behaviours over a range of domains. The Project Competence group's interest in resilience was on external measures of children's successful coping and social adaptation to their environment.

Other strands of resilience research have focused rather on internal measures of emotional health and wellbeing, and the process of coping with stress (Gore and Aseltine, 1995; Murphy and Moriarty, 1976). Fergusson and Lynskey (1996) too investigated resilience, but in their New Zealand study it was specifically in relation to family adversity, using the family adversity index described above. Protective factors associated with resilience in this sample were high IQ at age 8 years, low rates of seeking novelty at age 16 years, and less contact with delinquent peers.

Resilience research has consistently indicated a common set of systems that play a crucial role in adaptation to adversity (Masten, 2004). These are:

- learning systems to allow problem-solving, attachment system for development of close relationships
- mastery motivation system for enhancing self-efficacy and encouraging successful behaviour
- stress response systems to deal with difficult situations
- self-regulation systems for regulation of emotion and attention
- family system for effective parenting
- school system for education and learning standards and expectations
- peer system for friendships
- cultural systems for learning laws and values.

(Masten and Obradovic, 2006)

When these systems are working well, children can cope with adverse circumstances and are resilient to the risks. Where these systems are damaged, then problems to the child's development can occur. This seems to suggest that the same systems can operate as protective factors or, if damaged, as risk factors. Similarly, Rutter (1990) noted that lists of protective factors were essentially just the opposite poles of risk factors, e.g. high self-esteem is a protective variable while low self-esteem is a risk variable. That is to say that they are opposite ends of the same dimension, that of self-esteem. This offers a complex conceptualisation of resilience that involves a number of systems, processes and personality traits. Resilience is not simply a capacity that is internal to the individual but instead results from interplay between individual characteristics and external factors. Resilience is the end product of the interplay of these buffering processes with the risks and stresses experienced by the child (Rutter, 1987).

While the Gutman *et al.* (2003) study considered the role of early mental health competences as a *moderator* of the relationship between multiple risk and developmental outcomes in disadvantaged children (see QUISSET below about statistical definitions), other research has focused on possible *mediators* of the relationship between risk and various child behavioural, social, and academic outcomes. McWayne and Cheung's (2009) research, for example, examined the role of early competences as a mediator of the relationship between multiple risk and later behavioural outcomes. Their study indicated a chain of indirect effects from early behaviour problems through child competences across different educational, social and motor domains to later academic and social outcomes. This suggested that intervention aiming to build on developmental skill strengths can bolster poorer performance in other areas. In another study, maternal sensitivity was found to be a mediator of the relationship between parenting stress and children's social-emotional functioning (Whittaker, Harden, See, Meisch and Westbrook, in press), implying that intervention programmes can usefully target parenting quality to help improve child socio-emotional functioning.

QUISSET   *Now go beyond the text . . . look it up yourself!*

Explore your library's electronic databases to investigate 'moderators and mediators'.

- What is a moderator?
- What is a mediator?

Check that you understand the difference between these two terms.

Sektnan, McClelland, Acock and Morrison (in press) too were interested in developmental processes as mediators of risk, but in this case the outcome measure was academic achievement. Behavioural regulation refers to children's ability to apply skills such as attention, memory, planning, and inhibition of appropriate behaviours, such that they follow instructions, concentrate, and are able to carry out tasks and see them through to completion. Behavioural regulation is also known as executive function (Blair and Razza, 2007). Sektnan *et al.* found that it mediated the relationship between risk factors studied (disadvantaged minority status, low maternal education and family income and maternal depression) and academic achievement at school. Their findings suggested that behavioural regulation then is also a fruitful target for early intervention programmes for disadvantaged children. These meditational studies suggest that that intervention programmes could usefully aim to address mediating variables, as some of the risk factors we have discussed may actually have an indirect effect on child outcomes through these mediating variables.

QUISSET   *Now go beyond the text ... look it up yourself!*

Explore your library's electronic databases to investigate 'the definitions of terms used in the literature on resilience'.

- First satisfy yourself that you understand what is meant by 'resilience'.
- What are the specific statistical definitions of factors described as 'risk', 'protective', 'promotive' and 'vulnerabiity' in the resilience literature?

The paper by Gutman, Sameroff and Cole (2003) is a useful source for this.

- Are these meanings used consistently in other papers on resilience?

Reduce risk or optimise resilience?

Whether the focus of intervention should be on reducing risk or optimising resilience is still not clear, however (Rutter, 2000; Sameroff *et al.*, 1993). Gutman, Sameroff and Cole (2003) carried out a study that found personal characteristics such as intelligence and early mental health had no protective (moderating) effects in children who experienced multiple risk. This led them to argue that rather than trying to work to develop cognitive and social-emotional skills in the individual, intervention programmes might be better trying to tackle the multiple social risks faced by disadvantaged children, as these have cumulative effects on later development as discussed above. However, just as risk factors operate cumulatively rather than individually, it appears that protective factors too have little protective effect in isolation (e.g. Fergusson and Lynskey, 1996). Resilience then depends on the interplay of a range of factors which will have different protective effects depending on the outcome measure being examined. It also reflects a range of dynamic processes and mechanisms that will differ before, during, and after, and according to, different experiences of adversity, and at different life stages (Rutter, 2000; Werner, 2000). As mentioned earlier, this makes it difficult to infer 'one size fits all' policy implications for intervention programmes from current resilience research. Furthermore, trying to draw implications for early intervention programmes to promote resilience, from studies of 'resilient' children who haven't attended such programmes, is perilous as quite different processes might be involved (Werner, 2000).

Models of development and intervention

What models have been used to explain child development and to inform how we might intervene to change the developmental trajectory? Sameroff (2010) described four different types of models at different levels of analysis that are needed for us to understand how children grow and develop into fully functioning adults.

1 Personal change model

This model explains development and change at the level of the individual as s/he becomes more complex from infancy through childhood to adulthood. Piaget's model identifying stages of cognitive development from sensorimotor onwards to more complex cognitive levels may be viewed as an example of a personal change model of development.

 Revision activity

Revise Piagetian stages of intellectual development from your earlier studies of psychology. Consider them within the concept of a personal change model.

Can you think of any other developmental models that use the idea of stages to explain not engaging in the relevant tasks better but also, and more importantly, differently?

2 Contextual model

Here Sameroff (2010) pointed out that while developmental psychology is about the development of individuals, this development cannot occur without a social context. Thus experiences impact on individual development, so we need models that take account of social contexts. Bronfenbrenner's (1979) social ecological model provided a seminal conceptualisation of the social systems and settings that influence the child's development, either directly or indirectly. Bronfenbrenner envisaged these as a series of nested subsystems, much like a Russian doll, with each system nested within a larger one, each of which had an influence on the child's development. Thus the system comprising the child and parents is nested within the wider family subsystem, within the wider neighbourhood community subsystem, and within other wider systems, such as society and culture. You will recognise this model as the one that has been used to provide an overall structure for the different parts of this book, and which was outlined in the introduction to Part 2.

The immediate systems in which the child participates and which impact on development are known as *microsystems*, examples of which are the nursery school, the peer group and the family. *Mesosystems* are the systems that link the

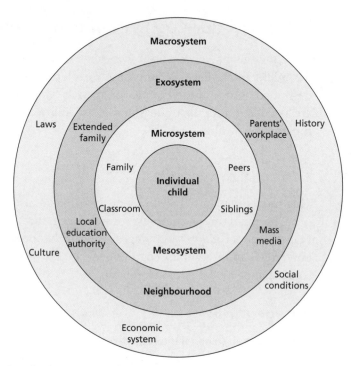

Figure 10.1 **Bronfenbrenner's ecological systems model**

microsystems, for example the relationship between the parents and the school, or between the parents and the neighbourhood. The richness of a mesosystem may be evaluated in terms of the number of its connections and the quality of these (Garbarino and Ganzel, 2000). In the case of the parent–school mesosystem, you might consider whether parents visit the nursery school, whether staff visit parents at home, whether the parents have children from the nursery school to their home to play with their child, and whether the child visits other peers from the nursery outside the nursery school. An *exosystem* is a system that the child has no direct contact with, for example the local council, but which can have an impact on the child's development and in his/her daily life, such as its decision to make a nursery place available or to offer free school meals.

The key point for us in this chapter in relation to models of developments is that Bronfenbrenner's model explains how multiple social contexts are interlinked and how they have an effect on the child's development.

3 Regulation model

A regulation model recognises the two previous models, that there is a developing individual, and that this development occurs within a social context. However, this model proposes that the social context does not simply passively offer experiences

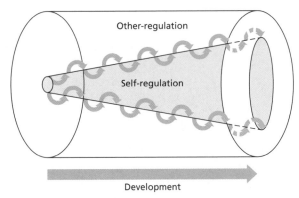

Other-regulation

Self-regulation

Development

Figure 10.2 Ice-cream-cone-in-can model
Source: Sameroff, 2010, reproduced by permission of John Wiley & Sons Inc

for the child to adapt to, but instead that the relationship between the child and the context is a dynamic one. Sameroff and Chandler's (1975) transactional model offered us an influential explanation of how transactional regulation might occur. Child development, within this model, is the outcome of continuous dynamic interactions between the child and the social context of the family. However, not only does the social environment have an effect on the child, but also the child has an effect on the social context in which s/he is developing.

Modelling how a child and her environment might regulate each other, Sameroff and Fiese (2000) used the 'ice-cream-cone-in-can' model. While the child is learning to adapt to the environment, i.e. self-regulation, the social environment is actively engaging in 'other'-regulation. There is a balance between the two such that as the child increases in self-regulation as she becomes more independent and takes on responsibility for self-management, i.e. as the cone in the can expands, then there is a corresponding decrease in other-regulation, the remainder of the space in the can.

This emphasis on the influences of the child and the environment on each other is the crucial thrust of the transactional model. Each influences the other and continues to do so over time. This operates to influence the child developmentally. An illustration may help to explain this (see Figure 10.3).

Let's consider an example to illustrate this idea. A mother has a baby who has breathing difficulties at birth. Although the mother is an experienced parent as she has already raised one child, she lacks confidence with this child and is anxious about his health. The mother does not enjoy interacting with this baby in the same way as she did with her older child, as she is constantly concerned that she is not managing things correctly. The baby takes a long time to feed, cries a lot and does not sleep well. Because she finds this child so difficult and is permanently exhausted, she interacts less appropriately with her baby, engaging in smiling, playing and talking to a limited extent. Thus the child's early difficulties have influenced his social context, resulting in a poorer social milieu for

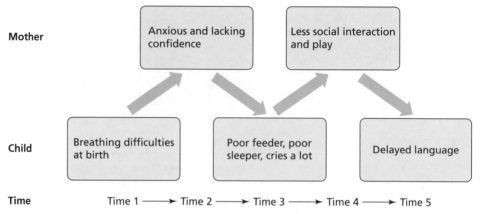

Figure 10.3 Example of how transactional developmental regulation might operate
Source: Shonkoff and Meisels (Eds.), 2000, reproduced by permission of Cambridge University Press

promoting development. Fewer opportunities for social interaction result in poorer language development, and by the end of the time period we are looking at in this example, this baby show delayed language development. If we simply look at the start of the sequence, birth complications, and then the end point of language delay, it might lead us to conclude that birth complications were responsible for causing the language delay, the outcome. This would suggest intervention should be targeted at the child only, to try to remediate the impairments he experiences, in order to improve developmental outcomes. Transactional developmental regulation helps us understand not only how the baby's developmental problems were shaped by the environment, but also how they shaped the environment (the mother's limited interactions with the child). The poor language outcome reflects not only the birth complications but also the mother's lack of confidence, and the decrease in mother–child social interaction and play. This model then helps us see that intervention should be targeted at the mother as well as the child.

4 Representational model

This model addresses the cognitions through which parents interpret and represent their experience, through which they understand the world and can make predictions and hold expectations about their children. As Sameroff (2010) pointed out, representations are not the same as what they represent. They may emphasise particular aspects and fail to take note of others. If we continue with the case example of the mother above, the representational model she had of her child seems to emphasise health problems and difficulties, and perhaps to ignore ways in which the child's feeding, sleeping, crying are just like those of other new babies before they get settled into a routine. When parents were asked to rate the temperament of (a) their own children and (b) six unknown infants, the correlation between parent ratings and those of neutral, trained observers were low for their own children and high for the unfamiliar children. This was because of the additional personal representations parents used in observing and making sense of their own children's behaviour (Seifer, Sameroff, Barrett and Krafchuk, 1994). What is important here is the impact that parental representations might have on the way parents interact with their children, their expectations, and ultimately on child functioning and developmental outcomes.

QUISSET *Now go beyond the text . . . look it up yourself!*

We have discussed above Sameroff's (2010) unified model of development which brings together into one model these four models:

– personal change

– contextual

– regulation

– representational.

Explore your library's electronic databases to investigate 'Sameroff's unifield model'.

● What are the implications of this model for targeting intervention?

Preschool intervention programmes

While the rearing of young children has been largely considered as something that takes place in the home and in which governments in the UK and the US have traditionally been reluctant to intervene, it has been argued that poor children living in disadvantaged communities have been the exception to this rule. From Victorian times, charities, nurses, social workers, and child development experts have intervened, aiming to change the child-rearing practices of poor mothers to something more in step with currently prevailing norms at any particular time. (Halpern, 2000). As Halpern (1998) pointed out, prevailing norms on disciplining children, and organising their feeding and sleeping, tended in particular to reflect middle-class norms.

Early educational provision targeting the parents of children living in poverty dates back to the 1960s with the HighScope Perry Preschool Project and the Head Start programme in the US. The purpose of these programmes was to eradicate early disadvantage in children who started their school careers already at risk of failure. The aim was for the vulnerable children to begin their formal schooling on an equal footing with their peers, and avoid having children repeat the year or be withdrawn from their classes for specialised support to help them catch up, as was common practice in the US of the 1960s.

Let's examine the content and aims of some of these programmes first, and then later in the chapter we will consider the findings of studies evaluating their effectiveness.

Early intervention programme aims and content

The Head Start initiative too started in the US in the 1960s and indeed there is some overlap between the two as some of the Head Start programmes used the HighScope curriculum, and the HighScope foundation has been involved in some

IN FOCUS

Perry Preschool Project

This project began in 1962 in Ypsilanti Public Schools in Michigan, US. David Weikart was the Director of Special Services there and was faced with the problem of at-risk children from poor and minority families who started their school careers already failing compared to their peers. At that time, it was common to use grade retention as a method of dealing with children who had difficulties, i.e. having them repeat the year (Schweinhart, 2002). Weikart wanted to try to avoid this situation and so started the Perry Preschool Programme for 3- and 4-year-olds to allow disadvantaged children in effect to begin their education earlier. This started initially just with a small group of staff, who, under Weikart's leadership, adopted a Piagetian cognitive-developmental philosophy of focusing on intellectual growth through active learning (Weikart, Kamii and Radin, 1967).

The Perry project evaluation is a longitudinal study of 123 African-American children who were 3–4 years old at the start of the study and who were from low-income families. The study used an experimental design randomly dividing the children into an intervention group (58 children) who received a preschool programme based on HighScope principles (see below), and a control group (65 children) who did not (Schweinhart, Weikart, Barnett and Epstein, 1993). These children had been identified as having low IQ scores. Many had scores so low that they would at that time have been classified as 'mentally retarded'. Indeed, half of the control group were later to require special education (Barnett, 1995). Children took part in the programme from October to June for two years. It comprised daily morning sessions plus a weekly teacher afternoon visit to the home.

Interest in the programme's methodology grew beyond the immediate school district and in 1970 Weikart and his team set up the HighScope Educational Research Foundation, a non-profit organisation focused on curricular approaches to early childhood education that have been validated by research. As well as the emphasis on active learning, a key HighScope programme element is the *plan–do–review* method, which goes beyond allowing children to choose their own activities, which is common in many preschool settings. The *plan–do–review* method requires children to plan activities with intention, carry them out and then reflect on what they have learned from them. Planning and reflection have been found to be associated with developmental progress (Epstein, 2003).

of the Head Start evaluations. As can be seen below, Project Head Start has a broader focus than the Perry Preschool Project, which was designed mainly to address educational outcomes.

IN FOCUS

Project Head Start

This project began in 1965 as a short summer pilot programme that was carried out in more than 2500 disadvantaged communities across the US and was staffed by volunteers. More than 560 000 children took part in this first demonstration programme, part of US President Johnson's 'War on Poverty'. The next year US Congress subsequently decided to extend this to full-time programmes with a variety of different options and emphases. There are now both centre-based and home-based programmes. In the centre-based programmes, children attend whole-day or half-day sessions and services are provided from the centre to the family. Programmes vary in length over the school year and in the number of days per week that are offered to children. The home-based programme service was added in 1973, where a home visitor visits weekly to work intensively with the parent in the family home. There are also combination programmes that combine these two elements, as well as programmes that offer variations as appropriate to the local community. Head Start programmes were designed to be sensitive to participating individuals' ethnic and cultural backgrounds.

Like the Perry project, Project Head Start's purpose was to provide a compensatory preschool programme to improve the development of children living in these communities and to enhance their readiness for school so that they were on a par with their peers (Schrag, Styco and Zigler, 2004; Zigler and Muenchow, 1992). It aimed to tackle multiple sources of disadvantage and so involved a corresponding range of educational, health and social services to target not only the child's intellectual and social development but also medical, dental, nutritional input. This early intervention model aiming to address multiple risks from different domains and placing a heavy emphasis on parental involvement, enhancing parenting, and parent–professional relationships is still influential today (Takanishi and DeLeon, 1994).

Children aged 3–4 years were randomly assigned either to a Head Start group or to a control group that received services that were not Head Start, i.e. the control group was not a no-treatment group. Most current early education initiatives in the UK owe a considerable debt to Project Head Start, particularly in the way that it targets two generations, parent and child, in its model of service service delivery, based on Bronfenbrenner's model of nested systems (Parker, Piotrowski, Horn and Green, 1995). Unlike Perry, Head Start did not recommend a particular curriculum, but instead encouraged local community variations (Zigler and Styfco, 1994).

In 1995, Early Head Start extended the Head Start focus on parent support so that services to parents were offered from birth and available up to age 5 years, by now targeting pregnant women and families with infants (Love, Kisker, Christine, Raikes, Constantine, Boller *et al.*, 2005). Families were offered access to both home-based and centre-based services. Early Head Start's framework included four cornerstones so that it aimed to address:

1 child intellectual, language, social, emotional and physical development

2 family development by empowering families to identify their own goals and develop individual family development plans that encompassed both their needs as a family as well as the child's individual needs

3 development in the broader community development by building a network of resources within the community according to need

4 development of staff who were involved in delivering services to the parents and children. This cornerstone recognised the extent to which programme success depended on staff capacity for building positive relationships with parents.

IN FOCUS

Carolina Abecedarian study

This project, based at the University of North Carolina, was influenced by General Systems Theory (von Bertalanffy, 1975), Sameroff's transactional model (Sameroff, 1985), and Bronfenbrenner's ecological model (Bronfenbrenner, 1986) in its conceptualisation of the need to target transactions between many different systems, involving child, parents, school, and the community (Campbell and Ramey, 1994).

It was designed as a randomised, controlled study. From 1972 to 1977, four cohorts of children from low-income families were recruited for the study, based on a High-Risk Index comprising 13 risk factors, such as low maternal education, single mother, unemployment (Ramey and Smith, 1977). These risk scores were used to match participants and by aged 3 months the matched pairs were randomly assigned to the intervention group (57 children) or the control group (54 children). Both groups received basic nutritional, social and medical services, so the control group was not a no-treatment control. Children in the intervention group, however, received a full-time, individualised, centre-based, preschool educational programme, 50 weeks a year from birth until 5 years, focusing on cognitive, social/emotional, language and motor development, as well as early literacy (Campbell and Ramey, 1995).

The Abecedarian curriculum, *LearningGames*, was devised by Sparling and Lewis (1979) for this purpose. It was based on Vygotskian principles, which recognise that children learn best through activities mediated by an adult or older peer. Adult language to support child learning was a key element. Adults, whether centre staff or parents, followed the programme's principles of *notice–nudge–narrate*, in which s/he notices what the child is engaged with, provides a nudge or prompt towards new learning, and then talks to the child about the child's activities, or uses language to direct the child. The programme then required mainly one-to-one adult support for children's learning, with some small group activity.

The Abecedarian study further involved a randomised crossover design: at school start matching again took place across the two groups, using IQ score at age 4 years. One of each pair was then randomly assigned to a school-age intervention or control group. For their first three years of primary school the intervention group received additional intervention in the form of a teacher who linked between school and home, and provided additional teaching (Campbell and Ramey, 1994, 1995). The purpose of the home teacher was to increase parental involvement in their children's education and so enhance children's academic development. Thus some children had eight years of intervention support (five years' preschool + three years' school), while others had no additional intervention, and others had preschool only or school only.

In 1978 the Abecedarian project was extended to Project Care also in North Carolina with another randomised design to compare centre-based and home-based programmes with a control. In 1985 the Abecedarian project was further extended to another eight sites throughout the US in the Infant Health and Development Programme.

In the UK Sure Start programmes were strongly influenced by the findings from US early intervention programmes such as Head Start, Early Head Start, and the Carolina Abecedarian Study. Sure Start local programmes were set up in 1999, as part of UK government action on poverty. They were locally driven to respond to the needs of the community neighbourhood in which they were set, with the purpose of expanding child-care provision to make it more widely available, and also to improve children's health and emotional development and support effective parenting. Sure Start programmes differed from these US predecessors in that they were based on a local geographical area, rather than targeted at specific groups of parents and children (Gray and Francis, 2007). The intention here was to widen access and to avoid any stigma that might be associated with participation for selected groups only. From 2004, these Sure Start local programmes provided the basis for Sure Start Children's Centres. By early 2010, 3500 Sure Start Children's Centres had been set up, offering services to over 2.7 million preschool children and their families in each community.

QUISSET   *Now go beyond the text ... look it up yourself!*

Explore your library's electronic databases to investigate 'early intervention programmes'.

Perry, Head Start, Early Head Start, and the Carolina Abecedarian Project are well-documented, indicative studies for which multiple longitudinal evaluations have been carried out. There are, however, many other early intervention programmes tackling disadvantaged preschoolers.
Search your library database to find out about other such projects.

● For each study, identify what the aims of the programme were and what the content was. Which participants were recruited? How was the study designed? What follow-up was carried out and what were the outcomes?

Starter clues: Project Care, Infant Health and Development Programme, Smart Start, Incredible Years, Sure Start Effective Provision of Preschool Education (EPPE)

Findings from early intervention evaluation studies

To what extent did these different projects succeed in achieving their stated school readiness objectives in order to eradicate social disadvantage at the start of formal schooling? This is not a straightforward question as there is still no consensus on how to evaluate children's readiness for school start (Parker, Boak, Griffin, Ripple and Peay, 1999), although language development, emotion regulation, social skills and phonemic awareness are typically viewed as useful indicators of success in the first school year (Foster, Lambert, Abbott-Shim, McCarty and Franze, 2005). The Head Start Bureau's recent guidelines on desired programme outcomes certainly recognised social, language and literacy outcomes as central to school readiness (Administration on Children, Youth, and Families, 2001). Many of the early evaluations, though, relied rather on IQ measurement.

Perry

The children who took part in the Perry project are of course now adults in their forties. This study has the longest follow-up of early intervention studies, as data were collected on this group of children each year from aged 3–11 years, and then at ages 14, 15, 19, 27, and most recently at aged 40 years. While improved school readiness and increased intervention group IQ scores at age 4 years were reported (Weikart, 1966), and continued through the early school years, they then seemed to fade out. Researchers, however, continued to investigate possible sleeper effects (Zigler and Styfco, 1994). An impressive series of longitudinal studies carried out by the HighScope Educational Foundation provided strong evidence that effects of participation in the Perry programme extended far beyond the initial aim of improved school readiness, to significant non-academic long-term outcomes in adult life, such as family relationships, health, criminality and economic performance. These include more intervention group participants having completed high school education, more took part in post-school education, higher employment, higher monthly income, higher home ownership, fewer criminal convictions, fewer teenage pregnancies, fewer in receipt of support from social services (Berrueta-Clement, Schweinhart, Barnett, Epstein and Weikart, 1984; Schweinhart et al., 1993; Schweinhart, Montie, Xiang, Barnett, Belfield and Nores, 2005). It can be seen that lasting benefits compared to the control group have been reported for the Perry participants over a range of outcome areas throughout the period from preschool to adulthood.

Head Start

Like the Perry Preschool Project, Project Head Start has also been extensively evaluated, although evaluations tended to have focused rather more on shorter-term outcomes than the Perry evaluations (Zigler and Styfco, 1994). Findings from

Head Start too reported short-term cognitive, academic and social benefits for disadvantaged children (Barnett, 1995; Malakoff, Underhill and Zigler, 1998). For example,. Abbott-Shim, Lambert and McCarty (2003) found improved phonemic awareness and understanding of vocabulary in Head Start participants compared to comparison group children. In examining data on 969 children, Lee, Brooks-Gunn and Schnur (1988) concluded there were indeed cognitive benefits associated with Head Start participation, particularly for those children who were most disadvantaged.

Again there has been evidence reported that positive short-term cognitive and academic gains 'wash out' in the early school years (Barnett and Hustedt, 2005). Currie and Thomas (1995), however, noted that when ethnicity is taken into account it seems that 'wash-out' findings might not apply equally to all children in the sample. They found that white and Hispanic children continued to demonstrate educational benefits at aged 8 years, but benefits faded in African-American children, a loss the authors suggested was likely to be related to unsatisfactory educational experiences for African-American children when they enter the school system. Unlike the Perry and Abecedarian studies though, which have been the subject of extensive longitudinal evaluations, longer-term 'sleeper' effects have only recently been examined for Head Start, now also establishing that programme participants were more likely to have completed a high school education, and less likely to have been arrested for criminal activities (Oden, Schweinhart, Weikart, Marcus and Xie, 2000).

Generally though, Head Start findings have been somewhat mixed, which may partly be explained by the variability of the programmes that all come under the umbrella heading of 'Head Start', variability not only in curriculum content but also in quality (Bryant, Burchinal, Lau and Sparling, 1994; Farran, 2000). Disappointingly, and like the other programmes discussed here, it does not seem to have resulted either in the elimination of school failure or criminal behaviour in the disadvantaged communities in which it was based (Farran, 2000; Takanishi and DeLeon, 1994).

Abecedarian

Evaluation data for the Abecedarian study were collected at ages 3, 4, 5, 6 and 8 years, and then followed up at ages 12, 15, 21. Age-30 data are currently being analysed. It should be pointed out that follow-up over this period of time is no mean feat as Abecedarian families moved addresses over time, some moving out of the state of North Carolina. Benefits have been reported for the intervention children who for the first three years of formal schooling showed both cognitive and academic gains compared to the control group (Campbell and Ramey, 1994). Allocation to the school-age intervention group did not result in any subsequent improvements on cognitive scores, but did show increases in academic outcomes where the number of years of intervention was related to both reading and, to a lesser extent, mathematics attainment scores. Results for social outcomes in the early school years were less positive with increased aggressive behaviour reported for the intervention group in comparison to the control group children (Haskins, 1985).

As with the Perry study, positive long-term outcomes were reported for the Abecedarian intervention group: higher IQ scores, higher academic attainments, more years in education, and more likely to undertake post-school education, and to become parents at an older age. Furthermore, positive outcomes extended beyond the children who took part in the intervention to their mothers, who achieved improved educational and employment outcomes compared to mothers in the control group (Campbell, Pungello, Miller-Johnson, Burchinal and Ramey, 2001; Campbell and Ramey, 1995; Campbell, Ramey, Pungello, Sparling and Miller-Johnson, 2002; Ramey and Ramey, 2004).

UK studies

US findings on early intervention have been further supported by studies carried out recently in the UK context – the Effective Provision of Pre-School Education (EPPE) project (1997 to 2003) (Sylva, Melhuish, Sammons, Siraj-Blatchford and Taggart, 2004), and also a longitudinal study of Sure Start programmes in England (Belsky, Melhuish, Barnes, Leyland and Romaniuk, 2006; Melhuish, Belsky, Leyland, Barnes, and NESS Research, 2008). The EPPE study, the first major longitudinal British research in this area, reported that attendance, whether full-time or part-time, at a preschool centre improved development across a range of academic and behavioural domains (Sammons, Sylva, Melhuish, Siraj-Blatchford, Taggart and Elliot, 2002a, 2002b).

QUISSET   *Now go beyond the text . . . look it up yourself!*

Explore your library's electronic databases to investigate 'findings from the EPPE project, Sure Start, and Incredible Years (UK) evaluations'.

- What have these UK studies found?
- What do the outcomes say about the effectiveness of early education programmes?

Reviews of the effectiveness of early childhood development programmes that have examined the outcomes of the seminal studies mentioned in this chapter as well as others have concluded that there is strong evidence for the effectiveness of these programmes. This has been demonstrated in cognitive developmental outcomes, in readiness for school, in standardised tests of achievement, and to a lesser extent in short-term social/behavioural outcomes, although more convincing 'sleeper' effects in this area were noted such as reduced criminality and delinquency (Anderson, Shinn, Fullilove, Scrimshaw, Fielding, Normand *et al.*, 2003; D'Onise, Lynch, Sawyer and McDermott, 2010; Geddes, Haw and Frank, 2010).

Group activity (for 2–6 people)

Join up with some friends to discuss.

You are a research team tasked with evaluating the effectiveness of a new early intervention programme being set up in an area of urban deprivation.

● How would you go about designing the evaluation study?

● Based on your examination of the limitations of previous evaluation studies, what methodological problems do you face and how might you address them?

Mechanisms

What mechanisms might be in place to result in the effects noted? Let us return to studies of risk and resilience to consider this question. It would seem that we are looking at possible sequences of indirect effects and complex pathways. McWayne and Cheung (2009) demonstrated that improved early developmental competences mediated the relationship between multiple risk and later academic, social, and behavioural outcomes through chains of indirect effects. Some studies have suggested that preschool programmes may utilise a cognitive-behavioural pathway from the educational element of the programme where cognitive gains cause improved school performance, and so increase motivation and behaviour in the classroom, and thus lead to improved academic outcomes in later school years (Campbell, Pungello, Miller-Johnson, Burchinal and Ramey, 2001; D'Onise *et al.*, 2010; Schweinhart, Barnes and Weikart, 1993). Sektan *et al.*'s (in press) study indicated that learning to regulate behaviour mediated the relationship between risk factors and academic achievement at school . The skill of learning at any early age how to regulate and manage one's behaviour, whether it was targeted directly by an intervention programme or learned by indirect means through participation in structured educational activities, may have contributed to academic and social outcomes reported in earlier evaluation studies

Intervention programmes may also contribute to parents viewing their children in a more positive light (Kazimirski, Dickens and White, 2008), or to changing their expectations of their children's development or social behaviour (Woolfson, Durkin and King, 2010), or to changing their beliefs about their capacity for parenting (Woolfson *et al.*, 2010). 'Parenting capacity' is the ability of parents to understand their children's needs and the role that they themselves themselves play as parents (Donald and Jureidini, 2004). With regard to parenting capacity, parents of children participating in early intervention programmes have been found to offer their children increased support, as well as experience less parenting stress and less household chaos and daily 'hassle' (Belsky, Melhuish, Barnes, Leyland and Romaniuk, 2006; Love, Kisker, Christine, Raikes, Constantine, Boller *et al.*, 2005; Woolfson *et al.*, 2010). We will return to the topic of parenting in greater depth in the next chapter when we examine research on parenting children with disabilities. Here we have just indicated how parenting factors might operate to influence the outcomes reported by these early intervention studies.

Classroom quality

It was suggested in this chapter that variations in classroom quality might contribute to mixed findings on Head Start outcomes. Programme standards are likely to be important for children's development (Burchinal, Roberts, Nabors and Bryant, 1996). Concerns about the quality of Head Start provision at the early stages may have been related to the speed at which new programmes were set up, inadequate funding, and the use of less than ideally qualified staff and volunteers (Gray and Francis, 2007). Improved funding, specification of programme performance standards, and the requirement of at least 50% of Head Start teachers to have a relevant degree qualification have all contributed to improved standards in the quality of programme delivery (Yoshikawa, Rosman and Hsueh, 2002). Certainly results from the EPPE study indicated that the quality of provision in programme centres was related to child developmental outcomes and associated with better qualified staff (Sammons *et al.*, 2002a, 2002b). Abbott-Shim, Lambert and McCarty (2000) tested out a model that demonstrated that teachers' education level did not have a direct effect on classroom quality but instead had indirect effects through teachers' beliefs and the teaching practices and classroom activities that resulted from these beliefs. The implications from Abbott-Shim *et al.*'s findings are that to improve classroom quality, it would be necessary to ensure suitable training and development opportunities for teaching staff, which would inform and change their beliefs about appropriate teaching practices.

Further, this issue of programme content, quality, and staff beliefs continues into school years. It has been argued that enhancing school readiness for children living in poverty and disadvantage can be viewed as being underpinned by an individual child/family deficit philosophy. While parents were encouraged to be involved in the programmes their children attended, there was a tension between an explicit parental empowerment agenda and an implicit parenting 'deficit' agenda (Gray and Francis, 2007). The focus on compensating for early social disadvantage so that children could start school having received an early education programme further assumed child deficits within a school environment where staff were not required to address the needs of children living in poverty. It seemed to be implied that it was the children who were experiencing multiple risk who had to change to make optimal use of a school programme that was not designed for them (Vernon-Feagans, 1996). Indeed, many of the children in the US evaluation studies were from impoverished African-American families who, once they started school, found themselves in educational environments that may have seemed unfamiliar and not well-matched to their particular circumstances. For example, after a tailored preschool curriculum, the Abecedarian children attended schools predominantly designed for the children of white, middle-class, university families (Farran, 2000).

Thirty years on, school systems and teaching staff are certainly much better at recognising the importance of accommodating the needs of a diverse range of learners than perhaps was the case when the Abecedarian children started school. Clearly it is important that any improvements in development that resulted from an intensive early education programme are supported in the school years too. This issue of the extent of carry-over of quality support after the individualised preschool programme is a neglected area of research (Farran, 2000).

Summary and conclusions

Good-quality early intervention programmes have a positive impact on both the children and parents who participate. Some of these effects are 'sleeper' effects and emerge many years after intervention participation, but serve to enhance the quality of the individual's life and that of the surrounding community. So far though, while these programmes may help protect against multiple risks associated with living in poverty in a disadvantaged community, they have unfortunately not yet succeeded in eradicating disadvantage. Perhaps such programmes need to tackle a broader range of risk and resilience factors than they have so far.

Further study

Go to the website www.pearsoned.co.uk/markswoolfson **for the following starter articles:**

Campbell, F., Ramey, C., Pungello, E., Sparling, J., and Miller-Johnson, S. (2002). Early childhood education: Young adult outcomes from the Abecedarian Project. *Applied Developmental Science, 6*(1), 42–57.

Gutman, L., Sameroff, A., and Cole, R. (2003). Academic growth curve trajectories from 1st grade to 12th grade: Effects of multiple social risk factors and preschool child factors. *Developmental Psychology, 39*(4), 777–90.

Sammons, P., Sylva, K.. Melhuish, E., Siraj-Blatchford, I., Taggart, B. and Elliot, K. (2002a), *The Effective Provision of Pre-School Education (EPPE) Project: Technical Paper 8a – Measuring the impact of pre-school on children's cognitive progress over the pre-school period.* London: DfES/Institute of Education, University of London.

References

Abbott-Shim, M., Lambert, R., and McCarty, F. (2000). Structural model of Head Start Classroom Quality. *Early Childhood Research Quarterly, 15*(1), 115–34.

Abbott-Shim, M., Lambert, R., and McCarty, F. (2003). A comparison of school readiness outcomes for children randomly assigned to a Head Start program and the program's wait list. *Journal of Education for Students Placed at Risk, 8*(2), 210–11.

Administration on Children, Youth and Families. (2001). *Head Start FACES: Longitudinal findings on program performance, third progress report.* Washington, DC: U.S. Department of Health and Human Services.

Anderson, L., Shinn, C., Fullilove, M., Scrimshaw, S., Fielding, J., Normand, J., *et al.* (2003). The effectiveness of early childhood development programs. *American Journal of Preventive Medicine*, 24(3S), 32–46.

Barnett, W. (1995). Long-term effects of early childhood programs on cognitive and school outcomes. *The Future of Children*, 5(3), 25–50.

Barnett, W. and Hustedt, J. (2005). Head Start's lasting benefits. *Infants and Young Children, 18*(1), 16–24.

Belsky, J., Melhuish, E., Barnes, J., Leyland, A., and Romaniuk, H. (2006). Effects of Sure Start local programmes on children and families: Early findings from a quasi-experimental, cross-sectional study. *British Medical Journal, 332*(7556), 1476.

Berrueta-Clement, J., Schweinhart, L., Barnett, W., Epstein, A., and Weikart, D. (1984). *Changed lives: The effects of the Perry Preschool programme on youths through age 19.* Ypsilanti, MI: High/Scope.

Blair, C. and Razza, R. (2007). Relating effortful control, executive function, and false belief understanding to emerging math and literacy ability in kindergarten. *Child Development, 78*(2), 647–68.

Bronfenbrenner, U. (1979). *The ecology of human development.* Cambridge, MA: Harvard University Press.

Bronfenbrenner, U. (1986). Ecology of the family as a context for human development: Research perspectives. *Developmental Psychology, 22*, 723–42.

Bryant, D., Burchinal, M., Lau, L., and Sparling, J. (1994). Family and classroom correlates of Head Start children's developmental outcomes. *Early Childhood Research Quarterly, 9*, 289–304.

Burchinal, M., Peisner-Feinberg, E., Pianta, R., and Howes, C. (2002). Development of academic skills from preschool through second grade: Family and classroom predictors of developmental trajectories. *Journal of School Psychology, 40*(5), 415–36.

Burchinal, M., Roberts, J., Nabors, L., and Bryant, D. (1996). Quality of centre child care and infant cognitive and language development. *Child Development, 67*, 606–20.

Campbell, F., Pungello, E., Miller-Johnson, S., Burchinal, M., and Ramey, C. (2001). The development of cognitive and academic abilities: Growth curves from an early educational experiment. *Developmental Psychology, 37*(2), 231–42.

Campbell, F. and Ramey, C. (1994). Effects of early intervention on intellectual and academic achievement: A follow-up study of children from low-income families. *Child Development, 65*, 684–98.

Campbell, F. and Ramey, C. (1995). Cognitive and school outcomes for high-risk African-American students at middle adolescence: positive effects of early intervention. *American Education Research Journal, 32*(4), 743–72

Campbell, F., Ramey, C., Pungello, E., Sparling, J., and Miller-Johnson, S. (2002). Early childhood education: Young adult outcomes from the Abecedarian Project. *Applied Developmental Science, 6*(1), 42–57.

Currie, J. and Thomas, D. (1995). Does Head Start make a difference? *American Economic Review, 85*(3), 341–64.

Deater-Deckard, K., Dodge, K., Bates, J., and Pettit, G. (1998). Multiple risk factors in the development of externalizing behaviour problems: Group and individual differences. *Development and Psychopathology, 10*(3), 469–93.

Donald, T. and Jureidini, J. (2004). Parenting capacity *Child Abuse Review,13*, 5–17.

D'Onise, K., Lynch, J., Sawyer, M. and McDermott, R. (2010). Can preschool improve child health outcomes? A systematic review. *Social Science and Medicine, 70*, 1423–40.

Entwhistle, D. and Alexander, K. (1992). Summer setback: Race, poverty, school composition, and mathematics achievement in the first two years of school. *American Sociological Review, 57*, 72–84.

Epstein, A. (2003), How planning and reflection develop young children's thinking skills. *Young Children, 58*(5), 28–36.

Farran, D. (2000). Another decade of intervention for children who are low income or disabled: What do we know now? In J. Shonkoff and S. Meisels (eds), *Handbook of early childhood intervention*, 2nd edn. Cambridge: Cambridge University Press, (pp. 510–48).

Fergusson, D. and Lynskey, M. (1996). Adolescent resiliency to family adversity. *Journal of Child Psychology and Psychiatry, 37*, 281–92.

Foster, M., Lambert, R., Abbott-Shim, M., McCarty, F., and Franze, S. (2005). A model of home learning environment and social risk factors in relation to children's emergent literacy and social outcomes. *Early Childhood Research Quarterly, 20*, 13–36.

Garbarino, J. and Ganzel, B. (2000). The human ecology of early risk. In J. Shonkoff and S. Meisels (eds), *Handbook of early childhood intervention* 2nd edn Cambridge: Cambridge University Press, (pp. 76–93).

Geddes, R., Haw, S., and Frank, J. (2010). *Interventions for promoting early child development for health. An environmental scan with special reference to Scotland*. Report for the Early Life Working Group of the Scottish Collaboration for Public Health Research and Policy. Edinburgh: Scottish Collaboration for Public Health Research and Policy.

Gore, S. and Aseltine, R. (1995). Protective processes in adolescence: Matching stressors with social resources. *American Journal of Community Psychology, 23*, 301–27.

Gray, R. and Francis, E. (2007). The implications of US experiences with early childhood interventions for the UK Sure Start programme. *Child: Care, Health and Development, 33*(6), 655–63.

Gutman, L., Sameroff, A., and Cole, R. (2003). Academic growth curve trajectories from 1st grade to 12th grade: Effects of multiple social risk factors and preschool child factors. *Developmental Psychology, 39*(4), 777–90.

Halpern, R. (1998). *Fragile families, fragile solutions: A history of supportive services for families in poverty*. New York: Columbia University Press.

Halpern, R. (2000). Early childhood intervention for low-income children and families. In J. Shonkoff and S. Meisels (eds), *Handbook of early childhood intervention*, 2nd edn. Cambridge: Cambridge University Press, (pp. 361–86).

Haskins, R. (1985). Public school aggression among children with varying daycare experience. *Child Development, 56*, 689–703.

Hauser-Cram, P., Sirin, S., and Stipek, D. (2003). When teachers' and parents' values differ: Teachers' ratings of academic competence in children from low-income families. *Journal of Educational Psychology, 95*, 813–20.

Kazimirski, A., Dickens, S., and White, C. (2008). *Pilot scheme for two year old children - evaluation of outreach projects*. London: National Centre for Social Research.

Lee, V., Brooks-Gunn, J., and Schnur, E. (1988). Does Head Start work? *Developmental Psychology, 24*(2), 210–22.

Love, J., Kisker, E., Christine, R., Raikes, H., Constantine, J., Boller, K., Brooks-Gunn, J., Chazan-Cohen, R., Tarullo, L., Brady-Smith, C., Fuligni, A., Schochet, P., Paulsell, D., and Vogel, C. (2005). The effectiveness of early head start for 3-year-old children and their parents: Lessons for policy and programs. *Developmental Psychology, 41*(6), 885–901.

Malakoff, M., Underhill, J., and Zigler, E. (1998). Influence of inner-city environment and Head Start experience on effectance motivation. *American Journal of Orthopsychiatry, 68*, 630–8.

Masten, A. (2001). Ordinary magic: Resilience processes in development. *American Psychologist, 56*(3), 227–38.

Masten, A. (2004). Regulatory processes, risk and resilience in adolescent development. *Annals of the New York Academy of Sciences, 1021*, 310–19.

Masten, A. and Coatsworth, J. (1998). The development of competence in favourable and unfavourable environments: Lessons from research on successful children. *American Psychologist, 53,* 205–20.

Masten, A. and Obradović, J. (2006). Competence and resilience in development. *Annals of the New York Academy of Sciences, 1094,* 13–27.

McLoyd, V. (1998). Socioeconomic disadvantage and child development. *American Psychologist, 53,* 185–204.

McWayne, C. and Cheung, K. (2009). A picture of strength: Preschool competencies mediate the effects of early behaviour problems on later academic and social adjustment for Head Start children. *Journal of Applied Developmental Psychology, 30,* 273–85.

Melhuish, E., Belsky, J., Leyland, A., Barnes, J. and NESS Research Team (2008). Effects of fully-established Sure Start Local Programmes on 3-year-old children and their families living in England: a quasi-experimental observational study. *Lancet, 372,* 1641–7.

Murphy, L. and Moriarty, A. (1976). *Vulnerability, coping and growing.* New Haven, CT: Yale University Press.

Oden, S., Schweinhart, L., Weikart, D., Marcus, S., and Xie, Y. (2000). *Into adulthood: A study of the effects of Head Start.* Ypsilanti, MI: High/Scope Press.

Parker, F., Boak, A., Griffin, K., Ripple, C., and Peay, L. (1999). Primary caregiver-child relationship, home learning environments, and school readiness. *School Psychology Review, 28,* 413–26.

Parker, F., Piotrokowski, C., Horn, W., and Green, S. (1995). The challenge for Head Start: Realising its vision as a two-generation program. In I. Sigel and S. Smith (eds), *Advances in applied developmental psychology: Two generation programs for families in poverty* vol. 9, Norwood, NJ: Ablex, (pp. 135–59).

Ramey, C. and Ramey, S. (2004). Early learning and school readiness: can early intervention make a difference? *Merrill-Palmer Quarterly, 50*(4), 471–91.

Ramey, C. and Smith, B. (1977). Assessing the intellectual consequences of early intervention with high-risk infants. *American Journal of Mental Deficiency, 81,* 318–24.

Rutter, M. (1979). Protective factors in children's responses to stress and disadvantage. In M. Kent and J Rolf (eds), *Primary prevention of psychopathology: Volume 3. Social competence in children.* Hanover, NH: University Press of New England, (pp. 49–74).

Rutter, M. (1987). Psychosocial resilience and protective mechanism. *American Journal of Orthopsychiatry, 57,* 316–31.

Rutter, M. (1990). Psychosocial resilience and protective mechanisms. In J. Rolf, A. Masten, D Cicchetti, K. Nuechterlein, and S. Weintraub (eds), *Risk and protective factors in the development of psychopathology.* New York: Cambridge University Press, (pp. 181–214).

Rutter, M. (2000). Resilience reconsidered: Conceptual considerations, empirical findings, and policy implications. In J. Shonkoff and S. Meisels (eds), *Handbook of early childhood intervention,* 2nd edn. Cambridge: Cambridge University Press (pp. 651–82).

Sameroff, A., (1985). Environmental factors in the early screening of risk. In W. Frankenburg and R. Emde (eds), *Early identification of the child at risk: An international perspective.* New York: Plenum, (pp. 21–44).

Sameroff, A. (2010). A unified theory of development: a dialectic integration of nature and nurture. *Child Development, 81*(1), 6–22.

Sameroff, A. and Chandler, M. (1975). Reproductive risk and the continuum of caretaking causalty. In F. Horowitz, M. Hetherington, S. Scarr-Salatapek, and G. Siegel (eds) *Review of child development research* vol. 4. Chicago: University of Chicago Press, (pp. 187–244).

Sameroff, A. and Fiese, B. (2000). Transactional regulation: the developmental ecology of early intervention. In J. Shonkoff and S. Meisels (eds), *Handbook of early childhood intervention,* 2nd edn. Cambridge: Cambridge University Press, (pp. 135–159).

Sameroff, A., Seifer, R., Baldwin, A., and Baldwin, C. (1993). Stability of intelligence from pre-school to adolescence: The influence of social and family risk factors. *Child Development, 64,* 80–97.

Sameroff, A., Seifer, R., Barocas, R., Zax, M., and Greenspan, S. (1987). Intelligence quotient scores of 4-year-old children: Social environmental risk factors. *Pediatrics, 79,* 343–50.

Sameroff, A., Seifer, R., Zax, M., and Barocas, R. (1987). Early indicators of developmental risk: The Rochester Longitudinal Study. *Schizophrenia Bulletin, 13,* 383–93.

Sammons, P., Sylva, K., Melhuish, E., Siraj-Blatchford, I., Taggart, B. and Elliot, K. (2002a), *The Effective Provision of Pre-School Education (EPPE) Project: Technical Paper 8a - Measuring the impact of pre-school on children's cognitive progress over the pre-school period.* London: DfES/Institute of Education, University of London.

Sammons, P., Sylva, K., Melhuish, E., Siraj-Blatchford, I., Taggart, B. and Elliot, K. (2002b), *The Effective Provision of Pre-School Education (EPPE) Project: Technical Paper 8b - Measuring the impact of pre-school on children's social/behavioural development over the pre-school period.* London: DfES / Institute of Education, University of London.

Schrag, R., Styco, S., and Zigler, E. (2004). Familiar concept, new name: Social competence/school readiness as the goal of Head Start. In E. Zigler and S. Styco (eds), *The Head Start Debates.* Baltimore, MD: Brookes Publishing Company, (pp. 19–25).

Schweinhart, L. (2002). How the HighScope Perry Preschool Study grew: A researcher's tale. *Phi Delta Kappa Center for Evaluation, Development, and Research, 32.*

Schweinhart, L., Barnes, H., and Weikart, D. (1993*). Significant benefits: The HighScope Perry Preschool Study through age 27.* Ypsilanti, MI: High/Scope Press.

Schweinhart, L., Montie, J., Xiang, Z., Barnett, W., Belfield, C., and Nores, M. (2005). *Lifetime effects: The HighScope Perry Preschool Study through age 40.* Ypsilanti, MI: High/Scope Press.

Schweinhart, L., Weikart, D., Barnett, W., and Epstein, A. (1993). *Significant benefits: The High/Scope Perry Preschool Project through age 27.* Ypsilanti, MI: High/Scope Press.

Seifer, R., Sameroff, A., Barrett, L., and Krafchuk, E. (1994). Infant temperament measured by multiple observations and mother report. *Child Development, 65,* 1478–90.

Sektnan, M., McClelland, M., Acock, A., and Morrison, F. (in press). Relations between early family risk, children's behavioural regulation, and academic achievement. *Early Childhood Research Quarterly.*

Sparling, J. and Lewis, I. (1979). *Learning Games for the first three years: A guide to parent-child play.* New York: Walker.

Sylva, K., Melhuish, E. C., Sammons, P., Siraj-Blatchford, I, and Taggart, B. (2004). *The effective provision of pre-school education (EPPE) project: Technical Paper 12 - The final report: effective pre-school education.* London: DfES / Institute of Education, University of London.

Takanishi, R. and DeLeon, P. (1994). A Head Start for the 21st century. *American Psychologist, 49,* 120–2.

Vernon-Feagans, L. (1996). *Children's talk in communities and classrooms.* Cambridge, MA: Blackwell.

von Bertalanffy, L. (1975). *Perspectives on general systems theory.* New York: Braziller.

Weikart, D. (1966). Preschool programs: Preliminary findings. *Journal of Special Education, 1*(2), 163–81.

Weikart, D., Kamii, C., and Radin, N. (1967). Perry Preschool Project progress report. In D. Weikart (ed.), *Preschool intervention: A preliminary report of the Perry Preschool Project* (pp 1–61). Ann Arbor, MI: Campus Publishers.

Werner, E. (1984). Resilient children. *Young Children, 40,* 68–72.

Werner, E. (2000). Protective factors and individual resilience. In J. Shonkoff and S. Meisels (eds), *Handbook of early childhood intervention,* 2nd edn. Cambridge: Cambridge University Press, (pp. 115–32).

Whittaker, J., Harden, B., See, H., Meisch, A., and Westbrook, T. (in press). Family risks and protective factors: Pathways to Early Head Start toddlers' social-emotional functioning. *Early Childhood Research Quarterly.*

Woolfson, L., Durkin, K., and King, J. (2010). Changing cognitions in parents of two-year-olds attending Scottish Sure Start Centres. *International Journal of Early Years Education, 18*(1), 3–26.

Yoshikawa, H., Rosman, E., and Hsueh, J. (2002). Resolving paradoxical criteria for the expansion and replication of Early Childhood Care and Education Programs. *Early Childhood Research Quarterly, 17,* 3–27.

Zigler, E. and Muenchow, S. (1992). *Head Start: The inside story of America's most successful educational experiment.* New York: Basic Books.

Zigler, E. and Styfco, S. (1994). Is the Perry Preschool better than Head Start? Yes and no. *Early Childhood Research Quarterly, 9,* 269–87.

Parenting children with developmental disabilities

Developmental disabilities are intellectual, physical, communication or sensory impairments, that are identified at birth or in the child's early years, and are likely to affect the child's day-to-day functioning and development, throughout the child's lifetime. However, intervention in the form of special education, speech therapy, physiotherapy or occupational therapy can help promote improved developmental outcomes.

The term 'developmental disabilities' covers a range of conditions that vary in nature, severity and complexity. For some children the impairment may be mild and related to one developmental domain only, e.g. unsteady walking due to mild cerebral palsy. For other children, the impairments may be severe and a number of domains may show significant delays, resulting in a complex pattern of disability in children with serious cognitive, physical and communication impairments who may never be able to walk or speak or feed or toilet independently.

In this chapter we will look at the experience of stress in families of children with developmental disabilities and the various stressors that might present. We will examine factors that influence family outcomes with a focus on those resulting in family resilience in the face of these challenges. We will consider models that address not only how the child and the family impact on, and change, each other, but that also take account of the influence of social factors that are outside the family system. In particular we will highlight the centrality of parental beliefs in the different models and the implications for intervention.

Learning outcomes

By the end of this chapter you should be able to:

- Show awareness of how parents adjust to a diagnosis of disabiity in their child
- Understand a range of potential stressors that may be experienced by parents of children with developmental disabilities
- Show awareness of models of family adjustment to stress
- Appreciate factors contributing to resilience in families of children with disabilities
- Understand how a transactional model underpins possible intervention approaches with parents and children with developmental disabilities
- Appreciate the influence of parental beliefs on child and family outcomes and how intervention might change these.

Adjustment to diagnosis

A diagnosis of disability in a child was once thought to be associated with parental 'chronic sorrow' (Olshansky, 1962). This described a pervasive sadness that parents experienced in acknowledging that their child was not the typically developing child that they had anticipated. 'Chronic sorrow' was thought to continue throughout the parent's life, and although it might subside at times it still recurred at key points in the child's development. An alternative conceptualisation was the idea that parents worked through stages as they adjusted to the diagnosis. The stage model was developed from Kübler-Ross's (1969) five stages of grief reactions to death or impending death, by applying these stages to other personal traumas. With regard to the specific emotional response to the experience of their child being diagnosed as having a disability, parents were viewed as working through a staged series of emotions: shock, denial, anger, sadness, detachment, reorganisation and adaptation (Hornby, 1994).

There are, however, criticisms of the application of this stage model to parents of a child with a disability (e.g. Seligman and Darling, 1997) because families are not all the same in how they adapt and may work through the stages in quite different ways, and with variations in length of duration of phases. Some families can work through the whole sequence of phases in a very few days while others might take years or never reach the final stage of adaptation (Hornby, 1994). It can generally be expected, though, that parents will have to adjust to the caregiving challenges that will be presented, the impact on family functioning and changed relationships within the family, as well as changes to previously established family routines (Marvin and Pianta, 1996; Seltzer and Heller, 1997, Turnbull and Turnbull, 1990).

Possible sources of stress

Considering the above, it is not surprising that studies have found that parents of children with developmental disabilities often experience stress to a greater extent than do parents of typically developing children (Blacher, Neece and Paczowski, 2005; Dumas, Wolf, Fisman and Culligan, 1991; Hastings and Beck, 2004; Hauser-Cram, Warfield, Shonkoff and Krauss, 2001; Johnston, Hessl, Blasey, Eliez, Erba, Dyer-Friedman *et al.*, 2003; Woolfson and Grant, 2006). Parental depression is often recognised and studied as a marker of this stress (Singer, 2006). In addition, it seems to be mothers of children with autism spectrum disorders (ASD) who experience stress and depressive symptoms to the greatest extent compared with mothers of children with other developmental disabilities (Dumas *et al.*, 1991; Estes, Munson, Dawson, Koehler, Zhou and Abbott, 2009). It is important to note that mothers and fathers within the same family may experience different levels of stress and a different pattern of stress across time (Gerstein, Crnic, Blacher and Baker, 2009). Mothers' stress seemed to increase over time while fathers' stress seemed to remain at a reasonably constant level (Baker, McIntyre, Blacher, Crnic, Edelbrock and Low, 2003; Crnic, Hoffman and Gaze, 2005; Gerstein *et al.*, 2009). This may be because it tends to be mothers who typically bear primary responsibility in dealing with day-to-day practical, parenting tasks.

As previously discussed, there may be a parental need to work through a process of grieving for the typically developing child that they expected but did not have: this can be a source of stress (e.g. McCubbin, Cauble and Patterson, 1982). Furthermore, parents and other family members may work through this process in different ways and at different rates. In addition, families of children with disabilities are likely to require to interact with a range of professionals and institutions regarding necessary medical treatment, or therapies for their child, or for the appropriate educational services or access to specialist resources. Dealing with the attitudes of professionals (e.g. Blacher and Hatton, 2007) who may hold some of the same prejudiced views about disability as does mainstream society (Evans, 1989) can also be stressful for families. Although intending to help, they do not always seem to parents to sufficiently recognise, understand or address their child's specific needs. Some families perceived themselves as having to fight professionals for control of decision-making about their child (Knox, Parmenter, Atkinson and Yazbeck, 2000).

Let us examine below some further potential sources of stress for families.

Nature and severity of disability

While there is some evidence that type and severity of disability influence parental stress (e.g. Gupta, 2007; Hauser-Cram *et al.*, 2001; Haveman, van Berkum, Reijnders and Heller, 1997), this is not clear-cut. Plant and Sanders (2007) certainly found the level of disability to have an effect on stress, i.e. that rearing a child whose impairments were more severe was more stressful. Their regression analysis showed that factors such as cognitive appraisal of the severity of the disability and the extent of social support available to the family exerted important influences on the relationship between disability severity and parental experience of stress. We will return to the themes of parental beliefs and also to social support in a later section of this chapter.

Children who have a developmental disability may have limited independent daily living skills and so are highly dependent on their parents for their day-to-day care, feeding, toileting, bathing, dressing, settling them at bedtime, for much longer than typically developing children. Carrying out these tasks of daily living may be even more difficult for parents where the level of disability is severe and where the child has very limited adaptive functioning. It may be this, rather than the severity of the disability itself, that explains increased parental stress. The findings on this, though, are mixed, with some studies finding an association between child adaptive functioning and positive maternal wellbeing and others not (e.g. Beck, Daley, Hastings and Stevenson, 2004; Tomanik, Harris and Hawkins, 2004). Current thinking seems to be that it is the other socio-economic and socio-contextual factors such as financial resources, time available for interaction and social support that predict stress better than measures of child functioning (Emerson, Hatton, Llewellyn, Blacher and Graham, 2006; Dempsey, Keen, Pennell, O'Reilly and Neilands, 2009; Smith, Oliver and Innocenti, 2010).

Problem behaviour

Problem behaviour is a consistent source of parental stress for parents of children with developmental disabilities (e.g. Estes *et al.*, 2009; Hastings, 2002; Hastings and Brown, 2002; Hauser-Cram *et al.*, 2001). In families of children with ASD, self-injurious behaviour too has been found to be a particularly strong predictor of parental stress (Konstantareas and Homatidis, 1989). As well as problem behaviour in general, difficult behaviour that occurs in relation to parents carrying out daily caregiving tasks with the child is associated with increased stress (Hastings and Brown, 2002; Plant and Sanders, 2007). As discussed above, if the level of disability is severe, children may be permanently dependent on caregiver help for these daily living activities. Difficulty experienced by parents in undertaking routine, daily caregiving tasks, the 'daily hassles' of parenting (Crnic and Greenberg, 1990, p. 1628) is another predictor of stress (McDonald, Couchonnal and Early, 1996). Indeed, difficulty in daily caregiving tasks was found to be a better predictor of the level of stress experienced by parents than were child behaviour problems themselves (Plant and Sanders, 2007).

Financial

There are economic stresses too associated with bringing up a child with a disability (Dobson and Middleton, 1998). There may be special treatment or equipment that parents would like that is not readily available and which has cost implications. Or the demands of child care might restrict the working opportunities available to the parents and result in a decrease in family income. The situation is even more difficult in the current recession. Bennett (2010), in a recent UK survey carried out by Contact a Family, reported that 34% of families with children with disabilities surveyed had fallen behind in debt repayments, mostly for loans and credit card debt; 23% were going without heating, which was an increase from 16% in 2008; and 73% were going without leisure activities compared to 55% in 2008. Close to 90% of families had financial worries that had an effect on their family life. A survey of over 440 families of children with developmental disability drawn from the UK's Millennium Cohort Study found that this group of children whose development was already compromised were at risk of further limitations on their life opportunities and wellbeing in terms of their likelihood of experiencing multiple socio-economic disadvantage (Emerson, Graham, McCulloch, Blacher, Hatton and Llewellyn, 2008).

Competing demands

As any parent can tell you, child-rearing in general can be a source of family strain. When rearing a child with a disability there are increased possibilities for strained emotional relationships in the family (e.g. Lobato, 1995; Powell and Gallagher, 1993; Risdal and Singer, 2004). At a practical level the mother, who is often the primary carer for the child with the disability, may have less time available for the child's siblings or for her partner. Her commitment to caring for a child with a developmental disability, the time demands of recommended rehabilitation and developmental activities for the child, and the lack of availability of suitable alternative child care may also mean that she is restricted in the time she has available to engage in paid work outside the home, leading to reduced hours of employment (Barnett and Boyce, 1995; Leiter, Krauss, Anderson and Wells, 2004; Warfield, 2005; Warfield and Hauser-Cram, 1996). These increased parenting demands have also been found to predict more absences from work (Warfield, 2001), and may limit employment possibilities such that mothers take less fulfilling jobs for which they are over-qualified (Freedman, Litchfield, and Warfield, 1995). Mothers often report working outside the home not only to have financial benefits for the family but also positive emotional benefits for the mother herself by providing personal respite (Freedman *et al.*, 1995), and mothers of children with developmental disabilities may be restricted in the extent to which they can access these benefits.

 Activity

What other stressors might there be for families of children with developmental disabilities?

Models of family adjustment to stress

Families differ in how they adapt to the stresses involved in rearing a child with developmental disabilities. The experience of stress is not a one-off occurrence but instead is ongoing and constantly changing. Let us consider next three models that identify the primary components of family stress and coping, and which have provided the basis for research studies examining the dynamic relationships between the different variables.

ABCX model (Hill, 1958)

Hill's ABCX model was the classic model of family stress. It was based on how families had responded to the stress of war, and to the separations and reunion that had been an inevitable part of this. The model recognised that families changed as a response to a stressful life event. These changes might be in their values, aspirations, the social roles ascribed to family members, how they interact with each other and with the wider community. In this model, A represented the characteristics of the stressor event, which for our focus of interest in this chapter is likely to be the nature and severity of the child's disability. B then represented the existing internal resources that were available to the family to help them manage the stressful event, and C was the meaning and definition of the stressor as it was perceived by the family. These variables, A, B, and C together, then contributed to X, which was the family 'crisis', either prevention of crisis or its occurrence. This model helped us to understand how the impact of the stressor event A, e.g. the child's disability, may be reduced by protective factors, e.g. family resources for dealing with crises (B), and the family's perception of the disability (C), to avoid, or contribute to, the onset of crisis in the family.

Double ABCX model (McCubbin and Patterson, 1981, 1983)

In the early 1980s Lazarus and Folkman (1984) were developing their seminal theory of stress and coping in individuals, in which cognitive appraisal was viewed as a key element in determining the extent to which individuals experienced stress. In this model the individual appraises the extent to which a stressor is threatening and the extent to which s/he has the resources to deal with the demands the stressor places on him/her. McCubbin and Patterson (1981, 1983) used similar principles to propose how families rather than individuals cope. They extended Hill's (1958) ABCX model to put forward a Double ABCX model that added four new post-crisis variables to the original ABCX model. Like Hill's model, this too was developed as a result of work with army families, in this case, post-Second World War, it was military families who had been posted overseas.

If the ABCX model is considered as an explanatory model of the variables contributing to the extent of family crisis at Time 1, the Double ABCX model may be considered as an explanation of the interaction of factors at Time 2, i.e. it deals with post-crisis adaptation. This model recognises that, as well as the stressor (A), it is likely that the family experiences other stressors because families do not usually just experience one stressor at a time. Thus aA represents the pile-up of additional stressors experienced by the family, with new stressors emerging after the changes in the family that have resulted from the crisis, all of which challenge family adaptation. To the family's existing resources (B), new expanded social and psychological resources (bB) now come into play, post-crisis, that the family now has at its disposal for meeting the demands of future crises. The final predictor variable is cC, which reflects more widely the family's appraisal not only of the crisis itself but the meaning the family attaches to the whole crisis situation that includes the original crisis as well as the family's perception of existing and new resources, the original stressor and any new stressors. In the Double ABCX model, the outcome variable, xX, refers to measures on a continuum of family adaptation ranging from maladaptation to good adaptation. The Double ABCX model has been found to be effective in predicting family stress and adjustment (e.g. Bristol, 1987, Saloviita, Itälinna and Leinonen, 2003).

EXAMPLE Understanding how the double ABCX model might work in practice

A family has a child who is born with significant physical disabilities (A). The parents also have financial and marital difficulties, which increase because the mother is unable to return to work after maternity leave. Thus we have a significant build-up of stressors (aA). Both parents have good coping skills (B) and in addition have now obtained social support from their extended family and from a local self-help group for parents of children with developmental disabilities (bB). The family's original appraisal of having a child with a disability (C) was problematic as they were struggling initially with a very negative definition of what this would mean for them as a family. However, there have been ongoing changes in their thinking about this through the contact they have had with other families in the support group (cC). These factors together (aA, bB and cC) can be used to predict family adjustment and adaptation (xX).

Family Adjustment and Adaptation model (FAAR; Patterson, 1988)

The FAAR model develops the same themes further, making explicit the contribution of three systems: the individual, the family and the community to family adaptation. Its key elements are: demands (i.e. stressors as previously discussed, unresolved ongoing strains within the family, and the general minor hassles of daily life) and capabilities. Balancing demands and capabilities is viewed as being mediated by the meanings that families ascribe to the events they are experiencing. The variable 'capabilities' is seen as encompassing:

1 **Resources**: these can be individual resources or can come from the family or indeed from the wider community. Thus this variable can include help from family and friends, support from statutory educational and health service professionals, as well as financial support. It can also encompass personal resources such as self-esteem.

2 **Coping behaviours** are included in the assessment of family capabilities using the FAAR model, and relate to what the family is able to do to manage the stressful situation and restore family equilibrium.

The FAAR model then sees the family as moving through cycles of adjustment and adaptation to crisis. Crisis is not a one-off event but this model takes instead a dynamic view of family processes that recognises that crises may recur within the family but that these will be different crises and indeed the family's resources and coping behaviours will have changed as a result of the previous crises it has had to deal with.

QUISSET   *Now go beyond the text ... look it up yourself!*

Explore your library's electronic databases to investigate 'models of family adjustment to stress'.

- Find studies that have used these models to evaluate child and family outcomes.
- Identify strengths and weaknesses of these studies.
- What other models have been used for this purpose?

Resilience

The models above each take account of the stressors and challenges experienced by families but they also recognise that many families successfully cope and adapt. We now understand that there is a complex interaction of factors that contributes to the extent to which families experience stress as an outcome of parenting a child with a disability, and that neither high levels of stress, family crisis nor maladaptation are inevitable outcomes. Singer's (2006) meta-analysis, for example, reported that 70% of mothers of children with developmental disabilities did not have increased symptoms of depression compared to mothers of typically developing children. A longitudinal study that collected data over 35 years similarly found no differences in parental wellbeing between the two groups of parents (Seltzer, Greenberg, Floyd, Pettee and Hong, 2001).

Not only do many parents cope very well with the challenges presented by having a child with a developmental disability in the family, some indeed perceive themselves to have benefited from this parenting challenge (Affleck, Tennen and Gershman, 1985; Green, 2007; Hastings and Taunt, 2002; King, Baxter, Rosenbaum, Zwaigenbaum and Bates, 2009). Rather than being defined by catastrophe and negative outcomes, Singer, Ethridge and Aldana (2007) suggested that family resilience over the long term may better characterise these families. The view of resilience here is as a complex multifaceted process, not a trait that belongs to an individual family (Gerstein *et al.*, 2009; Luthar and Zelazo, 2003).

Studies have indicated a variety of factors that may act as buffers against family stress. Let's look at some of these now.

Social variables

Social support

Social support has long been perceived as an important factor in helping people cope with stressful life events in general (Cobb, 1976), so it is not surprising that much of the research on support systems used by the family has shown that strong support systems help families deal better with the challenges they face (e.g. Bailey, Nelson, Hebbeler and Spiker, 2007; Crnic, Greenberg, Ragozin, Robinson and Basham, 1983; Dunst, Trivette and Deal, 1994; Hauser-Cram, Warfield, Shonkoff, Krauss, Sayer and Upshur, 2001). Social support in terms of the quality of the marital relationship has also been shown to be associated with coping and wellbeing (Friedrich, Wilturner and Cohen, 1985; Kersh, Hedvat, Hauser-Cram and Warfield, 2006).

Support systems may be formal, such as those provided by the team of professionals around the child or informal, comprising family and friends, (see Table 11.1). Informal networks may offer practical support such as babysitting, fund-raising for special treatment, or offering advice or emotional support. These informal supports have been demonstrated to have an important role to play in helping families cope with difficulties (Thompson, Lobb, Elling, Herman, Jurkiewicz and Hulleza, 1997). The mother's level of social support from her husband/partner, extended family and friends, has been shown to moderate the relationship between child disability and maternal stress (e.g. Plant and Sanders, 2007). Network size, the number of people available to offer different types of support to a family, may be an important factor in successful family adaptation (Kazak and Marvin, 1984; Kazak, 1987).

As already mentioned earlier in this chapter, having a child with a developmental disability can result in isolation from social and cultural activities (Marsh, 1992; Sanders and Morgan, 1997), which implies that the family have a reduced social network with less opportunity to receive the social support they need. For example, Heiman and Berger (2008) found that parents of children with Asperger Syndrome perceived themselves as experiencing lower levels of social support

Table 11.1 **Types of support with examples**

Formal	Informal
Paediatrician	Immediate family
Educational psychologist	Extended family
Speech and language therapist	Friends
Physiotherapist	Neighbours
Occupational therapist	Self-help groups
Home teacher	Charities
Health visitor	Wider community

compared to parents of children with a specific learning difficulty or parents of typically developing children. The authors pointed out that while this could indeed reflect deterioration in social relationships and isolation from friends and family, it could also signify an unmet need in this group. Enabling families to make use of, build on, and strengthen their existing informal support systems is now recognised as an important intervention goal for professionals (Bailey, Bruder, Hebbeler, Carta, Defosset, Greenwood *et al.*, 2006; Bailey *et al.*, 2007).

Attitudes

The social model of disability (Oliver, 1986, 1990) challenged the perception of disability as a medical problem. One implication of a medical perspective on disability is that a person with a disability is allocated the lifelong role of sick person, although s/he is not actually ill and indeed is not likely to recover with treatment (Oliver and Sapey, 1999). Oliver instead argued that over and above any medical aspects of disability – physical, cognitive or sensory aspects of impairment – there is a social construction of disability within society that is disabling for people with disabilities. Attitudes of fear, pity and disgust towards those with disabilities have been reported (Barton, 1996). Thus Oliver proposed that within Western societies, the dominant view of disability is that it is a personal tragedy that randomly happens to individuals, and that those individuals must be unhappy as a result.

With respect to children with disabilities, it has been argued by advocates of the social model of disability that in Western societies we expect children only to be dependent for a finite period and then to be independent and productive members of society. The argument runs that children with developmental disabilities cannot conform to this and so are viewed as problems for society with the resultant expectation that parents would feel raising such a child to be a burden (Priestly, 2003). This attitude of the burden of caregiving has in the past influenced a considerable amount of research on negative psychosocial aspects of parenting a child with a disability (Heiman, 2002), although as discussed earlier in the chapter this has changed to some extent with recent recognition of the benefits that parents experience in this role and research interest in resilience rather than negative outcomes (Green, 2007).

QUISSET *Now go beyond the text . . . look it up yourself!*

Explore your library's electronic databases to investigate 'the social model of disability'.

- What is meant by the social model of disability?
- How does it contrast with a medical model of disability?
- How have writers in this area recently moved towards a synthesis of these two positions?

(Hint: Shakespeare and Watson, 2002)

Parent variables

Studies have found a number of parent variables to be associated with good coping and adaptation to the challenges of having a child with a disability in the family. Although studies discussed here have used parental wellbeing as an *outcome* measure of the extent of family stress and coping (e.g. Friedrich *et al.*, 1985; Kersh *et al.*, 2006), other studies have instead shown it to be a *predictor* of family stress (Chang and Fine, 2007; Williford, Calkins and Keane, 2007).

In their study of parenting children with autism spectrum disorders, Hastings and Brown (2002) found maternal self-efficacy to mediate the relationship between child behaviour problems and maternal depression, i.e. parenting a child with problematic behaviour reduced feelings of efficacy, which was associated with increased depression. Hassall, Rose and McDonald (2005) similarly found parenting self-esteem to influence levels of stress experienced. They measured self-esteem using Johnston and Mash's (1989) Parenting Sense of Competence Scale which comprised a subscale that measured parenting efficacy with another that measured parenting satisfaction.

Parental locus of control has also been found to correlate with stress such that those parents who perceived themselves as having more personal (internal) control experienced stress to a lesser extent (Frey, Greenberg and Fewell, 1989; Friedrich *et al.*, 1985; Hassall *et al.*, 2005). We will return to examine attributions of control later in the chapter.

Lloyd and Hastings (2007) examined the influence of parental acceptance on maternal stress. They suggested that this was likely to be an important variable in the case of developmental disability where however successful child educational and rehabilitation interventions might be, it was unlikely that that they could totally overcome the developmental difficulties which were likely to present in the long term. Acceptance of present and future challenges then would seem to be a useful way forward for families and indeed Lloyd and Hastings found acceptance to be associated with maternal stress, such that higher levels of acceptance were associated with lower stress.

The quality of parenting and the parent–child relationship might have a role as a protective factor in the relationship between child disability and family stress (Gerstein *et al.*, 2009; Hauser-Cram, Warfield, Shonkoff, Krauss, Upshur and Sayer, 1999). Marfo's (1990) study found that parents of children with intellectual disabilities tended to be more directive than parents of typically developing children, i.e. an emphasis on firm parental control of behaviour, leaving little choice or decision-making to the child. Marfo found that although they were more directive in their approach, these parents of children with intellectual disabilities were not necessarily less warm or less positive in their parenting than parents of typically developing children. Confusingly though, while such *authoritative parenting* is associated with effective and appropriate parenting in typically developing children (Baumrind, 1971; Pettit, Bates and Dodge, 1997), it may actually be more stressful for parents of children with developmental disabilities to implement than for parents of typically developing children (Woolfson and Grant, 2006). One explanation for this higher stress could be that, because of their particular difficulties in understanding or in regulating their own behaviour, children with disabilities may need more repetition of parent directions before decreasing the particular target problematic behaviours.

Gerstein *et al.* (2009) studied some of the parent factors that we have discussed above, to see the extent to which they might operate as factors that promote resilience or protect from risk. They found that parental wellbeing, marital adjustment and positive father–child relationships contributed to resilience in mothers, with a different pattern in fathers, demonstrating that there was a complexity of interacting variables and also that the experience of stress and resilience to challenges was not the same for both parents. They argued that models of the processes involved in building resilience to stress in families of children with disabilities needed to encompass a considerable degree of complexity as well as multiple perspectives, recognising that processes contributing to resilience may be quite different in mothers than in fathers, and that, furthermore, mothers and fathers each affect the other's adaptation.

Parent variables are of particular interest within educational psychology as it is possible to work on these using psycho-educational approaches that teach parents new ways to manage their children's behaviour or new ways to understand it. Thus they are an important focus for intervention, particularly when we consider the impact changing parent variables can have on the caregiver–child system as a whole, and indirectly on child developmental outcomes. Furthermore, family belief systems are thought to have a key role in promoting resilience (Walsh, 2002, 2003) so we'll focus particularly on parental beliefs and cognitions in the latter section of this chapter.

Intervention

Let us move from considering family response to the child with developmental disability to examine how parents and professionals might intervene to promote optimal child developmental and behavioural outcomes.

Transactional developmental regulation (Sameroff and Fiese, 2000)

In Chapter 10 we discussed with respect to preschool development how child outcomes were the result of a series of transactions between the caregiver and the child over time. These principles of transactional developmental regulation still apply where the child has an identified disability. Disability is of course an important factor that influences child developmental outcomes; but just as factors other than child disability influence the extent to which increased parenting stress and other negative parenting outcomes are experienced within the family, so factors other than disability influence child developmental and behavioural outcomes.

The psychosocial context of parenting also contributes to child behavioural outcomes as it is through daily interactions with their parents that children with or without developmental disabilities learn how to behave and respond in ways that are appropriate to the culture in which they live (Moilanen, Shaw, Dishion, Gardner and Wilson, 2010), although clearly having a developmental disability may limit the extent to which a child can take advantage of this.

We know from Chapter 10 that transactional models view the child's development as resulting from continual interplay between a changing organism (the child) and a changing environment (the caregiving context) and that this points to a complexity of interactions over time between the parenting context and the child, that influence child behavioural outcomes. This suggests that rather than developmental and behavioural outcomes being directly caused by the child's disability, they are instead a product of the interplay between the child's presenting behaviour and the parents' response to it.

 Activity

Re-read the section in Chapter 10 that outlines Sameroff and Fiese's (2000) model of transactional developmental regulation.

Consider how this can be applied to families of children with developmental disabilities.

What then are the implications of a transactional model for intervention approaches for young children with developmental disabilities? Importantly, because of the reciprocal and sequential nature of these transactions in the child–parent relationship, targeting one part of the system for change is likely to result in change in another part of the system. Thus targeting the child's developmental difficulties directly with professional intervention is not the only useful form approach as a transactional model implies that tackling parent behaviour should have an effect on child development and behaviour. Sameroff and Fiese (2000) then suggested that intervention could be targeted in three ways: remediation, re-education, and redefinition. Each of these interventions targets the system quite differently (see Key Concepts box).

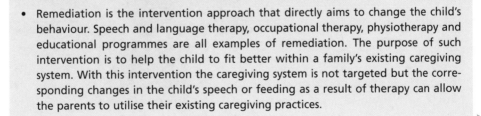

KEY CONCEPTS

- Remediation is the intervention approach that directly aims to change the child's behaviour. Speech and language therapy, occupational therapy, physiotherapy and educational programmes are all examples of remediation. The purpose of such intervention is to help the child to fit better within a family's existing caregiving system. With this intervention the caregiving system is not targeted but the corresponding changes in the child's speech or feeding as a result of therapy can allow the parents to utilise their existing caregiving practices.

- Re-education on the other hand does target the caregiving system. It aims to change parent behaviour by teaching parents new skills specific to their child's special developmental needs. So they might, for example, learn handling skills such as how to position a child who is floppy because of lack of muscle tone due to cerebral palsy. Learning how to position the child so that s/he can adopt a more upright position, see what is going on, receive more stimulation and engage more with their surroundings, is likely to have an effect on child developmental outcomes too. Or parents may learn new skills for supporting their child's feeding if their child has difficulty holding her head up in a good feeding position, or difficulty in chewing or swallowing. Examples of parent re-education in a preschool intervention programme for children with motor impairments were reported by Woolfson (1999), giving a good sense of skills that parents of young children with developmental disabilities found useful.

- Redefinition tackles neither child nor parent behaviour directly but instead focuses on parents' beliefs about parenting, about their child's development, about their perceptions of their role in facilitating this, and their interpretation of the meaning of the child's disability. Redefinition relates to cognitive appraisal as parents may be encouraged to reappraise, to redefine their beliefs about parenting their child with a developmental disability. With a redefinition strategy, the psychologist helps parents to engage in cognitive reframing and reappraisal so that they view some of the child's difficulties as a normal part of development rather than always as a function of the child's disability. This can help them respond in ways that are within the normal family repertoire of parenting behaviours, rather than always perceiving the child as requiring special management. Examples of parental redefinition can also be found in the Woolfson (1999) paper.

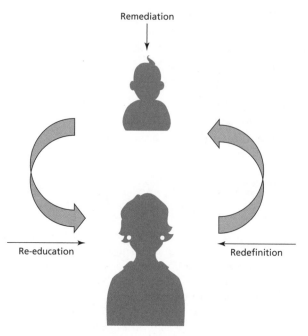

Figure 11.1 Intervention approaches with the mother–child caregiving system

QUISSET *Now go beyond the text . . . look it up yourself!*

Explore your library's electronic databases to investigate 'remediation, re-education and redefinition'.

● Access the Woolfson (1999) paper. How was a transactional model used to inform the evaluation in this study?

● What are the implications of a transactional model for designing intervention programmes for preschool children with disabilities?

Parenting beliefs and child outcomes

We know that remediation and reeducation approaches can have positive effects with children with developmental disabilities as shown by the success of behaviour management approaches (e.g. Levin and Carr, 2001; Mandal, Olmi, Edwards, Tingstrom and Benoit, 2000), and parent education programmes (e.g. Ozonoff and Cathcart, 1998; Woolfson, 1999). As we have just seen, Sameroff and Fiese's model of transactional developmental regulation also identified that parental beliefs and perceptions about child-rearing can be targeted by intervention approaches that aim to address redefinition. As the study of social cognition is of particular interest to psychologists, rather than examining biological aspects of disability or therapeutic rehabilitation and educational approaches that parents and professionals might undertake with children with disabilities (remediation and re-education), we will instead now focus on this more recent intervention approach (redefinition) by considering studies of parental beliefs about their child's disability as well as interventions that have attempted to change these beliefs.

Psychosocial model of disability-related behaviour problems (Woolfson, 2004)

In general, children with developmental disabilities exhibit more behavioural problems than do typically developing children (Baker *et al.*, 2003; Roberts and Lawton, 2001; Woolfson, Taylor and Mooney, (2010)). A range of parental beliefs and behaviours contribute to child behavioural and development outcomes in both typically developing children and those with developmental disabilities (e.g. Bernier, Carlsen and Whipple, 2010; Sameroff and Fiese, 2000; Woolfson, 2004). Let us now examine more carefully the relationship between parental beliefs and problematic child behaviours.

This is a model that takes as a starting point the negative social values identified earlier in this chapter by a social model of disability (Oliver, 1986, 1990). The model (see Figure 11.2) takes three societal views of disability proposed by Oliver, and suggests what these values might mean at the level of family beliefs about parenting their child with a disability, and then how this might impact on their parenting behaviour and then on the child's behaviour. The model predicts that these societal beliefs are problematic for effective parenting as parents

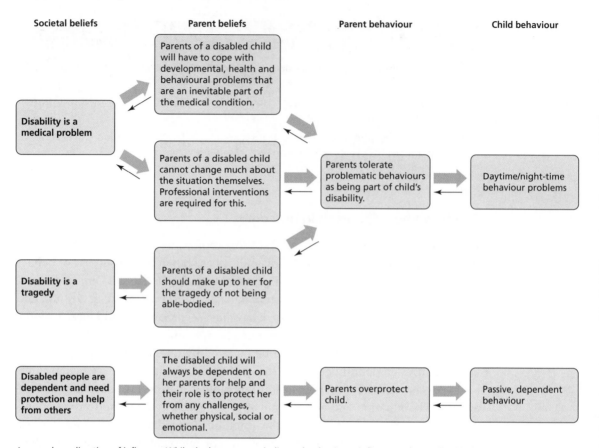

Arrows show direction of influence. While the large arrows indicate the dominant influences, the smaller black arrows show that the child's behaviour influences the parents' and societal views by confirming and strengthening them.

Figure 11.2 Psychosocial model of disability-related child behaviour problems

Source: Woolfson, 2004, reproduced by permission of John Wiley & Sons Inc

holding such perceptions about disability will not see themselves as having a role in the disciplining of their child to teach the rules of appropriate behaviour. Rather than viewing misbehaviour as the job of parents to try to tackle, they instead may view child problem behaviours, tantrums, lack of self-regulation, or lack of compliance with parental requests as a fixed part of the disability. Or they may feel sorry for their child and feel that they have to make up to their child for their impairments, so not perceive it as appropriate to try to discipline the child. Parents may feel that allowing their child to cry is harmful (Rickert and Johnson, 1988; Tse and Hall, 2007), and such a belief is likely to make it difficult for them to say 'no' to their child's demands. In their population-level study, McDermott, Coker, Mani, Krishnaswami, Nagle, Barnett-Queen *et al.* (1996) found 25.5% of children with cerebral palsy had behaviour problems, in particular on the head-strong subscale which relates to noncompliance at home, and which the authors suggested might be due to poor discipline and failure to set the child appropriate behavioural limits.

QUISSET *Now go beyond the text . . . look it up yourself!*

Explore your library's electronic databases to investigate 'the psychosocial model of disability-related behaviour problems'.

Access the Woolfson (2004) paper.

● What kinds of beliefs are suggested in the paper as being more useful for effective parenting?

● To what extent is there support in the literature for this?

The paper suggests that for effective parenting, the parents of children with developmental disabilities need to hold different views about disability from those that are dominant in society. For example, they may instead have high expectations for their child, expecting him/her to participate in society as fully as possible. They may view lack of compliance or tantrums not as part of the disability but instead as normal developmental problems that they as parents need to try to work on.

Changing parent beliefs

The models we have examined in this chapter suggest that there is a variety of parental beliefs of which some, more than others, are likely to contribute to improved child and family outcomes. It is therefore important for professionals working with families to take account of family worldviews and work with family belief systems (Bruce and Schultz, 2001; King, Baxter, Rosenbaum, Zwaigenbaum and Bates, 2009; King, Currie, Bartlett, Gilpin, Willoughby, Tucker *et al.*, 2007). Let's turn now to studies that have investigated parental cognitions around the child's disability.

Hastings, Allen, McDermott and Still (2002) reported that positive cognitive reframing of the child's disability predicted fulfilment, family strength, and maternal personal growth in their sample of mothers of children with intellectual disabilities. King *et al.*'s (2009) study of parents of children with autism spectrum disorder or Down syndrome too reported family changes in the realisation of what was important to them as a family. Their experiences were characterised by optimism, acceptance of challenge and difference, and striving to create change. The mothers in Larson's (1998) study were similarly hopeful about the future. King *et al.* concluded that for more effective practice in their work with families, professionals need to assess what parental priorities are for their child and what matters to the family, and then to use this more fine-grained understanding of individual family perspectives to help them better engage families in the process of adaptation.

Attribution theory provides us with a useful framework for studying parental beliefs about managing their children's behaviour. Within this framework, causes of behaviour are viewed as lying on three dimensions:

- locus of causality, whether the cause of the behaviour is internal or external to the child

- stability, whether the cause of the behaviour can change over time

- controllability, whether the child can act in a way that will change things.

(Weiner, 1985)

With regard to children with developmental disabilities, there has been a converging body of research on attributional beliefs of parents of children with ADHD which has consistently shown a relationship between their attributions and both child behaviour and their own parenting behaviour (Johnston, Chen and Ohan, 2006). Parents of children with ADHD tend to attribute ADHD behaviour problems to internal and stable factors and attribute little controllability of these to either child or parent (Johnston and Ohan, 2005). In particular they view attentional problems that are symptomatic of ADHD as caused by factors internal to the child, while they see more positive prosocial behaviours as being caused by external factors (Johnson and Freeman, 1997). This changes if the child is on medication for ADHD, when problematic behaviours are viewed as being located in causes outside the child, much more like the attributions used by parents of typically developing children (Johnston and Leung, 2001).

In addition, ADHD was found to be a moderator between parental controllability attributions and child behaviour (Johnston and Freeman, 1997), showing that parents of children with ADHD generally had different controllability attributions from parents of typically developing children. Correspondingly, Woolfson, Taylor and Mooney (2010) reported that parent controllability attributions may play a role in moderating the established relationship between child disability and behaviour in a sample of children with developmental disabilities other than ADHD.

There is, however, sensitivity around the study of parent attributions of child controllability for problematic behaviour as such attributions have been linked to negative emotions in parents of children with developmental disabiities (Chavira, Lopez, Blacher and Shapiro, 2000). It may be that when parents are asked about the extent to which the child has control over the cause of the problematic behaviour, they perceive issues of child responsibility, blame and whether the child has engaged in the behaviour intentionally as embedded within this question. Woolfson (2005) referred to it as a 'parenting paradox' that attributions of child controllability are associated with negative parental affect, as parents still need to see their children as having some degree of control over their actions if they are to expect them to learn acceptable ways of behaving. What is more, as teaching children how to behave is ultimately the responsibility of the parent, parents do need to view themselves as having a major role in controlling the child's behaviour. Perhaps beliefs of moderate child control over problem behaviour are necessary for effective behavioural management, while it is beliefs of high control that are associated with negative affect and harsh discipline (Mah and Johnston, 2008). Or perhaps even though an attribution of controllability is associated with negative emotion, that same attribution of controllability might be what is required for the mother to engage in effective parenting behaviour.

 ## Debate

Join up with some friends to discuss.

Discuss the issue of directionality of the relationship between attributions and child behaviour.

- Do parent controllability attributions influence child behavioural outcomes?
- Or does the experience of repeated unsuccessful attempts to manage child behaviour result in low parental attributions of controllability?

There is a small body of emerging evidence of successful outcomes for intervention targeting parental beliefs in families of children with disabilities. Dunst (1999) found that one of the best predictors of child outcomes was the extent to which programmes utilised family-centred practices that resulted in parents reappraising their own personal control. In their meta-analysis, Singer *et al.* (2007) analysed the outcomes of six studies that used cognitive-behavioural training with parents to help them better cope with stress and concluded that they were consistently effective. These included Nixon and Singer's (1993) study that aimed to change cognitive distortions and misattributions associated with parental guilt; reinforcing parental cognitions that promoted adaptation and changing parental beliefs that were detrimental (Pelchat, Bisson, Ricard, Perreault and Bouchard, 1999); modifying beliefs that were associated with distress (Singer, Irvin and Hawkins, 1988); and modifying negative thoughts (Singer, Irvin, Irvine, Hawkins and Cooley, 1989).

Singer *et al.*'s meta-analysis also examined parent education programmes and multi-component interventions. In terms of the transactional model used in this chapter, these may be considered as addressing both re-education and redefinition. They found that these multi-component interventions were more effective than just parent education or cognitive-behavioural training alone. The transactional model would further predict that these changes in parental beliefs and new parent learning would result in corresponding improvements in child outcomes, although this was not assessed in the above studies. This points to clear directions for future work for both academic researchers and professionals working with parents of children with disabilities.

Summary and conclusions

While parenting a child with a developmental disability may bring challenges that are stressful, there are factors that can operate as buffers and help to promote family coping and resilience. Similarly, while many children with developmental disabilities present behaviour problems, families can act to ameliorate the situation. Alongside educational and rehabilitation activities to help the child directly, and alongside parent education to teach the parents new skills, parental beliefs have an important role to play in moving the family towards improved child and family outcomes.

Further study

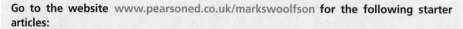

Go to the website www.pearsoned.co.uk/markswoolfson **for the following starter articles:**

Gerstein, E., Crnic, K., Blacher, J., and Baker, B. (2009). Resilience and the course of daily parenting stress in families of young children with intellectual disabilities. *Journal of Intellectual Disability Research.* 53(12), 981–97.

Woolfson, L. (1999) Using a model of transactional developmental regulation to evaluate the effectiveness of an early intervention programme for pre-school children with motor impairments. *Child: Care, Health and Development,* 25(1), 55–79.

Woolfson, L. (2004). Family wellbeing and disabled children: A psychosocial model of disability-related child behaviour problems. *British Journal of Health Psychology, 9,* 1–13.

References

Affleck, G., Tennen, H., and Gershman, K. (1985). Cognitive adaptations to high-risk infants: The search for mastery, meaning, and protection from harm. *American Journal of Mental Deficiency, 89,* 653–6.

Bailey, D., Bruder, M., Hebbeler, K., Carta, J., Defosset, M., Greenwood, C., *et al.* (2006). Recommended outcomes for families of young children with disabilities. *Journal of Early Intervention, 28,* 227–51.

Bailey, D., Nelson, L., Hebbeler, K., and Spiker, D. (2007). Modeling the impact of formal and informal supports for young children with disabilities and their families. *Pediatrics, 120,* e992–e1001.

Baker, B., McIntyre, L., Blacher, J., Crnic, K., Edelbrock, C., and Low, C. (2003). Preschool children with and without developmental delay: Behaviour problems and parenting stress over time. *Journal of Intellectual Disability Research, 49,* 217–30.

Barnett, R. and Boyce, G. (1995). Effects of children with Down syndrome on parents' activities. *American Journal of Mental Retardation, 100,* 115–27.

Barton, L. (1996). Sociology and disability: Some emerging issues. In L. Barton (ed.), *Disability and society: Emerging issues and insights.* London: Longman, (pp. 3–17).

Baumrind, D. (1971). Current patterns of parental authority. *Developmental Psychology Monograph, 4,* 1–103.

Beck, A., Daley, D., Hastings, R., and Stevenson, J. (2004). Mothers expressed emotion towards children with and without intellectual disabilities. *Journal of Intellectual Disability Research, 48*(7), 628–38.

Bennett, E. (2010). *Counting the costs 2010: The financial reality for families with disabled children*. London: Contact a Family.

Bernier, A., Carlsen, S., and Whipple, N. (2010). From external regulation to self-regulation: early parenting precursors of young children's executive functioning. *Child Development, 81*, 326–39.

Blacher, J. and Hatton, C. (2007). Families in context: Influences on coping and adaptation. In L. Odom, R. Home, M. Snell, and J. Blacher (eds), *Handbook of Developmental Disabilities*. New York: Guilford Press, (pp. 531–46).

Blacher, J., Neece, C., and Paczowski, E. (2005). Families and intellectual disability. *Current Opinion in Psychiatry, 18*, 507–13.

Bristol, M. (1987). Mothers of children with autism or communication disorders: successful adaptation and the double ABCX model. *Journal of Autism and Developmental Disorders, 17*, 469–86.

Bruce, E. and Schultz, C. (2001). *Nonfinite loss and grief: A psychoeducational approach*. Baltimore, MD: Brookes.

Chang, Y. and Fine, M. (2007). Modeling parenting stress trajectories among low-income mothers across the child's second and third years: Factors accounting for stability and change. *Journal of Family Psychology, 21*, 584–94.

Chavira, V., Lopez, S., Blacher, J., and Shapiro, J. (2000). Latina mothers' attributions, emotions and reactions to the problem behaviours of their children with developmental disabilities. *Journal of Child Psychology and Psychiatry, 41*, 245–52.

Cobb, S. (1976). Social support as a moderator of life stress. *Psychosomatic Medicine, 38*, 300–14.

Crnic, K. and Greenberg, M. (1990). Parenting stresses with young children. *Child Development, 61*(5), 1628–37.

Crnic, K., Greenberg, M., Ragozin, A., Robinson, N., and Basham, R. (1983). Effects of stress and social support on mothers and premature and full-term infants. *Child Development, 54*, 209–17.

Crnic, K., Hoffman, C., and Gaze, C. (2005). Cumulative parenting stress across the preschool period: Relations to maternal parenting and child behaviour at age 5. *Infant and Child Development, 14*, 117–32.

Dempsey, I., Keen, D., Pennell, D., O'Reilly, J., and Neilands, J. (2009). Parent stress, parenting competence and family-centred support to young children with an intellectual or developmental disability. *Research in Developmental Disabilities, 30*(3), 558–66.

Dobson, B. and Middleton, S. (1998). *Paying to care: The cost of childhood disability*. York: Joseph Rowntree Foundation.

Dumas, J., Wolf, L., Fisman, S., and Culligan, A. (1991). Parenting stress, child behaviour problems, and dysphoria in parents of children with autism, Down Syndrome, behaviour disorders, and normal development. *Exceptionality, 2*(2), 97–110.

Dunst, C. (1999). Placing parent education in conceptual and empirical context. *Topics in Early Childhood Special Education, 19*, 141–7.

Dunst, C., Trivette, C., and Deal, A. (1994). *Supporting and strengthening families: Volume 2 – methods, strategies and practices*. Cambridge, MA: Brookline.

Emerson, E., Graham, H., McCulloch, A., Blacher, J., Hatton, C., and Llewellyn, G. (2008). The social context of parenting 3-year-old children with developmental delay in the UK. *Child: Care, Health and Development, 35*(1), 63–70.

Emerson, E., Hatton, C., Llewellyn, G., Blacher, J., and Graham, H. (2006). Socio-economic position, household composition, health status, and indicators of the wellbeing of mothers of children with and without intellectual disabilities. *Journal of Intellectual Disability Research, 50*, 862–73.

Estes, A., Munson, J., Dawson, G., Koehler, E., Zhou, X., and Abbott, R. (2009). Parenting stress and psychological functioning among mothers of preschool children with autism and developmental delay. *Autism, 13*, 375–87.

Evans, D. (1989). The psychological impact of disability and illness on medical treatment decision making. *Issues in Law and Medicine, 5*, 277–99.

Freedman, R., Litchfield, L., and Warfield, M. (1995). Balancing work and family: Perspectives of parents of children with developmental disabilities. *Families in Society: The Journal of Contemporary Human Services, 76*, 507–14.

Frey, K., Greenberg, M., and Fewell, R. (1989). Stress and coping among parents of handicapped children: A multi-dimensional approach. *American Journal on Mental Retardation, 94*, 240–9.

Friedrich, W., Wilturner, L., and Cohen, D. (1985). Coping resources and parenting mentally retarded children. *American Journal of Mental Deficiency, 90*, 130–9.

Gerstein, E., Crnic, K., Blacher, J., and Baker, B. (2009). Resilience and the course of daily parenting stress in families of young children with intellectual disabilities. *Journal of Intellectual Disabiity Research, 53*(12), 981–97.

Green, S. (2007). "We're tired, not sad": Benefits and burdens of mothering a child with a disability. *Social Science and Medicine, 64*, 150–63.

Gupta, V. (2007). Comparison of parenting stress in different developmental disabilities. *Journal of Developmental and Physical Disabilities, 19*, 417–25.

Hassall, R., Rose, J., and McDonald, J. (2005). Parenting stress in mothers of children with intellectual disability: The effects of parental cognitions in relation to child characteristics and family support. *Journal of Intellectual Disability Research, 49*(6), 405–18.

Hastings, R. (2002). Parental stress and behavior problems of children with developmental disability. *Journal of Intellectual and Developmental Disability, 27*(3), 149–60.

Hastings, R., Allen, R., McDermott, K., and Still, D. (2002). Factors related to positive perceptions in mothers of children with intellectual disabilities. *Journal of Applied Research in Intellectual Disabilities, 15*, 269–75.

Hastings, R. and Beck, A. (2004). Practitioner review: stress intervention for parents of children with intellectual disabilities. *Journal of Child Psychology and Psychiatry, 45*, 1338–49.

Hastings, R. and Brown, T. (2002). Behaviour problems of children with autism, parental self-efficacy and mental health. *American Journal of Mental Retardation, 107*(3), 222–32.

Hastings, R. and Taunt, H. (2002). Positive perceptions in families of children with developmental disabilities. *American Journal of Mental Retardation, 107*, 116–27.

Hauser-Cram, P., Warfield, M., Shonkoff, J., and Krauss, M. (2001). The development of children with disabilities and the adaptation of their parents: theoretical perspective and empirical evidence. *Monographs of the Society for Research in Child Development, 66*, 6–21.

Hauser-Cram, P., Warfield, M., Shonkoff, J., Krauss, M., Sayer, A., and Upshur, C. (2001). Children with disabilities: A longitudinal study of child development and parent well-being. *Monograph of the Society for Research in Child Development, 66*, 1–126.

Hauser-Cram, P., Warfield, M., Shonkoff, J., Krauss, M., Upshur, C., and Sayer, A., (1999). Family influences on adaptive development in young children with Down Syndrome. *Child Development, 70*, 979–89.

Haveman, M., van Berkum, G., Reijnders, R., and Heller, T., (1997). Differences in service needs, time demands, and caregiving burden among parents of persons with mental retardation across the life cycle. *Family Relations, 46*, 417–25.

Heiman, T. (2002). Parents of children with disabilities: Resilience, coping and future expectations. *Journal of Developmental and Physical Disabilities, 14*, 159–71.

Heiman, T. and Berger, O. (2008). Parents of children with Asperger Syndrome or with learning disabilities.: Family environment and social support. *Research in Developmental Disabilities, 29*(4), 289–300.

Hill, R. (1958). Social stress on the family. *Social Case Work, 49*, 139–50.

Hornby, G. (1994). *Counselling in child disability*. London: Chapman and Hall.

Johnston, C., Chen., M., and Ohan, J. (2006). Mothers' attributions for behaviour in nonproblem boys, boys with attention deficit hyperactivity disorder, and boys with attention deficit hyperactivity disorder and oppositional defiant behaviour. *Journal of Clinical Child and Adolescent Psychology, 35*(1), 60–71.

Johnston, C. and Freeman, W. (1997). Attributions of child behaviour in parents of children without behaviour disorders and children with attention deficit hyperactivity disorder. *Journal of Consulting and Clinical Psychology, 65*(4), 636–45.

Johnston, C., Hessl, D., Blasey, C., Eliez, S., Erba, H., Dyer-Friedman, J. et al., (2003). Factors associated with parenting stress in mothers of children with Fragile X syndrome. *Journal of Developmental and Behavioural Pediatrics, 24*(4), 267–75.

Johnston, C. and Leung, D. (2001). Effects of medication, behavioural and combined treatments on parents' and children's attributions for the behaviour of children with attention deficit hyperactivity disorder. *Journal of Consulting and Clinical Psychology, 69*(1), 67–76.

Johnston, C. and Mash, E. (1989). A measure of parenting satisfaction and efficacy. *Journal of Clinical Child Psychology, 18*, 167–75.

Johnston, C. and Ohan, J. (2005). The importance of parental attributions in families of children with attention-deficit/hyperactivity and disruptive behaviour disorders. *Clinical Child and Family Psychology Review, 8*(3), 167–82.

Kazak, A. (1987). Families with disabled children: Stress and social networks in three samples. *Journal of Abnormal Child Psychology, 15*(1), 137–146.

Kazak, A. and Marvin, R. (1984). Differences, difficulties, and adaptation: Stress and social networks in families with a handicapped child. *Family Relations, 33*, 67–77.

Kersh, J., Hedvat, T., Hauser-Cram, P., and Warfield, M. (2006). The contribution of marital quality to the well-being of parents of children with developmental disabilities. *Journal of Intellectual Disability Research, 50*(12), 883–893.

King, G., Baxter, P., Rosenbaum, P., Zwaigenbaum, L., and Bates, A. (2009). Belief systems of families of children with autism spectrum disorders or Down Syndrome. *Focus on Autism and Other Developmental Disabilities, 24*, 50–64.

King, G., Currie, M., Bartlett, D., Gilpin, M., Willoughby, C., Tucker, M., *et al.* (2007). The development of expertise in pediatric rehabilitation therapists: Changes in self-approach, self-knowledge, and use of enabling and customising strategies. *Developmental Neurorehabilitation, 10*, 225–42.

Knox, M., Parmenter, T., Atkinson, N., and Yazbeck, M. (2000). Family control: The views of families who have a child with an intellectual disability. *Journal of Applied Research in Intellectual Disabilities, 13*, 17–28.

Konstantareas, M. and Homatidis, S. (1989). Assessing child symptom severity and stress in parents of autistic children. *Journal of Child Psychology and Psychiatry, 30*(3), 459–70.

Kübler-Ross, E. (1969). *On death and dying.* New York: Macmillan Publishing Company.

Lazarus, R. and Folkman, S. (1984). *Stress, appraisal, and coping.* New York: Springer Publishing Company.

Larson, E. (1998). Reframing the meaning of disability to families: The embrace of paradox. *Social Science and Medicine, 47*(7), 865–75.

Leiter, V., Krauss, M., Anderson, B., and Wells, N. (2004). The consequences of caring: Effects of mothering a child with special needs. *Journal of Family Issues, 25*, 379–403.

Levin, L. and Carr, E. (2001). Food selectivity and problem behaviour in children with developmental disabilities: Analysis and intervention. *Behaviour Modification, 25*, 443–70.

Lloyd, T. and Hastings, R. (2007). Psychological variables as correlates of adjustment in mothers of children with intellectual disabilities: Cross-sectional and longitudinal relationships. *Journal of Intellectual Disability Research, 52*(1), 37–48.

Lobato, D. (1995). *Brothers, sisters, and special needs: Information and activities for helping young children with chronic illnesses and developmental disabilities.* Baltimore: Paul H. Brookes.

Luther, S. and Zelazo, L. (2003). Research on resilience: An integrative review. In S. Luthar (ed.), *Resilience and vulnerability: Adaptation in the context of childhood adversity.* New York: Cambridge University Press (pp. 510–50).

Mah, J. and Johnston, C. (2008). Parental social cognitions: Considerations in the acceptability of and engagement in behavioral parent training. *Clinical Child and Family Psychology Review, 11,* 218–36.

Mandal, R., Olmi, D., Edwards, R., Tingstrom, D., and Benoit, D. (2000). Effective instruction delivery and time-in: Positive procedures for achieving child compliance. *Child and Family Behaviour Therapy, 22,* 1–12.

Marfo, K. (1990). Maternal directiveness in interactions with mentally handicapped children: An analytical commentary. *Journal of Child Psychology and Psychiatry, 31,* 531–49.

Marsh, D. (1992). *Families and mental retardation: New directions in professional practice.* New York: Praeger.

Marvin, R. and Pianta, R. (1996). Mothers' reactions to their child's diagnosis: Relations with security and attachment. *Journal of Clinical Child Psychology, 25,* 436–45.

McCubbin, H., Cauble, A., and Patterson, J. (eds) (1982). *Family stress, coping and social support.* Springfield, IL: Charles C. Thomas.

McCubbin, H. and Patterson, J. (1981). *Systematic assessment of family stress, resources, and coping.* St Paul: Family Stress Project, University of Minnesota.

McCubbin, H. and Patterson, J. (1983). The family stress process: The double ABCX model of adjustment and adaptation. In H. McCubbin and M. Sussman (eds) *Social stress and the family: Advances and developments in family stress theory and research* (pp. 7–37). New York: Haworth Press.

McDermott, S., Coker, A., Mani, S., Krishnaswami, S., Nagle, R., Barnett-Queen, L., *et al.* (1996). A population-based analysis of behaviour problems in children with cerebral palsy. *Journal of Pediatric Psychology, 21*(3), 447–63.

McDonald, T., Couchonnal, G., and Early, T. (1996). The impact of major events on the lives of family caregivers of children with disabilities. *Families in Society: The Journal of Contemporary Human Services, 10,* 502–14.

Moilanen, K., Shaw, D., Dishion, T., Gardner, F., and Wilson, M. (2010). Predictors of longitudinal growth in inhibitory control in early childhood. *Social Development, 19,* 326–47.

Nixon, C., and Singer, G., (1993). A group cognitive behavioural treatment for excessive parental self-blame and guilt. *American Journal of Mental Retardation, 97,* 665–72.

Oliver, M. (1986). Social policy and disability: Some theoretical issues. *Disability, Handicap and Society, 1,* 5–18.

Oliver, M. (1990). *The politics of disablement.* London: Macmillan.

Oliver, M. and Sapey, B. (1999). *Social work with disabled people,* 2nd edn. London: Macmillan.

Olshansky, S. (1962). Chronic sorrow: a response to having a mentally defective child. *Social Casework, 43,* 190–3.

Ozonoff, S. and Cathcart, K. (1998). Effectiveness of a home programme intervention for young children with autism. *Journal of Autism and Developmental Disorders, 28*(1), 25–32.

Patterson, J. (1988). Families experiencing stress: I. The Family Adjustment and Adaptation Response Model: II. Applying the FAAR model to health-related issues for intervention and research. *Family, Systems and Health, 6*(2), 202–37.

Pelchat, D., Bisson, J., Ricard, N., Perreault, M., and Bouchard, J.(1999). The longitudinal effects of an early family intervention programme on the adaptation of parents of children with a disability. *International Journal of Nursing Studies, 36,* 465–77.

Pettit. G., Bates, J., and Dodge, K. (1997). Supportive parenting, ecological context, and children's adjustment: a seven-year longitudinal study. *Child Development, 68,* 908–23.

Plant, K. and Sanders, M. (2007). Predictors of caregiver stress in families of preschool aged children with developmental disabilities. *Journal of Intellectual Disability Research, 51*(2), 109–24.

Powell, T. and Gallagher, P. (1993). *Brothers and sisters: A special part of exceptional families.* Baltimore: Paul H. Brookes.

Priestley, M. (2003). *Disability: A life course approach.* Cambridge: Polity Press.

Rickert, V. and Johnson, C. (1988). Reducing nocturnal awakening and crying episodes in infants and young children: A comparison between scheduled awakenings and systematic ignoring. *Pediatrics, 81,* 203–12.

Risdal, D. and Singer, G. (2004). Marital adjustment in parents of children with disabilities: A historical review and meta-analysis. *Research and Practice for Persons with Severe Disabilities, 29,* 95–103.

Roberts, K. and Lawton, D. (2001). Acknowledging the extra care parents give their disabled children. *Child: Care, Health and Development, 27,* 307–19.

Saloviita, T., Itälinna, M., and Leinonen, E. (2003). Explaining the parental stress of fathers and mothers caring for a child with intellectual disability: A Double ABCX model. *Journal of Intellectual Disability Research, 47(4/5),* 300–12.

Sameroff, A. and Fiese, B. (2000). Transactional regulation: the developmental ecology of early intervention. In J. Shonkoff and S. Meisels (eds), *Handbook of early childhood intervention,* 2nd edn. Cambridge: Cambridge University Press (pp. 135–59).

Sanders, J. and Morgan, S. (1997). Family stress and adjustment as perceived by parents of children with autism or Down syndrome: Implications for intervention. *Child and Family behaviour Therapy, 19,* 15–32.

Seligman, M. and Darling, R. (1997). *Ordinary families, special children.* New York: Guildford.

Seltzer, M., Greenberg, J., Floyd, F. Pettee, Y., Hong, J. (2001). Life course impacts of parenting a child with a disability. *American Journal of Mental Retardation, 106,* 265–86.

Seltzer, M. and Heller, T. (1997). Families and caregiving across the life course: Research advances on the influence of context. *Family Relations, 46,* 395–405.

Shakespeare, T. and Watson, N. (2002). The social model of disability: An outdated ideology? *Research in Social Science and Disability, 2,* 9–28.

Singer, G. (2006). Meta-analysis of comparative studies of depression in mothers of children with and without developmental disabilities. *American Journal of Mental Retardation, 111,* 155–69.

Singer, G., Ethridge, B., and Aldana, S. (2007). Primary and secondary effects of parenting and stress management interventions for parents of children with developmental disabilities: A meta-analysis. *Mental Retardation and Developmental Disabilities Research Reviews, 13,* 357–69.

Singer, G., Irvin, L., and Hawkins, N. (1988). Stress management training for parents of children with severe handicaps. *Mental Retardation, 26,* 269–77.

Singer, G., Irvin, L., and Irvine, B., Hawkins, N., and Cooley, E. (1989). Evaluation of community-based support services for families of persons with developmental disabilities. *Journal of the Association for Persons with Severe Handicaps, 14,* 312–23.

Smith, T., Oliver, M., and Innocenti, M. (2010). Parenting stress in families of children with disabilities. *American Journal of Orthopsychiatry, 71(2),* 257–61.

Thompson, L., Lobb, C., Elling, R., Herman, S., Jurkiewicz, T., and Hulleza, C. (1997). Pathways to family empowerment: Effects of family-centred delivery of early intervention services. *Exceptional Children, 64,* 99–113.

Tomanik, S., Harris, G., and Hawkins, J. (2004). The relationship between behaviours exhibited by children with autism and maternal stress. *Journal of Intellectual and Developmental Disability, 29,* 16–26.

Tse, L. and Hall, W. (2007). A qualitative study of parents' perceptions of a behavioural sleep intervention. *Child: Care, Health and Development, 34(2),* 162–72.

Turnbull, A. and Turnbull, H. (1990). *Families, professionals, and exceptionality: A special partnership.* Columbus, OH: Merrill.

Walsh, F. (2002). A family resilience framework: Innovative practice applications. *Family Relations, 51,* 130–7.

Walsh, F. (2003). Family resilience: A framework for clinical practice. *Family Process, 42,* 1–18.

Warfield, M. (2001). Employment, parenting and wellbeing among mothers of children with disabilities. *Mental Retardation, 39*, 297–309.

Warfield, M. (2005). Family and work predictors of parenting role stress among two-earner families of children with disabilities. *Infant and Child Development, 14*, 155–76.

Warfield, M. and Hauser-Cram, P. (1996). Child-care needs, arrangements, and satisfaction of mothers of children with developmental disabilities. *Mental Retardation, 34*, 294–302.

Weiner, B. (1985). An attributional theory of achievement motivation and emotion. *Psychological Review, 92*, 548–73.

Williford, A., Calkins, S., and Keane, S. (2007). Predicting change in parenting stress across early childhood: Child and maternal factors. *Journal of Abnormal Child Psychology, 35*, 251–63.

Woolfson, L. (1999) Using a model of transactional developmental regulation to evaluate the effectiveness of an early intervention programme for pre-school children with motor impairments. *Child: Care, Health and Development, 25*(1), 55–79.

Woolfson, L. (2004). Family wellbeing and disabled children: A psychosocial model of disability-related child behaviour problems. *British Journal of Health Psychology, 9*, 1–13.

Woolfson, L. (2005). Disability and the parenting paradox. *The Psychologist. Disability Special Issue, 18*(7), 421–2.

Woolfson, L. and Grant, E. (2006). Authoritative parenting and parental stress in parents of pre-school and older children with developmental disabilities. *Child: Care, Health and Development, 32*(2), 177–84.

Woolfson, L., Taylor, R., and Mooney, L. (2010) Parental attributions of controllability as a moderator of the relationship between developmental disability and behaviour problems. *Child: Care, Health and Development, 37*(2), 184–194.

Neuroscience and education

The final chapter of the book looks forward, to ways in which neuroscience, psychology and education can work together to help address educational problems. Neuroscientists are interested in how the brain learns new information and the factors that influence this. In recent years there has been an upsurge of interest from those in education in how neuroscientific findings might inform what and how teachers teach. In this chapter we will examine the gap that currently exists between neuroscientific research and its application to classrooms. The extent to which 'brain-based' educational packages fill this gap will be considered. We will then explore the role of cognitive psychology in establishing useful connections between neuroscience and classroom practice. We will cover some necessary basic background information about brain anatomy and methods of brain imaging in order to be able to understand findings from neuroscience investigations that are presented in the final sections of this chapter. Here new insights from neuroscience will be highlighted in two areas that have been the topics of earlier chapters: autism spectrum disorders and dyslexia.

Learning outcomes

By the end of this chapter you should be able to:

● Understand basics about brain structure

● Show awareness of neuroimaging techniques

● Separate fact from fiction in popular 'neuromyths'

● Appreciate how cognitive psychology can act as a 'bridge' between neuroscience and education

● Show awareness of current neuroscientific findings and their potential for impact on our understanding of autism spectrum disorders and dyslexia.

In the late 1970s, it was common practice for practitioner educational psychologists to perceive those children who had a specific learning difficulty, as opposed to generalised developmental delays across all areas, as having minimal brain damage. This was actually highly speculative as no neurological investigation had been carried out on which to base such a statement. It was simply assumed that where there was a presentation of specific difficulty in a child who otherwise showed typical development, there had to be a problem at brain level. Later it was rightly acknowledged that it was neither appropriate nor accurate to use this description. Instead of inferring spurious diagnoses of brain–behaviour links, educational psychologists then concentrated their assessment and intervention efforts only on functional and observable problems that presented in the classroom for the child with respect to their learning, behaviour and social interaction. They advised schools and parents on how best to intervene and manage.

Twenty years on from then, Morton and Frith's (1995) causal modelling framework (see Figure 12.1) provided a useful conceptualisation to aid our thinking about biological and cognitive contributions to developmental disorders. It identified three different levels of description that we might hypothesise to explain child learning and behaviour problems: biological, cognitive and behavioural. Thus it proposed a causal chain of links from brain to mind to behaviour within an overall context of environmental factors operating at each of the levels (Frith, 1997). From the late 1970s onwards, educational psychology, as described above, focused on developmental problems at the behavioural and cognitive levels, by using the cognitive level to provide psychological explanations for the observed behaviours. Biological-level study was the separate realm of the medical profession and not the business of educational psychology

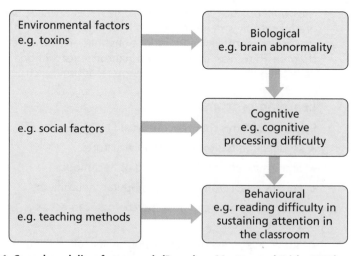

Figure 12.1 **Causal modeling framework (Based on Morton and Frith, 1995)**

at all: psychologists had focused on mind and behaviour, regardless of the actual workings of the brain.

Cognitive psychology: linking neuroscience and education

Since the 1990s, though, with the introduction of sophisticated new behavioural neuroimaging techniques that are discussed later in this chapter, it has become possible for cognitive neuroscientists to study the workings of the brain while children are engaged in particular cognitive tasks. This allows us to begin to put together more comprehensive explanations of the nature and extent of children's educational and behavioural problems by permitting the examination of functioning at each of the above three levels of Morton and Frith's causal modelling framework. Neuroscience then addresses the biological level, cognitive psychology the middle level, and classroom learning and social behaviour the third level. The second and third levels have been represented in preceding chapters in this book. This chapter deals with the biological level. Note, however, that there is a problem:

> Neuroscience has discovered a great deal about neurons and synapses, but not nearly enough to guide educational practice. Currently the span between brain and learning cannot support much of a load. Too many people marching in step across it could be dangerous.
> *Source*: Bruer, 1997, p. 15

For this reason, Bruer (1997) proposed that cognitive psychology is needed as a necessary bridge between neuroscience and educational practice. This mediational link has often been ignored (Geake, 2004). Cognitive psychology can provide us with theoretical explanations of processes that might underlie these behaviours and brain imaging techniques can provide neuroscientific evidence of these processes by showing us the inner working of the brain while children are engaged in these cognitive processes. This points to a new, interdisciplinary approach in which brain scientists, psychologists and teachers collaborate to identify what problems present in the classroom that teachers require solutions to, and which could usefully be informed by neuroscience findings (Blakemore and Frith, 2001; Fischer, Goswami, Geake, and the Task Force on the Future of Educational Neuroscience, 2010). This study of how the brain influences the mind is known as cognitive neuroscience, a discipline that has roots in neurology, neuroscience and cognitive science (Gazzaniga, Ivry and Mangun, 2008). This is our focus of interest in this chapter.

Neuromyths

Teachers are always interested in how they might utilise cutting-edge research findings to improve their practice. As indicated above, neuroscience itself has as yet little to offer to teachers directly (Bruer, 1997; Goswami, 2006). We cannot yet easily infer how new knowledge about neural development, brain structures and brain activity should influence classroom practice. To put it another way, 'brain scans cannot give rise directly to lesson plans' (TLRP, 2007).

There are at present, though, a number of educational packages that do claim to apply findings from neuroscience knowledge of the brain to the teaching plans in the classroom. Concern has been expressed that some of these packages may be misapplying or overclaiming: what is currently known in neuroscience as peddling 'neuromyths' (Blakemore and Frith, 2000). This refers to mythologies about brain functioning that seem to have gained currency among teachers and are influencing the curriculum and delivery of teaching in classrooms. Geake (2008) characterised them as either 'More is better' neuromyths where the idea is that teachers want to encourage more of the brain to 'light up' to facilitate learning, or specificity neuromyths where the idea is to encourage concentration on the 'lit-up' brain areas to enhance learning. Let us now examine some current neuromyths operating in education, and try to separate what is myth and over-interpretation of findings from the currently known neuroscientific facts embedded within the mythology.

Critical period for learning in early childhood

- *Neuromyth.* This myth propounds the principle that without teaching and stimulation within a critical developmental period, children's brains will not work properly and they will have missed the chance of learning particular skills or developing specific abilities. The actual timing of this window is reported to vary depending on what task or ability is being discussed, but it is reported variously as being birth to 3 years, birth to 6 years, birth to 10 years, and 3–10 years (Geake, 2008).

- *Fact.* Critical period research builds on work on animal sensory and motor systems that has demonstrated that specific stimulation is required at specific times for normal development to occur. Hubel and Wiesel's classic studies on the development of visual systems in cats are often referred to here. They showed that when kittens were deprived of all visual stimulation in one or both eyes in their first three months they were functionally blind, but the same effect was not found when older cats experienced similar deprivation (Wiesel and Hubel, 1965). However, while this effect was dramatic, subsequent studies demonstrated that the kittens could be trained to recover some visual function in the eye that had been occluded (Chow and Stewart, 1972).

Importantly it should be noted that research on critical periods in the main has involved visual and movement functions. It is not yet known how the principle of critical periods might apply to reading or number or other knowledge that is usually transmitted through a formally taught school curriculum (Blakemore and Frith, 2001; Bruer, 1997). In any case, now, our conceptualisation of the critical period is no longer that of a rigid time period when there is a window that is temporarily open and is then closed. What were called 'critical' periods are now more accurately referred to as 'sensitive' periods, where the brain responds particularly well to experiences due to its plasticity at that time (Daw, 1997). A 'critical' period, on the other hand, is one in which the absence or presence of an experience causes a change that cannot be reversed (Trachtenberg and Stryker, 2001). Fox, Levitt and Nelson (2010) also pointed out that we should not over-interpret from studies of the adverse effects of deprivation within sensitive periods such as that experienced by Hubel and Wiesel's cats, to reach conclusions about the necessity for educational enrichment programmes during sensitive periods.

 Activity

- How might the idea of a 'sensitive period' influence curriculum content in preschool and early years education?

Synaptogenesis

- *Neuromyth.* Related to the critical period neuromyth is the synaptogenesis neuromyth which states that learning will be more effective if it coincides with periods when there are synaptic growth and density of neural connections, i.e. during synaptogenesis (Geake, 2008).
- *Fact.* In infancy and through childhood, there is indeed a period of brain growth in which there is a proliferation in the number of synapses in the brain (Huttenlocher and Dabholkar, 1997). Neuroscience tells us that until the age of 10, there are more neural connections than in later years. Synapses that are used repeatedly are reinforced, but those that are less often used are subject to a process of synaptic pruning. Experience, however, affects not only the number of synaptic connections but even more importantly for brain function, it affects the pattern of synaptic connections (Bruer, 1997; Greenough, Black and Wallace, 1987). We also know now that synaptogenesis and pruning continue beyond childhood through adolescence for some areas of the brain, so while it is true that childhood is a good time to learn things because of changes in neural connectivity, it is not the only time to learn (TLRP, 2007). As for critical periods, we know little about the role of synaptogenesis in developing skills in subjects taught in schools and are not yet in a position to make inferences from neuroscientific knowledge about synaptogenesis and synaptic pruning to curricular content (Bruer, 1997).

Left brain, right brain

- *Neuromyth.* The left brain, right brain neuromyth, and the learning styles neuromyth below both rely on over-simplification and over-interpretation of the argument that functions are localised within the brain. It supposes that the two brain hemispheres work differently, with the left side more concerned with language, reasoning and logic, and the right side more creative and intuitive and dominant in the processing of pattern and images. Children can then be divided into 'left-brained' or 'right-brained' learners depending on their supposedly preferred way of processing information. This neuromyth further encourages teachers to ensure that teaching and learning activities in the classroom are balanced between left and right brain to optimise the match between learner preferences and classroom experiences (Geake, 2008; Goswami, 2006; TLRP, 2007; Hall, 2005).

- *Fact.* Based on studies of patients with abnormal brains in which the corpus callosum connections between the left and right hemispheres had been severed, it was found that the different brain hemispheres can indeed process different types of information in isolation. Certainly the processing of language, for example, is indeed *mainly* lateralised in the left hemisphere, but this is not to say that it is *totally* localised within the left hemisphere. Some language processing takes place in the right hemisphere too. In addition there are individual differences in the extent of lateralisation (Knecht, Deppe, Dräger, Bobe, Lohmann, Ringelstein, and Henningsen, 2000). In any case a normal brain has complex interconnections between the left and right hemispheres, so there is an interaction of activity between the two hemispheres. No part of the brain is normally completely inactive during a task, and learning tasks require both hemispheres working together (Blakemore and Frith, 2007).

Learning styles

- *Neuromyth.* For the past twenty years, a popular idea in education is that each child has a particular learning style that characterises how they best process information, a learning style that is based on visual, auditory and kinaesthetic (VAK) sensory modalities. Teachers following this approach in the classroom seek to identify for each child what their dominant learning style is and then aim to present material in a way that ensures the child can make use of their preferred style with the intention of optimising learning. It is sometimes even suggested that children wear a badge with V, A, or K on it so that teachers are reminded of children's learning preferences (Blakemore and Frith, 2007; Geake, 2008; Goswami, 2006).

- *Fact.* There is little evidence to demonstrate that applying a model of teaching based on these learning styles has any effect on learner outcomes (Coffield, Moseley, Hall and Ecclestone, 2004; Kratzig and Arbuthnott, 2006). In contrast, effective teachers for many years have implemented multi-modal strategies rather than focusing on a single modality. They might teach phonics, for example, by having children look at and sound out a phoneme, as well as having them handle plastic letter shapes, draw the letters in sand, or trace velvet letter shapes with their fingers. Teachers using multi-sensory methods aim to make use of visual and auditory modalities as well as the kinaesthetic modality; they do this in order to try to engage pupils' interest with variety in their method of presentation as well as to help them learn concepts more comprehensively.

A learning style approach focused on a single modality implies localisation of brain function, but, as already discussed in this chapter, we know that neuroimaging studies have provided evidence of connectedness across different parts of the brain rather than separateness. Imaging studies have further demonstrated that processing the same information through different modalities *at the same time,* a phenomenon known as crossmodal binding, has a greater effect than seeing the information and then subsequently hearing it (Calvert, Campbell and Brammer, 2000). Indeed, many teachers have taken on board VAK learning style ideas in a way that maximises presentation of material through different modalities in the classroom, that is to say they used multiple modalities. From their classroom experience, these teachers realise that individual learning styles seem to vary depending on what is being taught and on what the lesson demands are, and that children cannot be accurately characterised as always making use of a single VAK learning style across the curriculum (Geake, 2008).

Only 10% of the brain used

- *Neuromyth.* This is a popularly held notion that we only employ 10% of our brain. Implications of this neuromyth for educators then would be to devise activities for children to undertake in class that supposedly stimulate their using the other 90% and thus would make them smarter all round.

- *Fact.* This myth may have originated with the philosopher William James who in 1908 in his book *The Energies of Man* wrote that we only use a small amount of our potential mental resources. It may have been a misunderstanding from a 1920s radio interview with the scientist Albert Einstein who was attempting to explain his own superior intellect and encourage others to develop theirs. Studies in the 1800s by the French physiologist Flourens, in which he removed parts of the brains of rabbits and pigeons and noted what the animals could and could not subsequently do, may also have contributed to misinterpretation. Notions of a 'silent cortex' were further referred to in the 1930s, helping to perpetuate the 10% legend (Della Sala and Beyerstein, 2007; Geake, 2008). The idea has also been used in advertising for programmes to encourage people to buy into courses to develop their brain power. This neuromyth assumes extreme localisation of function, such that other parts of the brain are completely unused. We know from brain scans that this is not the case. Different functions certainly utilise different regions but neuroimaging has shown us that overall there are no inactive regions in the brain and that in the course of a day, a person going about his normal business will utilise all parts of his brain (Beyerstein, 1999). We would not have evolved in a way that permitted 90% redundancy of an organic structure (Beyerstein, 2004).

Determining the role of neuroscience within brain-based educational materials

Learning packages based on neuromyths have been marketed to teachers. Goswami (2006) reported that teachers attending a neuroscience teaching and learning conference received more than 70 mailshots each year inviting them to attend training on brain-based learning. Commercial programmes that claim to be brain-based are also available and have been taken up by many schools. Concern has been expressed by the neuroscience community that in general these products are not based on current knowledge within neuroscience but instead build on neuromyths or pseudoscience (TLRP, 2007).

Sylvan and Christodoulou (2010) have suggested a helpful framework to facilitate educators in making more informed and critical judgments about the extent to which educational materials do indeed build on neuroscientific findings. Firstly they suggested examining the material to determine if it is brain-based because it is underpinned in some way by neuroscience theory, principles or evidence. If it does indeed make use of neuroscience in this way, it can legitimately claim to be brain-based. Sylvan and Christodoulou proposed four sub-categories for the term 'brain-based' that reflect quite different ways neuroscience might be incorporated within these materials:

- **Brain-supported.** The effects of these products or programmes are supported by evidence from neuroimaging that shows changes in brain activation, structure or function, as a result of intervention using the programme.

- **Brain-derived.** Based soundly and directly on neuroscience theory, e.g. from fMRI information (see p. 262) about patterns of reduced brain activation in particular areas in, for example, dyslexia, a product might be developed to increase brain activation in that area. There are currently few examples of products that were initially based on neuroscience findings: they tend rather to be derived from cognitive domains and then informed by neuroscience findings at a later stage (Sylvan and Christodoulou, 2010).

- **Brain-driven.** Products in this category can be used to teach individuals how to manipulate brain activity to change behaviour. Such training targets changes in brain activity to change behaviour. For example, training might be designed to help children with ADHD regulate their behaviour using neurofeedback. Through awareness of their brain activity they can learn to monitor the neurofeedback and to modify their brain activity directly to change the feedback, thus changing their attentional behaviour too.

- **Brain-inspired.** These materials owe something to neuroscience principles or frameworks but are less directly derived from neuroscience principles and frameworks than brain-derived materials. Thus brain-inspired products have used neuroscience principles to some extent to underpin or inspire classroom activities or help teachers to better understand children's learning in ways that can be used to help guide teachers' practice. Sometimes the claims of underpinnings may credited to neuroscience but might more accurately be attributed to behavioural or cognitive neuroscience.

Another possibility, of course, is that the educational product makes claims about being brain-based and derived from neuroscience, but that none of the above applies and instead it uses pseudoscience concepts for commercial purposes.

 Activity

Carry out a web search to find examples of brain-based educational products.

Evaluate the products using Sylvan and Christodoulou's (2010) above sub-categories.

The brain

To understand the neuroscientific research findings that will be discussed in this chapter it is necessary to have a basic understanding of the structure of the brain and the nervous system. This will be kept simple and will be limited to developing an overview of brain anatomy and of brain imaging techniques.

The brain comprises two halves that are almost symmetrical. These are the left and right hemispheres that are joined by fibres (corpus callosum). We know that the two hemispheres perform different functions: the left has a particular role in language and speech, and in controlling the right side of the body; the right hemisphere's special role relates to perception of non-verbal information such as facial expression and music, and controlling the left side of the body. However, laterality is not absolute. For example, the right hemisphere also contributes to language (Kolb and Whishaw, 2009).

As can be seen from Figure 12.2, each hemisphere is further divided into four regions: frontal, temporal, parietal, and occipital. The crinkled outer layer

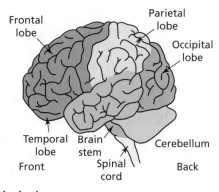

Figure 12.2 **Regions of the brain**

covering the brain is the cerebral cortex. Deeper within the brain lie structures other than the cortex, such as the hippocampus and amygdalae, that are important for learning, memory and emotional responses, but we will restrict our focus mainly to the cortex in this chapter. The word cortex means 'bark' in Latin, referring to the folds in this layer being like the folds in the bark of a tree and that the cortex covers the brain as bark covers a tree. Bumpy, protruding cortical folds are known as gyri (singular gyrus) and creases and lines in the cortex are referred to as sulci (singular sulcus). A fissure is the name given to some deeper sulci. For example, the lateral (or Sylvian) fissure separates the temporal lobe from the frontal and occipital lobes; the interhemispheric (or longitudinal) fissure separates left and right hemispheres (Gazzaniga, Ivry and Mangun, 2008; Kolb and Whishaw, 2009). In order to describe and identify brain sites with clarity, specific conventions derived from anatomy of the whole have been developed for referring to brain locations. Thus 'anterior' refers to anatomical structures 'in front' and 'posterior' to 'behind'. 'Superior' refers to the 'top' of the brain and 'inferior' to the 'bottom' of the brain.

Specific cognitive functions are associated with these regions. Frontal lobes have a major role in higher-order planning and reasoning, as well as in motor control. The auditory cortex is located in the temporal lobes, so these regions deal primarily with auditory processing as well as some memory functions. The parietal lobes deal with sensory processing of information from the body, i.e, somatosensory information, and are associated with spatial cognition and some mathematical skills. The occipital lobes contain the primary visual cortex, also known as striate cortex, which is associated with visual processing. It is important, though, not to view any one part of the brain as being solely responsible for executing any particular task as while there is localisation of brain function, communication goes on between regions throughout the brain's extensive and complex neural networks, so a number of different brain areas are required for any function (TLRP, 2007).

Neurons

The unit of structure within the brain is the nerve cell, the neuron. The human nervous system is estimated to comprise about 100 billion neurons, which interact with each other by sending signals with a chemical basis, known as *neurotransmission*. A neuron cell has three overall parts: its main part is the *cell body*, with many tree-like branches attached, known as *dendrites*. Connected to the cell body is one main root, called an *axon* (see Figure 12.3). Dendrites and axons extend the surface area of the cell. At the end of the axon are terminals that connect with the dendrites of neighbouring cells at points known as *synapses*, thus forming a complex network of neural connections. Communication between neurons is carried out via neurotransmitters, which are chemical substances.

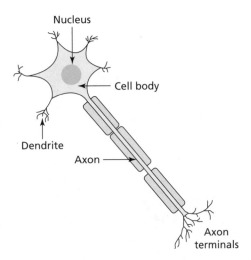

Figure 12.3 **A neuron**

Recording brain activity

Early studies of brain lesions provided researchers with useful information about brain function by identifying what the function of the missing area must have been by studying the subsequent changes in behaviour and task performance. Lesions were carried out on animals, and naturally occurring lesions were studied in humans. Broca's work in nineteenth-century France and Wernicke's research, investigating the responses of patients with brain lesions due to strokes, were highly influential in identifying the important role of the left hemisphere of the brain in language. While work on lesions in neural structures has produced important findings, it may be that damaged brains function differently from non-damaged brains. Perhaps another part of the brain compensates for the damaged area. New technology in brain science allows us now to research how the brain functions in healthy people whose brains are intact. Let us now familiarise ourselves with some of these methods so that we can better understand the research findings of neuroscience applications to education that will be presented in this chapter.

Electroencephalogram and event-related potentials

When we learned about brain cells, neurons, in the previous section, we learned that neural networks communicate with each other by electrochemical signals being passed from neuron to neuron. Electrical activity in the brain, 'brain waves', can be measured by placing electrodes on the scalp, usually in a cap that fits onto the head. The resulting measurement is an electroencephalogram (EEG). EEG measurements can show us abnormalities in brain function as neuroscientists know what normal

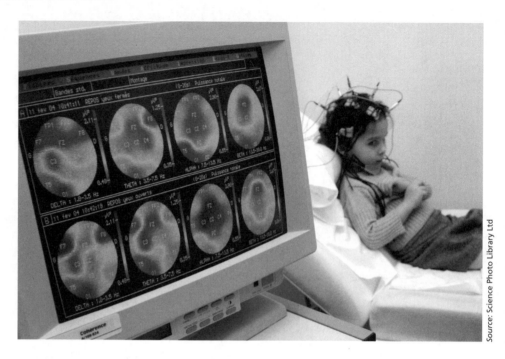

EEG patterns should look like. They can also show us how the brain responds to a particular task of interest by recording what is known as an event-related potential (ERP). This is where, following sensory stimulation, the brain changes from a resting EEG response over the time period during which it processes that information. ERPs then can be used to record brain activity in response to a stimulus such as response to speech sounds (e.g. Molfese, Molfese and Espy, 1999). ERPs provide temporal information about when the brain responds to a stimulus. A map of ERPs produced by particular areas of cortex can therefore be generated, representing cortical function in response to that stimulus. This is a non-invasive technique and as such is suitable for use with children. For visual images of a (living) brain, however, we need to make use of the techniques described below.

Computerised tomography

This is the procedure by which a CT scan is produced. The individual has to lie flat in the long metal cylinder of a scanning machine while X-rays are rotated so that they are projected through the head at different angles. X-rays conventionally produce two-dimensional pictures, but CT scanning instead takes many X-ray pictures at different angles and then the computer combines these multiple cross-sectional images of views from a variety of directions to construct a three-dimensional picture of the brain. The extent to which X-rays are absorbed

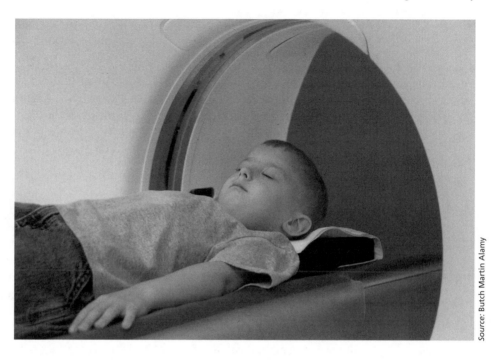

depends on the density of organic tissues, so bone, which is high density, absorbs a lot of radiation and shows up on the scan as light in colour while brain tissue absorbs less and shows up as dark coloured. CT scans are commonly used in hospitals to produce visual images of anatomical structures that can be used to help diagnose many medical conditions. They are quick to do and relatively inexpensive.

The next three, even more sophisticated, image reconstruction methods were inspired by CT scan methodologies and allow study of the brain in action (Kolb and Wishaw, 2009). Using these methods cognitive neuroscientists can see which brain regions are in use while individuals are engaged in particular cognitive processing tasks. It should be noted, though, that unlike EEG, they do not themselves directly record activation of neural networks but instead measure associated metabolic processes, such as blood flow.

Positron emission tomography (PET)

With this method, the individual lies in the scanner with his head surrounded by a circle of radiation detectors. Radioactive molecules in, for example, water are injected into the individual and the PET camera detectors can pick these up to produce a brain image of higher and lower levels of blood flow. Active brain areas use more blood, so this method can be used to study mental activity in cognitive processing. Typically the injection of radioactive tracers is administered twice, once as a control condition and one during the activity of interest. Note that the control condition could be a resting condition, but could equally be a different activity. It is the change in cerebral blood flow between the two conditions that is measured in this procedure. This tells us which areas of the brain are active in the different conditions. This methodology can also be used to compare brain activity across groups of individuals, e.g. those with dyslexia and those without, to discover if there are differences in brain functioning between the groups. Because of its use of radioactive tracers, though, it is not suitable for use with children (Goswami, 2004).

Magnetic resonance imaging (MRI) and functional magnetic resonance imaging (fMRI)

MRI is a non-invasive technique that uses a large magnet and radio waves at a particular frequency to generate a three-dimensional visual image of the area of the brain that is of interest. As it uses electromagnetic energy rather than radiation, it is safe for children and also for repeated usage. Most hospitals have MRI scanners as, like CT scans, they are commonly used for examining brain structures for the purpose of medical diagnoses of brain abnormalities from illness or injury. However, to study the brain in action, rather than these structural imaging techniques we look to functional imaging techniques. We have already discussed one of these above, PET. The other functional imaging technique we will consider here is fMRI.

MRI scanners can be adapted for functional MRI. Like PET, fMRI also utilises the principle of increased blood flow when there is neural activity. It measures increases in the ratio of oxygenated to deoxygenated haemoglobin in the blood, that occur when there is neural activity in an area of the brain. A method known as event-related fMRI is used to track change in brain activity over time during a particular cognitive event. As for CT and PET, the individual needs to lie flat and still, confined in a metal cylinder, while the images are recorded. This of course limits the techniques that can be used for stimulus presentation and the kinds of behaviours that can be investigated because of restrictions in responses that can be made in this environment. Often participants in studies are required to look at study stimuli presented on mirrors and press buttons held in their hands to signal responses. Results of studies using fMRI techniques have made a major contribution to the study of cognitive neuroscience (Gazzaniga et al., 2008). Because fMRI does not require radioactive tracers to be injected, the same person can undergo this process many times, allowing multiple measurement of neural activity.

Having familiarised ourselves with some neuroimaging techniques, let's now see how they have been applied to two areas that we have already discussed in this book: autism spectrum disorders (Chapter 5), and dyslexia (Chapter 7). You might find it useful to revisit these chapters before proceeding.

Autism spectrum disorders (ASD)

Structural brain imaging

With respect to children with ASD, MRI studies have indicated anatomical differences between this group and typically developing children. Cerebellum and brainstem areas (see Figure 12.2) were found to increase in size with age, but to be smaller in children with ASD than in the control group (Carper and Courchesne, 2000; Hashimoto, Tayama, Murakawa, Yoshimoto, Miyazaki, Harada *et al.*, 1995). Within the cerebellum are contained special neurons called Purkinje cells, and autopsies have shown that the number and size of Purkinje cells in the cerebellum were substantially reduced in individuals with ASD compared to typically developing controls (Bauman, 1991; Fatemi, Halt, Realmuto, Earle, Kist, Thuras *et al.*, 2002; Ritvo, Freeman, Scheibel, Duong, Robinson, Guthrie *et al.*, 1986). This finding from post-mortem studies was supported by in vivo MRI research (Courchesne, Yeung-Courchesne, Press, Hesselink and Jernigan, 1988) as well as by a more recent meta-analysis (Stanfield, McIntosh, Spencer, Philip, Gaur and Lawrie, 2007).

MRI studies have also indicated that in autism, there is a reduction in the size of the corpus callosum, a white matter bundle containing many millions of axons (Stanfield *et al.*, 2007; Verhoeven, De Cock, Lagae and Sunaert, 2010), This could mean that connectivity between the two hemispheres is reduced as a result, which might explain some of the clinical features of autism discussed in Chapter 5. Parietal lobes in an autistic sample have also been reported as reduced in volume, with an increase in sulcal width in this region (Courchesne, Press and Yeung-Courchesne, 1993). The volume of the amygdala, an area associated with expression of the emotion of fear, is reported as increased in children with ASD (Schumann, Hamstra, Goodlin-Jones, Lotspeich, Kwon, Buonocore *et al.*, 2004).

QUISSET *Now go beyond the text . . . look it up yourself!*

Explore your library's electronic databases to investigate 'brain imaging in autism spectrum disorders'.

Carry out a literature search on neuroimaging in ASD using the databases that are available to you in order to identify further studies on this topic.

- What brain structures are associated with ASD in addition to those mentioned above?

Functional brain imaging

While MRI studies provide valuable information about anatomical differences between individuals with ASD and typically developing individuals, what we as psychologists are even more interested in is what processes are involved when the brain is actively engaged in a cognitive task. As already mentioned, for that we look to functional imaging. This provides us with some initial findings about neuro-functioning and cognitive processes that contribute to explanations for features of the triad of impairments associated with ASD (see Chapter 5).

Social interaction

Unlike typically developing controls, children with ASD, when they were required to observe and imitate emotional expressions, showed minimal mirror neuron activity in a fold in the lower part of the frontal cortex known as the inferior frontal gyrus (Dapretto, Davies, Pfeifer, Scott, Sigman, Bookheimer *et al.*, 2006; Verhoeven *et al.*, 2010). 'Mirror cells' have been identified in macaque monkeys in a series of ingenious studies carried out in Italy, as cells were activated not only when a monkey undertook a particular action such as, say, reaching for food, but also when a monkey *observed* another animal making that action (Rizzolatti, Fogassi and Gallese, 2006). The 'mirror cells' seem to respond to both the monkey's actions and the actions of others, by matching them and investing them with the same meaning. Could this then be the beginning of understanding others' actions and intentions, possibly the beginning of a theory of mind (TOM) in humans? Perhaps humans use the mirror neuron system not only to understand others' actions like the monkeys but to understand emotion by translation of an observed facial expression (action) through imitation (Carr, Iacoboni, Dubeau, Mazziotta and Lenzi, 2003; Goswami. 2006; Verhoeven *et al.*, 2010). The assumption for children with ASD then is that imitation has a core role to play in the development of theory of mind, and that impairment in imitation due to reduced mirror neuron activity could result in impairment in the development of theory of mind and in social interaction which requires understanding of the emotions and intentions of another (Meltzoff and Decety, 2003). It seems likely that there are altered patterns of brain activation in ASD, possibly due to poor integration between areas of the brain that serve visual, motor, somatosensory and motor functions: it is this poor integration that may affect development of TOM through a cascade of developmental impairments (Williams, Waiter, Gilchrist, Perrett, Murray and Whiten, 2006; Williams, Whiten, Suddendorf and Perrett, 2001).

Communication

As mentioned earlier in this chapter, an area in the left inferior frontal gyrus, is involved in language processing. This is known as Broea's area. fMRI studies have suggested that reduced activity in Broca's area alongside increased activity in Wernicke's area may contribute to difficulties in communication that are characteristic of ASD – excessive focus on individual words and lack of integration of these into a meaningful whole conceptual structure (e.g. Harris, Chabris, Clark, Urban, Aharon, Steele, *et al.*, 2006; Just, Cherkassky, Keller and Minshew, 2004). Harris *et al.* (2006) further noted that in their study the ASD group (of adults) showed reduced differences in activation between concrete and abstract words compared to the control group. There is also fMRI evidence from a memory study of adults with high-functioning autism that while in behavioural terms, the autism group performed the task similarly to the control group, in terms of neural networks, different patterns of neural activation were recorded, with the autistic group using verbal processing mechanisms to a lesser extent (Koshino, Carpenter, Minshew, Cherkassky, Keller and Just, 2005). In this study, participants were asked to remember a target letter which was projected on to a viewing screen inside the scanner and viewed through mirrors. Participants were then presented with a sequence of letters and asked to press the response button when the target letter reappeared on the screen. There were no significant differences between the groups in terms of error rate or reaction time to respond. Koshino *et al.* found less activation in left hemisphere frontal regions in the autism group compared to the control group. As the left prefrontal cortex is associated with verbal working memory, and right prefrontal with nonverbal working memory, Koshino *et al.* interpreted this as indicating that the autism group processed the letters in a non-verbal, visual way, rather than verbally as did the control group.

Similarly, the processing of social information from faces is important in social interaction. This involves reading faces to interpret affect, expressions and eye gaze. Typically developing babies attend to faces from early in infancy (Pascalis, Haan and Nelson, 2002), but autistic individuals do not show improved processing of faces that are presented in a normal orientation compared to inverted faces. Instead of processing faces as a whole, they process features (Speer, Cook, McMahon and Clark, 2007). fMRI studies have shown this deficit in adults who have lesions of the temporal lobe fusiform gyrus, as well as in individuals with autism who showed reduced neural activation of the fusiform gyrus in a facial processing task compared to controls (Schultz, Gauthier, Klin, Fulbright, Anderson, Volkmar *et al.*, 2000, Verhoeven *et al.*, 2010). Neuroscience research is suggesting that, for both verbal and non-verbal communication, the brain network of individuals with autism is organised differently from that of controls.

QUISSET *Now go beyond the text . . . look it up yourself!*

Explore your library's electronic databases to investigate 'the role of the fusiform gyrus in face processing in autistic individuals'.

Review the literature on the role of the fusiform gyrus in face processing in individuals with autism.

- Which studies confirm the activation pattern discussed above and which do not?
- How might these apparently different findings be reconciled?

Repetitive behaviours

As discussed in Chapter 5, repetitive stereotyped behaviours are common in children with autism. Arm-flapping, toe-walking, running in circles, humming are examples of these (Turner, 1999), and are viewed as being related to deficits in inhibition control, and cognitive and behavioural inflexibility, which are aspects of executive function (Ozonoff, Pennington and Rogers, 1991). One of the main brain locations for executive function is the frontal cortex, although few studies have so far been carried out to examine associations between these repetitive behaviours and neural activations (Verhoeven *et al.*, 2010). One such study was carried out by Schmitz, Rubia, Daly, Smith, William and Murphy (2006), who found no difference in executive function performance between the ASD and control groups but significant differences in brain activation. The ASD group showed higher activation of frontal and parietal cortices, which Schmitz *et al.* interpreted as abnormal brain development and different connectivity to other brain regions involved in executive functioning compared to controls.

QUISSET *Now go beyond the text . . . look it up yourself!*

Explore your library's electronic databases to investigate 'the tests of executive functioning'.

One of the tests used in the Schmitz *et al.* (2006) study was the Stroop test.

- What is the Stroop test?
- What does it assess?
- What other tests of inhibitory control and set shifting did Schmitz *et al.* use in this study?

Search your database to see what other studies you can find that link repetitive behaviours to neuroimaging findings in individuals with autism.

 Debate

Join up with some friends to discuss.

Consider the above findings on neuroscience findings regarding the triad of impairments.

- What are the implications of these findings for intervention in the classroom for children with ASD?

Dyslexia

Neuroimaging studies with adults have shown us which brain regions are activated when they engage in the cognitive task of reading. Fiez and Petersen's (1998) review of nine neuroimaging studies presented converging evidence of a network of areas within the left hemisphere, in particular the frontal, temporo-parietal and occipito-temporal regions, that are active when adults read. However, as well as identifying where reading takes place, we want to know more about the processes that underlie reading. We know from our earlier chapter on literacy that reading involves complex processes, so neuroscience may be able to contribute to a better understanding of how these operate. PET and fMRI scans have been used to compare phonological processing in dyslexic adults with non-impaired adults who are able to read normally. Also, brain imaging studies in dyslexic adults have indeed shown a reduction, or even a complete absence, of activity in the left temporo-parietal cortex while engaged in auditory phonological processing tasks, i.e. rhyme detection presented auditorily, and visual phonological processing tasks, i.e. rhyme detection with visually presented letters, and pseudoword reading (Temple, 2002).

While studying adults provides us with important information, one has to be cautious about drawing inferences from adult studies, where reading strategies are already well established, to the development of reading difficulties in children. We cannot tell from adult studies whether the findings from brain imaging indicate the causes of the reading difficulties or rather reflect the effects of having had reading difficulties for a lifetime. They may indicate compensatory mechanisms that adults have had to resort to because of a difficulty in reading, rather than reflecting neural differences that were present in these dyslexic adults from early on in their development. It is therefore important to study children directly, and fortunately the non-invasive imaging techniques that are available to cognitive neuroscientists now allow this to be carried out (Beaulieu, Plewes, Paulson *et al.*, 2005). While fMRI has fewer obvious risks than PET, there are still concerns about the possible effects on children taking part in such studies. The effects of exposure to a magnetic field are not fully known, and restrictions on movement and the confined space required by scans are not pleasant experiences for young children who cannot give informed consent (Dowker, 2006).

To give a flavour of the kinds of findings that are emerging from neuroscience research and their implications for classroom practice, let's consider evidence from neuroimaging studies on the involvement of two key brain regions in dyslexia: left superior temporal cortex, and left inferior frontal gyrus. It should be noted that there is evidence that other left hemisphere areas too are involved in the complex neural network that is required for reading, e.g. infero-temporal, ventral extrastriate, occipito-temporal, perisylvian and extrasylvian temporal cortices (Fiez and Petersen, 1998; Goswami, 2006; Pugh, Menci, Jenner, Katz, Frost, Lee *et al.*, 2001; Shaywitz, Shaywitz, Blachman, Pugh, Fulbright and Skudlarski 2004; Sun, Lee and Kirby, 2010), as well as some indications of possible right temporo-parietal involvement (Hoeft, Hernandez, McMillon, Taylor-Hill, Martindale, Meyler *et al.*, 2006). In this chapter, however, we will focus our attention on findings regarding the two specific regions of left superior temporal cortex and inferior frontal gyrus.

 Activity

Join up with some friends.

Work together using internet resources to identify on a diagram of the brain where the above-mentioned brain regions are located.

Left superior temporal cortex

fMRI studies on children have reported similar findings to the adult studies above. Gaillard, Balsamo, Ibrahim, Sachs and Xu (2003), for example, reported left hemisphere brain specialisation in young children who were learning to read. In a cross-sectional study of reading development covering the whole period of reading acquisition from 6 to 22 years, Turkeltaub, Gareau, Flowers, Zeffiro and Eden (2003) noted that as children learned to read there were changes in brain activity in the temporo-parietal cortex, in particular in an area known as the left superior temporal sulcus. This area matured early in the learning process and continued to be involved in adult reading. Activity in this brain region correlated with the development of phonological awareness (Turkeltaub *et al.*, 2003; Wagner and Torgesen, 1987). As we know that phonological awareness predicts reading achievement (see Chapter 7), it is an exciting possibility that measures of activity in the left superior temporal sulcus could predict later reading abilities.

IN FOCUS

Use of false fonts in Turkeltaub *et al.*'s (2003) study

When measuring neural activity in individuals engaged in cognitive tasks such as reading, one important issue in fMRI measurement is that differences in effort, between individuals, can present as differences in measured brain activity, even where exactly the same neural networks are being used. Thus the cognitive skill being measured needs to be something that can be undertaken equally well by novices and experts (Turkeltaub, Weisberg, Flowers, Basu and Eden, 2005) To avoid this potential confound, and also in order that the same task could be administered to measure brain activity changes in reading acquisition across a very wide 6–22-year-old age group, Turkeltaub *et al.* (2003) used what they referred to as an 'implicit' task. Rather than requiring the participants to read actual words, the task required them to detect visual features, such as tall letters, in words. For example, the word

alarm

has a tall letter, the letter 'l', but the word

sauce

has no tall letters – all letters are the same size.

As you can see, successful completion of this task does not actually require reading; a non-reader can respond correctly to it, allowing measures of accuracy and reaction time to be collected for different age groups.

However, as Turkeltaub *et al.* wanted to study brain activity specifically related to reading, they utilised a control task in which participants were similarly asked to detect tall characters but this time they used 'false fonts', which were unreadable strings of nonsense characters of the same length and complexity as the actual words.

Participants in this study then had to press a button held in their right hand if the stimulus contained a tall letter, as in the word 'alarm' on page 268 or to press a button in their left hand if the stimulus did not contain a tall letter, as in the word 'sauce'. Brain activity on words and false font strings was compared with baseline brain activity for 41 healthy, good readers across the age range 6–22 years. Younger readers aged 6–9 years activated the left superior temporal sulcus when they were identifying the tall characters in words compared to when they processed the false fonts. The left superior temporal sulcus therfore seemed to be involved in word reading and not in nonsense character processing. This area was the same one that was activated in adult readers, along with other regions in the temporal and parietal cortex (Turkeltaub *et al.*, 2005).

alarm ⊓⏀∧⊏

parry ∑∧⊃⊃⍴

Example of false font
Source: Turkeltaub *et al.* 2005, reproduced by permission of Taylor & Frances

Other studies too have indicated the role of the left superior temporal cortex in children's reading. fMRI studies comparing dyslexic and non-dyslexic groups found different brain activation patterns in these two groups when engaged in word recognition tasks and phonological processing tasks. The dyslexic, reading-impaired group not only showed reduced activation in left temporo-parietal areas compared to the non-dyslexics, but also displayed activity in right temporo-parietal areas, suggesting that there may be possible compensation by the right hemisphere (Shaywitz *et al.*, 2002: Simos, Breier, Fletcher, Bergman and Papanicolaou, 2000). In contrast other studies had found that there was a disengagement of right inferotemporal cortex in good readers as they learned to read (Turkeltaub *et al.*, 2003).

Furthermore, Turkeltaub, Flowers, Verbalis, Miranda, Gareau and Eden (2004) provided evidence of increased left superior temporal cortex activity in hyperlexia, precocious reading ability, from a case study with a 9-year-old boy with an autism spectrum disorder whose reading performance was six years ahead of his chronological age. In addition to left hemisphere systems, though, this hyperlexic reader also demonstrated greater activation of the right posterior inferior temporal sulcus than reading-age-matched controls. This is an area that seems to be important for visual form recognition and as mentioned above, is a region that typically shows disengagement of activity during normative development. Thus it seemed that hyperlexic reading might make use of both the left hemisphere's phonological systems as well as the right hemisphere's visual systems (Turkeltaub *et al.*, 2004).

In addition, intervention studies also show changes in this brain region. Temple, Deutsch, Poldrack, Miller, Tallal, Merzenich *et al.* (2003) used fMRI to measure changes in neural mechanisms during and after a computerised intervention programme that focused on auditory and language processing. Twenty 8–12-year-olds with dyslexia took part in this and showed behavioural improvements in their processing of oral language and in their reading performance. Neuroimaging showed increased activity in left temporo-parietal cortex and also in the left inferior frontal gyrus. Left temporo-parietal activity after intervention was closer to that observed in control normal readers, suggesting a partial improvement of the disrupted temporo-parietal response as a result of the intervention.

These studies indicate that there is an association between the left temporo-parietal cortex and reading, but in addition there is evidence from another type of neuroimaging technique, diffusion tensor magnetic resonance imaging, that there are further differences in underlying neural connections in brain white matter in this region. In a study of children aged 8–12 years who were mostly average readers, Beaulieu, Plewes, Paulson, Roy, Snook, Concha *et al.* (2005) found an association between brain connectivity and reading ability. This is to say that there was increased brain connectivity in the better readers within neural networks in the left temporo-parietal region of the brain, compared to the weaker readers. Beaulieu *et al.* suggested that more efficient neural processing, perhaps due to increased myelination, could be a critical factor in the ability to learn. While it might be tempting to infer a causal connection between these neural networks and reading ability, Beaulieu *et al.* cautioned that we do not yet know whether efficient neural networks are a prerequisite for reading or an outcome of improvement in reading ability. The above studies suggest then that activity in left temporo-parietal cortex correlates with reading and also that within this region of the brain, neural connectivity in white matter correlates with reading ability.

Left inferior frontal gyrus

While the left superior temporal cortex matures relatively early and was shown to be activated by both children and adults in the studies reported above (Balsamo, Xu, Grandin, Petrella, Braniecki, Elliott *et al.*, 2002), in contrast the left inferior frontal gyrus does show developmental changes as individuals learn to read. In Turkeltaub *et al.*'s (2003) implicit reading task, this area was not activated in the children who participated but was strongly activated by the adults in the study. Activity in this area of the frontal cortex correlates with reading ability (Georgiewa, Rzanny, Gaser, Gerhard, Vieweg, Freesmeyer *et al.*, 2002; Turkeltaub *et al.*, 2005). Development of phonological awareness seems to be an important factor in the activation of this area too (Pugh *et al.*, 2001). Some studies with older dyslexic readers, though, have reported *increased* activation in the left inferior frontal gyrus compared to control groups in particular in Broca's area, which, as we have mentioned, is involved in the generation of language (Georgiewa *et al.*, 2002; Shaywitz, Shaywitz, Pugh, Fulbright, Constable, Menci, *et al.*, 1998). Shaywitz *et al.* (2002) suggested that these apparently different findings might be explained by frontal neural systems being engaged in older dyslexic readers to a greater extent during difficult phonological tasks in order to compensate for reduced activity in temporo-parietal regions.

Dyslexic children who took part in the auditory processing programme referred to above also showed increased activation in left inferior frontal gyrus post-intervention (Temple *et al.*, 2003). Similarly Shaywitz *et al.* (2004) provided fMRI evidence that 37 6–9-year-olds who took part in a phonologically based intervention demonstrated increased activation in the left inferior frontal gyrus, relative to the comparison groups. Further, in comparison with children of the same reading ability this brain region in the hyperlexic case study, with a child who had exceptional phonological skills, showed a greater degree of activation (Turkeltaub *et al.*, 2004). In a study that compared neural activation in normal and impaired readers aged 9–15 years in their attempts at reading phonologically consistent (i.e. regular) versus irregular words, the left inferior frontal gyrus was one of the brain regions (along with middle frontal and left fusiform gyri) that showed differences between the two groups of readers (Bolger, Minas, Burman and Booth, 2008). In reading irregular, low-consistency words, normal readers here were found to activate these areas to a greater extent than impaired readers in order to respond to the conflict between orthographic presentation and its irregular phonology. This network of regions is likely to be involved in the matching of written to spoken word, i.e. phonological processing (Bolger *et al.*, 2008; Fiez and Petersen, 1998). Bolger *et al.* further suggested that these findings did not provide support for a dual-route model (see Chapter 7), as this would imply lower consistency, irregular words are processed by a separate mechanism from regular words. Instead Bolger *et al.*'s results indicated a single-route model with lower-consistency words producing greater neural activation than regular words in brain regions that process orthography and phonology. Here we can begin to see the potential for neuroscientific findings to illuminate our understandings of cognitive processes.

How can neuroscience knowledge aid intervention?

Neuroimaging studies can help us identify which neural networks might contribute to autism spectrum disorders, and to dyslexia. They can even identify which neural changes are associated with behavioural changes in reading as a result of intervention programmes, although it is not yet possible to infer from neuroscience what exactly teachers can do in the classroom to intervene in the case of either autism or dyslexia (Goswami, 2006).

There is great potential and new possibilities are beginning to be explored. Several studies have found relationships between ERPs and reading and have noted that children with reading disabilities show different ERP responses to typically developing readers (e.g. Goswami, Thomson, Richardson, Stainthorp, Hughes, Rosen *et al.*, 2002; Molfese, 2000; Penolazzi, Spironelli, Vio and Angrilli, 2006). ERP differences that have been noted relate not only to differences in phonological processing between dyslexic and non-dyslexic readers (Molfese, Molfese and Modgline, 2001), but also to differences in visual outcomes (Lovrich, Cheng and Velting, 2003), and attentional outcomes (Bernal, Harmony, Rodriguez, Reyes, Yanez, Fernandez *et al.* 2000). Longitudinal studies have shown that newborn ERPs can predict later reading outcomes (e.g. Molfese *et al.*, 2001), and that this is a particularly useful imaging technique for potential use in schools as while ERP measurement requires specialised personnel it does not require such specialised laboratory settings as do fMRI and PET techniques (Lemons, Key, Fuchs, Yoder, Fuchs, Compton *et al.*, in press). ERP measurement is also cheaper to carry out than these other methods and less threatening for children than lying still in an enclosed scanner. Perhaps this neuroscience knowledge can help predict which children will require intensive intervention to develop reading skills. Lemons *et al.* (in press) considered that in addition to using ERPs to predict outcomes over a long-term period, it would be useful if they could be used to predict responsiveness to reading tuition over a shorter-term intervention period, that of the school academic year. They studied 29 children aged 6–8 years and found that ERP responses were indeed significant predictors of reading change over the school year. Lemons *et al.* viewed this study as providing preliminary evidence of the potential of neuroscience techniques such as ERP for practical application to school settings. Lemons *et al.* suggested that maybe in the future as new technologies become available, brain scans like this could be used in addition to behavioural assessments of, for example, rhyming, non-word reading, and letter naming to predict which pupils would require intensive support to develop reading and which could make progress in their reading without such intervention.

Summary and conclusions

Neuroscience offers us exciting possibilities for the future for understanding developmental problems such as dyslexia and autism. Currently there is still a gap between neuroscience findings and direct implications for educational intervention practices. Cognitive psychology offers a useful bridge between the two by providing psychological models to help us understand underlying processes: neuroscience can then test out these models. It is likely that in the not-too-distant future we will be able to integrate neuroscience, cognitive psychology and educational practices in ways that impact directly on the classroom. We can see the beginnings of this in the studies presented in this chapter.

Further study

Go to the website www.pearsoned.co.uk/markswoolfson **for the following starter articles:**

Schmitz, N., Rubia, K., Daly, E., Smith, A., Williams, S., and Murphy, D. (2006). Neural correlates of executive function in autistic spectrum disorders. *Biological Psychiatry, 59*(1), 7-16.

Sylvan, L. and Christodoulou, J. (2010). Understanding the role of neuroscience in brain based products: A guide for educators and consumers. *Mind, Brain and Education, 4*(1), 1-7.

Temple, E. (2002). Brain mechanisms in normal and dyslexic readers. *Current Opinion in Neurobiology, 12*, 178-83.

References

Balsamo, L., Xu, B., Grandin, C., Petrella, J., Braniecki, S., Elliott, T., et al. (2002). A functional magnetic resonance imaging study of left hemisphere language dominance in children. *Archives of Neurology, 59*(7), 1168–74.

Bauman, M. (1991). Microscopic neuroanatomic abnormailities in autism. *Pediatrics, 87*, 791–6.

Beaulieu, C., Plewes, C., Paulson, L., Roy, D., Snook. L., Concha, L., and Phillips, L. (2005). Imaging brain connectivity in children with diverse reading ability. *NeuroImage, 25*, 1266–71.

Bernal, J., Harmony, T., Rodriguez, M., Reyes, A.,Yanez, G., Fernandez, T., *et al.* (2000). Auditory event-related potentials in poor readers. *International Journal of Psychophysiology, 36*, 11–23.

Beyerstein, B. (1999). Whence cometh the myth that we only use ten percent of our brains? In S. Della Sala (ed). *Mind-myths: Exploring everyday mysteries of the mind and brain.* New York: John Wiley and Sons.

Beyerstein, B. (2004). Ask the experts: Do we really use only 10% of our brains? *Scientific American* 290 (6), 86.

Blakemore, S. and Frith, U. (2000). *Report on the implications of recent developments in neuroscience for research on teaching and learning.* Teaching and Learning Research Programme/ESRC.

Blakemore, S. and Frith, U. (2001). *The implications of recent developments in neuroscience for research on teaching and learning.* Research Intelligence No. 75.

Blakemore, S. and Frith, U. (2005). *The learning brain: Lessons for education.* Oxford: Blackwell.

Bolger, D., Minas, J., Burman, D., Booth, J. (2008). Differential effects of orthographic and phonological consistency in cortex for children with and without reading impairment. *Neuropsychologia, 46*, 3210–24.

Bruer, J. (1997). Education and the brain: a bridge too far. *Educational Research, 26*, 4–16.

Calvert, G., Campbell, R., Brammer, M. (2000). Evidence from functional magnetic resonance imaging of crossmodal binding in human heteromodal cortex. *Current Biology 10*(11), 649–657.

Carper, R., and Courchesne, E. (2000). Inverse correlation between frontal lobe and cerebellum sizes in children with autism. *Brain, 123*, 836–44.

Carr, L., Iacoboni, M., Dubeau, M-C., Mazziotta, J., and Lenzi, G. (2003). Neural mechanisms of empathy in humans: A relay from neural systems for imitation to limbic areas. *Proceedings of the National Academy of Sciences of the United States of America, 100*(9), 5497–502.

Chow, K., and Stewart, D. (1972). Reversal of structural and functional effects of long-term visual deprivation in cats. *Experimental Neurology, 34*, 409–33.

Coffield, F., Moseley, D., Hall, E., and Ecclestone, K. (2004). *Learning styles and pedagogy in post-16 learning: A systematic and critical review*. Report No. 041543. London: Learning and Skills Research Centre.

Courchesne, E., Press, G., Yeung-Courchesne, R. (1993). Parietal lobe abnormalities detected with MR in patients with infantile autism. *American Journal of Roentgenology, 160*, 387–93.

Courchesne, E., Yeung-Courchesne, R., Press, G., Hesselink, J., and Jernigan, T. (1988). Hypoplasia of cerebellar vernal lobules VI and VII in autism. *New England Journal of Medicine, 318*(21), 1349–54.

Dapretto, M., Davies, M., Pfeifer, J., Scott, A., Sigman, M., Bookheimer, S., et al. (2006). Understanding emotions in others: Mirror neuron dysfunction in children with autism spectrum disorders. *Nature Neuroscience, 9*(1), 28–30.

Daw, N. (1997). Critical periods and strabismus: What questions remain? *Optometry and Vision Science, 74*, 690–4.

Della Sala, S. and Beyerstein, B. (2007). Introduction: The myth of 10% and other tall tales about the mind and brain. (p. xvii). In S. Della Sala (ed.). *Tall tales about the mind and brain: Separating fact from fiction*. Oxford: Oxford University Press.

Dennison, P. (1994). *Brain gym* (Teachers edition: revised). Ventura, CA: Edu-Kinaesthetics Ltd.

Dowker, A. (2006). What can functional brain imaging studies tell us about typical and atypical cognitive development in children? *Journal of Physiology - Paris 99*, 333–41.

Fatemi, S., Halt, A., Realmuto, G., Earle, J., Kist, D., Thuras, P., et al. (2002). Purkinje cell size is reduced in patients with autism. *Cellular and Molecular Neurobiology, 22*(2), 171–5.

Fiez, J. and Petersen, S. (1998). Neuroimaging studies of word reading. *Proceedings of the National Academy of Sciences, 95*, 914–21.

Fischer, K., Goswami, U., Geake, J., and the Task Force on the Future of Educational Neuroscience (2010). The future of educational neuroscience. *Mind, Brain and Education, 4*(2), 68–80.

Fox, S., Levitt, P., and Nelson, C. (2010). How the timing and quality of early experiences influence the development of brain architecture. *Child Development, 81*(1), 28–40.

Frith, U. (1997). Brain, mind and behaviour in dyslexia. In C. Hulme and M. Snowling (eds) *Dyslexia: Biology, cognition and intervention*. London: Whurr (pp. 1–19).

Gaillard, W., Balsamo, L., Ibrahim, Z., Sachs, B., and Xu, H. (2003). fMRI identifies regional specialization of neural networks for reading in young children. *Neurology, 60*, 94–100.

Gazzaniga, M., Ivry, R., and Mangun, G. (2008). *Cognitive neuroscience: The biology of the mind*, 3rd edn. New York: Norton.

Geake, J. (2004). Cognitive neuroscience and education: Two-way traffic or one-way street? *International Journal of Research and Method in Education, 27*, 87–98.

Geake, J. (2008). Neuromythologies in education. *Educational Researcher, 50*(2), 123–33.

Georgiewa, P., Rzanny, R., Gaser, C., Gerhard, U., Vieweg, U., Freesmeyer, D., et al. (2002). Phonological processing in dyslexic children: A study combining functional imaging and event related potentials. *Neuroscience Letters, 318*, 5–8.

Goswami. U. (2004). Neuroscience and education. *British Journal of Educational Psychology, 74*, 1–14.

Goswami, U. (2006). Neuroscience and education: From research to practice. *Nature Reviews Neuroscience, 7*, 406–13.

Goswami, U., Thomson, J., Richardson, U., Stainthorp, R., Hughes, D., Rosen, S., and Scott, S. (2002). Amplitude envelope onsets and developmental dyslexia: A new hypothesis. *Proceedings of the National Academy of Sciences, 99*(16), 10911–6.

Greenough, W., Black, J., and Wallace, C. (1987). Experience and brain development. *Child Development, 58*, 539–59.

Hall, J. (2005). *Neuroscience and education: What can brain science contribute to teaching and learning?* Research Report 121. Glasgow: Scottish Research in Education Centre, University of Glasgow.

Harris, G., Chabris, C., Clark, J., Urban, T., Aharon, I., Steele, S., et al. (2006). Brain activation during semantic processing in autism spectrum disorders via functional magnetic resonance imaging. *Brain and Cognition, 61*(1), 54–68.

Hashimoto, T., Tayama, M., Murakawa, K., Yoshimoto, T., Miyazaki, M., Harada, M., and Kuroda, Y. (1995). Development of the brainstem and cerebellum in autistic patients. *Journal of Autism and Developmental Disorders, 25*(1), 1–18.

Hoeft, F., Hernandez, A., McMillon, G., Taylor-Hill, H., Martindale, J., Meyler, A., *et al.* (2006). Neural basis of dyslexia: A comparison between dyslexic and nondyslexic children equated for reading ability. *The Journal of Neuroscience, 26*(42), 10700–8.

Huttenlocher, P. and Dabholkar, A. (1997). Regional differences in synaptogenesis in human cerebral cortex. *Journal of Comparative Neurology, 387,* 167–78.

Just, M., Cherkassky, V., Keller, T., and Minshew, N. (2004). Cortical activation and synchronization during sentence comprehension in high-functioning autism: Evidence of underconnectivity. *Brain, 127*(8), 1811–21.

Knecht, S., Deppe, M., Dräger, B., Bobe, L., Lohmann, H., Ringelstein, E-B., and Henningsen, H. (2000). Language lateralization in healthy right-handers. *Brain, 123*(1), 74–81.

Kolb, B. and Whishaw, I. (2009). *Fundamentals of human neuropsychology*, 6th edn. New York: Worth.

Koshino, H., Carpenter, P., Minshew, N., Cherkassky, V., Keller, T., and Just, M. (2005). Functional connectivity in an fMRI working memory task in high functioning autism. *NeuroImage, 24,* 810–21.

Kratzig, G. and Arbuthnott, K. (2006). Perceptual learning style and learning proficiency: A test of the hypothesis. *Journal of Educational Psychology, 98*(1), 238–46.

Lemons, C., Key, A., Fuchs, D., Yoder, P., Fuchs, L., Compton, D., *et al.* (in press). Predicting reading growth with event-related potentials: Thinking differently about indexing 'Responsiveness'. *Learning and Individual Differences.*

Lovrich, D., Cheng, J., and Velting, D. (2003). ERP correlates of form and rhyme letter tasks in impaired reading children: A critical evaluation. *Child Neuropsychology, 9,* 159–74.

Metltzoff, A. and Decety, J. (2003). What imitation tells us about social cognition: A rapprochement between developmental psychology and cognitive neuroscience. *Philosophical transactions of the Royal Society of London. Series B: Biological Sciences, 358*(1431), 491–500.

Molfese, D. (2000). Predicting dyslexia at 8 years of age using neonatal brain responses. *Brain and Language, 72,* 238–45.

Molfese, D., Molfese, V., and Espy, K. (1999). The predictive use of event-related potentials in language development and the treatment of language disorders. *Developmental Neuropsychology, 16*(3), 373–7.

Molfese, V., Molfese, D., and Modgline, A., (2001). Newborn and preschool predictors of second grade reading scores: An evaluation of categorical and continuous scores. *Journal of Learning Disabilities, 34,* 545–54.

Morton, J. and Frith, U. (1995). Causal modeling: A structural approach to developmental psychopathology. In D. Cicchetti and D. Cohen. (eds) *Manual of developmental psychology*. Wiley: New York (pp. 357–90).

Organisation for Economic Co-operation and Development. (2002). *Understanding the brain: Towards a new learning science.* Paris: OECD.

Ozonoff, S., Pennington, B., and Rogers, S. (1991). Executive function deficits in high-functioning autistic individuals: Relationship to theory of mind. *Journal of Child Psychology and Psychiatry, 32*(7), 1081–105.

Pascalis, O., Haan, M., and Nelson, C., (2002). Is face-processing species-specific during the first year of life? *Science, 296,* 1321–3.

Penolazzi, B., Spironelli, C., Vio, C., and Angrilli, A. (2006). Altered hemispheric asymmetry during word processing in dyslexic children: An event-related potential study. *Cognitive Neuroscience and Neuropsychology, 17,* 429–33.

Pugh, K., Menci, W., Jenner, A., Katz, L., Frost, S., Lee, J., *et al.* (2001). Neurobiological studies of reading and reading disability. *Journal of Communication Disorders, 34*(6), 479–92.

Rizzolatti, G., Fogassi, L., and Gallese, V. (2006). Mirrors of the mind. *Scientific American, 295*(5), 54–61.

Ritvo, E., Freeman, B., Scheibel, A., Duong, T., Robinson, H., Guthrie, D. *et al.* (1986). Lower Purkinje cell counts in the cerebella of four autistic subjects: Initial findings of the UCLA-NSAC Autopsy Research Report. *American Journal of Psychiatry, 143*(7), 862–6.

Schmitz, N., Rubia, K., Daly, E., Smith, A., Williams, S., and Murphy, D. (2006). Neural correlates of executive function in autistic spectrum disorders. *Biological Psychiatry, 59*(1), 7–16.

Schultz, R., Gauthier, I., Klin, A., Fulbright, R., Anderson, A., Volkmar, F. *et al.* (2000). Abnormal ventral temporal cortical activity during face discrimination among individuals with autism and Asperger syndrome. *Archives of General Psychiatry, 57*(4), 331–40.

Schumann, C., Hamstra, J., Goodlin-Jones, B., Lotspeich, L., Kwon, H., Buonocore, M. *et al.* (2004). The amygdala is enlarged in children but not adolescents with autism: The hippocampus is enlarged at all ages. *Journal of Neuroscience, 24*(28), 6392–401.

Shaywitz, B., Shaywitz, S., Blachman, B., Pugh, K., Fulbright, R., Skudlarski, P., *et al.* (2004). Development of left occipitotemporal systems for skilled reading in children after a phonologically-based intervention. *Biological Psychiatry, 55*, 926–33.

Shaywitz, S., Shaywitz, B., Pugh, K., Fulbright, R., Constable, R., Menci, W. *et al.* (1998). Functional disruption in the organization of the brain for reading in dyslexia. *Proceedings of the National Academy of Sciences, 95*, 2636–41.

Shaywitz, B., Shaywitz, S., Pugh, K., Mencl, E., Fulbright, R., Skudlarski, P., *et al.* (2002). Disruption of posterior brain systems for reading in children with developmental dyslexia. *Biological Psychiatry, 52*, 101–10.

Simos, P., Breier, J. Fletcher, J., Bergman, E. Papanicolaou, A. (2000).Cerebral mechanisms involved in word reading in dyslexic children: a magnetic source imaging approach. *Cerebral Cortex, 10*, 809–16.

Speer, L., Cook, A., McMahon, W., and Clark, E. (2007). Face processing in children with autism: effects of stimulus contents and type. *Autism, 11*(3), 265–77.

Stanfield, A., McIntosh, A., Spencer, M., Philip, R., Gaur, S., and Lawrie, S. (2007). Towards a neuroanatomy of autism: A systematic review and meta-analysis of structural magnetic resonance imagingstudies. *European Psychiatry, 23*, 289–99.

Sun, Y., Lee, J., and Kirby, R. (2010). Brain imaging findings in dyslexia. *Pediatric Neonatology, 51*(2), 89–96.

Sylvan, L. and Christodoulou, J. (2010). Understanding the role of neuroscience in brain based products: A guide for educators and consumers. *Mind, Brain and Education, 4*(1), 1–7.

Temple, E. (2002). Brain mechanisms in normal and dyslexic readers. *Current Opinion in Neurobiology, 12*, 178–183.

Temple, E., Deutsch, G., Poldrack, R., Miller, S., Tallal, P., Merzenich, M., et al. (2003). Neural deficits in children with dyslexia ameliorated by behavioral remediation: Evidence from functional fMRI. *Proceedings of the National Academy of Sciences, 100*(5), 2860–5.

TLRP (Teaching and Learning Research Programme) (2007). *Neuroscience and education: Issues and opportunities.* London: TLRP/ESRC.

Trachtenberg, J. and Stryker, M. (2001). Rapid anatomical plasticity of horizontal connections in the developing visual cortex. *Journal of Neuroscience, 15*, 3476–82.

Turkeltaub, P., Flowers, L., Verbalis, A., Miranda, M., Gareau, L., and Eden, G. (2004). The neural basis of hyperlexic reading: An fMRI Case Study. *Neuron, 41*, 11–25.

Turkeltaub, P., Gareau, L., Flowers, L. Zeffiro, T., and Eden, G. (2003). Development of neural mechanisms for reading. *Nature Neuroscience, 6*, 767–73.

Turkeltaub, P., Weisberg, J., Flowers, D., Basu, D., and Eden, G. (2005). The neurobiological basis of reading: A special case of skill acquisition. H. Catts and A Kamhi (eds), *The connections between language and reading disabilities*. Mahwah NJ: Lawrence Erlbaum (pp. 103–130).

Turner, M. (1999). Annotation: Repetitive behaviour in autism: A review of psychological research. *Journal of Child Psychology and Psychiatry, 40*(6), 839–49.

Verhoeven, J., De Cock, P., Lagae, L., and Sunaert, S. (2010). Neuroimaging of autism. *Neuroradiology, 52*, 3–14.

Wagner, R. and Torgesen, J. (1987). The nature of phonological processing and its causal role in the acquisition of reading skills. *Psychological Bulletin, 101*, 192–212.

Wiesel, T. and Hubel, D. (1965). Extent of recovery from the effects of visual deprivation in kittens. *Journal of Neurophysiology, 28*, 1060–72.

Williams, J., Waiter, G., Gilchrist, A., Perrett, D., Murray, A., and Whiten, A. (2006). Neural mechanisms of imitation and 'mirror neuron' functioning in autistic spectrum disorder. *Neuropsychologia, 44*, 610–21.

Williams, J., Whiten, A., Suddendorf, T., and Perrett, D. (2001). Imitation, mirror neurons and autism. *Neuroscience and Biobehavioural Reviews, 25*(4), 287–95.

Index